History of Ideas: Importance of the Legal Semantics

History of Ideas: Importance of the Legal Semantics

Maverick Ingram

CLANRYE INTERNATIONAL
www.clanryeinternational.com

Clanrye International,
750 Third Avenue, 9th Floor,
New York, NY 10017, USA

ISBN: 978-1-64726-624-0

Cataloging-in-Publication Data

History of ideas : importance of the legal semantics / Maverick Ingram.
p. cm.
Includes bibliographical references and index.
ISBN 978-1-64726-624-0
1. History. 2. Idea (Philosophy)--History. 3. Philosophy--History.
4. Intellectual life--History. I. Ingram, Maverick.

D16.9 .H57 2023
901--dc23

For information on all Clanrye International publications
visit our website at www.clanryeinternational.com

CLANRYE INTERNATIONAL

Contents

	Preface	**VII**
	An Overview of History of Ideas and Language of Law	**1**
Part 1	**Understanding the Global History of Ideas**	**32**
Chapter 1	**Concept of Idea and Importance of Disciplines**	**43**
Chapter 2	**A Comprehensive Study of Intellectual Fields and Legal Spaces**	**53**
Chapter 3	**History of Ideas and Knowledge: An "Entangled History" Approach**	**70**
Part 2	**Global History of Ideas: Locating the Language and Functions of Law**	**84**
Chapter 4	**Law and its Language: Functions of Abstraction and Transformation**	**85**
Chapter 5	**An Integrated Study of Conflict Resolution, Language of Law and Order**	**94**
Chapter 6	**Resonance and Law: Types of State and "Their" Law**	**102**
Part 3	**Role of Legal Regimes and Concepts**	**121**
Chapter 7	**A Comprehensive Study of Natural Law and Enlightenment**	**122**

Chapter 8 **Rethinking International Law and its Language** **143**

Chapter 9 **Human Rights and Language: A Political Perspective** **174**

Chapter 10 **History of Political Ideas: Significance of Language of the Rule of Law** **198**

Part 4 **Global History of Political Ideas: Major Legal Concepts** **221**

Chapter 11 **The Concept of State and its Authority** **222**

Chapter 12 **Sovereignty and the Modern State: Legal and Political Perspectives** **236**

Chapter 13 **Diverse Perspectives on the Constitution** **244**

Chapter 14 **Contract as a Legal Concept** **256**

Permissions

Index

Preface

This book has been a concerted effort by a group of academicians, researchers and scientists, who have contributed their research works for the realization of the book. This book has materialized in the wake of emerging advancements and innovations in this field. Therefore, the need of the hour was to compile all the required researches and disseminate the knowledge to a broad spectrum of people comprising of students, researchers and specialists of the field.

Semantics refers to the branch of linguistics and logic which focuses on meaning. It can be broadly categorized into lexical semantics and logical semantics. Lexical semantics deals with word meanings and connections between them, and logical semantics focuses on topics such as sense and reference, and presupposition and implication. The legal language refers to any language which is used for the purpose of legal writing. It is different from the day-to-day language in terms of semantics, vocabulary, morphology and syntax. The legal language focuses on consistency, validity, completeness and soundness. This makes the study of meaning within the legal language an important area of inquiry. This study is conducted under the umbrella of legal semantics. This book offers valuable insights into the field of legal semantics. It is an essential reference guide for lawyers, historians, and students seeking to understand the meaning of law and legal language.

At the end of the preface, I would like to thank the authors for their brilliant chapters and the publisher for guiding us all-through the making of the book till its final stage. Also, I would like to thank my family for providing the support and encouragement throughout my academic career and research projects.

Maverick Ingram

An Overview of History of Ideas and Language of Law

A. The history of ideas as a history of languages

Studies on what is referred to as universal history, world story, or, more and more frequently, global history are enjoying a heyday.[1] This can also be said for the global history of ideas,[2] which can be considered a variety of global history.[3] Different methodological approaches can be adopted in a global history of ideas. Some authors, like David Armitage, concern themselves with the origins and spread of "big ideas."[4] This is not our chosen path; with Martin Mulsow, we consider such a narrow concept of "idea" not very useful.[5] A second and particularly popular approach is to treat the history of ideas as a history of interaction[6] looking at "intermediaries, translations, and networks."[7] This is a tempting perspective,[8] and we shall be considering it in some detail at a later stage. At present, however, we will be looking at a

1 See Bayly (2006); Budde et al. (eds.) (2006); Conrad et. al. (eds.) (2007a); Sachsenmaier (2011); Conrad (2013).

2 On the global history of ideas see, above all, Moyn / Sartori (eds.) (2013); Osterhammel (2015); Mulsow (2016); Mulsow (2015).

3 In the view of Conrad – which we share – global history is more a perspective than a subject. A vast range of subject matter can accordingly be examined from a global history perspective: "Basically, a global history perspective can be adopted by all historiographical approaches", Conrad (2013) 13.

4 See Armitage (2012).

5 Mulsow (2015) 19: "Ideas, theories, portions of theory, points of view in a broad sense are conveyed together with the concomitant informational elements, religious attitudes, physical carriers, and cultural practices. It cannot be helpful to subject the history of ideas to puristic reduction."

6 Mulsow (2015) 1–21.

7 Moyn / Sartori (eds.) (2013) 3–30.

8 See Schuppert, G. F. (2014); Schuppert, G. F. (2015).

"third way," at writing a history of ideas as a history of languages: the languages used in public discourses on the common good and on the good and just order of things – the languages, for instance, of theology, philosophy,[9] law, and, increasingly, economics.

Centre stage in the history of ideas as a history of languages is John G. A. Pocock, who, along with Quentin Skinner, founded the reputation of the "Cambridge School of Intellectual History."[10] As the name suggests, it is really a style or school of thought,[11] whose influence is difficult to overestimate.

What this "Cambridge School" is about is perhaps best explained by John G. A. Pocock in his now classic 1962 essay "History of Political Thought."[12] Pocock names his point of departure already in the second paragraph: discussions in the higher spheres of politics are conducted in one or more languages that can be described as *political language(s)*: "… a political scientist may … be interested in the relations between the political activities, institutions and traditions of a society and the terms in which that political complex is from time to time expressed and commented on, and in the uses to which those terms are put; in short, in the functions within a political society of what may be called its language (or languages) of politics."[13]

Quentin Skinner,[14] too, posits that political thought is embedded in the context of the political life and action of a social community[15] and that the language used by the people involved is also socially embedded: "*The political thinker is a social being and his thoughts are social actions or events*. The words and concepts he uses are part of a shared inheritance which severely constrain his liberty to conceptualize and theorize. It is shared inheritance, variously named traditions, universes of discourse, *languages of legitimation*,

9 Mulsow (2015) 9: "Decisive frameworks for ideas are often philosophical and philosophico-theological languages. They determine and influence the speech acts performed in them."

10 See the articles in: Mulsow/Mahler (eds.) (2010); the outstanding introduction in Rosa (1994).

11 See Fleck (1980).

12 Pocock (1962).

13 Pocock (1962) 183.

14 See, above all, his key article: Skinner (1988).

15 Rosa (1994) 199.

vocabularies, and paradigms, which must provide the context in which individual thinkers perform their social actions."[16]

On closer inspection, the public discourse in a society uses not only *one* political language but several such languages: "Any stable and articulate society possesses concepts with which to discuss its political affairs, and associates these to form groups of languages. There is no reason to suppose that a society will have only one such language; we may rather expect to find several, differing in the departments of social activity from which they originate, the uses to which they are put and the modifications which they undergo."[17]

Does the language of law have its place in this repertoire? Pocock believes so: "Some [of those political languages] originate in the technical vocabulary of one of society's institutionalized modes of regulating public affairs. *Western political thought has been conducted largely in the vocabulary of law*, Confucian Chinese in that of ritual. Others originate in the vocabulary of some social process which has become relevant to politics: theology in an ecclesiastical society, land tenure in a feudal society, technology in an industrial society."[18]

Quentin Skinner, too, not only testifies to the important role of the language of law in the political discourse but complains of the predominance of a "law-centric paradigm"[19] that needs to be balanced by a humanistic-republican paradigm as a sort of counter ideology.[20]

This brief review of the "Cambridge School" indicates that political languages are used in every society where policy design and political ideas are discussed: until the advent of modernity first and foremost the language of theology, in early modern times theological-philosophical language, and, in the present age, often the language of economics – reflecting the economization of almost all areas of life. Above all in early modernity, the language of law predominated among these political languages.

It is our impression that the language of law no longer plays a key, or even major role in the history of ideas. At an international conference "Towards a

16 Boucher (1985) 155; quoted from Rosa (1994) 199.
17 Pocock (1962) 195.
18 Pocock (1962) 195.
19 Skinner (1978).
20 Rosa (1994) 208.

Global History of Ideas" staged by the Max Weber College for Cultural and Social Science Studies at the University of Erfurt in July 2017, law was not mentioned. And in his paper on "elements of a globalized intellectual history of premodernity," Martin Mulsow[21] failed to mention the language of the philosophy of law when discussing the globalization of philosophical languages.

The marginalization of the language of law to be observed in discourses on the global history of ideas and knowledge does not do justice to the undeniably prominent role it played in early modernity and fails to recognize the *important potential of the language of law for a future history of ideas and knowledge*.

This is the concern of this book: to explain *the language of law as a language of politics* in discourses on the good and just order of society. As the following five points convincingly show, it is well worth examining the potential of the language of law for a global history of ideas and knowledge.

B. The language of law as a language of politics relevant to the history of ideas: five functions in five contexts

I. The language of law as a language of discourses on the legitimacy of political authority

As Hartmut Rosa has clearly demonstrated for the Cambridge School, discourses conducted in political language are above all *discourses about legitimacy*, a function that comes to the fore principally when old and outdated orders are to be overcome. The success of such ventures can be substantially furthered if a *new language* with new concepts is available that is able to convey the new content. With reference to John G. A. Pocock, Hartmut Rosa writes:

> "Revolutions and changes in paradigm occur … Where social or societal changes can no longer be adequately captured, legitimized, or explained in the prevailing vocabulary; where, to use Kuhn's terminology, societal anomalies occur. As in Kuhn's theory, anomalies in science impose adaptation of the prevailing paradigm, and, if this fails, produce 'scientific revolutions.' According to Pocock, a political community (in the shape of its political thinkers) seeks to adapt the existing lin-

21 Mulsow (2016).

> guistic system to new situations or to replace it by a different 'language.' … An example of such a process that Pocock cites are the upheavals in the English political system in the 1640s. In the first half of the seventeenth century, the political vocabulary in England was dominated by such ideas and concepts as tradition, convention, and custom. The key concepts were 'ancient constitution' and 'common law.' But this vocabulary could be applied only to situations characterized by continuity; it was completely unsuited for explaining, let alone justifying radical change."[22]

With Pocock's remarks in mind, we turn to two examples of how the legitimacy of political authority is handled discursively *in two sublanguages of the language of law*. The first is the language of global constitutionalism with its two legal sublanguages, the language of human rights[23] and the language of the rule of law.[24]

The language of global constitutionalism

In the debate about models of global order,[25] the concept of global constitutionalism[26] plays a prominent part, not in the sense of a utopian call for a world constitution, and not – as Anne Peters suggests[27] – in the sense of "compensatory constitutionalism" to make up for national constitutions' lack of reach, but as a "*global legal script*" in discourses on the justification of political authority wherever and in whatever guise. Mattias Kumm et al. have set out this claim to global validity in an editorial marking the third year of publication of the journal "Global Constitutionalism." They first address the "Trinitarian mantra of the constitutionalist faith," namely "human rights, democracy and the rule of law":

> "The publication record over the first couple of years also reflects the fact that constitutive and fundamental norms that implicate questions of legitimate authority generally include a commitment to human rights, democracy and the rule of law. The commitment to human rights, democracy and the rule of law – *the Trinitarian mantra of the constitutionalist faith* – is part of the deep grammar of the

22 Rosa (1994) 206.
23 On the concept of universal human rights as a "juridified revolution" see Schuppert, G. F. (2015) 247 f.
24 On the globalization of rule of law principles as an applied case of discursive lawmaking, Schuppert, G. F. (2015) 257.
25 See Zürn (2011b) 78.
26 Law/Versteeg (2011) 1163; Schwöbel (2011) 1.
27 Peters (2015) 1484.

> modern constitutionalist tradition. It provides an abstract template of principles in the light of which concrete arrangements are negotiated and policies are forged in contemporary constitutionalist settings. Within this constitutionalist framework, wherever political and legal authority is constituted or exercised, it can be criticized or justified with reference to these concepts."[28]

On closer inspection, the core of the "global constitutionalism" concept consists – secondly – in a *global language* to be employed in discourses on the justification or limitation of political authority. On this *claim to universality*, the authors comment:

> "The '*legitimatory trinity*' as a central feature of a modern constitutional discourse came into the world with the French and American Revolutions and was internally connected to ideas of individual and collective self-government at the time. It went through various challenges and permutations before it re-emerged after World War II to become a globally hegemonic discourse since the 1990s, both in and beyond the state. There is no liberal constitution enacted after 1990 that does not pledge allegiance to the trinity in some way. The European Union asserts that these are its foundational values, the Council of Europe has embraced it, the UN claims to be committed to it and various General Assembly Resolutions have endorsed it. In global public discourse *this is the language most likely to be used* and most likely to be effective when either contesting or resisting authority or using it to justify the imposition of restrictions on others."[29]

The language of legal pluralism

The critical and emancipatory potential of the language of law is demonstrated by one of the most prominent representatives of legal pluralism, Boaventura de Sousa Santos (* 1940). His 1977 essay on "The Law of the Oppressed: The Construction and Reproduction of Legality in Pasargada"[30] reveals the political thrust of his work: he opposes the state monopoly on law and wants to give, or return, a degree of autonomy to the normative order, especially in socially disadvantaged communities. In contrast to other well-known theoreticians of legal pluralism such as John Griffith[31] and Marc Galanter,[32] "he does not look for legal pluralism in indigenous commun-

28 Kumm et al. (2014) 1.
29 Kumm et al. (2014) 4.
30 de Sousa Santos (1977).
31 Griffith (1986).
32 Galanter (1981).

ities. He looks for it in the precarious conditions on the fringes of urban centres of modernity: in the favelas of Rio de Janeiro. He has given the name Pasargada to this urban time-space he studies."[33]

He wants to liberate the various social spheres existing in differentiated societies from the hegemony of state law and have their intrinsic normative value recognized. Innate to the "*new legal common sense*"[34] he propagates is a clear *emancipatory tendency*, which Ralf Seinecke outlines as follows:

> "This demands not an instrumental but an emancipatory juridification of social affairs. His postmodern law gives back their intrinsic law to social spheres, frees them from the exclusive hegemony of state and formal law. This postmodern or plural law lends the various social spheres greater potential for reflection because it places their (autonomous) law, their (autonomous) power, and their (autonomous) knowledge in competition with the law, power, and knowledge of the state and of other structural spaces. This juridification of the social measures actual social structures by the normative standards of the law and puts it under greater *pressure for legitimation.* Law and rightness are more closely related than social authority, social power, and social justice."[35]

In the emancipation of non-state "normative spaces," Santos suggests that an important role could be played by the language of law, which imagines these social spaces and provides not only orientation like a map but can also generates its own reality.

> "My argument is that there are many unresolved problems in the sociological study of the law that may be solved by comparing law with other ways of imagining the real. Maps are one such way. There are, in fact, striking similarities between the laws and maps – both concerning their structural features and their use patterns. Obviously, laws are maps only in the metaphorical sense. But, as rhetoric also teaches us, the repeated use of a metaphor over a long period of time may gradually transform the metaphorical description into a literal description. Today laws are maps in a metaphorical sense. Tomorrow they may be maps in a literal sense."[36]

Closely related to the language of law as a language of discourses on the legitimacy of political authority is its application as a language of political change, which brings out its ability to convey new ideas particularly clearly.

33 Seinecke (2015) 209.
34 For more detail see de Sousa Santos (2002).
35 de Sousa Santos (2002) 229.
36 de Sousa Santos (1987) 286.

II. The language of law as a language of political change

As we have seen, using a language – whether that of theology, philosophy, or law – as a language of politics is not about the inconsequential instruction of the reader but about achieving something, about changing a social reality no longer considered acceptable. To quote John L. Austin, it is about "how to do things with words."[37] Heinrich Heine, one of the most acute and sharp-tongued observers of political affairs in both Germany and France, had this to say about the *incantations* circulating in the political debate on the French Revolution: "... they are incantations mightier than gold and guns, words with which the dead are called out of their graves and the living sent to their death. Words that make giants out of dwarves and shatter giants, words that sever all your power like the guillotine a king's neck."[38]

Some will find this too dramatic and will prefer to formulate the issue in linguistic terms, speaking of the *performative use*[39] of every language of politics. This also holds for the language of law in this capacity.

1. The language of law used in legal policy as "performative language"

In a recent article on "Law as the Subject of Jurisprudence and Law Production", Thilo Kuntz[40] complains of the self-imposed, narrow limitation of jurisprudence to the law "in force". He shows that not only classical law-making but also its realization and interpretation involve producing law in and through language. Kuntz calls this *performative law production*:[41]

> "Law is constituted linguistically whether it is written or unwritten law. The only medium available is the linguistic utterance. The type of legal source, law, or ruling, whether precedent or some other form is immaterial. There is a 'fundamental ... dependence of legal rules and values (requirement, validity, normativity, and obligation) on a legal culture tied to language and its media.'[42] The dependence of law on language is apparent on (at least) two levels: law is not only linguistically *constituted*, it is also *produced* in and through language. The production of law is based on speech acts by the competent authorities. It is an example of the possibility of not

37 Austin (1962).
38 Heine (1971) 103. Transl. R. B.
39 On performativity see Wirth (ed.) (2002); Bachmann-Medick (2009) 104–143.
40 Kuntz (2016).
41 Kuntz (2016) 18.
42 Vesting (2011b) 42.

> only describing the world by means of speech act but also of *changing* it. In other words, the production of law is an example of a performative speech act:[43] if someone with the relevant authority makes a linguistic utterance to the effect that certain conduct is liable to prosecution or that a certain option is available, for instance a company limited by shares, performance of these speech acts bring about criminal liability and creates the company limited by shares as a legal form. These are examples of "performance of an act *in* saying something."[44]

If we apply these reflections of Thilo Kuntz on the performative production of law to the language of law concerned with political change – that is to say, as a language of politics – we can rightly speak of the language of law as performative language. This performative language of law can be used in two ways: first to defend the existing order – under such headings as tradition and acquired rights – and as a fanfare for revolution.[45] The latter almost inevitably invites brief consideration of the French Revolution and its revolutionary (legal) language.

2. Revolutions and their revolutionary (legal) language: the example of the French Revolution

When it comes to discussing the French Revolution, it is only right to give the floor to a Frenchman. Particularly eloquent is Pierre Rosanvallon, who has this to say about the language of the French Revolution:[46]

> "From the beginning of the Revolution it was clear that a new vocabulary was needed to describe the motives and principles of the new political order that was being established. One no longer spoke of subjects, for example, but of citizens; not of a kingdom but of a nation; and so on. It was a time of extraordinary inventiveness in this connection, and *a novel political language* did in fact emerge. But not only was it a language in flux, it was liable to be corrupted as well. Some of the most bitter recriminations expressed during the Terror concerned just this point. Thus Sieyès, the father of the first French Constitution, scathingly denounced "the infamous prostitution of the words most dear to French hearts, Liberty, Equality, People," considering "the abuse of what once was a common language" to be by no means

43 Monography: Müller-Mall (2012).

44 Müller-Mall (2012) 8.

45 On the role of the lawyer, see Schmitt (2008) 491: "Of every revolutionary movement it can be said that the lawyer, the 'theologian of the prevailing order' is seen as its special enemy, while, vice versa, it is precisely the lawyers in particular who are on the side of the revolution and who lend it the pathos of oppressed and insulted law."

46 Rosanvallon (2018) 228.

the least source of the misfortunes of the age, words having now lost their natural meaning and been made to "conspire with the enemies of our country."[47]

In view of the susceptibility of probably all political language to abuse, it is no surprise that in turbulent revolutionary times attempts were made to discipline the use of language; Rosanvallon reports:

"Condorcet's purpose in founding the *Journal d'instruction sociale*, in 1793, was more pedagogical than punitive. Its objective was to 'combat political charlatans'[48] by elucidating the key terms of an orthodox political lexicon and thereby limit variant and illegitimate interpretations. The journal's motto was simply stated: 'Reason is one, and has only one language.'[49] In the same spirit, Sieyès proposed that an attempt be made to 'fix the language,' giving it a stable and permanent form by means of conventions, and thus to provided politics with a 'proper language' uncontaminated by the imprecision of 'natual language.' Sieyès was seconded in this by Destutt de Tracy, author of five-volume *Éléments d'idéologie* (1801–1815), who sought to create an 'analytic language' that would help modify and improve the practice of democracy.[50] The utopian conception of linguistic purity as the condition of plain speaking came to nothing in either case, but there was no getting around the necessity of confronting fundamental questions arising from the indefinite character of political semantics. Democracy is, after all, a regime that unavoidably involves continual and perpetual debate over is basic concepts and terminology."[51]

The plausible conclusion is that democracy is a form of political sociation whose task it is to permanently reflect on the type and quality of the performative language practised within it.

Finally, we take a look at the particularly interesting language of institutional legal thought under the National Socialist regime.

3. The institutional legal thinking of the Carl Schmitt School: an example of the susceptibility of the language of law to abuse

This is not the place to go into the interesting history of institutional legal thought[52] or to examine, let alone question, whether we are witnessing a

47 Guilhaumou (2002) 31, as quoted by Rosanvallon (2018) 228.
48 Condorcet (1793), prospectus of this journal, 10.
49 Condorcet (1793), prospectus of this journal, 10–11.
50 See Schlieben-Lange (1996).
51 Schlieben-Lange (1996) 232–233.
52 See Rüthers (1970); also Meinel (2011).

renaissance of the institutional perspective[53] or its replacement by an individual basic rights perspective, such as Hans-Michael Heinig and Christian Walter propagate for public ecclesiastical law.[54] Instead, we shall examine the *concrete order thinking* of Carl Schmitt, because this example can teach us a great deal about the *susceptibility of the language of law to instrumentalization*.

a) *The concept and function of concrete order thinking*

The concept of *concrete order thinking* goes back to the treatise Carl Schmitt published in 1934 under the title "On the Three Types of Juristic Thought",[55] which introduces the notion of "concrete order and formation thinking" as follows: "every lawyer who consciously or unconsciously bases his work on the concept of '*law*' understands this law either as a *rule*, or a *decision*, or as a concrete *order and formation*. This determines the three types of juristic thinking that are distinguished here."[56]

- *Changes in the property regime*

In 1935, Franz Wieacker, then teaching law at the University of Freiburg i. Br., author of the later "History of Private Law in Europe"[57] and professor at the University of Göttingen (where the present author attended his lectures on Digest exegesis), published a brief work under this heading.[58] It reflects what a circle of professors of law, young in 1933, understood and propagated by "national legal renewal" ("*völkische Rechtserneuerung*").

The preface and foreword send a clear message: a new age requires a "new" jurisprudence[59] and thus *new figures of thought* – as the example of the property concept illustrates:

> "After the upheavals of 1933, the clear and precise *definition of the forms of thought* within which the property concept is still meaningful in the law of this state must be attempted. Even though the National Socialist state promises to care for and

53 See Vesting et al. (eds.) 2014.
54 See Heinig / Walter (eds.) (2007).
55 Schmitt (1993); English translation by J. W. Bendersky: Schmitt (2004).
56 Schmitt (2004) 7.
57 Wieacker (1996); Wieacker (1967).
58 Wieacker (1935).
59 See Grimm (1985).

> uphold property, there can be no doubt that this decision is grounded in *materially new values content*; all work on renewing property law surely needs to begin with an explanation of this content. For it is precisely the property commitments behind the legal provision of Article 903 that, in the merging economic regime, determine the *concrete validity content of the institution 'property'*. In seeking clarity about its structure, we should not once again posit a new generic concept in the sense of normativist positivism from which a new property regime is derived by rigid necessity; such a concept imposed on the *realities of life* would be taken to the point of absurdity by ongoing legislation. Considering new ways of thinking about property serves a different, essentially pedagogical purpose: to present acceptable and unequivocal ideas that obviate any return to obsolescent forms of civil law."[60]

The postulated redefinition of the property concept is explained in the following passage. What the new national order (*Volksordnung*), divided into defined "order circles" (*Ordnungskreise*), requires is a "bounded property regime":

> "This formal version of the task of legal policy will bear no fruit if we do not take the concrete structure of the new order into account. This structuring tendency, as the Farm Succession Act and the Labour Promotion Act show, leads to the replacement of *destructive dialectical group formation in the body of the nation*: workers – employers; tenants – landlords; city and country by ... formations such as the Labour Front (*Arbeitsfront*) and works community (*Betriebsgemeinschaft*), food producers, and farmers. Lawmaking in pursuit of this structural principle is justified by the notion that fronts and occupations are subdivisions of the natural order of the nation, in which lawmaking through occupational group regulation presents itself as the optimal principle for the unconstrained and ordering growth of law. The closer these subdivisions are to the *given circles of the national order*, the more thoroughgoing, comprehensive, and stable regulation will be. Thus, family property law, which in the Civil Code still purports to represent a concrete basic order, is joined by agricultural property law, and in outline also property law pertaining to the industrial enterprise. This is the structure we mean when using the ambiguous term '*bounded property order*'."[61]

- *Changes in the work regime*

Without a doubt, "concrete order thinking" left its mark particularly on the work regime. Writing about "civil law theory and fascism", Ingeborg Maus remarks:[62]

60 Wieacker (1935) 9.
61 Wieacker (1935) 21.
62 Maus (1980).

> "Carl Schmitt's theory of concrete order thinking is most concrete where it refers to the 1934 'Act on the Order of National Labour': 'the collective wage agreement is replaced by a wage order; employers, employees, and workers are the leaders and followers of an enterprise who work together in pursuit of business objectives and for the common good of the nation and state; the two are members of a common order, a community under public law.'[63] This definition, especially under Section 1 of the Act, of a *community ideology of the undertaking*, in which group freedom of contract disappears and the limits to the justiciable legal obligation of the individual are abandoned in favour of a duty of loyalty, offers a classical example of perverted legislation typical of a constitution-making prerogative state and grounded in 'concrete-order thinking'."[64]

What two then standard commentaries on the "Act on the Order of National Labour" have to say about Article 1 is both informative and revelatory. Ingeborg Maus:

> "The first paragraph, a form of preamble, sums up the meaning, content, and ethic of the law, so that the following provisions can be understood largely as elaborations of these basic ideas ... The Act treats this community of all working in the enterprise as *part of* a *national community* (*Volksgemeinschaft*). With every single provision, it calls upon this spirit of national community, demanding and expecting that all individuals fulfil their duties in this sense, but also exercise their rights in this sense. The Act deliberately waives all casuistic regulation, being satisfied to establish general guidelines and generally define duties and rights. Basically, it leaves detailed interpretation to the responsible and conscientious decision of the individuals called upon to decide. It places almost unlimited confidence in all those entrusted with interpretation."[65]

And in the commentary by Mansfeld / Pohl / Steinmann and Krause we find the following complementary remarks: "We are dealing not so much with legal norms inapt to interpretation by old methods ... as with an Act whose main sections are less juristic than *ethical in import*. The aim of the lawmaker is rather to educate and form members of the German nation (*Volksgenossen*) than to establish an external legal order for social life, that will become less and less necessary as this education succeeds."[66]

63 Schmitt (1993) 64.
64 Maus (1980) 133–134.
65 Hueck et al. (1934) 20–21.
66 Mansfeld et al. (1934) 75.

These passages invite the following conclusion:

A regime like that of National Socialism shaped by political struggle and a specific political ideology had to rely on translating its political goals into the language of law, as well, and placing law at the service of regime policy. The ruling elite of the Nazi state were fully aware that it would be useful if they could point to theoretical grounding for such instrumentalization of law and present it as "amenable to theory". In this situation the formulation "concrete order thinking" was to prove invaluable. The conclusion of Schmitt's treatise on the three types of jurisprudential thought shows that, with concrete order thinking, he presented the Nazi regime with an *"apposite" mode of reasoning* on a silver platter. A somewhat lengthy perusal of this "customized" gift is therefore called for:

> "… to traditional positivist thinking, the indisputable advance of a new mode of juridical thought appears to be only a corrective to its old method, a limbering up as in earlier free law movements, as mere adjustment to a new situation for perpetuation and self-preservation of the prevailing type. But the change in jurisprudential thinking comes now in conjunction with a change in the entire structure of the state. As we have seen, all changes in a mode of legal thought are to be seen in a vast historical and systematic context, which places them in the given situation of the community's political life. … The state of today is no longer divided into two in terms of state and society, but into three series of orders in terms of state, movement, and people. The state as a special order level within the political entity no longer holds a monopoly of politics, but is only an organ of the leader of the movement. The old decisionist, normativistic or combined positivist legal thinking is no longer adequate for a political entity thus structured. What is now needed is a concrete order and formation thinking that can deal with the numerous new tasks imposed by the state, national, economic, and world-view situation and which can cope with the new forms of community. Intrinsic to this advance of a new jurisprudential thinking is therefore not mere correction of old positivist methods but a transition to a new type of legal thought able to cope with the coming communities, orders, and formations of a new century."[67]

b) *Radical order thinking and the organization of totalitarian rule*

Under this heading, the historian Lutz Raphael presents ground-breaking reflections[68] on how the totalitarian National Socialist regime managed

67 Schmitt (1993) 54–55. Translation R. B.

68 Raphael (2001).

– without any resistance to speak of – to organize a close relationship between the regime and academia,[69] gaining justification of its political goals. At the same time, Raphael shows the indispensable role played by jurists in *translating the language of ideology into the language of law*, in transforming political ideology into enforceable official language. With reference to National Socialist race theory, he explains that an irrational ideology like that of the Nazi state, if it was to be implemented in administrative practice, in a bureaucratic, i. e., *rule-bound administrative state*, had to be translated into manageable decisions, that is, into statutory law, regulations, or decrees that an administrative staff, generally with legal training, could execute.[70] It was the job of jurists to transpose ideological policy programmes into a language that could be comprehended and carried out by an administration operating in the functional mode of rational legal government. Lutz Raphael describes this "metamorphosis" of irrational ideology into the ostensible rationality of legal and administrative language:

> "As professors, judges, and administrative officials, jurists performed key functions in reshaping private and constitutional law to meet the political goals of the regime, continuously legitimating the wrongful practices of the regime through commentaries and decisions. Notably, the important role played by institutionalized racism shows the need to take the contribution of legal experts into account when examining the applied human sciences. Legal expertise was the indispensable prerequisite for transforming the defamatory propaganda of the regime or the discriminatory allegations of scientists and scholars into *the official language of legally relevant classifications and distinctions*. The contribution of jurisprudence must therefore be seen in this genuinely 'political work':[71] 'The legal facts strengthened the belief in the scientificity of race theory and eugenic practices. In turn, the latter were raised to the

69 Academia was not only unable to oppose the aggressive governmental policy of the National Socialists, but, as Raphael notes, experienced a "*wave of self-mobilization*" for the Nazi cause, abandoning prevailing standards of scholarly morality and professional ethics: "The willing participation of a broad majority in the academic professions and university circles in the 'national revolution' was a decisive precondition for the regime itself, after eliminating basic critique, to adapt to the existing relation of forces in the universities, permitting a limited measure of intellectual freedom of opinion, which established a pluralism of discipline-specific theories and schools for all who accepted *the official language of the new regime and, above all, its political claim to binding interpretation and designation of the social world*." Raphael (2001) 12.

70 See Bertrand (2012).

71 Pollak (1990) 25.

status of research areas at the universities. Vice versa, these disciplines contributed to the legitimation of conditions that had been created by the new legal framework.'"[72]

4. A brief interim appraisal

The language of law as a language of politics, being a performative language, is always at risk of political instrumentalization. This is demonstrated by the French Revolution and by the advent of the National Socialist regime as linguistic-conceptual seizure of power. The latter example is so interesting because it shows how, through the agency of jurists who saw themselves as representatives of a "new jurisprudence," could be translated into the language of law, thus legitimating the totalitarian regime and enabling its bureaucratic application. This particular example demonstrates how the language of law as a language of politics also operates as an institutional language at constant risk of political instrumentalization and even abuse. Not only the language of law is necessarily close to the exercise of power: so is the legal profession, as Bernd Rüthers has convincingly shown.[73]

III. The language of law as a language of rights

When the law comes under discussion in its function of creating and guaranteeing rights, whether in relations between individuals or between the individual and the governance collective to which he or she belongs,[74] we expect to hear about conceptual classics of the language of rights such as subjective public law,[75] basic rights,[76] and the constitutional guarantee of effective legal protection.[77] For the moment, however, our attention turns elsewhere: to two matters we consider particularly important from the point of view of the history of ideas.

72 Raphael (2001) 1–16.
73 Rüthers (1992).
74 Moore (1973).
75 Bühler (1914) 21, 224; Kraft (2008) 14.
76 Comprehensive treatment in: Pieroth / Schlink (2010) 23.
77 Wahl (1985) 222–223.

1. Hardening political ideas through translation into the language of constitutional law

Those who have successfully carried out a revolution or have emerged victorious from a political dispute tend to record the result as a perceptible turn of events – preferably in the language of law with its promise of permanence and stability. In legal and constitutional history, this is demonstrated by the fact that almost all legal acts marking revolutions and upheavals are formulated as documents of rights. Wolfgang Knies has this to say:

> "Not only the French Déclaration but also the *American declarations of rights* is the outcome of revolutionary history. In formulating individual rights, they could draw on the model and material of the seventeenth century English freedom documents, which blazed the trail in the dispute between Crown and Parliament, and which set out the civil liberties of Englishmen – partly as political demands, partly as concessions by the Crown. In the *Petition of Rights* (1628), the first *Agreement of the People* (1647), the *Habeas Corpus Act* (1679), and finally in the *Bill of Rights* (1689), we find not only such important, forward-looking principles and rights as equality before the law, freedom of religion, no taxation without representation, procedural guarantees for detainees, and due process of the law with respect to any encroachment on freedom and property; also the notion of certain natural, innate human rights (birth rights, native rights), which – systematically developed by English theoreticians of the state, notably John Locke (1632–1704) – already find expression in them."[78]

Clearly, the strategy of couching the victory of a political idea or other course-setting political decision in the form of a constitutional act lends palpable shape to the characteristics of a constitution that, following Peter Badura,[79] can be defined as follows:[80]

Constitution

- *a law set out in a constitutional document*, distinguished from the rest of the legal order by its legal effect and the import of its subject matter;
- the most outstanding expression of the *legal culture of a society*, politically documenting and constantly renewing its unity and self-conception;

78 Knies (1971) 45.
79 Badura (1987) cl. 3757 ff.
80 Schuppert, G. F. (2003) 743.

- *legally effectuating*, through the exercise of state authority, *the political ideas promulgated in making the constitution*, and hence, above all establishing the unity of the legal order;
- imposing the exercise of power under a legal order, eliminating the arbitrary and inconsistent exercise of this power, lending it *predictability and stability* through "juristic baptism".

Every constitution is hence a historical snapshot that breaths and reflects the spirit of the times, but which also signals the dawning of a better world.[81] Presumably, a "good" constitution would therefore have something to say even if somewhat antiquated. Writing in the Süddeutsche Zeitung on the occasion of the seventieth anniversary of the Bavarian Constitution, Heribert Prantl confirmed this in an article entitled "State Love Letter":

> "Although this constitution is a love letter it is not mere waffle. When it addresses work, the economy, and social policy, it sounds as if Fidel Castro and Pope Francis helped draft it. 'Every man has the right to gain an adequate livelihood through work,' we read. And: 'Work enjoys the special protection of the state.' And: 'Every man has a right to security against the vicissitudes of life.' And 'Every worker has a right to recreation.'
>
> As we see, this is not taken from a brochure for the 125th jubilee of the German Metalworkers' Union, not from a papal social encyclical, let alone an old socialist constitution of an erstwhile Eastern Bloc country. It comes from the Bavarian Constitution of December 1946. This provision on co-determination above establishment level is also there, very clear and very forceful: 'Workers as equal members of the economy participate in formative economic activities together with all other persons engaged in the economy.'
>
> All these statements convey a vision and a lesson – the lesson from the mass unemployment in the twenties and thirties of the twentieth century, which helped bring the Nazis to power. Seventy years ago, this lesson was so clear to the CSU and the SPD that agreement on fundamental economic issues proved possible. Even if the language sounds a little antiquated and traditionalist here and there, one sometimes has the feeling that this constitution foresaw the difficulties of globalization and pointed in the right direction. 'All economic activity serves the common good' according to Article 151, and 'the economic freedom of the individual finds its limits in consideration of others.' If we hear this nowadays, the old Heiner Geißler comes to mind, or perhaps Sahra Wagenknecht."[82]

So much – with regard to the weight of political ideas – for the hardening of constitutional law in the mould of the constitution.

81 Preuss (1994).
82 Prantl (2016) 49.

2. The language of law as dynamic language: "extending the combat zone"

In a recent article we posited that – in contrast to the classical notion of a system upholding and developing a static order – law has to be understood as a thoroughly *dynamic system*,[83] because only in this sense can law perform its function as the central steerage system for the democratic constitutional state, the state under the rule of law.[84] If this is so, the language of law can also be described as a dynamic language. This is indeed the case.

a) The endogenous dynamics of basic rights

At an early date, basic rights, the focus of the language of rights, moved beyond the closed ranks of defensive rights to steadily extend their *rich functional potential*. The history of basic rights can in so far be written as a *history of expansion*.

In his seminal work on the system of subjective public rights,[85] Georg Jellinek had, in addressing the position of the individual vis-à-vis the state, already drawn a distinction between "status negativus", "status positivus", and "status activus". "Status negativus" concerns basic rights as defensive rights against the state; "status positivus" is determined and guaranteed by basic rights in their capacity as *entitlements, participatory rights, rights to performance*, and *procedural rights*. Finally, "status activus" refers to the situation "where the individual exercises his *freedom in and for the state*, helps to shape and participate in the state. It is fashioned and safeguarded by civil rights."[86]

Taking up and developing this approach, the *basic rights theories*[87] so dominant in the jurisprudence of the Bonn Republic took note of constant change in basic rights and fostered the process[88] in an effort to meet the constantly changing challenges of societal reality. The Federal Constitutional

83 Schuppert, G. F. (2016a); see also Zeh (2006) 123–138.
84 On the law see: Schuppert, G. F. (ed.) (1998).
85 Jellinek (1919) 87 ff.
86 Pieroth / Schlink (2010).
87 Still instructive: Böckenförde (1974).
88 See from the perspective of the transition from the Bonn to the Berlin Republic: Krüper (2015).

Court, in particular, has shown considerable initiative with avant-garde innovations in basic rights.[89] In terms of the problem addressed in this introduction, it could be said that, through its rulings on basic rights, the Federal Constitutional Court has not only safeguarded the expressive capacity of the language of law but has also made it sustainable.

b) *The language of human rights as a language of intervention in political discourses*

If what we have said at the beginning of this introduction about the language of law as a language of discourses on the legitimacy of political authority is correct, the language of law as a language of politics will always tend to be a language of intervention in political discourses and debates. The genuinely political dimension of the language of law is impressively demonstrated by the discourse on human rights:

- *Human rights as "enabling narrative"*

Writing about human rights as a translation problem, Doris Bachmann-Medick[90] addresses the translational potential of the idea of human rights, which unfolds above all when the human rights discourse in the sense of Dipesh Chakrabarty[91] links up with other, politico-social discourses, forming critical-strategic alliances. With reference to Joseph Slaughter, Doris Bachmann-Medick sees such a link in the coupling of human rights and an "emancipatory" literature such as the bildungsroman:[92]

> "Like Lynn Hunt,[93] Slaughter maintains that the programmatic development perspective of individual legal claims in the human rights discourse since the eight-

89 A good example is the "fundamental right of the confidentiality and integrity of information systems", BVerfGE 120, 274, 313 ff.; see Hoffmann-Riem (2016) § 35: Grundrechtsinnovationen im Spannungsfeld von Präventionsstaat und technologischer Entwicklung.

90 Bachmann-Medick (2012).

91 Chakrabarty (2013).

92 On the question of how "human rights function as narrative constructions" can be linked to "story-telling" as the facilitation of "self-representation" of the subjects, see Slaughter (2007), http: //docs.lib.purdue.edu/cgi/viewcontent.cgi?article=1031&context=clcweb&seiredir=1#search=%22clc+web+jospeh+Slaughter+narration%22.

93 Hunt (2007).

> eenth century goes back to the humanistic idea of the spiritual development of the individual. Like literature, it operates as 'enabling fiction.'[94] It is thus certainly no accident, albeit astonishing, that, in drafting Article 29 of the UN declaration of 1948,[95] some delegates controversially invoked a prime literary example of personality development: Daniel Defoe's 'Robinson Crusoe'.[96] But 'enabling' has come to mean a great deal more. It also covers giving impetus to political activism through 'life narratives,' 'testimonios,' and other forms of self-testimony[97] such as those of well-known writers: Arundhati Roy writing against the construction of the [...] Narmada Dam[98] and the Nobel Prize winner and human rights activist Rigoberta Menchú with her support for the rights of the Quiché-Mayas in Guatemala, which she develops in a testimonio.[99] Scandalous and moving is the case of the Nigerian writer and human rights activist Ken Saro-Wiwa, who for many years championed the rights of the Ogoni in Nigeria, a minority whose land has for decades been exploited and contaminated by the oil company Shell against the backdrop of their oppression and impoverishment. In this struggle for indigenous rights, Ken Saro-Wiwa was executed – despite all appeals to human rights and despite the constitution of a local human rights declaration,[100] the Ogoni Bill of Rights of 1990."[101]

But Bachmann-Medick points to another interesting connection, which we shall consider in brief in concluding this look at the language of law as a language of rights.

94 Slaughter (2006) 1406.

95 Article 29:
Everyone has duties to the community in which alone the free and full development of his personality is possible.
(1) In the exercise of his rights and freedoms, everyone shall be subject only to such limitations as are determined by law solely for the purpose of securing due recognition and respect for the rights and freedoms of others and of meeting the just requirements of morality, public order and the general welfare in a democratic society.
(2) These rights and freedoms may in no case be exercised contrary to the purposes and principles of the United Nations.

96 Slaughter (2006) 1405 f.

97 Schaffer / Smith (2004) 1–34.

98 See Roy (1999).

99 Menchú (2010).

100 Under: http://www.waado.org/nigerdelta/RightsDeclaration/Ogoni.html.

101 Bachmann-Medick (2009) 354.

* *From a "needs-centred approach" to a "rights-centred one"*

The link between the human rights discourse and the development discourse has proved particularly fruitful, notable in the discussion of *resource rights*;[102] Doris Bachmann-Medick:

> "Further new translational links arise where, for example human rights issues are translated into the development discourse, particularly apparent in the *Declaration of Development Rights*.[103] Vice versa, the translation of development debates into human rights discourses proves fruitful for human rights praxis. In this fashion, subsistence rights such as food, water, and work – as we have seen – are reformulated as human rights.[104] At any rate, the translation perspective reveals how marginalized sections of the population can advance their self-empowerment and assert their interests; for instance by translating an orientation on needs into an orientation on rights: 'The *needs-centred approach* is being *replaced by a rights-centred approach*'[105] – in rural areas, for example, by reclaiming fishing, land, and forest rights; in urban areas through claims to housing and residential rights or rights to a power supply."[106]

If this perspective is extended to include the ever more urgent problem of climate change, the "rights-centred approach" and the threats to it posed by climate change can be described as follows, to quote Oxfam International:[107]

102 See further: Schuppert, F. (2012); Schuppert, F. (2014).

103 See Eckert (2009) 318: "Der Aufstieg von Entwicklungs- und Menschenrechtsdiskursen verläuft parallel, institutionell gibt es zahllose Überlappungen. Der Frage nach der gegenseitigen Prägung dieser Felder wurde bisher nur sehr unsystematisch nachgegangen."

104 Sachs (2003).

105 Sachs (2003) 30.

106 Bachmann-Medick (2009) 357.

107 Oxfam International (2008).

How climate change undermines human rights

Human-rights norms in international law	Current and projected impacts of climate change upon human rights
The Right to Life and Security "Everyone has the right to life, liberty and security of person." (UDHR, Article3)	• There will be more deaths, disease, and injury due to the increasing frequency and intensity of heat waves, floods, storms, fires, and droughts. • Rising sea levels will increase the risk of death and injury by drowning. Up to 20 percent of the world's population live in river basins that are likely to be affected by increased flood hazard by the 2080s. • Heat weaves are likely to increase deaths among elderly or chronically sick people, young children, and the socially isolated. Europe's 2003 heat wave – induced by climate change – resulted in 27.000 extra deaths.*
Right to Food "The State Parties to the present Covenant, recognize the fundamental right of everyone to be free of hunger …" (ICESCR, Article 11)	• Future climate change is expected to put close to 50 million more people at risk of hunger by 2020, and an additional 132 million people by 2050. • In Africa, Shrinking arable land, shorter growing seasons, and lower crop yields will exacerbate malnutrition. In some countries, yields form rain-fed agriculture could fall by up to 30 per cent in central and South Asia by 2050. • In parts of Asia, food security will be threatened due to water shortages and rising temperatures. Crop yields could fall by up to 30 per cent in Central and South Asia by 2050.
The Right to Subsistence "Everyone has the right to a standard of living adequate for the health and well-being of himself and of his family, including food, clothing, housing …" (UDHR, Article 25) "In no case may a people be deprived of its own means of subsistence." (ICCPR, Article 1.2 and ICESCR, Article 1.2)	• Water: By 2020, between 75 million and 250 million people in Africa are likely to face greater water stress due to climate change. Reduced water flow from mountain glaciers could affect up to one billion people in Asia by 2050s. • Natural resources: Approximately 20–30 per cent of plant and animal species assessed so far are likely to be at increased risk of extinction if average global temperatures rise more then 1.5–2.5 C. Coral bleaching and coastal erosion will affect fish stocks – currently the primary source of animal protein for one billion people. • Property and shelter: Millions more people risk facing annual floods due to sea-level rise by 2080s, mostly in the mega-deltas of Asia and Africa. On small islands, too, sea-level rise is expected to exacerbate inundation, storm surge, and erosion, threatening vital infrastructure, settlements, and facilities that support the livelihoods of island communities.
The Right to Health "The State Parties to the present Covenant, recognise the fundamental right of everyone to be free from hunger …" (ICESCR, Article 11)	• Child malnutrition will increase, damaging growth and development prospects for millions of children. • Increasing floods and drought will lead to more cases of diarrhea and cholera. Over 150.000 people are currently estimated to die each year from diarrhea, malaria, and malnutrition caused by climate change. • Changing temperatures will cause some infectious diseases to spread into new areas. It is estimated that 220–400 million more people will be at risk of malaria. The risk of dengue fever is estimated to reach 3.5 billion people by 2085 to climate change.

Sources: Universal Declaration of Human Rights (UDHR); International Covenant on Civil and Political Rights (ICCPR); International Covenant on Economic, Social and Cultural Right (ICESCR); the Intergovernmental Panel on Climate Change (IPCC) 2007, Working Group II; *World Health Organisation.

3. A second interim appraisal

The language of rights is clearly a classical *subdivision of the language of law*, since it conveys the promising message of individual freedom. But, as we know from our examination of "semantic shifts",[108] semantics change and must change if they do not only reflect societal change but also accompany or even induce it. If the language of rights as a language of politics is to claim such a critical-strategic thrust for itself, it assumes the function of equipping a vast range of "agents of justice"[109] with the vocabulary and conceptual repertoire needed for legal discourse as social critique. It is then only a short step to the language of law as a language of justice, as we shall see.

IV. The language of law as a language of justice

If, in concluding our tour d'horizon of the functions and contexts of the language of law, we now turn to the justice dimension, it is not with the intention of losing ourselves in the vast terrain of law as justice.[110] We are concerned with a specific perspective, namely the role of the language of law in the current intensive political discourse on justice; the language of law makes itself distinctly heard in these debates.

1. Justice discourses as social critique: the language of law as social-critical language

There is currently no escaping the call for "more justice". In 2016, the Social Democratic party staged a major "Values Conference: Justice",[111] and the Greens, too, give the highest priority to justice – witness their efforts to develop a consistent taxation concept. These justice discourses naturally address the everlasting topic of all social policy – associated above all with the name of John Rawls – *distributive justice*,[112] but especially with social

108 On the role and function of "semantic shifts" see SCHUPPERT, G. F. (2010) 115 ff.
109 See O'NEILL, O. (2001); DRYZEK (2015).
110 For a good overview on law and justice see: RÜTHERS et al. (2010) § 9 (222–264).
111 On 9/5 2016 in Berlin; see the speech by party leader Sigmar Gabriel, https://sigmar-gabriel.de/wp-content/uploads/sites/3/2016/05/Rede_Sigmar_Gabriel_beim_Wertekongress.pdf.
112 RAWLS (1999).

justice, represented in political philosophy primarily by "social egalitarians",[113] who focus not so much on the distribution of material goods but – as Fabian Schuppert has shown – on the demand to treat people as "being equal":

> "According to its proponents, social equality is valuable because it protects every person's status as a free and equal member of society. Social equality is concerned with the relationships people stand in and what people can do and be within these relationships. Phrased differently, social equality concerns more the harmful effects of certain social relationships and their associated inequalities, than the equal distribution of a particular set of goods or the provision of equal initial opportunity. This reading of equality distinguishes social egalitarians from classic distributive egalitarians, whose focus is determining the adequate currency for egalitarian distributions and the exact principles of such distribution. [...] Social egalitarians thus primarily worry about the negative effects of certain inequalities."[114]

This "social egalitarian approach" is particularly convincing and promising because it connects three functionally related dimensions. First, it focuses on the *justifiability of existing inequalities*, a highly charged issue from the social critique point of view; second, it addresses concrete experiences of inequality, how social groups[115] are affected;[116] thirdly and finally, this social-egalitarian approach – and this where law comes in – also addresses the *remedial dimension*, exploring how, by what means and by whom unjustified inequalities can be eliminated or compensated.[117]

2. The demand for global justice as a paradigmatic shift in the history of ideas

Where justice is concerned, the question automatically arises of whether justice is to be conceived of as local, regional, national, or even global: "what is the scope of justice?" As Stefan Gosepath puts it:

> "Is justice global, universal, boundless? Or are there reasons of any sort, conceptual, normative, or pragmatic, to conceive of justice locally – to rather start at home, in a

113 See especially Anderson (1999); O'Neill, M. (2008); Schuppert, F. (2015a).

114 Schuppert, F. (2015b).

115 On the concept of group in a sociology of inequalities, see Schuppert, G. F. (forthcoming).

116 O'Neill, M. (2008); Schuppert, F. (2015a).

117 See Anderson (2012).

> community or state-society and therefore require less from foreigners than from our fellow citizens? In order to find an answer to such questions, I will start […] by outlining what I see as a relatively plausible, and not uncommon, egalitarian conception of justice. According to this conception, justice is – at least prima facie – immediately universal, and therefore global. It does not morally recognize any judicial boundaries or limits. […] My conclusion that there is such a [global] dimension will consequently lead to many normative-pragmatic questions […] especially how best to construct and establish global (or international) institutions securing global justice."[118]

According to Christoph Broszies and Henning Hahn, the widespread view that justice can be conceptualized only in global terms is nothing less than a paradigmatic shift:

> "The idea that the domain of justice extends beyond the limits of one's own polity or empire marks no less than a paradigmatic shift in the history of ideas. To a certain extent, cosmopolitanism follows on from antiquity, the Middle Ages, and modernity, but ultimately it responds to genuinely modern experiences and challenges. In brief: global justice is a prerequisite of globalization. The associated global mechanisms of exclusion, exploitation, and domination are a basic condition for global justice to come to the fore. It is therefore no surprise that the cosmopolitanism-particularism debate opens a new chapter in the history of ideas."[119]

Nevertheless, the notion of global justice has older historical roots:[120]

> "Leafing back through the history of ideas can … prove informative. After all, the Stoics introduced the cosmopolitan at an early date, the citizen of the world who understands himself as a member of the human race and part of the overall world order – and who is consequently not intimidated when threatened with exile because of his independent attitude. However, in the ethical cosmopolitanism of the stoics, there is little sign of any justice-theoretical cosmopolitanism explicitly concerned with the legitimacy of global rule. The same can be said of divine justice in the Christian Middle Ages. It was not until modern times that a sustainable change is to be observed in state-centric legal thinking and consequently in the state-centric understanding of justice. Although the aim of early modern international law was mainly to embed (religious) peace in an international legal order, the idea of cosmopolitan individual rights was already taking root in the soil of natural law. In this connection, Martha Nussbaum points out that Hugo Grotius (1583–1645) grounded international law in human dignity, and already in *De Jure Belli ac Pacis* (1625) argued in favour of universalizing legal relations between individuals."[121]

118 Gosepath (2001) 145.

119 Broszies / Hahn (eds.) (2013) 9–52, here 13.

120 Broszies / Hahn (eds.) (2013) 1–14.

121 Nussbaum (2006) 36–39; see also: Fraser (2005).

Be that as it may. In a globalized world one can think only in global terms, which – see Stefan Gosepath – leads directly to the problem that *international institutions* are needed in order to realize justice at the global level. To this extent, justice – as we have shown elsewhere[122] – is to be conceived of primarily as *institutional justice*, a conclusion that Christoph Broszies und Henning Hahn draw in their introduction to the cosmopolitanism-particularism debate:

> "'The world in which we live is not just.' With this remark, Thomas Nagel begins his already seminal article on 'The Problem of Global Justice.'"[123]… Nagel describes a world that as a whole *cannot* be just, at least as long as it is divided into separate spheres of dominance. This world quite simply lacks the necessary institutions for coordinating action and enforcing rules. Seen in this light, the world as it is can be neither just nor unjust, so that asking about global justice is pointless. Nevertheless, Nagel, too, asserts that the world is unjust. Not perhaps in the same sense as when a state apportions well-being unequally across society, denies people democratic participatory rights, or discriminates against certain groups. The familiar principles of social justice, according to Nagel, are adapted to the nation-state. In many ways, however, it makes sense to speak of global injustice phenomena, for instance the distribution of climate change costs, veto rights in the Security Council of the United Nations, global seed and medicine patents, the exploitation of people and nature in the global market, or malnutrition among some billion human beings."[124]

This brings us to our last, brief topic.

V. The language of law as the language of a new global order

1. The transformation of statehood as a problem of description and analysis

Statehood has of course always been subject to change,[125] inviting the amiable depiction of various stages in its development. One example of such scenario painting is offered by Udo di Fabio, who offers a five-stage model:

> "The first stage is the arrival of the new idea of the state, which to some extent presented itself in the revival context of the Renaissance as a return to antiquity's

122 Schuppert, G. F. (2017a).

123 Nagel, T. (2013).

124 Broszies/Hahn (eds.) (2013) 9.

125 See, for instance: Leibfried/Zürn (eds.) (2006); see also the article by Schuppert, G. F. (2008c) with the reply by Genschel/Leibfried (2008).

> notion of polity. The next stage is abstraction and detachment from the concrete ruling figure, which made the state into more than the ideational amplification of a monopoly of authority claimed by the prince and his house. A further stage is national magnification and merging with the community defined in national terms. The trend from the outset, and still predominant today, has been towards rationalization, demystification, and complete legal subjugation of state authority in the constitutional state. However, a new stage seems to be emerging: the functional dismemberment of the state, the loss of state unity and of its ideational significance in a marked shift towards an open and integrated state, which – apparently in rejection of the order concepts of modernity – is reverting to a complex web of authority."[126]

Whether we take this model or that of the shift described by Philipp Genschel and Bernhard Zangl "from authority monopolist to authority manager",[127] every far-reaching change in statehood is a challenge for all scholarly disciplines that address the state, obliging them to examine whether their methodological tools suffice to adequately describe and analyse these processes of change.

In the first volume of the Jahrbuchs für Staats- und Verwaltungswissenschaft, Claus Offe reflects on a "theory of the state in search of its subject",[128] and Juliane Kokott and Thomas Vesting from the board of the Association of German University Teachers of Constitutional Law were commissioned to examine public law theory and changes in the subject matter.[129] Other examples of similar efforts could be cited.[130]

However, if any scholarly approach is particularly suitable for investigating change in statehood, it is the governance approach. This is at any rated suggested by the more recent governance literature, as the following examples show.

First, writing about the connection between changes in statehood and the governance perspective, Julia von Blumenthal has this to say:

> "A link is often established between the increasing scholarly interest in governance and political changes. Apart from the processes of globalization already mentioned, the financial crisis in the public sector and an 'ideological shift towards the market' in politics and science are cited in explaining the popularity of the concept. The discussion on governance thus belongs in the context of analysing and describing changes in statehood. To some extent, governance research adopts a contrary stance to scenarios of crisis or even of an end of statehood, seeing in governance proof of the adaptability of states to external social and economic changes."[131]

126 di Fabio (2003) 20.
127 Genschel / Zangl (2008).
128 Ellwein et al. (eds.) (1987) 30–320.
129 Kokott / Vesting (2004) 7 ff., 41 ff.
130 See Ladeur (2000) 101 ff.; Neyer (2004).
131 Blumenthal (2005) 1150 ff.

The second example is from Hans-Heinrich Trute, Doris Kühlers, and Arne Pilniok, who conclude their article on the governance approach as an analytical approach in administrative jurisprudence with the following succinct remark: "One important achievement of the governance approach is that it provides a *framework for discussing changes in statehood* while ensuring mutual interdisciplinary connectivity."[132]

The suitability of the governance approach for analysing change in statehood is even more obvious if this approach is seen as specifically process-oriented. In my view, the special "competence" of the governance approach, indeed, its specific added value, is its processuality and dynamics.[133] It is, however, demanding in that, unlike many approaches, it addresses neither the sequence of governance levels (local governance, regional governance, metropolitan governance, European governance, global governance) nor the sequence of governance areas (Internet governance, environmental governance, governance of financial markets). Instead, it takes a processual perspective that seeks to analyse changes in governance structures and explain observable processes of change. This processual perspective can unfold in four dimensions,[134] namely:

- *Changing and new actor constellations*, drawing on the actor perspectives of control theory but "dynamizing" them processually;
- *Changing and new institutional arrangements and regulatory structures*, drawing on the institutionalist turn called for by Renate Mayntz,[135] enriching it primarily from an institutional culture point of view;
- *Dissolving or blurring boundaries*, such as those between national and international, public and private, internal and external, etc., on the assumption that observable changes in statehood are above all processes of dissolving and blurring boundaries;
- *Changing or new legitimation concepts* that overcome the security offered by national lines of legitimation, making legitimatory demands on new, notably transnational forms of governance.

This brings us to the next point.

132 Trute et al. (2008) 173–189.
133 See Botzem et al. (eds.) (2008).
134 Botzem et al. (eds.) (2008).
135 Mayntz (2005).

2. In what language is a new global order really described?

The answer is pretty obvious: above all in the language of law, when – informed by governance theory – it thinks in terms of regulatory structures. It suffices to cite Michael Zürn's "four models of a global order in cosmopolitan intent" in which, as the following overview shows, the language of law plays a key role.[136]

Four models of a global order in cosmopolitan intent

	Intergovernmental model of global order	*Cosmopolitan pluralism*	*Cosmopolitan federalism*	*Cosmopolitan democracy*
Representatives (examples)	Dahl, Maus, Moravcsik, Scharpf	Dryzek, Forst, Krisch, Kumm	Habermas, Höffe, Schmalz-Bruns	Archibugi, Caney, Held, Pogge, Marchetti
Basic norms	State sovereignty; prohibition of the use of force; principle of non-intervention; democratic organization of states	Human rights; rule of Law; due process; practical reasoning; discursive democracy	Human rights; democratic legitimation of the monopoly of force; discursive justification of regulation	Democratic legitimation of all regulation; justice; fundamental rights
Statehood	Territorial states concentrate all the functions of statehood	Statehood unravels in different legal orders; the monopoly of force remains on the nation-state level; sovereignty is bound by basic norms	Legitimate monopoly on preserving peace and protecting fundamental rights shifts to the global level; democratic states continue to exist and maintain their dominance in many fields	Emergence of a rudimentary world state; nation-states

This instructive overview concludes our tour d'horizon of the five functions of the language of law we consider the most important.

136 Zürn (2011b).

C. In conclusion

As we remarked at the outset, we are concerned with the *potential of the language of law* as a language of politics for making a meaningful contribution to a future global history of ideas and knowledge. To judge by what we have so far "dug up", this potential can be considered extremely high.

It begins with the observation that discourses on the legitimacy of political authority as social-critical discourses generally take the form of legal discourses. This brings us to the second observation that revolutionary seizures of power are always legalo-semantic seizures of power, in which the "new cause" always comes in the guise of a new language requiring new concepts or reinterpreting existing legal concepts.

Third, it is evident that the language of law can make a particularly important contribute to the *global dimension of a history of ideas*. Something in the way of a language of global constitutionalism has meanwhile developed, a particularly interesting phenomenon because it takes up the function of constitution-making, "hardening" political ideas with all the legal consequences for impact and durability. Fourth, this globalization "gene" of the language of law as a language of politics is also evident in the spread of justice discourses at the global level, where, as inevitable response to ongoing globalization, global justice is in increasing demand, thus broadening the very concept of justice (catchwords: environmental justice, climate justice).

Fifth, a future world order – however conceived – cannot, it would seem, be described without the language of law. Zürn's overview of the subject "speaks volumes".

In sum: the language of law as a language of politics is, in our view, an essential component of a global history of ideas and knowledge, a conclusion we shall be justifying in detail in the course of this book with abundant reference to the literature. To begin with, however, the first section considers what is to be understood by global history and a global history of ideas. The contribution of the language of law cannot be meaningfully discussed without first defining these concepts.

Part 1
Understanding the Global History of Ideas

Introduction

A. How ideas and knowledge travel: a little story to begin with

When people write about the history of ideas and knowledge, they mostly focus on how knowledge and ideas spread – not only within a narrow compass but also throughout the world or what the people of the time consider to be "their" world, for instance Christendom or Islam. Ideas and knowledge seem to find it difficult to stay put: they like to be "on the move."[1] This suggests it would be useful to look at how ideas and knowledge voyaged before the advent of telegraphy and the Internet. A novel, "The Thousand Autumns of Jacob de Zoet,"[2] gives us a pointer. The hero is a young clerk in the employ of the Dutch East India Company (Vereenigte Oost-Indische Compagnie or VOC). In 1799 he takes up his post at a trading factory at the gates of the Japanese port of Nagasaki. Since the Japanese government is determined to prevent Western, notably Christian ideas from entering the country unfiltered, the baggage of foreign arrivals is thoroughly searched. Including Jacob's sea chest. Its contents include a "scarred Psalter bound in deerskin," a family heirloom Jacob's father has entrusted to him for his journey to Asia with instructions to "protect it with your life." When Jacob learns that the bibliophile inspector Ogawa is to examine the chest, he fears all is lost:

> "Mr. de Zoet," says Ogawa, "I wish to speak about a book you bring. It is important matter …"

1 See, for instance, Smith, P.H. (2009); Secord (2004).
2 Mitchell (2011). The magazine *Spiegel* has described the work as "a literary travel dream and linguistic orgy."

> Jacob loses the next clause to a rush of nausea and dread. … My career is destroyed, thinks Jacob, my liberty is gone …
>
> "In Mr. de Zoet's chest I found book of Mr. … Adamu Sumissu." Jacob opens his eyes: … "Adam Smith?"
>
> "Adam Smith – please excuse. The Wealth of Nations … You know?"
>
> I know it, yes, thinks Jacob, but I don't yet dare hope. "The original English is a little difficult, so I bought the Dutch edition in Batavia."
>
> Ogawa looks surprised. "Adam Smith is Englishman?"
>
> "He'd not thank you, Mr. Ogawa!" Smith's a Scot, living in Edinburgh. But can it be The Wealth of Nations about which you speak?"
>
> "What other? I am rangakusha – scholar of Dutch science. Four years ago, I borrow Wealth of Nations from Chief Hemmij.[3] I began translation to bring" – Ogawa's lips ready themselves, 'Theory of Political Economy' to Japan. But lord of Satsuma offered Chief Hemmij much money, so I returned it. Book was sold before I finish."
>
> … "Then, this morning, in your book chest, Adam Smith I find. Very much surprise, and to speak with sincerity, Mr. de Zoet, I wish to buy or rent …"
>
> "Adam Smith is neither for sale nor rent," says the Dutchman, "But you are welcome, Mr. Ogawa – very welcome indeed – to borrow him for as long as ever you wish."[4]

The theory of political economy might well have come to Japan in this fashion – on a ship of one of the world's biggest trading companies in the sea chest of a company officer.

So far so good.

The brief episode from this novelistic "historical cabinet of curiosities"[5] has a certain déjà-vu effect, recalling Christopher L. Hill's assertion in "Conceptual Universalization in the Transnational Nineteenth Century,"[6] that it is immaterial whether the "circulation of ideas by circulation of books"[7] involves the original publication, a translation, or a popularized version:

3 The then director of the trading factory before the gates of Nagasaki.
4 Mitchell (2011) 28 f.
5 To quote a review in the *Tageszeitung*.
6 Hill (2013).
7 See Gamsa (2011).

> "The fact that many of the concepts arrived in mediated form – through the intellectual vulgate, through translation – means it was not necessary to go to the origin to get the concepts, which by this time may have been more recognizable in their popularized than in their original forms anyway. Such recognizability came from the reproduction of concepts, not their original production. And as much as geopolitics inflected the creation of equivalents – a key part of the circulation of ideas – the readiness with which equivalents were accepted shows that these concepts' lingering associations with particular parts of the globe did not leave them looking any less universal."[8]

With these considerations in mind, *three points* should be noted:

* *Ideas and knowledge: typical "fellow travellers"*

The history of ideas and knowledge repeatedly draws attention to the fact that ideas and knowledge[9] like to travel in company – riding piggyback, as it were, on trade, religion, and the military;[10] in our example on the shoulders of a group of merchants[11] – a species of globalization actor we have dealt with elsewhere and whom we shall be looking at more closely in the course of this book.

* *Transport media for knowledge and ideas*

Even though we are not told the titles of all the books Jacob de Zoet had in his sea chest – there were some fifty – we nevertheless learn that at least two "bodies of thought" were being transported: Dutch Protestantism and the economic theory of the Scot Adam Smith. Books were thus particularly suitable transport media; a global history of ideas and knowledge always has to be a "history of books,"[12] as well.

Now, books and printing are not only an important medium for philosophical and economic theories and knowledge but also a key *medium of law*, as two examples will show. The first is Hugo Grotius' famous work "De Jure Belli ac Pacis," which Thomas Nicklas in 2010 described (albeit with a question mark) as "*international law for the saddlebag*",[13] because King Gustav

8 Hill (2013) 145.
9 On "knowledge as fellow traveller" see Renn/Hyman (2012).
10 See Mulsow (2016) 6.
11 Mulsow (2016) 6.
12 See Rose, J. (1998).
13 Nicklas (2010).

Adolf of Sweden, "who landed with his army in West Pomerania in 1630, claimed to have it always at hand during his military campaigns."[14]

Our second example comes from Thomas Vesting, "Die Medien des Rechts: Buchdruck,"[15] ("The Media of Law: Printing"), in which he describes the Christianity of late antiquity as a sort of "*pocketbook religion*" because of the important role played by the parchment codex as a writing material:[16]

> "These changes in the materiality and format of communication are closely associated with the religious transformations of late antiquity, notably the rise of Christianity following Constantine's victory at the Battle of the Milvian Bridge (312), which also proved an institutionally stabilizing movement. While the importance of orality for (early) Christianity ought not to be underestimated, Christians were eager readers from the outset. They are repeatedly noted as owning books and often have to explain themselves, as did the Christians of Scilium arrested and brought before the proconsul Saturnius in Carthage; when asked what they had in their luggage, they responded: 'The books and letters of Paul, a just man'. As writers, however the apostles had always preferred the parchment codex, which towards the end of the second century was practically a Christian innovation, establishing Christianity in a certain sense as a 'pocketbook religion'[17]."[18]

* *Receptivity for the Other and New*

In our first example, it was the "third rank" interpreter Ogawa who was eager to translate the theories of Adam Smith in order to introduce them to Japan. Thus the spread of ideas and knowledge appears to depend very much on the openness of elites in the recipient country; in this connection, Martin Mulsow has pointed to receptiveness at the Chinese imperial court:

> "Also prominent is naturally the receptiveness of the Chinese imperial court, notable that of the Kangxi Emperor, the second of the Quing dynasty at the turn of the

14 Nicklas (2010) 61.

15 Vesting (2013); see also Vesting (2011b) and (2011a) as well as the fourth and final volume (2015).

16 On its qualities, see Vesting (2013) 10: "The parchment codex fundamentally changed the technical form of the book. It ended the monopoly of papyrus as writing material, which since the second millennium before Christ had been made from the papyrus plant harvested on the banks of the Nile and glued together into rolls. … [I]n the Mediterranean region of late antiquity, calf, goat, and sheepskin was laboriously washed, depilated, bated, dried, smoothed, and then folded once, twice or three times When all surfaces had been written on and or painted, they were bound together into a codex, which, with its layered rectangular pages came very close to the the compact format of the printed book."

17 Stroumsa (2011) 67 f.

18 Stroumsa (2011) 10–11.

> seventeenth to the eighteenth century, for European mathematics and astronomy brought to China by the Jesuits. Catherine Jami tells the story not, as usual, from the European perspective but from that of the Chinese.[19] Only then does the process as a genuine "entanglement" become apparent, for we see how the emperor adapted the ideas received and used them to consolidate the Manchu dynasty while the Jesuits proved open to adopt Chinese ideas in other areas."[20]

So much for our introductory example. What, however, are we to understand by global history and a global history of ideas and knowledge? In considering this question we must constantly keep in mind ("casting our eyes to and fro"[21]) what this means for the language of law as a "language of politics" relevant for the history of ideas.

B. What are global history and the global history of ideas?

As Jürgen Osterhammel has repeatedly and knowledgeably shown, there are old and new approaches to world history, and, above all, methodologically differing ones.[22] There is no need to go over them here. Since the concept of "global history" appears to be gaining ground and is also more apposite to our present project than the somewhat bombastic "world history",[23] we shall be drawing on Sebastian Conrad's[24] exemplary definition of global history, identifying three approaches.

19 Jami (2012).
20 Jami (2012) 16.
21 A process familiar to all lawyers. The formulation ("Prozess des Hin- und Herwandern des Blicks") goes back to Engish (1963), who discusses the process of applying the law and the need to cast one's eyes to and from between the facts of the case and the legal consequences.
22 Osterhammel (2005); Osterhammel (ed.) (2008) 9–32.
23 It seems to us that Martti Koskenniemi's scepticism about the term "global history" expressed in discussion with Alexandra Kemmerer applies to "world history": "For me the call for global history implied a ridiculously exaggerated ambition, perhaps even the old European endeavour to find the place where one's own statements can be stamped 'global', where one can say 'that is global' whereas that there is not." Kemmerer (2015) 38.
24 Conrad (2013); see also Conrad et al. (eds.) (2007b).

I. Fields and topics of global history

In his highly differentiated introduction to global history, Sebastian Conrad presents a tour d'horizon, identifying seven topic areas with a strong affinity for global issues:[25]

- *Global commodities*
- *Expansion*
- *History of the oceans*
- *Migration*
- *Empire*
- *Nation*
- *Environmental history*
- *Race*

There can be no doubt that taking a "*global view*" of these fields is particularly fruitful, and Conrad's exposition of the topics is extremely interesting, with abundant examples, from the global product history of sugar and tea[26] to oceans as interactional spaces – which we shall be looking at – and the global history of migration, a subject of almost depressing topicality: in some regards, the treatment of migrants recalls the times of the slave trade.[27]

Be that as it may, we will not be pursuing this *issue-specific approach* any further. The various levels of analysis – products, geographical determinants,[28] governmental structures, global processes – are too heterogeneous; this approach offers far too much temptation to include fields – such as the global history of communication,[29] not to mention the global history of ideas and knowledge – that an author might consider just as important.

25 Conrad (2013) 202 ff.

26 On sugar, see Mintz (2007); on tea, see Vries (2009).

27 Consider the growing practice of countries targeted by current migration flows of spending billions to induce governments in migrants' countries of origin to "keep" would-be refugees, or to persuade governments in transit countries to take back the people who have passed through them. To this extent, we can speak of the economization of the refugee problem.

28 Marshall (2015).

29 See Schuppert, G. F. (2015).

II. Key concepts and figures of thought

In a 2015 article on "globalification," Jürgen Osterhammel introduces six "figures of thought of the new world,"[30] using what we can describe as key concepts.[31] This arouses our interest: the key concept[32] has proved a particularly useful device for mapping out an extensive terrain – for instance, "changes in statehood."[33] Since by definition no other subject matter is likely to have a broader wingspan than global history, the three essential functions of key concepts outlined by Andreas Voßkuhle will be helpful:

> "The function of key concepts is to make overarching ideas of order fertile for given argumentational contexts by concentrating, structuring and rendering comprehensible a mass of information and thoughts in a repository term. While reducing complexity they also serve as an inspirational platform by stimulating association, lending first shape to ideas still in the making, bringing various perspectives together, and offering guidance for the future. In this sense they resemble 'theories' ... – but the format is smaller and the proposition at first glance more simplistic. Key concepts are therefore particularly dependent on concretisation; they supply no answers but give direction to thought."[34]

With these three functions in mind, we turn briefly to Osterhammel's six figures of thought and, in much abbreviated form, to what he has to say about them:[35]

- *Expansion*
  "It is no wonder that more recent global history has developed essentially out of the history of imperial and economic expansion ... Expansion remains the *founding figure of thought of global history*."
- *Circulation*
  "The cross-boundary dynamics of expansion processes are often contained and channelled in the figure of circulation ..." What do we mean [however] by the 'circulation of ideas'? Older, somewhat patinated categories like 'transfer' and 'reception' were in many regards more differentiated.
- *Channelling systems*
  "Circulation necessarily presupposes a channelling system." In this context *network* is the concept often used: "Analytically, the network remains the most productive figure of thought for globality, because it allows stable system for-

30 Osterhammel (2015).
31 See Baer (2004).
32 Schuppert, G. F. (1999).
33 See Schuppert, G. F. (2008c).
34 Vosskuhle (2001b); Schuppert, G. F. (1999) 198.
35 Osterhammel (2015) 12 f.

mation through the institutional consolidation of such interconnected complexes. The transitive concept of networking includes intentional action: there is no network without *networkers*."

- *Densification*
  "Densification means, for example, multiplying elements and their interrelations in a finite world, reducing spacing, increasing the speed and frequency of contact, compressing cause-effect chains. ... Densification is relatively easy to describe; where it occurs, even statistics will have a great deal to say – for instance, statistics on book production and the book trade in the modern history of ideas and knowledge."
- *Standardization and universalization*
  "Standardization and universalization have become fundamental figures of a global teleology .... Only rarely is simple convergence meant .... The focus is rather on two things: first, on the development of world-society legal norms, headed by the much-discussed human rights, and, second, the development of systems of technico-economic coordination, such as standard world time or the rules of international payments."
- *Spatial asymmetry of power*
  "If we take the originally critical impulse of global history seriously, it does not reduce itself to the genesis of the all-round integrated present. The uneventful, creeping filling and densification of the planet – more and more people having more and more to do with one another – would be a framing narrative of dubious triviality. For this reason, a figure of thought from the dependence and world-system theories of the 1970s has remained important, namely spatial *asymmetry* of power, the asymmetry of subjugation and resistance. The gap between rich and poor, between strong and weak corresponds at the international level to social inequality within national societies. ... The discussion is only getting under way on how the history of ideas, especially for the age of European world dominance, reacts to such conflictual plurality. At any rate, widespread dichotomies such as Occident / Orient, export / import of ideas, and Westernization / local knowledge are no longer adequate."

These six figures of thought look promising and do justice to the basic functions of key concepts outlined by Andreas Voßkuhle. The productiveness of this approach encourages us to look for key concepts in the global history of ideas to allow comparison with the figures of thought discovered there with those of Osterhammel for global history.

III. Global history as perspective

Under this heading, we return to Sebastian Conrad's introduction to global history. He begins by asking whether global history is a subject or a perspective. His answer is clear: global history is primarily a perspective.

> "Is global history … a subject of study or a perspective? Primarily, it is the latter – and thus an approach that focuses on certain aspects and contexts. The Kulturkampf in Bavaria in the nineteenth century, to take an example, can be examined from the point of view of local history, as an issue of cultural or gender history, or as part of German history. But it can also be placed in the context of global history – as an element in the struggle between the liberal state and the churches that occurred in the nineteenth century in many parts of the world: throughout Europe, but also in Latin America and Japan. These conflicts were interconnected through various channels. *Global history is therefore primarily a perspective, and it brings other dimensions, other questions to the fore*."[36]

I agree with this assessment, above all in the light of my far-reaching experience with "governance," my concern at the Berlin Social Science Center (WZB) as holder of the research professorship in "New Modes of Governance" established in 2003. Here, too, the question was whether governance was to be seen rather as a subject of study – as implied by such topic blocks as "local," "regional," and "global governance" to be found in every governance manual[37] – or as a perspective from which the governance structures of modern statehood are investigated in their diversity and specific "mix." After more than ten interesting years in the governance field, we are as convinced as Sebastian Conrad that governance is above all a perspective, and a non-statist one: a non-state-centric point of view operating with institutional categories, a standpoint from which the regulatory structures and governance regimes obtaining in any policy sector can be examined.[38]

If global history is primarily a perspective – a view repeatedly echoed in Jürgen Osterhammel's presentation of various "globalizations"[39] and which has recently been affirmed by Philip McCarty[40] – it can also be *a perspective* in a broad range of topic areas, as Sebastian Conrad concludes:

> "Global history is currently a broad trend in both research and teaching. In journals and publication series, at meetings and conferences concerned with global history, forums for scientific exchanges and discussion on research have developed. They do

36 Conrad (2013) 12.
37 Benz (ed.) (2004).
38 See Schuppert, G. F. (ed.) (2005) 371–469; Schuppert, G. F. (2007c); Schuppert, G. F. (2014).
39 Osterhammel (2011).
40 McCarty (2014) 290: "Whatever the object of study or field of inquiry, global perspectives shape the kinds of questions we ask, the analytical approaches we take, and the ways we engage the world."

> not operate alongside the rest of the discipline, they are not a luxury one must be able to afford. In the twentieth century things were different: then world history was an occupation for well-established and mostly older historians. Today, global history is even on occasion addressed by theses and dissertations. The approach has also found its place in theory, in individual seminars or entire courses of study. Also striking is that widely different fields are discussed. Environmental and economic historians no less than social and cultural historians lay claim to global history. *In principle, a global history perspective can be combined with all historiographical approaches.*"[41]

If this is the case, a global history perspective would not only be amenable to legal history but also necessary in the interests of connectivity. Anticipating this observation – which dates from August 2016 – the Max Planck Institute for European Legal History launched a series of publications on "Global Perspectives on Legal History," starting in 2014 with "Entanglements in Legal History,"[42] fully in agreement with the definition of a global history of ideas as "histoire croisée" or "entangled history."[43]

Thomas Duve, director of the Frankfurt Max Planck Institute, who has taken up the cause of this global perspective for legal history[44] and launched the publication series mentioned, (in which our book "The World of Rules" has also appeared[45]), notes in his introductory contribution to the entanglement volume that a global history dimension has always been immanent in legal historiography:

> "[...] Legal History may nearly always have harboured a 'transnational' dimension in the broad sense of the word, especially in consideration of history before and after the spread of nationalism in Europe. Our work has addressed a wide array of questions relating to the 'transfer', 'transplantation' or 'translation' of normativity. It has almost always had to confront the challenge of describing and analyzing processes of normative reproduction in rapidly changing historical settings, not similar, but neither that different from those we observe today. The globalization of law, and of legal thought, is not a new phenomenon.[46] Thus, legal history should be able to make a contribution to the growing reflection on how different normative orders emerge, interact, develop."[47]

41 Conrad (2013) 13.
42 Duve (ed.) (2014).
43 Mulsow (2015).
44 See also his programmatic treatise: Duve (2012).
45 Schuppert, G. F. (2016b).
46 Kennedy (2006).
47 Schuppert, G. F. (2016b) 6.

Before considering what is to be understood by a global history of ideas, it should be noted that where in the course of this book we use the now current term global history, we mean not a subject but a *perspective* on certain historical events or processes. We can then, like the Max Planck Institute for European Legal History, write of "global perspectives on legal history."

When working with such a global history perspective, it is useful to make use of various key concepts or figures of thought that have proved their worth in analysing global history interrelations. Jürgen Osterhammel has convincingly shown what key concepts come into question.[48]

IV. Global history of ideas – three searchlights

To get at what a "global history of ideas" might mean, it is not helpful to proceed "globally" like Marcus Llanque, who presents a history of political ideas from antiquity to the present day without omitting a single major political philosopher in the long trajectory.[49] Of necessity Plato and Aristotle take the lead with Thomas Hobbes, Montesquieu, and Rousseau in midfield, while the concluding chapter describes the present as the age of human rights without, for a change, assigning responsibility to any philosophical thinker. We prefer to sweep the broad terrain of a global history of ideas to map out a history of ideas in keeping with the times in the light of the following questions:

- What ideas?
- "Global intellectual fields" and "global legal spaces" – What constitutes an intellectual field and a legal space?
- The history of ideas as entangled history?

48 Osterhammel (2015); also McCarty (2014), has identified nine "Integrated Perspectives in Global Studies": "1. Global and Local – Issues at Scale, 2. Interconnecting and Interdependence, 3. Decentralized and Distributed Processes, 4. Synchronic Contextualization, 5. Historical Contextualization, 6. Critical and Constructive, 7. Breaking Down Binaries, 8. Hybridity and Flexibility, 9. Multiple Perspectives and Voices."

49 Llanque (2016).

1

Concept of Idea and Importance of Disciplines

A. A narrow or broad concept of idea?

We must first clarify what sort of ideas we are actually thinking of when tracing the contours of a global history of ideas: Are we concerned primarily with so-called "big ideas"[50] and major philosophical conceptions, or ought we to use a *wide-angle lens* so as not to leave out too much of interest?

As far as presenting "big ideas" is concerned, Martin Mulsow has identified a clear trend in this direction: "The big themes are once again being pursued across the centuries and now also across the continents. ... The focus is once again be on thinking itself and its efficacy ...". Can we therefore expect a – modified – return to Lovejoy's "unit-ideas"? By this he meant basal ideas[51] that have kept going for hundreds or thousands of years, assuming ever new forms of expression and entering into different relationships.[52]

With Martin Mulsow, we take a decidedly different view in the conviction that such mega-concepts as "idea" or "knowledge" ought not to be too closely tailored from the outset. "Knowledge" – as Wilfried Rudloff remarks with reference to the knowledge of local social welfare authorities in Germany[53] – "is a complex, flexible, but also, because of its universal application, fuzzy concept. It covers everything that individual or collective actors use to interpret situations or produce action: know-how and information, techniques, world views, experience, customs, values, etc."[54]

The same holds for the concept of idea; we therefore agree with Martin Mulsow that, in addressing the history of ideas as entangled history, a narrow concept of this history makes no sense: "What do transfers convey? ... Ideas, theories, bits of theory, points of view in a broad sense are conveyed together with the concomitant informational elements, religious attitudes, physical carriers, and cultural practices. Puristically narrowing down intellectual history cannot be helpful."[55]

50 See Armitage (2012).
51 Lovejoy (1936), Introduction; also Lovejoy (1940).
52 Mulsow (2015) 4–5.
53 Rudloff (2003).
54 Rudloff (2003) 33.
55 Mulsow (2015) 19.

In what follows we therefore adopt a broad concept of idea.

B. Do disciplines matter?

A closer look at the literature on the history of ideas raises the question whether there has been a *lead discipline* "responsible" for the production of successful ideas on a global scale. Depending on what periods are under scrutiny and perhaps in varying order, the candidates are theology, political philosophy, legal philosophy, and – last but not least – the comparatively young discipline of political science. On closer examination, however, it seems doubtful whether thinking in terms of separate disciplines within the history of ideas makes any sense at all, and whether such an approach will not neglect the increasingly obvious need to *contextualize* the *production of ideas*.[56] The following observations also suggest that a discipline-oriented approach is inappropriate:

- *The difficulty of assignment to a discipline*

Turning once again to Marcus Llanque,[57] we find the following icons of the political history of ideas, to each of whom a specific substantive focus is attributed:

(1) Plato, Aristotle, and antique democracy
(2) Augustine of Hippo and Marsilius of Padua: faith, church, and politics in the Middle Ages
(3) Thomas More and Niccolo Macchiavelli: politics between Utopia and the preservation of power

56 Particularly clear in this sense: Koskenniemi (2014) 123: "No doubt the turn to context provides an important corrective to ways of doing international legal history. It situates past rules and practices in their institutional, economic and political environments, portraying the jurists and politicians as active agents in their milieus with distinct interests and purposes to advance. ... It brings legal principles down from the conceptual heaven and into a real world where agents make claims and counter-claims, advancing some agendas, opposing others. Meaning cannot be detached from intention, and intention, again, appears in action – in the way words are used to attain effects in the world. Historians of political and legal thoughts should pay attention to the specific moments when a text was produced and ask the question of who produced it and for what purpose – making agency visible while simultaneously demonstrating the way ideas function within linguistic and social conventions agents must follow so as to attain the persuasive effects they look for."

57 Llanque (2016).

(4) Thomas Hobbes, John Locke and modern contractualism
(5) Montesquieu and Rousseau: politics and society in the Enlightenment
(6) "Federalist Papers" and Immanuel Kant: the constitutional state and the rule of law in the Age of Revolutions
(7) Hegel, Marx, and the modern contradictions in society and politics
(8) Alexis de Tocqueville and John Stuart Mill: the individual and democracy in the modern age
(9) Max Weber and John Dewey: the idea of democracy between realism and idealism
(10) Carl Schmitt and Max Horckheimer: political thought in the epoch of totalitarian regimes
(11) The present: the age of human rights

This list of names almost automatically invites enquiry of the various disciplines as to their choice of icons for their ancestral portrait galleries. Legal philosophy would go for Hegel and Kant, but, quite rightly, so would philosophy. Thomas Hobbes, Montesquieu, and Carl Schmitt would be claimed not only by the general theory of the state (*allgemeine Staatslehre*) but naturally also by political science.[58] Particularly interesting, of course, is the case of Max Weber, one of the greatest legal sociologists. He was also a sociologist of religion, a national economist, and, above all, a theoretician of power and bureaucracy. This disciplinary diversity in one person was the inspiration behind the founding of the "Max Weber Centre for Advanced Cultural and Social Studies" at the University of Erfurt,[59] whose fellows are drawn from the various disciplines covered by Weber's research programme. For some years now, the present author has been of their number, not least as standard-bearer for legal science.

But there is a further aspect. Many of the great names in the history of ideas were not only theorizing scholars but also to a greater or lesser degree actively involved in the political affairs of their country as what we would now call "political consultants." This was the case for Thomas More and Jean

58 Interestingly, the frontispiece of the Leviathan not only adorns the front page of the eponymous social science journal but – on my initiative when chairman of the organization – also featured on the official letterhead for the circular of board of the Association of German University Teachers of Constitutional Law until removed on a motion by several members on the grounds that Thomas Hobbes was no worthy forbear of the democratic / liberal theory of constitutional law; nonsense, of course.

59 https://www.uni-erfurt.de/max-weber-kolleg.

Bodin, and particularly for the putative founder of modern international law Hugo Grotius – whose world – as Martti Koskenniemi shows[60] – was a *multi-disciplinary* one:

> "It has become increasingly common to read and understand Hugo Grotius from the perspective of his advocacy work *De jure praedae* (1604–1606) for the Dutch East India Company (Vereenigde Oostindische Compagnie, VOC) and thus at the service of the colonial pursuits of his countrymen.[61] But surely this welcome corrective to the old image of the great humanist may also blind us to the significance of his ecumenical projects and writings that manifest his specific religious convictions that, again, cannot be dissociated from his belonging to a cosmopolitan social class that was viewed with suspicion by the country's strictly puritan majority. Theology, politics and economy – and law – all frame the world in which Grotius operated. How to conceive the relations between these contexts is of course subject to ongoing methodological debate. Each of the alternatives provide us with a different 'Grotius' and none with any *intrinsic* epistemological priority."[62]

So much for our first observation.

* *The emerging modern territorial state as a state in need of ideas and knowledge*

The developing modern territorial state, whose emergence – as Ernst-Wolfgang Böckenförde has notably shown[63] – can be seen as a process of emancipation from the all-embracing grasp of the lead discipline theology, required specific legitimation to consolidate its self-standing as a genuinely political entity as well as the "know-how" that we could now call "governance knowledge." Historically, they were supplied by what in German was referred to as '*Staatswissenschaft*,'[64] inseparably associated with the rise of the territorial state in modern times, a discipline that managed to satisfy both requirements of modern statehood: with a specific theory of the purpose of the state – to further the happiness of subjects[65] – firstly as theory of legitimation while also providing the necessary *governance and administrative*

60 Koskenniemi/Orford (2015) 119–135.
61 In the same vein, Van Ittersen (2006); Wilson, E. (2008).
62 Van Ittersen (2006) 125.
63 Böckenförde (2007).
64 See Schuppert, G. F. (2003).
65 See Stolleis (1988) 334 ff.

knowledge[66] with the combined efforts of the subdisciplines *Policeywissenschaft, Kameralwissenschaft*, and *Ökonomie*.

The princely foundation of universities in Göttingen and Halle are also to be seen in this context, flagships for the thought of the Enlightenment and natural law, which also had to be *useful state institutions*.[67] Chairs of natural law were established less in the pursuit of legal philosophy than because of the *practical value* of natural law "in education of administrators and officials, in law reform, in recasting the law of nations, in civic education and its association with civic religion".[68]

In this context, it is particularly worth noting that natural law, although regarded as a "Protestant discipline," was also taught in Catholic territories at the explicit wish of Catholic authorities. Katharina Beiergrösslein, Iris von Dorn und Diethelm Klippel in "Das Naturrecht an den Universitäten Würzburg und Bamberg im 18. Jahrhundert"[69] have this to say on the subject:

> "... the introduction of natural law as a branch of study also appears to have been considered some years prior to Schönborn's broad programme of reform: already in the 1720s, Johann Georg von Eckert, former Hanover councillor and historian, as well as professor of history in Helmstedt, who in 1723 had been appointed court and university librarian by Johann Philipp Franz von Schönborn in 1723, called for the establishment of a chair in natural law. Schönborn's predecessor Christoph Franz von Hutten (1724–1729), too, had already recognized the importance of jus publicum and jus naturae, and had demanded that the professors of the law faculty hold regular lectures on natural, international and constitutional law. ... This trend was reflected in Schönborn's reform programme, which set the number of full professorships at four. The required syllabus included not only canon law and Roman law but also jus publicum, natural and international law, jus feudale, and legal praxis. Friedrich Karl von Schönborn saw natural law in relation to jus publicum, '*whose true and proper science is of the greatest importance for every ecclesiastical and secular principality*'. In fact, natural law provided the basis for the theory of jus publicum, particularly that part of natural law that dealt with public law, *jus publicum universale*.[70] ... The instructions for the professor juris naturae et gentium also clearly show that, although natural law continued to be regarded as a basic subject, this was no longer only because of jure publico, and thus in relation to *Publizistik*

66 On state modernization policy during the Enlightenment see Stollberg-Rilinger (2016) 208 ff.

67 Stolleis (1988) 298 ff.

68 Haakonssen (2012) 50.

69 Beiergrösslein et al. (2013) 178–179.

70 See Klippel (2010); Klippel (2013).

> (constitutional law). It was now a general basic subject, designed to acquaint law students with the structure of all legal scholarship and its methods."[71]

So much for our second observation.

- *The cross-disciplinary history of the reception of ideas*

Carl Schmitt once said that all important constitutional law concepts had once been theological concepts.[72] This teaches us that ideas tend to leave their original river bed and wend their own way. Developing Schmitt's dictum somewhat further, it could be said that originally legal concepts transmute into political concepts, indeed by preference into *tools of political discourse*: for – as Thomas Niklas has put it – "*The language of law can sometimes be very useful*."[73] Niklas cites the example of the Grotian concept of "freedom of the seas" as a "means of compensating the power deficits of small states."[74] Another particularly impressive example is Bodin's concept of sovereignty, in itself a constitutional law concept,[75] whose triumphal progress was more or less predestined, since it satisfied the needs of the rising territorial state to perfection.[76]

C. The phenomenon of contact zones between disciplines

Turning to the concept of contact zones, we leave aside the spatial sense of the term current in the history of ideas,[77] which addresses *communicatively shaped interactional spaces* such as the Silk Road or the Mediterranean, applying it primarily to *institutionalized cross-disciplinary interfaces*. Taking the example of the *relationship between the cultural and legal sciences*, we shall then consider exchange relations between disciplines.

71 Beiergrösslein et al. (2013) 178–179.
72 Schmitt (2009) 43.
73 Vesting (2013) 65.
74 Vesting (2013) 65.
75 See Quaritsch (1970).
76 Schuppert, G.F. (2003) 157 ff.
77 The concept of "contact zones" was coined by Pratt (1992) – primarily with reference to contact between "imperial and indigenous subjects" within territories under imperial rule.

* *Institutionalized contact zones*

Two, perhaps even three examples can show what we mean by institutionalized contact zones. The first is *natural law*, a discipline always characterized by remarkable *internal plurality*.[78] But, as Knud Haakonssen has shown, natural law, despite its internal plurality, had a strong *institutional identity*, marked by a Europe-wide network of chairs in natural law, filled with the aid of transnational "headhunters":

> "While natural law as a philosophical and religious doctrine may be of uncertain age, address and origins, it is indisputable that the subject took on a distinct *institutional* identity at a particular time – at least, within a limited span of time – in relatively well defined places, namely as an academic discipline in the European university faculties from the latter half of the seventeenth century until the end of the eighteenth century and, in several places, until well into the nineteenth century. There had of course been teaching of natural law as part of philosophy and theology since the Middle Ages, but the renewal of the subject that was perceived to happen with Hugo Grotius' *De iure belli ac pacis* (1625) had a nearly immediate academic impact in the context of the new *politica*. For example, Grotius's natural law had begun to be taught by Henrik Ernst in Sorø Academy in Denmark already in 1634. And in 1655 the subject had a special chair devoted to it at the University of Uppsala, when Petrus Eliæ Gavelius was appointed to a post in the Law Faculty specifically devoted to teaching the law of nature and nations, and, it was understood, to do so on the basis of Grotius's *De iure belli*. From then on chairs in the subject began to be founded with great intensity. In Germany the first was in 1661 in Heidelberg, although not in name certainly in fact, for this was the start of Samuel Pufendorf's career. It was from this position that he was head-hunted to become foundation professor of the law of nature and nations at the new Swedish University of Lund in 1668. But before that, similar chairs had already been instituted in Kiel (1665) and in Greifswald (1666), which had recently become part of the new Swedish empire. The Swedish concern with the teaching of natural law was extended from Lund, Greifswald and, in particular, Uppsala to Dorpat (Tartu) and Åbo, although separate chairs were not provided in the Estonian and Finnish institutions. Similarly natural law was taught at the Ridderakademi in Copenhagen from 1692, though at the University a chair was not established until 1732."[79]

The second example for an institutionalized contact zone is the aforementioned *Staatswissenschaft*, not only a science of legitimation and and purveyor of governance and administrative knowledge but also a contact-zone disci-

78 See, for example, Seelmann (2010) 131 ff.

79 Haakonssen (2012) 47.

pline uniting various fields of study useful to the modern territorial state.[80] Attempts to carry on this tradition of communication under the umbrella of *Staatswissenschaft*, or even to proclaim a "new" discipline under this heading have, as far as we can judge, enjoyed no great success.[81]

A third example of a scholarly discipline or a research institution seeking to relate various perspectives could be governance research,[82] which has now been institutionalized[83] to a considerable degree and whose approach cannot be claimed exclusively by any established discipline. Under the friendly applause of colleagues,[84] we have therefore labelled governance a bridging concept,[85] which unites various scholarly perspectives, thus sharpening analytical acuity.

So much for institutionalized contact zones between disciplines.

- *The relationship between culture and law: dynamic exchanges*

Thomas Vesting has shown –notably under the heading *contact zones*[86] – that the relationship between culture and law, between the cultural sciences and legal science has to be understood as one of dynamic exchange.

Vesting takes it as given that people have to rely on symbolic forms of culture for *orientation*. "If, as does older ethnology, we describe culture as the 'quintessence of knowledge, faith, art, morality, law, custom, and all the other abilities and habits that a person acquires as a member of society',"[87] it is clear that the specific function culture provides is orientation: "If one argues thus, the concept of culture occupies the sphere of transcendence abandoned by God and transforms the metaphysical vacuum of modernity into an incessant inner-world search for 'legible' meaning. For this reason,

80 See Stichweh (1991).

81 This is also true of "new" theory of the state posited by Vosskuhle (2001a), and for the attempt by the present author to revive "Staatswissenschaft" (2003).

82 See Schuppert, G. F. (ed.) (2005) 371–469.

83 In addition to an international network of governance research and the journal *Governance*, of which I have long been a member of the board of trustees.

84 See Benz et al. (ed.) (2007) 16: "Governance is thus no more, but also no less that a scholarly 'bridging concept' (…), which enable problem-oriented communication between different subdisciplines of political science and between scholarly disciplines."

85 Again in: Schuppert, G. F. (2007c).

86 Vesting (2015) 131 ff.

87 Vesting (2015) 127, with reference to Tylor (1871), quoted there by Baecker (2013) 211.

too, one can now posit that the 'question about culture' is a form of the 'question about the world', and not only a question about the cultural and intellectual as opposed to the technical / economic / material."[88]

"This insight into the embedding of individual conduct in cultural contexts that go beyond his or her person, the ties of the human being to the 'traditions within us' have" – according to Vesting[89] – "been elaborated by Aleida and Jan Assmann into a theory of cultural memory: the memory has not only a neuronal and social dimension, it is not only corporeally embodied and linguistically networked memory: it is also shaped by a cultural dimension inscribed in landscapes, places, buildings, pictures, and texts. Cultural memory includes not only the '*functional memory*', the symbolically present world, but also a '*storage memory*', the stocks of tradition that are not directly available for communication and which include what has not only been forgotten but also repressed."[90]

We agree with Vesting that these orientational aids are closely *linked to institutions and rules*, which brings us directly to law and its storage function – which we will be considering later in greater detail – and thus to the relationship between law and culture. Since Vesting describes this relationship between law and culture, cultural studies, and legal science as *entangled history*, we quote the relevant passage in full:

> That for the law of the liberal state a polycentric network of different national cultures is constitutive and that this network, like the individual cultures themselves are initially cultivated by the printing press could, according to David Wellbery and Kart-Heinz Ladeur, be described as the 'semantic intermediate input' of culture for the legal structure of the liberal state.[91] From this point of view, the orientation that the culture of printing provides for the liberal state would consist – to put it somewhat differently – in the production of 'formative texts', in *jointly inhabited narratives*, on which law docks as 'normative text', as expression of enhanced binding

88 Vesting (2015).
89 Vesting (2015) 128.
90 See Assmann, A. (2011) 181 f., 188: "In the storage memory, sources, objects, and data are collected and preserved regardless of whether they are needed at the present moment; we can therefore speak of a passive memory of society. The functional memory, by contrast, is the active memory of a we-group. Just as the autobiographical memory supports the identity of an individual, the cultural functional memory supports the identity of a collectivity. It contains a small selection from the abundance of handed down stocks important for the identity of this group."
91 Ladeur (2012) 173 ff.

> force.[92] Niklas Luhmann would perhaps have said that the symbolic forms of the culture of printing would then be responsible for a specific 'cognitive' infrastructure of liberal law over and beyond its normative closure.[93] These various conceptual strategies for the literary, cultural- science, and systems-theory context (semantic input, formative / normative, cognitive / normative) is likely to be particularly useful where the *relationship between culture and law* is seen as dynamic, as a discontinuous shift in the density of a contact zone, but not as a rigid boundary and insurmountable dividing line. In contrast to Luhmann's closed legal system that operates only within its own boundaries, we must now look for constructions that allow more possibilities: on the one hand, the figure of the boundary of the legal system cannot be abandoned, nor the structure and intrasystemic ordering competence intrinsic to law; on the other hand, the legal system must always be incomplete. It cannot process all and every 'environmental irritation' in accordance with its own rules. And the relationship of the liberal state with culture and the media must be thought of and theoretically conceptualized as a locus of transition, of exchange, as a contact point, a space of entanglement of cultural-formative and legal-normative phenomena."[94]

After this excursion into the relationship between culture and law, we turn to a particularly interesting question: what actually constitutes intellectual fields and legal spaces.

92 On this terminology see Assmann, J. (2000) 38 f., 146 f.

93 See Luhmann (1993) 77 ff.

94 Vesting (2015) 131–132.

2

A Comprehensive Study of Intellectual Fields and Legal Spaces

A. Global intellectual and knowledge fields and legal spaces as communication spaces

We take the view that global intellectual fields, fields of knowledge, and legal spaces are primarily spaces of communication, that it is communication that constitutes them. To underpin this thesis, we invite the reader to join us in exploring two paths towards understanding this assertion. First, we cast a brief glance at the nature of communication spaces.

I. The workings and forms of communication spaces

Communication scientists largely agree that what constitutes communication communities is the presence of a common *communication code* by which members make themselves understood and which performs functions typical of a community, namely internal identity consolidation and external demarcation. Hubert Knoblauch explains:

> "We can speak of *communication communities* only if the commonalties of communication and their objectivization are also realized in social structures. Whereas only very weak social structures develop, for instance, in relation to television – referred to as a 'public' (with the exception of fan groups for popular soaps, who actively form communities) – the interactive media enable social structures to form: actors that build networks in which common topics (job hunting, homosexuality, dental phobia) or forms (games, gambling, auctions) are treated communicatively, quite clearly form communication communities. As such they share not only *common codes* and forms but also the notion of a community to which one belongs. Still more important in the framework of decontextualized communication is the *communicative marking of an identity* corresponding to the community."[95]

The religious community is a particularly apt example, which we will be looking at below. As Enzo Pace has convincingly shown, an experience of faith or an act of faith becomes "religion" only through the *development of a community-specific communication code*:

95 Knoblauch (2008) 85.

> "To sum up, religion as a means of communication therefore means at least three things: suggesting the idea of a God that speaks, always choosing privileged interpreters to whom He transmits a symbolic code, giving the latter the power to establish social links that can no longer be conceived in purely ethnic, territorial, tribal and parental terms – worlds that end to wrap individuals up in details (ethnic group, tribe, family, territory) – the links must be traced back to a higher code that separates individuals from these particulars and makes them feel and act as if they *belonged to a universal community.*
>
> The *symbolic boundaries* of this community are *defined by a communication code*, the key to which cannot be infinitely duplicated, because it is guarded by those who programmed the code and only made accessible (as a sign of their goodwill) to someone they trust. Religions basically ask human beings to place their trust in the person that a god has trusted with the opening and closing of the communication code. Seen from this point of view, faith thus means primarily trust in somebody (be it a prophet, a spiritual master, guide or shaman); *the community of faith* that is created *relies on a constant process of ritualized communication*, by means of which its members renew their pact of loyalty to the code transmitted to them, learning to discriminate true signs from false, confirming the socio-linguistic evidence that enables the community to consider itself as such. Its unity is essentially the product of a communicative investment, of a successful communication that publicly ensures a formal understanding of the evidence, of the fact that everything is continuing true to memory. The rites and liturgies of religions can be seen as great public communication systems that serve specifically to reiterate (so as to acknowledge and have acknowledged) the content and confines of the communicative pact that the community of 'faithful' has signed in order to come into being."[96]

It is only the existence of such a *communication* code not tied to a defined territory that ensures the functioning of deterritorial communication communities, which – as the overview below shows[97] – include both religious communities and social movements, which, like the anti-slavery movement, are held together by a common idea, in this case human dignity.

96 Pace (2009) 215.
97 Hepp (2008) 135.

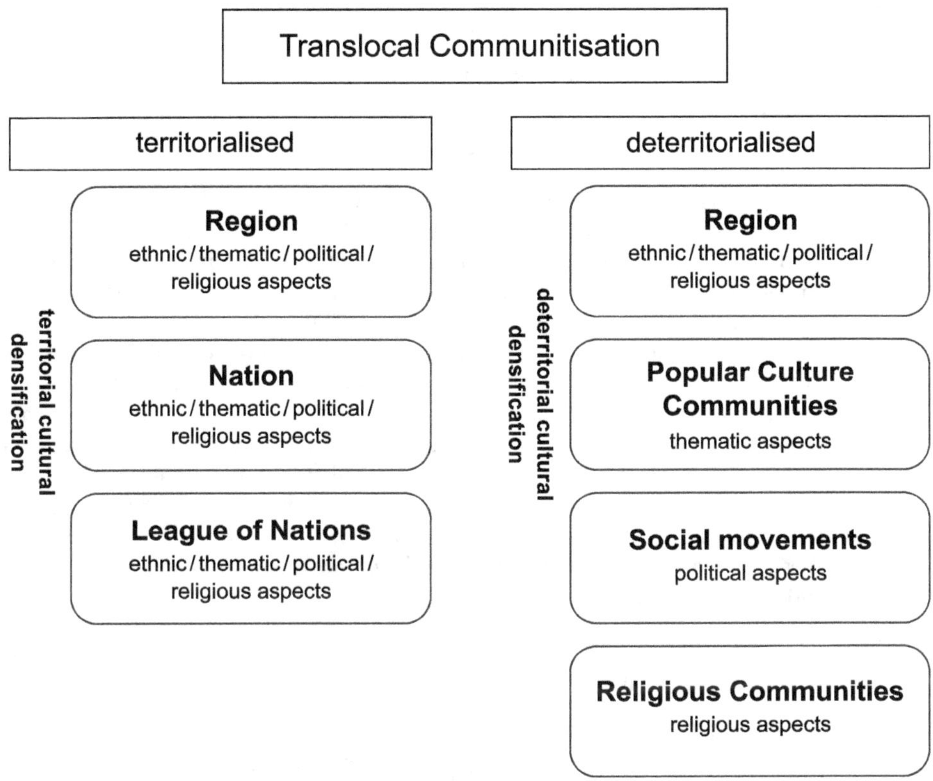

But in speaking of communication spaces, we are concerned not only with the nature of communication codes and their decoding, but also with the actors communicating with one another, the members of the communication community and especially with the prominent social group that determines communication style and exercises interpretational sovereignty over the means of communication used.[98] This brings us to forms of community building in the professions, which generally operate as intensive communication communities and, as such, develop their own technical language as a communication code.

98 See GEBHARDT (ed.) (1999).

II. Professions and their language

It is interesting to see what *type of professionalized actor* "calls the tune" from one period of history to the next. Back in the – hardly conceivable – "age without lawyers"[99] it was the clergy:

> "... the clergy were the leading personalities. The *institutional responsibility* they took on themselves made them the guardians and interpreters of the Ten Commandments, the Holy Scriptures, and the earthly standards of divine justice. Their daily contact with the faithful, particularly in the confessional, meant that they were constantly obliged to judge human conduct. Within the communities of the time it was quite normal to turn to the parish priest, the bishop, the monk, or the canon, not only in matters of spiritual welfare but also for advice in secular questions, or for help and moral support in the business of everyday life (the just price for buying or selling, or the right choice of an heir, etc.). It was, it seems, just as usual for the cleric who had been consulted to take up his pen and record on parchment the decisions and agreements of the parties to a legal transaction. The man of the Church was therefore a judge in matters both divine and secular; he was theologian and lawyer, rhetor and notary. He knew and judged evil deeds and forbidden thoughts as sin, and at the same time as unlawful conduct under civil or criminal law."[100]

But the clergyman soon found himself in company. Under the heading "Between old and new social estates," Manlio Bellomo has this to report:

> "In the cities a new circle of people took the stage. They included the specialized jurists trained in schools of law. These schools became increasingly important; they were the cradle of the modern university. They included physicians (now called *physici*), who took over many positions and logical procedures for analysing reality from the rediscovered Aristotelian texts, and tested and refined their professional qualifications through direct observation. They included scholars, who now attained social and political weight, which reached its zenith in the Humanism of the fifteenth and sixteenth centuries. They included artists, above all painters and sculptors. But the money changers – exchange brokers and the highly esteemed financial brokers (the modern banking system was coming into being) were also among them, contributing to the economic and cultural unity of the emerging Europe with major international transactions."[101]

We have opted for this actor-specific approach because professions tend to develop their own professional language as communication code, with the aid of which they can make themselves understood worldwide, wherever

99 This is the heading of chapter two in Bellomo (2005) 35.
100 Bellomo (2005) 48.
101 Bellomo (2005) 59.

they happen to be. John G.A. Pocock calls these professional languages "institutional languages," which are to be distinguished from the "languages of politics,"[102] which arise only in political discourse. In their informative article on the Cambridge School and its critics ("Die Cambridge School und ihre Kritiker" [2001]), Eckhart Hellmuth and Christoph von Ehrenstein remark that:

> "For Pocock there are basically two different types of 'political language'. First there are the so-called institutional languages. By this Pocock means idioms that have their origin in specific milieus. Pocock cites the example of the cultivation of *common law* and the idea of the *ancient constitution* by English jurists in the seventeenth century. Secondly, there are 'political languages', which develop in the discourse itself. They include, for instance *civic humanism*, whose genesis and transformation Pocock describes in his 1975 magnum opus 'The Machiavellian Moment'. In this monograph, which has remained influential to this day, he traces out the history of the participatory civic ideal from Machiavelli's Florentine city republic to the American constitutional debates in the late eighteenth century. With the discovery of the tradition of civic humanism, Pocock dramatically changes the way the intellectual household of early modernity is seen. In the Anglo-American culture of the seventeenth and eighteenth centuries, it now became clear that, alongside natural law, which had hitherto been regarded as the dominant idiom, there was a second key 'political language' in use – that of *civic humanism* – which contemporaries turned to in reasoning on the state, society, and law."[103]

Our interest focuses on "institutional languages"; Pocock names examples of such languages specific to a given profession: "Some will have originated in the institutional practices of the society concerned: as the professional vocabularies of jurists, theologians, philosophers, merchants, and so on that for some reason have become recognized as part of the practice of politics and have entered into political discourse."[104] Of these four, we are particularly interested in the language of jurists and theologians because their *institutional framing* is especially pronounced. In what follows – and this is the second path we wish to explore – we consider two "global intellectual fields": the world of law and the world of religion.

102 On the function of "languages of politics" in discourses on the good and just order of a polity see Pocock (1962).

103 Hellmuth/Ehrenstein (2001) 159 f.

104 Pocock (1973) 3–41.

B. Two examples of deterritorialized communication about law and life-determining ideas

I. The "jus commune" as communicatively generated and disseminated universalist legal thought

In considering the law of the Middle Ages, *various legal regimes* have to be distinguished, which have in turn to be *ranked*. Precedence is taken by enacted local law, such as local government statutes or the royal prerogative, be it that of the Regnum Sicilia or in Castile and Léon, then came customary law, and, finally – if the first two levels offered no solution – the jus commune, which in turn was based on the tenets and principles of the "corpus juris civilis" and the "corpus juris canonici."[105] What are we to understand by "jus commune"?

The particularity of the jus commune is best understood when it becomes clear how it was made and disseminated. It was made by a particular species of legal actor, who in legal history go by the names of "glossarist" and "commentator," who processed the rediscovered Roman law in the form of glosses and commentaries in such a way that the "corpus juris civilis" gradually came into being alongside the canon law of the Church in the shape of the "corpus juris canonici."[106] Together, the two legal regimes formed the "utrumque jus," whose two pillars had to be mastered by prospective "doctors of law." The jus commune was taught in the schools of law scattered across Europe, for example in Bologna, Padua, Perugia, Montpellier, Toulouse, Orleans, and Salamanca – to mention the most renowned. Entire generations of students from everywhere in Europe made their way to these places of learning, a process that Manlio Bellomo describes as follows:

> "On the road, they met other students from Sicily or the distant British Isles, and they made chance acquaintance with fellow travellers and experienced, prudent merchants. Their sense of community, of solidarity grew through such contacts, and in comparing habits and customs in conversation, they harmonized their various vulgar tongues through the lexical and grammatical medium of a living, sim-

105 On the overall complex of jus commune see Bellomo (2005) 155 ff.: "Das System des ius commune."

106 On the function and importance of glossarists and commentators, see Wesel (1997) 311 ff.

> ple, and flexible language, Latin. Thus, they helped promote a cultural unity that was to play a prominent role in the cities."[107]

But what was really particular to the jus commune was that it taught jurists *how to argue legally*. Its chief function was thus less to establish a system of legal rules than to provide jurists everywhere with a *fund of argumentation* on which to draw when dealing with local law – "jus proprium" – or enacted law. Bellomo sums up:

> "Even if the binding point of reference was a rule of *jus proprium* (royal prerogative, municipal, etc,) or a term in a contract, the judge or lawyer could not ignore the generally accepted meaning of the technical terms that he found in the law or notarial document. In other words, he could not ignore the *jus commune*, which had determined the meaning of these terms and which designated what Gaius called the *variae causarum figurae* – the legal *figurae*, which were the heritage and wealth of every jurist. It was immaterial whether the content of the norms or contractual terms tallied with *jus commune* rules, and it was irrelevant whether the *jus commune* as the applicable positive law ranked first or last among the legal sources. What counted was only the *figurae* that embodied the *jus commune*, the principles and their underlying values.
>
> Associated with the conception and knowledge of the *figurae* was the conviction that they were eternal and non-modifiable, since they embodied a system of values and supreme, absolute principles. This provided a standard of value, a presentation model, and a means of reaching agreement that surpassed the arbitrariness and randomness of *jus proprium*. The *jus commune* in its objective and meta-historical nature thus also served to protect the interests of jurists and their profession. It was immaterial whether they were aware of this, or whether they acted out of conviction grounded in reason or out of naive, unthinking trust in the universality of *jus commune*."[108]

In his treatment of law in European history,[109] Paolo Grossi provides an excellent description of jus commune. He begins with the particularities of its emergence:

> "Legal experts developed this law, people at home in the law: judges, notaries, advocates, but especially scholars and professors teaching at universities throughout Europe. Deeply involved in the concrete practice of the law, they served rulers as legal advisers; appeared in court as barristers or counsel to the bench; successfully

107 Wesel (1997) 121.
108 Wesel (1997) 159.
109 Grossi (2010).

> exercised the professions of solicitor and notary. The law grew out of a complex dialogue with both the requirements of their age and the antique Roman texts."[110]

Also important was that the jus commune could operate as a uniform *voice of the legal community*:

> "It was law that presented itself as the uniform voice of the legal community, as the mouthpiece of a class of experts who were endeavouring to erect a great legal edifice, a law free of the state, which was to prevail throughout the later Middle Ages. The great Italian legal historian Francesco Calasso rightly spoke of 'common law as an intellectual fact'."[111]

Above all, however, the jus commune was essentially law without borders, law – we could say – with a *globalization gene*:

> "This law knew no borders, just like science, which addresses the universal and to which artificial political barriers are anathema. This is shown by the great *migrations of teachers and students*, moving from one university to the next as cultural pilgrims and citizens of a republic of letters in which no-one felt himself to be a foreigner. This law created the legal unity of Europe and had a *universal orientation*, which alone enjoyed scholarly legitimacy. One of many instructive examples is offered by the main representative of the commentator school, Bartolus de Saxoferrato, an Italian jurist in the first half of the fourteenth century. At one point in his *Commentarii*, for the most part notes on lectures that record lively dialogues with students, Bartolus supplemented his text with reference to a German scholar who on a particular morning had presented the views of a university professor from Orléans. The small lecture hall at the University of Perugia where Bartolus taught was not sealed off from the outside world by the walls of the central Italian city but was at the centre of an *intellectual network* that spanned Italy, Germany, and France and was located geographically at the centre of the entire civilized world."[112]

In sum, we note that the jus commune was a legal regime disseminated communicatively, which consisted essentially in a *legal idea* and a *methodological regime* rather than constituting a closed system of legal rules, and which was therefore suitable for application wherever legal experts were at work. However, the globalization gene of the jus commune – and this is the inevitable actor perspective – could develop a global effect only because there was a class of jurists able to exert their interpretive sway over this *jurists' law* to establish its position in politics and society.

Now to our second example.

110 Grossi (2010) 58.
111 Grossi (2010) 59.
112 Grossi (2010) 59.

II. Religious communities as important communication communities in the history of ideas

1. The history of religion as a history of ideas

To take the religious community as an example of a communication community important in intellectual history can be justified on the undeniable grounds that religious thinking plays a key role in the history of political thought. For this reason, such names as Augustine, Thomas Aquinas, and Marsilius of Padua have their place in every ancestral portrait gallery of the political history of ideas.[113] At this point, however, we are concerned not with these great thinkers but with political thought as theological thought and with the role of religious language as a language of politics.

In his recent history of political thought, Otfried Höffe[114] offers provides an admirable introduction to the topic. We begin with his assessment of the *role of Christianity* in the political history of ideas as a *revolutionary force*:

> "With Christianity, a new intellectual and social force entered political thought. … Whereas Plato had connected political thinking with just about all the fields of his philosophy, Aristotle and Cicero limited themselves to interlocking politics with ethics and a philosophically demanding rhetoric. … Although the outstanding thinker of the early period, St. Augustine, went along with this, the continuity was interrupted by a discontinuity with revolutionary implications. Political thought was profoundly, essentially charged with religion. Mere politics, coupled at best with ethics and rhetoric, had lost its rights. Permeated to the core by religion, genuinely political thinking transmuted into political theology and theological politics."[115]

As the introductory remarks in this book on the role of the language of law would lead us to expect, this "new intellectual and social force" employed a new language and new concepts, as Höffe explains:

> "Augustine's propositions are without a doubt both innovative and provocative, and both radically so. Innovative is the focal topic of the second part, *fundamentally new* vis-à-vis the philosophical tradition: a civitas dei, a city of God, with its just as *fundamentally new concepts and arguments*. No less provocative is the lack of interest

113 See, for example, Llanque (2016) 24 ff. on "Augustinus von Hippo und Marsilius von Padua: Glaube, Kirche und Politik im Mittelalter".

114 Höffe (2016).

115 Höffe (2016) 92.

in usual political thought. Political philosophy is displaced by political theology. However, what was meant was not the Roman, 'heathen' theology of the state-controlled cult of the gods totally rejected by Augustine in Books VI to VII. Augustine's *city of God* is not political thinking *as* political theology but rather political theology *instead* of political philosophy."[116]

If, as we feel, there is something to Höffe's assessment of the innovative and radical nature of the *Christian gospel*, this brings two aspects into focus: first, the question of how and by whom this good news was told and how it was institutionally "managed."

2. Religious communities as narrative communities

One thing they the monotheistic religions Judaism, Christianity, and Islam have in common is that they clearly cannot manage without a founding story, a *foundational narrative*: religious communities can with good reason be described as *narrative communities* in which a particular narrative form – the so-called *revelation narrative* – plays a key role. What such revelation narratives are and what function they have can be illustrated by two particularly apt examples:

* *Revelation as inspiration or "sending down" – the case of the Koran*

According to the usual account, the word of God was revealed *only orally* by the Archangel Gabriel to the Prophet, and by the Prophet to the faithful. In his introduction to the Koran, Hartmut Bonzin gives us an excellent idea of how this revelation is to be imagined and what it means for understanding the Koran.

> "Sura 20; 114 brings us closer to the *process of revelation*:
>
> And do not be hasty with the Koran before its inspiration to you is concluded. From this we learn that first an inspiration or revelation is given Mohammed by God, which is then recited by the Prophet. This 'recitation' of the revealed text is called Koran (Quran, Qur'an). And to describe the process of revelation which precedes this recitation, two main concepts are used, namely '*inspiration*' (wahy) and '*sending or coming down*' (tanzíl)."[117]

116 Höffe (2016) 107.
117 Bobzin (2007) 19.

The revelation story of Islam thus describes a multi-stage process; the first recitation is ascribed to the Archangel Gabriel, the second, based on this first, is made by the Prophet Mohammed; in all, according to Bolzin, "Koran" thus means *four different things*:

- The recitation of a revelation text to Mohammed himself
- The public recitation of this text by Mohammed
- The text itself that is recited
- The totality of the texts to be recited, i. e., the Koran as book.[118]

God's revelation of the Ten Commandments as surely the most impressive legislative act in legal history

How God revealed the Ten Commandments to Moses on Mount Sinai has been portrayed over and over again, and we all remember the pictures from bible class, if not from Cecile B. DeMille's "The Ten Commandments." "The revelation on Mount Sinai," comments Graf, "is a primal scene in the religious narratives of monotheism, a constellation of inexhaustible abundance of meaning. No Jew and no Christian would not immediately associate the Ten Commandments with the idea of biblical law." And then the act of legislation itself, a religious representation whose suggestive power could hardly be more intensive:

> "Yahwe's Sinai theophany is accompanied by fearsome natural signals of divine transcendence: thunder, lightening, dense clouds, mighty trumpeting, quakes, smoke, and fire. In ancient European emblematics, smoke and fire were symbols of transience, ephemerality, of the self-consumung, the unobtainable. By contrast, *the law of the eternal God written in stone had an aura of eternal validity, immutability, which should govern all dimensions of human conduct.*"[119]

But it is not only a matter of being impressed; we want to understand what was special about this law revealed and made by God. As Matthias Köckert[120] has shown, this can best be achieved by comparing the revelation of the Ten Commandments with the conferring of legislative power on King Hammurapi by the sun god Shamash:

118 Bobzin (2007) 20.
119 Graf (2006) 44.
120 Köckert (2007).

> "Before Shamash to the left stands the king, recognizable from his bowl-like cap. It is doubtless Hammurapi. But Shamash presents him not with the collection of laws but with ring and sceptre, the insignia of power and dominion. In relation to the laws set out below, *the relief depicts the king as lawmaker under divine commission*. Contravention of the legal order enacted by the king was therefore also an offence against the commissioning divinity, even though *gods in the ancient Orient were merely the guardians of the law and not lawmakers* …
>
> *Lawmaking in the Ancient Orient was prerogative of the king.* For this reason, kingship and lawmaking were closely associated. However, through the mediation of the king, the law also had a religious foundation, for the monarchy was – if not of divine origin or nature – always kingship by the grace of God."[121]

It was quite a different matter with the revelation of the Ten Commandments; in this case, lawmaking power was not conferred: it was the *lawmaker God*[122] Himself who enacted the law. Köckert notes:

> "How very differently the Old Testament tells of the imparting of the Decalogue and the laws. Although it depicts Moses in kingly guise: he alone may approach God, he is representative of the people, intermediary for God's will, military leader, and many other things, but not a lawmaker. *Unlike King Hammurapi, Moses receives not insignia of power from the hands of God but the Tables of the Law*, which not Moses but God Himself has written on the tablets with his finger. Whatever laws Moses wrote after receiving the Decalogue, such as the Book of the Covenant etc., he had first received from God. Although the laws in themselves do not indicate the authorship of God, and even the Decalogue presents itself only at the beginning as the word of God, in the context of the framing narrative they are all styled as statements of God. In the Old Testament, God himself authorizes law and justice in lieu of the king."[123]

Before turning to *religious communities as institutionalized loci* of religious and of legal communication, it is well worth taking a look at the narrative foundations of another governance collective, the modern constitutional state. In considering this parallel world, what Otto Depenheuer and Christian Waldhoff have to say on the subject is helpful.

• The narrative foundations of the modern constitutional state

Otto Depenheuer set out recently in "search of the narrated state."[124] He has identified various "state narratives." As examples he cites the idea of the "Holy Roman Empire" and the associated notion of "translatio imperii" – and

121 Köckert (2007) 23 f.
122 See Graf (2006) 36.
123 Graf (2006) 24.
124 Depenheuer (ed.) (2011) 7–34.

competition between state narratives in which states take part as narrative communities; the relevant passage is worth quoting not least because it is tempting to replace the term "state" by that of "religion":

> "There is competition between state narratives. States that vouch for a dream and represent hope for people have much more attractive narratives than others that close themselves off from the outside world in a narrative. The state that can tell the better story is courted and self-confident. The unavoidable and disagreeable flip side of this narrative creation of particular identity is exclusion of the Other: whoever does not understand the stories, who cannot or does not wish to apply the narratives to himself does not belong to the *narrative community*. This can give rise to exaggerations, delusions and aversion vis à vis 'others',– the 'barbarians', 'foreigners', 'outcasts', 'enemies'–, as history shows over and over again. Such absolutization, however, is neither an historically necessary nor logically inevitable consequence of these narratives. One can love one's own narration while respecting others and gaining enrichment from them. This is also life-serving because everyone is caught in a network of stories: all narratives passing judgement on inclusion and exclusion are therefore always relative; each refers to only one of many narrated communities: that of a country, a region, a city, a religion, a party, a firm, etc. There is not only one, big story; the present reality is shaped by the reality of a *plurality of narratives*. The abuse of a narrative, which can never be excluded, therefore does not speak against it, and certainly not against the inevitability of narratives. 'Abusus non tollit usum', ['Abuse does not take away use'] say the Digest, and this should not be seriously disputed with regard to the narratives of the state, either."[125]

The quite remarkable parallels between religious revelation narratives and the foundational narratives of constitutional states is stressed by Christian Waldhoff, writing about "The Foundational Narrative of the Constitution as Idea of the State." Concluding our consideration of religious communities as narrative community, we cite him as follows:

> "As we shall see, the constituent power thrives on the notion that the new constitution as idea of the state to come is born in full facticity through the revolutionary act, the 'supreme accomplishment' of constitutional theory ….
>
> Literally spelling out this idea and transporting it into time is the real objective of constitution-making. *The constituent power thus becomes the foundational narrative of the later constitutional state*, the myth of the nation. This narrative – as Napoleon demonstrates with the confidence of a sleepwalker – is not a historical account but a novel. Making a constitution is, furthermore, one of those 'conditional beginnings' of which Thomas Mann writes, 'that constitute the primal origin of the special tradition of a given community, ethic entity, or religious family in a practical and actual sense (Mann 1969, p. 9) and thus bring the eternal search for ever more distant origins in infinite regression to an end. This could well explain the kinship

125 Depenheuer (ed.) (2011) 26.

> with aesthetic categories; it is more a matter of fathoming sensory perception than juridical rationality. The sets the theory of constituent power in stark contrast to the prosaic full positivity of constitutional law. Napoleon again: once the novel of revolution is over, the task is to govern, not to philosophize."[126]

3. The institution "Church" as an important communication space in the history of ideas

The sociology of space and communication science tell us three things about the nature of communication spaces: first, that a container-like understanding of communication spaces is inadequate; second, that communication itself has a space-generating function; and, third, that different social groups can be understood as different communication spaces.[127] The first point obviously requires no further discussion. The second – the space-generating function of communication – also seems perfectly plausible on condition that there is a certain density of communication. Thomas Wetzstein argues in this vein in writing about the contribution the papacy made to the development of new communication spaces:

> "A 'communication space' is to be understood as a space defined by longer-term *exchange relations*. The term 'communication space' has only recently been taken up by historiography … With reference, mostly in studies on the early modern period, to 'a dense network of informal relationship matrices and communications contacts' (Keller 2004). And the motto 'Communication and Space' for the 45th Biennial Meeting of German Historians in Kiel in 2004 indicated that the science of history had opened up a new field of research, albeit without devoting too much attention to the significance of this compound concept.
>
> That German medieval studies, in particular, are only now gradually coming to focus on large historical spaces again is perhaps due to the risk of political exploitation. In light of twentieth-century debates on the 'West' and a European Union still thirsting after historical identity, the temptation to use spatial categories for political purposes is by no means a phenomenon from the distant past. Be that as it may, there can be no doubt about the importance of historical communication spaces, especially in investigating transfer and homogenization processes. The eleventh and twelfth centuries, in particular, are seen by historians as a phase of intensive exchanges and concentration processes."[128]

126 Waldhoff (2011) 62.

127 As representative of the sociology of space, see Löw (2001); for communications science, Jarren (1987).

128 Wetzstein (2008).

The third point – social groups as communication spaces – invites an argumentation chain from religious communities as governance collectives to religious communities as institutionalized collectives and then to religious communities as loci of institutionalized communication. We end up with "Church" as locus and space of institutionalized communication.

This *connection between institution and communication* seems to have been wantonly neglected by media-centric communication science; in our view *institutions* are also *communication spaces*, and the institution "Church" is an excellent example of this. Our view is confirmed by Helmut Schelsky, who has gone into the question "Can permanent reflection be institutionalized?" Institutions, he claims, are not only loci of communication but, as the example of churches shows, also entities *needful of communication*:

> "The step to knowledge of developing institutional forms for religious faith based on the permanent reflection of interiority is now no longer all that difficult to take. It is clearly a matter of the production and communication, steered organizationally by the temporal outside world, of permanently reflected subjectivity in the religious field, which in consciousness is reduced to trivially banal commonplace. This seems to me to be the case for all social forms of present-day religious life, which is based on conversation and discussion, and thus on the conscious meeting of individual subjectivities, as form of organization and communication. The fundamental institutional requirement of this form of faith appears to be that 'people talk to one another'. This *conversation principle* underlies all modern attempts to achieve the socially effective animation of faith, reconversion, or safeguarding of religious existence. What is at issue are not only 'structurally pure' institutions of this sort like the Protestant academies, the churches and 'Katholikentage', church industrial work, youth work, etc.: 'discursive partnership' is increasingly becoming the normal form per se of religious church activity, both within the inner life of the community – the oratory becomes an assembly room – and in the overall societal presentation of the churches, apparently reducing the importance of older forms of religious communication – ritual, scripture readings, singing, even preaching."[129]

The history of the papal creation of communication spaces shows that it makes sense to regard the institution "Church" as an important such space in the history of ideas. As a rule, the rise of the papacy is recorded as institutional history, describing how this organizational model gained the upper hand over other institutional options such as conciliarism. As Thomas Wetzstein shows, the growing importance of the papacy can be described from

129 Schelsky (1957).

the perspective sociology of space and communication theory, yielding interesting insights.

The first is that the strengthen of the papal office was accompanied by a "*novel claim to space penetration*":

> "Although the horizon of the Roman bishops had briefly broadened under Nicolas I (858–867) and again in the tenth century with activities in Spain, Scandinavia, and Eastern Europe, it was a quite new development in the history of the papacy when the vicarius Petri in the person of Leo IX not only laid theoretical claim to the leadership of Christendom but also pursued the practical implementation of his reform demands by seeking to impose a completely new relationship with space. Also for the successors of the pope Emperor Henry III had placed on St. Peter's throne, this novel claim to space penetration was a prototypical innovation whose causes are to be found not only in a new conception of the papal office, but also in the 'de-Romanization' of the papacy itself through the appointment of non-Roman bishops and in the example of the episcopal visitation."[130]

Whereas ecclesiastical legal history often describes important pontiffs as "*judicial popes*" because they pursued the judicialization of the Church, from a communication science point of view it might also be appropriate to speak of popes who made their mark through their high *communication potential*. As Wetzstein points out:

> "Particularly under Gregory VII (1073–1085), the new relationship of the popes to space took on a new quality (1073–1085) Not only is his correspondence permeated, as it were, by a programmatic postulate of spatial domination: his address book listed rulers and prelates in Germany, Italy, France, England, and the three Spanish empires, along with the kings of Denmark, Norway, and Sweden, the Duke of Poland, the kings of Russia, Hungary, Serbia, Croatia, and Dalmatia, the Emperor in Constantinople, rulers in Ireland and even in Islamic Mauritania. Recent research on papal records shows that in document production, the papacy began as early as the pontificate of Leo IX to overtake the Holy Roman Emperor as competing, space-dominant authority. Over a period of five years (1154–1159), for instance, the chancellery of Frederic I issued 148 documents, whereas over the same period Pope Hadrian IV produced no fewer than 1000.
>
> Above all in critical situations – already during the Investiture dispute, but particularly in the context of schisms – the popes began to implement their newly won communicative potential in intensive public relations work, often with the support of wide personal networks. Alexander III, in particular, was well aware of the effectiveness of this tool when, after the controversial election of 1159, he sought systematically to inundate Western Christendom with electoral propaganda, finally

130 Wetzstein (2008) 60.

> – with the aid of two centralized orders with a communicative potential at least equal to that of the papacy – emerging as victor from the 'war of propaganda'....”[131]

We conclude this point with Thomas Wetzstein's summary of the history of the papacy as communication history:

> “To return to the initial question of the contribution the papacy made to expanding the communication spaces of Latin Christendom, there can be no doubt about the impressive achievement of the popes since Leo IX – even though the twelfth century offered institutions that in no way lagged behind the papacy in their spatial impact: universities with far-reaching personal networks often maintained by correspondence, and the new, centralized orders of the Cistercians and Premonstrensians with general chapters almost revolutionary in communication history.
>
> The communications techniques of the papacy demonstrated a striking development in keeping with a general trend in Latin European communication history: in propagating their reform programme, Leo IX and many of his successors quite clearly took the communicative habits of a face-to-face society into account when they placed great value on personal contact through travel, synodical activities, and the attachment of external functional elites to their persons. The twelfth century saw a gradually break with such communicative practices, as the written word gained increasing importance in organizing 'rule from afar'. The Fourth Lateran Council with its impressive list of participants can be seen as marking the end of this era, opening the door on a new epoch of papal communicative praxis. Although, until well into the fifteenth century, the papacy was unable to carry out its reforms or collect financial resources without sending out representatives, from the twelfth century onwards it displayed more and more decided characteristics of governance based on the written word.”[132]

After these observations and findings on intellectual fields, fields of knowledge, and legal spaces as communication spaces, we turn to the popular subject of the history of ideas and knowledge as histoire croisée or entangled history.

131 Wetzstein (2008) 61 f.

132 Wetzstein (2008) 73–74.

3

History of Ideas and Knowledge: An "Entangled History" Approach

As the founder of the history of ideas in America in the 1940s Arthur O. Lovejoy rightly stressed, "Ideas are the most migratory things in the world."[133] With this in mind, I presented some thoughts on the mobility of the rule of law principle under the heading "Can the Rule of Law Travel?" at a 2012 workshop at the Erfurt Max Weber Center.[134] Given the incontestable wanderlust of ideas, writing a history of ideas as entangled history is an increasingly popular approach – witness Martin Mulsow's "Ideengeschichte als Verflechtungsgeschichte. Impulse für eine Global Intellectual History"[135] and the introductory essay by the editors Samuel Moyn and Andrew Sartori in "Global Intellectual History".[136]

Certain reflections and examples of our own could prove helpful at this stage. Before presenting them, however, we shall attempt to place the "entangled history" approach to a global history of ideas and knowledge in a somewhat more general context as a contribution to understanding the history of ideas as entangled history.

A. Globalization history as entangled history: the need for systematic entanglement research

Two books I published in 2014 and 2015 discussed the history of globalization from two different, rather unusual perspectives. I first examined what *governance structures* and *governance actors* can be regarded as characteristic of the globalization process – globalization as a history of governance[137] – and, second, I sought to depict the history of globalization as essentially a history of communication,[138] since *globalizing communication* has been the chief factor leading to the shrinking of the world and the "death of distance."

133 Lovejoy (1940) 4.
134 Schuppert, G. F. (2012a).
135 Mulsow (2015).
136 Moyn / Sartori (eds.) (2013) 3–32.
137 Schuppert, G. F. (2014).
138 Schuppert, G. F. (2015).

From the standpoint of governance research[139] and of communication science, *entanglement structures* were in clear evidence almost everywhere.

The first book was therefore given the title "*Entangled Statehood*" ("*Verflochtene Staatlichkeit*") and focused on the following *five entanglement regimes*:[140]

- Statehood entrepreneurs, such as the East India Company as pioneers in globalization
- Empires and networks as entanglement structures typical of globalization
- The state in the entangled world of finance – between the Rothschilds and the International Monetary Fund
- The partnership practised between State and Church; and
- The history of globalization as missionary history – the triad of commerce, civilizational sense of mission, and Christian missionaryship

The second publication, which addresses the phenomenon of globalization from the point of view of communication history, deals not only with entanglement structures but focuses more strongly on specific *globalization actors*, as they can be called. Seven are particularly typical and interesting:

- The postal entrepreneurs Thurn and Taxis
- The operators of news and press agencies as communication entrepreneurs of the "Victorian Internet"
- Siemens as a communications and infrastructure company
- The Reformation as a communication event and Luther as media star
- The inhabitants of the "blogosphere"
- The members of the Republic of Letters, and
- Human rights activists

These rich pickings invite us to outline what we could call *entanglement research*, which would have to be pursued as a *multi-disciplinary project*. In what follows we make a start with a list of five fields that any entanglement research worthy of the name would have to address. The list shows which discipline could assume "responsibility" for the given field of study.

139 See the overview in Schuppert, G. F. (2015) 371–469.
140 Schuppert, G. F. (2014) 356 ff.

* To begin with, *entanglement structures* and *entanglement actors* need to be identified. Although they are difficult to keep apart – as governance studies show, actors operate within the structures that frame their action[141] – it is analytically useful to treat structures and actors separately while keeping their interrelatedness in mind. And this is how we shall proceed, looking first at some typical entanglement structures and then at particularly "conspicuous" entanglement actors.
* Our second concern is to examine the *causes of entanglement* and also whether we are dealing with institutional pathologies rather than institutional responses to certain processes and problems not or scarcely amenable to handling without entanglement. One interesting example is the so-called *European composite administration*,[142] an informational, decision-making, and monitoring network that is to be understood as an answer to the institutional structure of the European Union. From a still more general perspective, the investigation of governance structures in multi-level systems – so-called "multilevel governance"[143] – has to seen as entanglement research: "The focal subject matter of political-science analysis [of multilevel governance] is the causes, forms, and consequences of entanglement."
* Third and last, entanglement research would have to capture the diversity of existing entanglement forms and attempt to systematize them in some way; I have, very provisionally, identified *four types of entanglement structure typical of globalization*:
  - *Entanglement structures* between the state and commerce: from the privileged trading companies to the symbiotic relationship between state and multinational corporations
  - *Entanglement structures* between the state and religion: from alliance between throne and altar to military chaplaincies and the division of labour in meaning production.
  - *Entanglement structures beyond national statehood*: from transnational network cooperation to fraying statehood[144] as an applied case of entangling statehood.
  - *Imperial entanglement structures*: from "informal empire" to "indirect rule."[145]

141 Mayntz (2005).
142 See Schmidt-Assmann / Schöndorf-Haubold (eds.) (2005).
143 Greater detail in Benz (ed.) (2004) 125–146.
144 Genschel / Zangl (2007).
145 Greater detail in Osterhammel (2003).

* Fourthly, entanglement research would have to examine the intended and, above all, the *unintended consequences* of entangled political decision-making processes. In this connection, the reader is referred to the now classical study by Fritz W. Scharpf on the so-called *political interdependence trap*,[146] in which he convincingly traces the phenomenon of the European butter mountain back to the entanglement structures of European governance, which favour status-quo decisions, prevent dramatic surges of reform,[147] and generally enable a policy of blockade.
* Fifth – which brings us to the second part – entanglement research has to investigate whether there is a *dynamic between the entangled parts* and what this dynamic is. What actually happens there? What is transported and exchanged through the *entangled channels*?

The European Union is a highly instructive example. The EU governance system is characterized by, among other things, *performance competition* between member states. Arthur Benz describes the functional logic involved:

> "In the EU, governance by performance competition takes place under the heading '*open method of coordination*' above all in the fields of economic, employment, social, and environmental policy. At the European level the commission defines goals and standards to guide member states and leaves it to them to implement them by the means of their choice. *Benchmarking* by member-state experts and the commission provides the incentive for member states to meet these goals and standards. The publication of best practices aims to trigger *learning processes* and public critique of bad practices is intended to prompt the states involved to adapt their policy to meet European standards."[148]

"Benchmarking" and "open method of coordination" (OMC) involve not only confrontation with and exchanges between different political styles and administrative cultures but also a meeting of different notions of the public good and political ideas. These are extremely communication-intensive processes, which justifies speaking of "governance as communication."[149]

146 Scharpf (1985).
147 See Schuppert, G. F. (2008a).
148 Scharpf (1985) 107.
149 Schuppert, G. F. (2007a).

We now take a closer look at typical entanglement structures and entanglement actors.

B. Communication-intensive networks as a prime instance of entanglement structures: two historical examples

The network concept is a fine example of entanglement structure. Despite its ambivalence, this successful concept cannot be avoided.[150] Jürgen Osterhammel shows this: while expressing his scepticism about the concept ("the network is a both graphic and deceptive metaphor"), he stresses how useful it is: "The network metaphor is particularly useful because it permits the notion of a *multitude of contact points and nodes*."[151]

The metaphor is useful, and therefore so successful, because – as Andreas Wald and Dorothea Jansen rightly stress – networks are "application-neutral."[152] Its all-round usefulness explains why the network concept is to be found in so many contexts. It can be used as an analytical tool in micro-political history; Wolfgang Reinhard does so in his study on "The Nose of Cleopatra" ("Die Nase der Kleopatra").[153] He has this to say about the ubiquity of the metaphor:

> "Networks are an omnipresent historico-anthropological phenomenon, just as convincingly demonstrated by the old Chinese variant Guanxi and its adaptation to the present as by a network-theoretical interpretation of St. Paul's first letter to the Coninthians.[154] But its importance was recognized only when it was promoted to a *form of societalization of the information world* of our age. The connection with the growing importance of the Internet is obvious. Since 1990, 'network' has become an absolute concept that no scientific or non-scientific publication can now do without.[155]
>
> However, closer examination of the 'nodes', 'edges', and overall form of networks shows how very much networks are modified by historical and cultural environmental influences. Once again, the given *political culture* as the quintessence of political praxis plays an important role. Basically, a role of societal power leads to a better position in networks, for power is the raw material of micropolitics. But

150 See JANSEN / SCHUBERT (eds.) (1995).
151 OSTERHAMMEL (2009) 1010.
152 JANSEN / WALD (2007) 188.
153 REINHARD (2011).
154 GOLD et al. (eds.) (2002); CHOW (1992).
155 SCHÜTTPELZ (2007).

> because political power roles have changed historically, membership of parties or associations, of the Free Masons or the Rotary Club now play a far greater role than kinship or regional origins, which in premodernity were micropolitically more important. Accordingly, the importance of 'connections' arising from a common education, place of work, and membership has increased in the modern age.[156] It should also be remembered that the Internet opens up quite new possibilities for micropolitics owing to its network character."[157]

However, network can also be understood as a concept typical of globalization[158] that explains the spread of globalizing capitalism, as Sven Beckert shows in his study of the cotton trade empire under the heading "Information flow and trust":

> "Although the cotton empires did not manage to integrate the growers, the most important characteristic of this first modern processing industry was its globality. *This globalization needed globalizers*, people who recognized the opportunities offered by the new order and who persuaded others, not least their governments, to take collective action. The most important globalizers were not the often very local-minded planters or factory owners but … the merchants, who were specialized in *establishing networks* linking up producers, manufacturers, and consumers.
>
> Developing such global networks required courage and vision. When in 1854 Johannes Niederer applied for a position with the Swiss trading firm Gebrüder Volkart, he offered to sound out the market opportunities in Batavia, Australia, Macassar, Mindanao, Japan, China, Rangoon, Ceylon, and Cape Town. Such globetrotter merchants 'ruled over industry'. Indeed, manufacturers and planters regularly complained about the power of these traders, and many merchants looked down on factory owners as provincials and gamblers. To become powerful actors in the cotton empire and to conduct this trade profitably, the Rathbones, Barings, Lecesnes, Wätjens, Rallis, and others established *close-knit networks in which information, finance, and merchandise could reliably flow*."[159]

And the network concept is extremely useful in analysing governance structures beyond the nation state, as I have done with respect to *transnational administrative networks*.[160]

Two other examples are particularly instructive from the history of ideas perspective, namely the closely related phenomena of the so-called Republic of Letters and the network of the Enlightenment.

156 Emrich et al. (1996); Döscher (2005); Karsten / Thiessen (eds.) (2006).

157 Reinhard (2011) 638–639.

158 As I have done in Schuppert, G. F. (2014), chapter 2: "Globalisierung als 'institution building' – Imperien und Netzwerke als globalisierungstypische Verflechtungsstrukturen".

159 Beckert (2014) 217–218.

160 Schuppert, G. F. (2013b).

I. The Gelehrtenrepublik/Republic of Letters/République des Lettres as communication network

The Republic of Letters should not be overlooked in this study, for it operated through and was fuelled by networked communication.

> "Republic of Letters has to be conceived of as part of the Scholarly Culture in the Early Modern Age, primarily under the aspects of its links to community, in general of communications, i. e. institutions, ideas and their diffusion, production/reception / distribution of texts, nature and history of text genres – but always in the analytical context of communication: of its participants, centres, channels, instruments, media. We should be aware of the fact that analyzing Scholarly Culture under the leading aspect of Republic of Letters means to accept an implicit bias of its analysis towards communication."[161]

The name of this virtual republic is essentially a self-description of a specific scholarly culture of the sixteenth and seventeenth centuries, held together by communication:

> "*Republic of Letters*, more than nobilitas litteraria, is a *metaphorical manner of speech*, a façon de parler used to characterize this kind of communication among scholars, i. e. the internal communication within the (status-bound or status-transcending?) community of scholars, under the aspect of its conditions and state as well as, and more so, of the claims and norms the scholarly community should conform to, that is under the aspect of *communication as it should be.* Thus, *Republic of Letters* thematizes scholarly communications with respect to *normative* expectations, to definitions of limits, e. g. of tolerance, of room for criticism etc. [...] As a subject of historical research, *Republic of Letters* does not assume its proper, specific contour until it is conceived of as the *self-concept*, the *self-description* of (a representative part of) early modern scholarly communication, or to put it more precisely: of scholarly culture under the specific aspect of its communications."[162]

With Anthony Graften we must ask, "If this state had no maps, no administrative officials, and no borders, how do we know it existed at all?"[163] Any answer to this question calls for a visit to the republic to gain better acquaintance with its characteristics.

In his *Sketch Map of a Lost Continent*, Grafton describes this imaginary country as follows:

161 Jaumann (2011) 12.
162 Jaumann (2011) 13 ff.
163 Grafton (2009) 8.

> "This essay offers a historical traveler's report on a strange imaginary land, one that had few of the distinctive marks by which we usually identify a state. It did have a distinctive name: *Respublica literarum,* the Republic of Letters. Its citizens agreed that they owed it loyalty, and almost all of them spoke its two languages – Latin, which remained the language of all scholars from 1500 to 1650 or so, and still played a prominent role thereafter, and French, which gradually replaced it in most periodicals and almost all salons. But it had no borders, no government, no capital. In a world of sharp and well-defined social hierarchies – a world in which men and women wore formal costumes that graphically revealed their rank and occupation – its citizens insisted that all of them were equal, and that any special fame that one of them might enjoy had been earned by his or her own efforts. As one observer put it in 1699, 'The Republic of Letters is of very ancient origin [...] It embraces the whole world and is composed of all nationalities, all social classes, all ages and both sexes ... All languages, ancient as well as modern, are spoken. The arts are joined to letters, and artisans also have their place in it ... Praise and honor are awarded by popular acclaim' ... The Republic of Letters imagined itself as Europe's first egalitarian society, even if it did not always enact these high ideals in the grubby reality of its intellectual and professional practices."[164]

Particularly interesting, of course, is the question of how citizenship of this virtual republic was to be gained. According to Anthony Grafton, it was quite simple: required were good language skills, a certain social behaviour, and a letter of recommendation from a senior scholar:

> "The citizens of the Republic carried no passports, but they could recognize one another by certain marks. Not wealth, of course; then as now, scholar did not rhyme with dollar. But they looked for learning, for humanity, for generosity, and they rewarded those who possessed these qualities. Any young man, and more than a few young women, could pay the price of admission. Just master Latin – and, ideally, Greek, Hebrew, and Arabic; become proficient at what now seem the unconnected skills of mathematics and astronomy, history and geography, physics and music; turn up at the door of any recognized scholar from John Locke in London to Giambattista Vico in Naples, bearing a letter from a senior scholar, and greet your host in acceptable Latin or French – and you were assured of everything a learned man or woman could want: a warm and civilized welcome, a cup of chocolate (or, later, coffee); and an hour or two of ceremonious conversation on the latest editions of the classics and the most recent sightings of the rings of Saturn."[165]

The architecture of this republic thus consisted of a network of mutual correspondence: "The strands of long-term correspondence formed a capillary system along which information could travel from papal Rome to Cal-

164 Grafton (2009) 1 f.
165 Grafton (2009) 8.

vinist strongholds in the north, and vice versa – so long as both had inhabitants, as they did, who wished to communicate."[166]

Interestingly, Anthony Grafton draws clear parallels between the Republic of Letters he describes and the present-day information and knowledge society. They are evident not only in the common problem of "information overload,"[167] but also in the *incessant transfer of information and ideas*, which calls to mind the bloggers of today:

> "Trade had become global again in the fifteenth century. Now information also joined the global flow, as Huguenots in exile in Berlin and Potsdam informed the European world about recent science and scholarship in French. Kircher, admired and envied in Rome, drew information from fellow Jesuits around the world as he charted the underground movements of rivers and lava flows and the ancient migrations of peoples. Vico, isolated but well-informed Catholic, southern Naples, used Dutch journals published in Latin as his primary sources for the new theories of Spinoza and Locke. Like the blogs that have accelerated the movement of facts and ideas in recent years, the new journals and publishing houses had a profoundly unsettling effect on political and social authorities. The Republic of Letters stood, in the first instance, for a kind of intellectual market – one in which values depended, in theory at least, not on a writer's rank but on the quality of his or her work."[168]

II. The Enlightenment as a process of transnational coproduction of knowledge

I have long been a friend of the notion that what we call statehood is not produced exclusively by the state but is also co-produced in collaboration between the state and other actors. This could explain why we find Sebastian Conrad's comment particularly interesting that the so-called Enlightenment – a second and somewhat later Republic of Letters – can be seen as a process of global co-production.[169] In the Enlightenment, inseparably associated with the name of Immanuel Kant, he sees above all an answer to the growing global processes of entanglement:

166 Grafton (2009) 9.
167 Rosenberg, D. (2003).
168 Grafton (2009).
169 Conrad (2012).

> "The production of knowledge in the late eighteenth century was structurally embedded in larger global contexts, and much of the debate about Enlightenment in Europe can be understood *as a response to the challenges of global integration.* The non-European world was always present in eighteenth-century intellectual discussions. No contemporary genre was more popular and more influential than the travelogue. Accounts of the Hurons in North America, of the Polynesian Omai who was taken to England by Captain Cook in 1774, and of the Mandarins at the Chinese court reached a broad readership and found their way into popular culture. Most direct was the impact of the idealization of the reign of the Qing emperors Kangxi (1661–1722) and Qianlong (1736–1795); China was posited as the incarnation of an enlightened and meritocratic society – and instrumentalized for criticisms of absolutist rule in Europe.
>
> But the appropriation of the world was not confined to its function as a mirror. In many ways, central elements of the cultural transformations that are customarily summarized as 'Enlightenment' *need to be understood as a reaction to the global entanglements of the times.* The expansion of Europe's horizons that had begun in the Age of Discovery and culminated in the voyages of James Cook and Louis de Bougainville resulted in the incorporation of the 'world' into European systems of knowledge. In particular, the emergence of the modern sciences can be seen as an attempt *to come to terms with global realities.* Further examples include the discussions about the character of humanity following the interventions of Bartolomé de las Casas; the idea of the law of nations and an international world order as proposed by Hugo Grotius; the ethnological and geographical explorations of the globe; the comparative study of language and religion; the theories of free trade and the civilizing effects of commerce; and the notions of race, on the one hand, and cosmopolitanism, on the other. The perception *of an increasingly interlinked globe posed a cognitive challenge* that was gradually met by reorganizing knowledge and the order of the disciplines."[170]

Conrad avoids a Eurocentric view of what we are accustomed to calling the Enlightenment, instead stressing the global perspective and the trend towards global thinking that entered the world of ideas and knowledge with the Enlightenment:

> "The Enlightenment of the eighteenth century, however, was not the intellectual monopoly of Europeans. It needs to be understood *as a result of the transnational co-production of knowledge by many contributors around the world.* This is not to deny that particular debates were also deeply embedded in European traditions, and were shaped by specific situations in places such as Edinburgh, Halle, and Naples. But the intellectual dynamic as well as the revolutionary impact of the transformation of the late eighteenth century was very much *energized by global conditions*.
>
> Moreover, the Enlightenment was not confined to its Atlantic moment in the eighteenth century; it had a much longer course. This was a history not so much of

170 Conrad (2012) 1009 f.

> its diffusion as of its permanent reinvention. Groups and social milieus that pressed for social and cultural change invoked the authority of the Enlightenment while fusing it with other traditions. In the process, what was seen as the core of the Enlightenment changed profoundly, both because of the creative merging of elements from a variety of cultural backgrounds, and because these ideas were proposed in geopolitical contexts that differed greatly from eighteenth-century Europe. Increasingly, Enlightenment was employed *as a concept that allowed historical actors to think globally and to position their communities on a world stage.*"[171]

C. Two types of entanglement actor at work: "state nomads" or "empire agents" and "go-betweens in a brokered world"

When different cultures encounter one another, meeting spaces develop that Mary Louise Pratt calls "contact zones."[172] These zones[173] are home to specific entanglement actors that play an important role in the circulation of ideas and concepts. We conclude this first part with a look at this interesting species:

I. State nomads and empire agents

In her fascinating book "The Secret War," Eva Horn[174] addresses, among other things, the imperial thirst for knowledge. She comes across a type of actor Thomas Richards[175] has labelled "state nomad." Writing about the British Empire, Horn has this to say:[176]

> "The British Empire was a power structure rooted in the administration and control of an immense and extremely heterogeneous space. As Thomas Richards has argued, it took a specific regime of knowledge to guarantee its spatial coherence, an 'imperial archive' designed to collect, store, and classify information from all parts of the world. 'They surveyed and they mapped. They took censuses, produces statistics. … In fact they often could do little other than collect and collate information, for any exact civil control, of the kind possible in England, was out of question. The Empire was too far away …'.[177] Pursuing the ideal of a unified and complete representation

171 Conrad (2012) 1026.
172 Pratt (1992).
173 Greater detail in Smith, V. (2013).
174 Horn (2013).
175 Richards (1993).
176 Richards (1993) 164–165.
177 Richards (1993) 3.

> of the world, the *imperial thirst for knowledge* arose from its specific spatial structure: and empire spanning the globe with Britain as its undisputed political, economic, and military center that nonetheless had to nurture and facilitate a certain amount of 'local' self-organization to maintain control over such a vast domain. Local features in colonial territories had to be harmonized with imperial centralization – that is, remote control and self-control had to be coordinated. The *Victorian colonial will to knowledge is a will to power* grounded in control over space. Geography and hydrography, institutionalized in the *Royal Geogrphical Society* (founded in 1830), are the basis for the administration and military control of the colonial territory. As such they are not simply areas of knowledge among others but the royal disciplines of colonialism. 'State nomads', that is, world travelers, explorers, cartographers, and the empire's more or less amateurish secret agents, are the actual heroes of this kind of spatial power: 'nineteenth-century geography was the continuation of politics by other means'."[178]

But in addition to the state nomad, there is another type of actor, whom Eva Horn calls the "*empire agent*." She cites "Kim" from Rudyard Kipling's famous novel[179] as an example. About the function of the empire agent, which she also refers to as a cultural chameleon, she remarks:

> "… Kipling's novel depicts in singular clarity a transformation of imperialism from the reliance on ethnocide, enslavement, or unfettered exploitation, that is, from the direct use of violence, to the skilled management of information – and of intelligence, for that matter. … However, colonial intelligence as the accumulation of knowledge pertaining to the control of colonial territory is already encumbered by problems of communication and interpretation. Hence there is an urgent need for multilingual agents familiar with *the many cultural codes, laws, and taboos* of an extremely heterogeneous society such as India. In other words, the political and military reconnaissance of colonial space involves more than scouting and spying missions to explore the terrain and eavesdrop on the enemy; it also requires cultural fluency and social acumen. In short, it depends on '*local knowledge*'. As the British had been forced to learn during the Indian uprising of 1857, they could not secure their rule if they disregarded local codes and customs."[180]

II. Government by go-betweens in a brokered world

In "The Brokered World. Go-Betweens and Global Intelligence 1770–1820, "the editors Simon Schaffer/Lissa Roberts/Kapil Raj and James Delbourgo

178 Richards (1993) 17.
179 Kipling (1987).
180 Horn (2013) 182.

write expressis verbis of "government by go-betweens,"[181] making these mediators into key governance actors. In effect, this is a concept transfer from the world of literature to the world of "global intellectual history." In literature, the 'go-between' is the intermediary who "through swift and willing services as postillon d'amour joins lovers separated from one another by a plethora of moral and social barriers, but who remains in ignorance of the delicate substance and purposes of his actions."[182] This is the concept as we know it exemplified by the classic novel by L. P. Hartley.[183] Now – in global intellectual history – he no longer operates as postillion d'amour but as intermediary and interpreter between different cultures: "The go-between in this sense is thus not just a passer-by or a simple agent of cross-cultural diffusion, but someone who articulates relationships between disparate worlds of cultures by being able to translate between them."[184]

Kapi Raj takes us somewhat deeper in the world of "go-betweens" in this study on "Mapping Knowledge Go-Betweens in Calcutta, 1770–1820,"[185] where he shows that all merchants, whether 14th century Arabs or officers of the East India Company had to rely on the services of intermediaries if they were to trade successfully with the locals. "*Knowledge go-betweens*" of wide-ranging provenance were therefore indispensable.

> "In the circumstances, it is not difficult to perceive that go-betweens were indispensable to ensure passage between the varied languages, customs and accounting techniques of the merchants and those of local communities of producers and suppliers. They were designated by special appellations, such as *dallāl* in Arabic, but often looked upon with contempt and suspicion, referred to variously as 'arrogant, rebellious and audacious' or 'shameless, bold, cunning, debauched [and] liars.' Nonetheless, they constituted an obligatory passage point for all transactions and, already in the 14th century, Arab merchants were advised to use the services of such factotums, as the following extract from an Arabic trader's manual emphasizes: 'The merchant who arrives in a locality unknown to him must also carefully arrange in advance to secure a reliable representative, a safe lodging house, and whatever besides is necessary, so that he is not taken in by a slow payer or a cheat.' In addition to translators, interpreters, moneychangers, bankers and moneylenders, the regional trade network was predicated upon specific maritime knowledge and skills. Pilots,

181 Schaffer et al. (eds.) (2000) xi ff.
182 Breidecker (2008) 14.
183 Hartley (2000).
184 Schaffer et al. (eds.) (2000) xiv.
185 Raj (2000).

> navigators and theorists of navigation helped guide ships around maritime Asia and East Africa, thus forming yet another *intermediary profession*."[186]

The colonial powers, in particular, starting with the Portuguese, learned by bitter experience that fruitful exchanges between themselves and "civil societies" could not be organized without the assistances of professionalized go-betweens:

> "At the turn of the sixteenth century, west Europeans thus entered a highly organized and complex economic network in the Indian Ocean with well-established trade conventions, of which they had some notion through various travel accounts and reports. But over which they lacked mastery. For a start, the Portuguese – the first west European power to enter the region – had to rely on the services of different local Muslim pilots to direct them up the Swahili coast and then to Calicut, their final destination. And when, after initially carrying out armed attacks on local powers, merchants and populations, they finally embarked on establishing an empire in the region, based on fortified littoral colonial settlements, private trade, and political and commercial treaties with regional polities, their interaction with the various communities and political authorities concerned was rendered possible only *through the mediation of professional go-betweens with specific literary, technical, juridical, administrative and financial* skills. The pattern set by the Portuguese in the 16th century was to continue into the following centuries and formed the basis of subsequent European interaction and maritime settlements in the Indian Ocean.
>
> In the context of the relationship between maritime Asia and western Europe, we can distinguish *at least five major functional types of intermediaries* – the interpreter-translator, the merchant-banker, the comprador or procurer, the legal representative or attorney, and the knowledge broker. In the South Asian context, each of these types could be composed of Asians, North Africans or Europeans, missionaries or footloose strangers, men or women."[187]

186 Raj (2000) 107.
187 Raj (2000) 108.

Part 2
Global History of Ideas: Locating the Language and Functions of Law

The first part of this book was about what Pocock has called the "languages of politics" in which the nature of the good and just order of a community is spoken and written about. The key questions were what legitimizes admitting the language of law to the concert of these languages, and whether its voice should be marginal or central.

In tackling these questions, we propose distinguishing between five functions of the language of law:

- The language of law as the language of discourses on the legitimacy of political authority
- The language of law as the language of political change
- The language of law as the language of rights
- The language of law as the language of justice, and
- The language of law as the language of a new global order

In the second part, we focus on two aspects of the capabilities of law and its specific language as a language of politics. First, we ask what the language of law does particularly well in comparison with other "languages of politics", and second why the language of law can consequently deal a particularly "good hand" in discourses on the order of the polity.

We present the indulgent reader with three key functions of law and its language in examining these questions.

4

Law and its Language: Functions of Abstraction and Transformation

A. Two examples of the abstraction functions of the language of law

I. The "invention" of the legal person

In "Sapiens: A Brief History of Humankind",[1] Yuval Noah Harari cites the French automotive firm Peugeot, founded in 1896, as an example of what this momentous invention is all about.

> "... Armand Peugeot, who had inherited from his parents a metalworking shop that produced springs, saws and bicycles, decided to go into the automobile business. To that end, he set up a limited liability company. He named the company after himself, but it was independent of him. If one of the cars broke down, the buyer could sue Peugeot, but not Armand Peugeot. If the company borrowed millions of francs and then went bust, Armand Peugeot did not owe its creditors a single franc. The loan, after all, had been given to Peugeot, the company, not to Armand Peugeot, the Homo sapiens. Armand Peugeot died in 1915. Peugeot, the company, is still alive and well."[2]

Harari seeks to explains that the firm Peugeot as an object of juridical attribution can be kept apart from the natural person Armand Peugeot by a 'legal conjuring trick' – which, in a certain sense, it is:

> "Peugeot is a figment of our collective imagination. It can't be pointed at; it is not a physical object. ... But it *exists as a 'legal fiction'*. ...
>
> In the case of Peugeot SA the crucial story was the French legal code, as written by the French parliament. According to the French legislators, if a certified lawyer followed all the proper liturgy and rituals, wrote all the required spells and oaths on a wonderfully decorated piece of paper, and affixed his ornate signature to the bottom of the document, then hocus pocus – a new company was incorporated. Once the lawyer had performed all the right rituals and pronounced all the necessary spells and oaths, millions of upright French citizens behaved as if the Peugeot company really existed."[3]

1 Harari (2015).
2 Harari (2015) 45.
3 Harari (2015) 43, 46.

If this account is a little to colourful and the role of the lawyer as shaman[4] somewhat overdrawn, Jürgen Kocka provides a more sober description.[5] He sees the invention of the limited liability company or corporation as playing a decisive role in the development of capitalism. The founding of the "Vereenigde Oostindische Compagnie" (VOC) in 1602 provides a good illustration of the innovative nature of this institution:

> "Trade enterprises had already existed, but through the sixteenth century primarily as partnerships that brought together a small number of merchants working and keeping accounts relatively independently. The *VOC*, however, *came into being as a public corporation*. Its impressive capital of 6.45 million guilders was raised by 219 shareholders, each with limited liability. They regularly received dividends (18 percent on average annually) but had little influence on the management of the company. The VOC stayed together until 1799, while *its shareholders changed*. They could do this because they could trade their shares on the newly emerging stock exchanges. The management of the company lay in the hands of directors. They ran the extensive, vertically integrated organization and its many branch offices (especially in Asia) out of Amsterdam with the aid of an ingenious system of committees, a systemic reporting system, and a central office that soon employed a staff of 350 salaried employees. The company operated the purchase, transport, and sale of a variety of goods. But it also expanded selectively to become a manufacturing company by incorporating, for example, saltpetre works and silk-spinning plants in India. In all these respects, the VOC seemed *unusually modern*."[6]

But the public corporation, which experienced a veritable boom during the industrial revolution in the form of the limited liability company, was not only modern: it was also – a *condition for the spread of ideas and knowledge* – adapted to the political needs of the time:

> "The huge capital requirements and complexity of services to be performed are not the only factors explaining the emergence of this *unique organization*. The Dutch East India Company also fit in with the political needs of government in this era, since business, politics, and military force were most intimately mixed, and intensive competition between states often brought to a standstill competition between enterprises within one and the same country. The VOC was formed as an alliance of merchants and trading companies from all the provinces of the Netherlands under pressure from the government, as a pooling of resources in international competition with an anti-Spanish, and then soon also an anti-English, thrust. Much the same can be said of other trading companies of the time, such as the much smaller

4 Harari (2015) 41, pos. 478: "The principle difference between them and tribal shamans is that modern lawyers tell far stranger tales."

5 Kocka (2016).

6 Kocka (2016) 50.

> English East India Company, which existed between 1600 and 1858, but also the Dutch West-India Company and comparable establishments, for example in Scandinavian countries."[7]

However, the consequences that the abstraction function of depersonalized economic actors in the form of limited liability companies and public limited companies had for the history of ideas were far outdone by the invention of the state as a legal person and thus as a form of depersonalized government. Ernst Forsthoff has described the juridification of the state and depersonalization of power this implies:

> "This theory goes back to a book review published by the Göttingen historian Albrecht in the 'Göttingische Gelehrte Anzeigen' in 1837. It has recently attracted much attention among constitutional lawyers. And rightly so: classifying the state as a legal person was the most momentous intellectual attack on the monarchical constitution. The monarch, in whose person the state had hitherto been embodied was converted into an *institution of the legal person 'state*,' with which he could no longer be equated. His *sovereign rights were transformed into integrated powers* defined by the constitution and thus also limited. … The rapid spread of this theory is to be explained by the intention prevailing in constitutional law on the threshold of rule-of-law constitutionalism, which triumphed in the Prussian constitution of 1850. This intention was juridification of the state, transformation of governing relations between the state and the individual into legal relations – that were as bilateral as possible. The service that the theory of the state as legal person rendered towards realizing this intention was outstanding. This theory underpinned a specific conception of the rule of law."[8]

The same direction – the depersonalization of power through the functionalization of the ruling person into an agent of the abstract entity "state" – had already been indicated by the *reason of state concept* in the political philosophy of early modern times; Herfried Münkler comments on this topos in relation to the *institution of the state*:

> "*Reason of state* has a *double function* for those who cite it – first, it allows decisions to be made and action taken in breach of legal norms and moral bounds, while rigorously subordinating such decisions and action to an *objectivizable interest of the state* not only as orientation but also as the later measure and touchstone of efficiency. As Reinhard Kreuz has shown,[9] the reason of state is born when the purposes of power, or to be more precise, of the state, begin to constrain the arbitrary personal rule of power holders and to *transform them successively into agents*:

7 Kocka (2016) 51.
8 Forsthoff (1971b) 13 f.
9 Kreuz (1978) 199.

'While the reason of state allows the prince to be "worse" than subjects ought to be, it also requires him to be "better" than the ruling individual, swayed by his passions and therefore needful of strict control, actually is." The prince, who at first glance appears to gain from the transformation, is etatized until he is finally no more than an executive institution of the reason of state, the first servant of the state, to quote Frederick the Great. The reason of state is thus – also – a milestone on the road to the *depersonalization of power*."[10]

II. The reception of Roman law as acquisition of a new language

The reception of Roman law has received a great deal of attention[11] – also from the present author.[12] This is not the place to revisit this subject. What we will do briefly at this point is to recall[13] *the special quality of Roman law* that made it especially suitable for reception. Experts appear to agree that this quality lies in what the particular *"conceptual strength"* of Roman law, which permits a high degree of abstraction. Uwe Wesels notes: "In civil law, the Romans created the global pattern of a law that is founded on private property and free will. In this form it spread throughout Europe in the Late Middle Ages after Justinian's codification had come to Northern Italy in the eleventh century. It has accordingly become the basis of our law, not only our civil law but, *with its abstract conceptuality* also of our criminal law and administrative law, and even of our constitutional law."[14]

Peter G. Stein takes a similar view in "Roman Law in European History":[15]

> "Within the borders of the Holy Roman Empire, reference to Roman sources could be explained on the grounds that it was imperial law, but it was justified not for its formal authority but for its *technical superiority over every possible rival.* Unlike the canon law, however, no court applied just Roman law. The Church courts applied canon law to such matters as marriage and personal status; the courts of feudal lords applied feudal law to questions of landholding; the traditional community courts

10 Münkler (1987) 168.
11 See Wieacker (1967).
12 Schuppert, G. F. (2003) 95 ff: "Frühneuzeitliche Staatsbildung und die Bedeutung der Rezeption des römischen Rechts."
13 See also my treatment of the "jus commune" as communicatively generated and diffused universalist legal thought, in this volume p. 59.
14 Wesel (1997) 156.
15 Stein (1999).

> applied the local customary law to claims for compensation for wrongdoing. What the civil law supplied was a conceptual framework, a set of principles of interpretation that constituted a kind of universal grammar of law, to which recourse could be made whenever it was needed."[16]

This description of Roman law as a universal grammar of law brings us without much of a detour to the legal historian Christoph H. F. Meyer, who, fully in line with our argument, describes the reception of Roman law as the *acquisition of a new language*:

> "In the history of scholarship, widely differing reasons for this success have been mooted, for instance the quality of Roman law as ratio scripta, its *claim to be imperial law*, or its scientific presentation. In what follows, no explanation of the 'miracle of Bologna' is offered, or any answer to the question what the acquisition of Roman legal knowledge brought substantively, that is, in innovation from an institutional or dogmatic historical point of view. The point of departure is rather the question of what was new, what use was made of it, and how it spread. The focus is first on the stations of a particular way of juridification, which in the twelfth century led from Northern Italy to far reaches of the Occident. Characteristic of this process was work on written law, the acquisition and recording of knowledge from ancient texts of Roman law, and effort to use the resulting knowledge for contemporary concerns.
>
> Looking, however, at the *spread of this juridification strategy*, things look different: quite new agreement was to be reached on what (secular) law ought to be. *The communicative side of the process* is thus also involved, *which in some respects recalls the imparting of a new language*. A *language of law* that possesses a vast vocabulary of norms and concepts together with a learned grammar that sets the rules for deontological statements. The metaphor helps perhaps to better understand not only the general phenomenon but also the remarkable diffusion processes. For *the success of the new language of law lay in the first place in successful communication* and only secondly in norm enforcement. Whoever accepted the new idiom, answered in it, placed himself on the same legal and deontological footing as his interlocutor. Even partial success was effective, for instance if someone had only an incomplete mastery of the new language or wished to make only selective use of it."[17]

With respect to this *analogy between law and language*, Meyer refers the reader to the famous work by Rudolf Jhering published in 1852, "Geist des römischen Rechts" (The Spirit of Roman Law"); we quote a brief passage on the *alphabet of law*:

> "Allow me to use another analogy, namely, to liken the systematic or logical structure of law to an alphabet. *The relationship between a case-centred legal code and law reduced to its logical form is the same as that between written Chinese and our written*

16 Stein (1999) 61.
17 Meyer, C. (2010) 312 f.

> *language*. For every concept the Chinese have a special sign; a lifetime hardly suffices to learn them all, and for each new concept its sign has to be determined. We, by contrast, have a small alphabet that allows us to reduce each word to its constituent parts and assemble it: easy to learn and dependable. The case-centred legal code thus contains a great many signs for particular, individual cases; a law reduced to its logical elements, however, offers us an alphabet of law that allows us to decipher and depict even the most unusual word formations of life."[18]

These two passages confirm our conviction that *learning the law* is really not about learning certain legal norms, the content of law (which is naturally also useful; such proficiency is required up to the usual final law examinations) but about *learning a certain method* of thinking, whose mastery allows the lawyer to *communicate with colleagues in the same language*.

B. Two examples of the transformation functions of law and its language

I. Transformation of power into authority: the "invention" of public office

In early modern state building, the institution of "office" plays a key role because it accomplishes two things. First – like the "reason of state" – it *depersonalizes power*: the person is replaced by a function, a job title, and it is this office concept that *abstracts from the person*. The abstraction function is accompanied by a *transformation function* – transformation in so far as public office transforms power into government, since *office vests the holder with power.*

- From a historical point of view the *Church played a leading role* in achieving abstraction from the person. After the fall of the Roman Empire, the Church was the "sole coherently organized institution"[19] left, and it continued to function well not least because it had adopted the organizational principles of the Empire:

  > "The Church took over the administrative subdivisions of the late Roman Empire as its own, which involved the acceptance of a whole range of concepts, such as the

18 Jhering (1926).
19 Blockmans (1997) 115.

> *territorial nature of authority*, the *hierarchy of official competences* and functions and, more fundamental still, *the concept of office itself*. These were all *abstract ideas* which the Germanic and Slavic peoples had not yet reached by the tenth century. ... The maintenance of hierarchically arranged and well-defined territorial offices was of such importance because in the period from the fifth to the eleventh century the mass migrations of peoples had blurred all ideas of frontiers. Among the Germans, and even more among the equestrian hordes who overran central Europe and the Balkans, power was linked to individuals and not to specific territories."[20]

Wim Blockmans describes the central role that the concept of office played in the organizational and functional model of the Church:

> "The Church also took over from the late empire the concept of exemptions, which the senatorial class of large landowners had deployed to protect their patrimonies from taxation by the state. Pleading its otherworldly mission, the Church claimed immunity for its property and sacrosanctity from worldly judges for its servants. By doing so it created for later ages its role as a special order, the First Estate. Apart from its separate legal status, this also rested on education and consecration. These two components added to the interpretation of the concept of office, which the Church took over from the Romans. As an abstract concept this consisted of a well-defined sum of qualifications which the holder needed to satisfy, and powers which he might or might not exercise. The role of an office-holder is strictly defined, and quite separate from the individual filling it. The criteria he has to satisfy, the procedure for appointment and, where necessary, for dismissal from his office if he exceeds his powers or neglects his duties all exist quite separately from the individuals who have to fill the roles. This kind of *abstract thought* was wholly alien to the Germans and Slavs; their vision was a direct one of individuals who by virtue of the trust placed in them were given extensive but vaguely defined opportunities for exercising power. Some were able to develop and expand their power. Dismissal was barely thinkable without a bloody conflict with those challenging them."[21]

* But public office is not only a successful model transferred from a traditional bureaucratic hierarchical institution – the Church – to a new type of bureaucratic hierarchical institution – the early modern territorial state. And the exercise of power through office is not only an institutional backbone of bureaucratic administration in the sense of Max Weber: *public office is more than a mere organisational-sociology category*. Public office transports the regime of power into the world of law, turns power into authority by institutionalizing it. Whether this justifies the claim that

20 Blockmans (1997) 115.
21 Blockmans (1997) 115 f.

public office "ennobles" rule[22] is another matter. The *decisive function of public office is its catalytic effect:* as a catalyst, office translates power into responsibility,[23] converts the power of command into the right to command, makes forced obedience into obligatory obedience.[24] Office conveys *entitlement to power,* a *transformation function* that, as Ralf Dreier has shown, means not only the limitation but also the *legitimation of social power*:

> "Fundamental is … the *notion of limitation*. The understanding of rule as office implies its interpretation as service; i. e., as *entrusted power to be exercised with responsibility.* For practical purposes, however, everything depends on whom this responsibility is owed to and what legal form it takes. If we draw a simple distinction between natural and conferred rule, the latter is typically defined in terms of accountability towards those subject to rule. By contrast, 'natural' rule characteristically sees limitation only as moral accountability to a higher authority, namely God, and does not consider itself subject to institutional control by the governed. This also shows the *importance of the notion of office as a legitimation category.* The same moral and (or) legal norms that constitute rule as service also justify its existence. No proof is needed that this legitimation function of the office concept, i. e., its interpretation as entitlement to power, has been more effective historically than the limitation principle. But the one should not be forgotten because of the other."[25]

II. Law as congealed politics: the transformation function of constitutional law

One of the key functions of constitutions identified by Rudolf Smend[26] is integration: "Among the essential achievements of the modern constitutional state is its considerable integrative force. It can provide divergent political forces common legal ground on which conflicts can be peacefully resolved in accordance with set rules of the game. The condition is consensus to place greater value on the constitutional order than on any substantive decision."[27]

This function of a constitution to codify the *consensus on certain fundamental values and political procedures* prevailing at the time of its enactment

22 See Gneist (1879) 15, cited with approval by Krüger (1964) 270.
23 See Isensee (1987), § 57, r. 10.
24 Schluchter (1985) 146.
25 Dreier, R. (1972) 130 f.
26 Smend (1994) 119–276.
27 Pauly / Sielinger (1999) 83.

significantly eases the burden on the political process, because the rules of the constitution are no longer an issue but a premise of politics:

> "The written form given to the consensus dissociates it from any subjective interpretation by the parties involved and lends it verifiable certainty. Enrichment with legal normative force divorces it from the historical will of the authors and lends it validity over time. In that it comprises rules, it is divorced from the purposes for which it was drawn up and can find application in later implementation.
>
> This involves substantial achievements. Binding written form reduces the possibility of later dissension about the content of the consensus. When opinions differ, rules laid down by the constitution make it easier to establish how the state is required to act in specific cases. The permanence consensus gains from legal validity relieves politics from the need to find it in each and every case. If decisions had constantly to be made on the basis of competing proposals, such a procedure would bring immeasurable costs. The political decision-making process depends on being spared incessant discussion on finding consensus. The constitution provides this relief because its rules are no longer a political issue but a premise for politics."[28]

On closer inspection, the high normative ranking of constitutional provisions *deprives politics of decision-making autonomy* that accrues inversely to the domain of law – and hence in effect to constitutional courts as the guardians of the constitution. Dieter Grimm explains this functional interplay of political and legal effects:

> "Legal norms are plurifunctional. The lawyer tends to absolutize the dispute settlement function. Systems theory, in contrast, stress the disburdening function of norms. *Through lawmaking, issues are withdrawn from decision and rendered binding.* Legal rules thus reduce the decisional load by setting a frame for decision-making authorities. They operate henceforth as meaning-constituting premises and no longer as topics of decision. Legal rules can perform this function on various levels: so that only a principle is taken out of dispute while its elaboration is left open politically; so that its elaboration is also settled while it remains to be applied in the individual case. The scope for action narrows from stage to stage. The reduction function is also performed by constitutional provisions that are not directly applicable. To this extent they are more than mere 'proposals', as Burdeau posits.[29] That they still require specification and development says nothing about their normative nature but does indicate the level of reduction: their addressee is primarily (not exclusively) the lawmaker."[30]

28 Grimm (1990) 22 f.

29 Burdeau (1962) 398.

30 Grimm (1972) 489 ff.

5

An Integrated Study of Conflict Resolution, Language of Law and Order

A. The language of law as a language of order

The guarantee of legal certainty as the "idée directrice" of law

Certainty and law have been closely related from the very outset: "Securitas" in the sense of a guarantee that obligations will be met is already to be found in Roman law …. In the personalized governance relations of the Middle Ages, too, securitas is the focus of the oath of fealty and urban defence leagues."[31] The term *legal certainty* has long been used to describe this close relationship between certainty and law, notably with respect to its most important aspects *certainty of expectation, certainty of meaning, and certainty of compliance*.

Certainty of expectation and of meaning constitute what amounts to an "*idée directrice of law*." "Together with justice and purposiveness", according to Andreas von Arnauld,[32] "legal certainty is a fundamental element in the idea of law. In all more or less developed legal systems, legal certainty is an idée directrice of law; every reasonably well-developed legal system will create institutions seeking to realize the demand for knowable, reliable, and predictable law."

If, as perhaps needful in the more general context of this discussion, we wish to operate not so much with the concept of legal certainty, of certainty as to the law, with its connotations of state law – which is, moreover perceived by most people solely as a legal concept – we can with Andreas Anter[33] opt for the broader concept of certainty of order (*Ordnungssicherheit*) to place greater emphasis on production of the public good "certainty as order". The two concepts, legal certainty and the certainty of order, although not identical, do largely overlap; and it is this functional perspective that is of interest for our purposes:

31 Arnauld (2006) 76.
32 Arnauld (2006) 691.
33 Anter (2004).

> "Under the conditions and prerequisites of legal-rational governance, however, law is an essential, if not decisive factor for the certainty of order. Law plays a decisive role because its function is ultimately to guarantee certainty. This notion culminates in the idea and practice of the modern rule of law, whose legitimacy is based primarily on the guarantee of 'legal certainty.' *The concept of legal certainty points to the elementary function of law to provide order.* Legal certainty can also be understood as certainty of order and vice versa. *In both cases one knows where one stands* and what one can expect. Although the two concepts are closely related, they are by no means synonymous, since certainty of order is the somewhat more comprehensive of the two."[34]

According to Anter, orders have at their disposition a special form of capital offering members or subjects a specific type of certainty, which can be called certainty of order, a concept that Heinrich Popitz describes as follows: "People enjoy certainty of order if they have certain knowledge about what they and others may and must do; if they can gain certainty that all parties involved will also, with some reliability, really behave as expected of them. ... In short, people have to know where they stand."[35]

Thus, if the certainty of order is based on the justified expectation of certain consequences of action, we could with Hermann Heller[36] propose the following simple equation: "order is predictability", an equation that also implies that predictability does not necessarily have to be based on state law; it can be provided by private governance or by non-state regulatory regimes.

Turning to certainty of compliance, he points to the mandate of the constitutional state not only to provide a legal system that guarantees certainty of expectation but also to put it into effect if trust is not to be disappointed. This aspect of *law enforcement is therefore an essential element of the rule-of-law principle*; Markus Möstl:

> "The *mandate to enforce the law* is in many regards immanent in the principle of the rule of law. On the one hand, it follows from the fundamental rule-of-law mandate to preserve and safeguard the public peace and legal certainty. Both historically and dogmatically, *keeping the peace through legal order* is among the original and constitutive properties of the rule of law. However, the public peace and certainty as to the law (legal certainty in the broader sense of the term) presuppose that the legal order of the state, which is to provide this peace and certainty, not only exists but is actually efficacious, which in turn requires the legal order to be sufficiently efficient

34 Anter (2004) 105.

35 Popitz (1992) 35.

36 Heller (1927).

> and actually enforced. *The efficacy and enforcement of the law are therefore a permanent demand of a state governed by the rule of law.* But even if – second – the focus is less on peace than on freedom as a conceptual cornerstone of the rule of law, the result is no different: if the essential property of the rule of law is to ensure lawful freedom and self-determination through the law, this presupposes that lawfulness and the law are actually realized and enforced, not only in relation to the state as freedom from unlawful coercion but also in relation to third parties as security against unlawful encroachment; for only the all-round enforcement of the law produces the state of lawful freedom that the rule of law seeks to guarantee."[37]

However, since we are concerned not only with the legal point of view, we now cite an author – political scientist, governance scholar, and institutional theoretician in one – who stresses the key *importance of chiefly formal* but also informal *rules* for the *stability* of the political system and its institutional structure:

> "Institutions are permanent regulatory systems recognized in a society. Their purpose is to steer individual behaviour and to coordinate it with the behaviour of other institutions in order to enable collective action. In the constant flow of events, institutions also ensure order, orientation, coordination, and *stability*, thus easing the persistent pressure on actors to justify themselves and make decisions. ...
>
> The *stability* of institutions depends above all on *formal rules*. However, the governance, orientation, and coordination effects of institutions also depend on how actors in the institution interpret and apply the rules. Furthermore, the reality of institutions also includes informal rules and social norms, so-called 'standard operation procedures,' the routines, decisional styles, and normative self-descriptions of organized reality that collaborating actors have agreed on."[38]

However, the extent to which the language of law is a language of order is particularly evident in the production and guarantee of order and stability through rule-boundedness. It is rule-boundedness and the consequent repeatability of courses of action that lead to their *institutionalized concentration*. This process of creating institutions from ritual also holds, in particularly strong measure, for law, as the numerous studies show on the *importance of legal rituals*, notably in early and medieval legal history.[39] Later in this book, we will be looking more closely at the importance of ritual knowledge as a particularly striking example of so-called 'rule knowledge'.

37 Möstl (2002) 65.

38 Benz (2004) 19–20.

39 See Kannowski (2002); Ebel (1975); Sellert (1997). In particular on the history of the oath, see Esders (ed.) (2007) 55–77; Esders (2009).

B. The language of law as a language of conflict resolution

I. Political culture as conflict culture

1. *Conflicts as sources of social change*

Obviously, conflict is ubiquitous in modern societies,[40] we have consequently to learn how to deal with it: "It is an axiom of the modern political and social sciences that conflict is inherent in all known societies. However, societies differ in how that handle it."[41] How conflicts are dealt with can be described (as I have done[42]) as the conflict culture of a polity and as part of its political culture.

It is also agreed that there is nothing pathological about conflict: if peacefully resolved,[43] it has, from a sociological point of view, a positive capacity to further the social change society needs.[44] Conflict is socially productive: within itself it develops the elements of its own limitation and regulation. It builds not only on an existing wealth of common interests but also creates new norms and rules and modifies old ones. From this point of view, conflict can be regarded as a source of social change."[45]

If the social function of conflict is thus positive rather than negative, it must obviously be tackled and *somehow regulated*. Ralf Dahrendorf comes to the following conclusion:

> "The attitude towards conflicts that, unlike repression and 'solution', promises success because it takes account of social realities, I shall call the *regulation of conflicts*. The regulation of social conflicts is the decisive tool for reducing the violence of almost all types of conflict. Conflicts do not disappear through regulation; they do not even necessarily become less intensive; but to the extent that they can be successfully regulated they become controllable and their creative force is put to the service of the gradual development of social structures."[46]

40 On the many types and fields of conflict see MEYER, B. (ed.) (1997).

41 BÜRZER et al. (1996) 15.

42 SCHUPPERT, G. F. (2008b) 465–598: "Drittes Kapitel: Politische Kultur als Konfliktkultur."

43 On the basic decision between "peaceful or unpeaceful" see, from the historical perspective, WESEL (1985).

44 COSER (1965).

45 NOLLMANN (1997) 20.

46 DAHRENDORF (1961) 227.

However, conflicts can be successfully regulated only if conflicts are recognized by all those concerned to be justified and useful, if the aim is not their final elimination, and if conflicts manifest themselves in organized conflict parties. Only then does the next step make sense: that the parties agree on specific 'rules of the game' for settling their differences; but it must be seen in the context of the other preconditions. '*Rules of the game*', framework agreements, constitutions, statutes, and so forth can operate as such only if they do not advantage or disadvantage any party from the outset, if they limit themselves *to formal aspects of the dispute* and if they presuppose the binding channelling of all differences."[47]

It should, however, be added that, where *rules of the game, constitutions, or statutes* are involved, the legal system comes into play, whose task it is to *provide* such rules of conflict processing. This brings us to an old favourite of mine, the 'providing' function of law.

2. *The providing function of law*

We have long spoken of the providing function of law, initially in relation to the task of state and administrative law to provide all the forms of action and organization required for effective, citizen-friendly administrative action subject to discipline by the rule of law.[48] It is not only a matter of administration but also of conflict parties being provided with the rules and institutional arrangements required for propitious conflict processing. An important effect of the providing function of law is to make the individual, that is in principle everyone, *capable of conflict*:

> "Legal norms enhance the riskability of conflicts. They create better prospects for 'noes' by producing adversarial institutions. A farmer can face a dispute about the use of a service road with confidence if the relevant right of use is entered in the land register. Even an impecunious student can oblige his landlord to repair a washbasin if such repairs are covered by the tenancy agreement. For his part, the landlord as owner can serve notice on the student as tenant if he can plausibly demonstrate that he needs the premises for personal use. However one judges the justice of legally normativized relations – there can be no doubt that the law enhances conflict

47 Dahrendorf (1961) 228.
48 Schuppert, G. F. (1993).

> competence.[49] The initiation of conflicts through legal norms backed by physical force succeeds because force is withheld from society and reserved to the state but then made available for non-state purposes through legal mediatization. Force as a means of conflict resolution is barracked, legally re-specified and, finally, socially redistributed. Under no circumstances is a landlord permitted to evict tenants himself, even if notice has been correctly served and the period of notice observed. He has to apply for eviction to the competent authority – only then is, if need be, forceable eviction legalized."[50]

This second step – the withdrawal of force – presupposes that the legal order of the state is prepared to make conflicts communicable and resolvable:

> "More possibilities will not prevent many conflicts from occurring but can lend tolerable form to them. The typically modern combination of political monopolization, legal specification, and societal redistribution of force acts in this direction. The outdifferentiation of the rule of law follows on from here. *Law clears the path, so to speak, by which reproduced contradictions can work their way towards processing. Paths are provided* by which contradictions are easier to communicate. Contradictions become effectively operative because their immanent indeterminacy can be made determinable by the law always looming on the horizon."[51]

II. The need for a "modus vivendi" and "modus procedendi" for normative conflicts – formulated in the language of law

Growing cultural, especially religious plurality in modern societies raises the increasingly urgent problem of how to deal with often conflicting diversity – a problem we have addressed under the heading "governance of diversity."[52] More and more people apparently see the practical solution to such normative conflicts in *proceduralization and institutionalization* – in the search for a "modus vivendi" and "modus procedendi" to defuse conflict.[53] The language of law is not only available for formulating this arrangement, it is probably also indispensable for the purpose.

A particularly apt historical example is the so-called Religious Peace of Augsburg of 1555, which sought to deal adequately with the confessional

49 See Luhmann (1995) 397 ff.
50 Nollmann (1997) 176 f.
51 Nollmann (1997) 178 f.
52 Schuppert, G. F. (2017b).
53 See especially Willems (2012b); Willems (2012a).

schism that had led to dissolution of the universal ecclesiastical and secular unity in medieval *Christianitas* and the development of the confessional state.[54] A brief glance at how this peace accord worked is therefore à propos:

It should be noted that the Augsburg Peace did not bring religious peace; it was unable to do so because it did not resolve the religious crisis: "The crisis of faith was *not resolved*: the Religious Peace did not bring religious peace; it could not, and did not even seek to do so. Spiritual agreement and consensus in faith were not achieved, and the aim had been precisely to avoid any forced unity of faith and law in the Empire."[55]

Martin Heckel concludes, that "… the Religious Peace of 1555 established an *order of political peace and legally guaranteed coexistence* between the two confessional power blocs";[56] it was therefore an order of peaceful coexistence. Heckel:

> "This order of peaceful coexistence was thus both secular and political in nature: it henceforth gave both confessions the same imperial protection and legal recognition; it guaranteed their political existence, internal spiritual self-determination, and the external freedom of development for confession and church organization. It also guaranteed that each could lay absolute claim to identity with the true Church of Christ and hence to being the sole true confession and that the two could engage in *spiritual* combat. In the Tridentine ordinances and in both early and later Protestant confessionals, this spiritual repudiation and dissociation were then emphatically proclaimed. But the legal freedom of spiritual self-realization and dispute was hedged in and contained secularly by the manifold distributive, protective, and barrier norms of imperial church law, which were intended to prevent the spiritual blaze from enveloping and razing the secular structure of the empire."[57]

This order of coexistence was the outcome of arduous negotiations and took the legal form of a contract: "The Religious Peace laid the foundations for the further development of the Empire in peace and freedom amidst the raging European religious struggles. In both practice and theory, it had gained the status of a constitutional basic contract and – law. It had *two aspects*: first, it was an agreement between estates, between the head of the Empire and the estates of the Empire (like every imperial 'recess' or reso-

54 Important on this subject: Reinhard (1977); Reinhard (1995).
55 Heckel (2001) 45.
56 Heckel (2001).
57 Heckel (2001) 46.

lution) and a confessional agreement between the Catholic and Protestant parties. It effected the decisive merging of estate / federalist dualism and confessional dualism, which had a lasting impact on the development of religion and the spiritual life, on the conflict between monarchy and estates, unitary statehood and on federalism and particularism in Germany."[58]

Marin Heckels shows that we are dealing with a professionally managed *conflict culture*, with a mode of conflict resolution that, although it did not eliminate the substantive conflict, did consistently *juridify* and *proceduralize* it – in the language of law.

58 Heckel (2001) 49–50.

6

Resonance and Law: Types of State and "Their" Law

In pursuing and modifying our examination of law as a dynamic system,[59] we now turn to law as a sphere of resonance, which Hartmut Rosa has addressed in his inspiring book (in June 2018 the English translation was forthcoming) "Resonance – A Sociology of the Relationship to the World" (in press: Cambridge UK, Polity Press).[60]

A. What is resonance and what does the answer teach us about our topic?

Our point of departure is Rosa's thesis that resonance is not, for example, an emotional state, but a *relationship mode*.[61] For our topic of law and its language, this means that the focus is on the relationship between the dynamic societal and political reality and the legal system (and its language) and whether it can be considered a resonance relationship. Rosa suggests that this is indeed the case.

He explains that resonance occurs only if the *resonant (or natural) frequency* of a body is excited by the oscillation of another:

> "Even at this acoustic physical level it can thus be said that when two bodies are in a resonant relationship each speaks with a 'voice of its own'. The oscillation of two bodies in a resonant relationship can in turn lead to mutual amplification … Resonant relationships can also develop in a process of mutual adaptive movements, which can be understood as *responsive oscillation* … The essential idea is that the two entities in the relationship affect one another in an oscillatory medium (or resonant space) in such a way that they respond to one another while *each speaking with its own voice*, i. e. 'resounding.'"[62]

Having established that resonance consists in mutual reaction between two entities, the important complementary concept of *axes of resonance* needs to be introduced. Rosa identifies two types: *horizontal axes of resonance* such as family, friendship, and politics, and *vertical axes of resonance* such as religion, nature, art, and history. It is thus not only a matter of the relation of the

59 Schuppert, G. F. (2016a).
60 Rosa (2016).
61 Rosa (2016) 288.
62 Rosa (2016) 282.

individual subject to the world, but also of *collective spheres of resonance*, such as *democracy* as an – ideally – self-determined order of the social:

> "The great promise of democracy ... is essentially that the structures and institutions of public life can be changed in and through the medium of democratic politics and its representatives, the *rulers*, placed in a responsive relation to the subjects. Because and to the extent that – taking up a basic constitutive idea of modernity – human beings can themselves determine the social, political, and economic order in which they live and act and can so (democratically) shape society, they can experience this order as a responsive and reactive sphere of resonance and make it their own."[63]

Thus Hartmut Rosa. All we have to do now is to translate this for the *field of law*, which presents no major difficulties.

If we substitute 'politics' or rather 'democratically self-made political order' by 'democratically self-made *legal order*,' we are dealing *in law with a collective sphere of resonance*, which can be experienced as and made one's own. If we also assume that there is a resonant relationship between dynamic societal and political developments and the legal system in which the two entities articulate themselves independently, we have to substitute Rosa's concept of 'voice' by that of 'language', bringing us to the *language of law* in which the collective sphere of resonance of law responds to the surrounding world.

However, this response in the language of law is, it is important to note, not to be understood as an echo in the natural-science sense of the word but as the language peculiar to the legal system, which still has to be articulated – in the institutionally formed political process by which "law" is produced. The successful novelist Juli Zeh, herself a doctor at law,[64] has described this process:

> "Legislative competence is part of state authority. In the democratic system, the authority of the state emanates from the people. Legal authority accordingly also emanates from the people and is delegated by them to representative institutions. In parliamentary legislative procedure, the concerns of interest groups are deliberated until a distribution of forces is attained that enables a majority decision to be reached. On the one hand, such a procedure is highly accommodating to societal developments and the interests they produce. On the other, it is phlegmatic and protracted. This is one of the key paradoxes of lawmaking in the modern democratic state. A complex society marked by ever faster change requires law that assimilates dynamic impulses and translates them into action at a pace amenable to develop-

63 Rosa (2016) 364–365.
64 Zeh (2012); see the favourable review by Kilian (2014) 285 f.

> ment while reflecting the democratic balance of interests. And it should avoid the unwieldy, wishy-washy outcomes that precipitate compromise brings. This is three wishes in one. The conservational nature of a system of rules resistant to change is therefore not the primary obstacle to dynamic law; It is the democratic idea itself, which requires the plural crystallization of opinions and their representation in the legislature."[65]

We now turn in more detail to the resonant relationship between the dynamic world and the legal system responding in its specific language. First, we look at selected types of state and "their" law. Second, we examine whether a "successful" legal system and its language not only reacts to the external world but helps shape it as a "language of politics." Third, we venture into the worlds of law to examine the autonomy of these nomoi and their order – the nomos of the nomoi.[66]

B. Types of state and "their" law

Taking up our own preliminary reflections on the subject,[67] we identify various types of state, as well as typical regulatory structures and regulatory regimes. The aim is to show how the legal system and – as an element thereof – jurisprudence reacts to societal and political change in the sense of a sphere of resonance; and not only – technically and instrumentally – by *providing the necessary forms of action and regulation* but also by *creating new concepts and new methods*, thus affecting its subject – government and administration. We consider two examples of this interactive relationship between societal reality and responding jurisprudence, the "manager" of the language of law.[68] The first state is that of industrial society.

65 Zeh (2006) 123–138, here 127–128.
66 See Seinecke (2015) 262, 273.
67 See above all: Schuppert, G. F. (2001).
68 On the relationship between law and language and in particular the "crisis of law as crisis of language," see Forsthoff (1971a).

I. The state of industrial society and the existential responsibility of the state as ordering idea of the modern administrative state

1. The development of the interventionist state in response to societal and political modernization

The history of German administration and administrative history in the late nineteenth century and the first third of the twentieth century shows this to have been a period of societal, legal, and administrative modernization,[69] which set in with the industrial revolution[70] and entered a *phase of acceleration* between 1880 and 1930: "In the history of society, these decades were marked by industrialization and urbanization, by the dissolution of traditional, estate-based milieus and by the political rise of the labour movement. These … factors were also important determinants of political development in Germany at the turn of the century. With the "great turn" in Bismarck's domestic, economic, and social policy after the end of his alliance with the liberals, a period of massive statization began in Germany. Many social fields *become subject to sovereign regulation and control by the state.*[71]

To describe the role of the state in the face of these modernization processes, the term *interventionist state* has often been used,[72] playing a role that, as Michael Stolleis stresses, the state could not avoid:

> "In a very broad sense, every modern state is interventionist because lawmaking and enforcement and the administrative regulation of individual cases incessantly constrains, induces, or inhibits societal processes, so that we can meaningfully speak of the 'interventionist state' only when legal influence reaches a certain level of density and systematization. The changes must therefore be 'structural and qualitative … And not merely a quantitative inflation of functions already in place'. For legal and constitutional history, it is decisive whether, from a certain point in time, industrial society urgently needed constant state intervention in the form of new legislation because it was no longer a self-supporting construction. As soon as this point was reached, the state had to intervene if it was to maintain its double role as guarantor of the rules of the game and as player; it intervened not from a position of strength but from one of weakness. Where intervention was to take place was increasingly determined in consultation between the politico-administrative system and societal groups. This had far-reaching consequences, not least in the style of legislation and

69 Greater detail in Schnabel (1949) 101 ff.
70 See Maetschke et al. (eds.) (2013).
71 Meinel (2011) 108.
72 On the concept and the problems it poses, see Gall (1978) 562 ff.; Stolleis (1989).

> the administration of justice, political will-formation, and, ultimately in the attribution of sovereignty. The question, debated since the end of the nineteenth century, of whether the epoch of (internal) sovereignty was coming to an end, had its origins in this complex."[73]

We now turn from the interventionist state and its interventionist law[74] to the question of how jurisprudence reacted to this far-reaching modernization. In the role of '*resonant actor*', one of the major figures in the administrative law of the period, Ernst Forsthoff, formulated better than anyone the answer of administrative jurisprudence. As we shall see with regard to the Enlightenment and natural law, there are authoritative *resonant places* and *resonant persons* in a sphere of resonance like law.

2. *Ernst Forsthoff and the "discovery" of responsibility for providing services of general interest as an objective of the modern administrative state*

Unlike natural scientists, jurists are generally said to invent and discover nothing. This may well be so, but there are exceptions. One is Ernst Forsthoff, who in his seminal work on the administration as service provider[75] responded to the modernization processes of the late nineteenth and early twentieth centuries, a period Jürgen Osterhammel has knowledgeably described and analysed under the heading "The Transformation of the World."[76] Reading Forsthoff – preferably also through Florian Meinel's spectacles in his ground-breaking dissertation "The Jurist in Industrial Society"[77] – does indeed leave one with an impression of *resonant oscillations*, concentrating conceptually towards the provision of services of general interest as a notion of order in the modern administrative state. Methodologically, Forsthoff sets out from a sociological finding: that individuals are increasingly dependent on services provided by the state, since the life space

73 Stolleis (1989) 135 f.

74 According to Puhle (1973). Three structural and qualitative changes are characteristic of law in the interventionist state: 1. The sharp rise in the need for regulation in industrial society; 2. The 'seizure of power' by public law and administrative law as growth sector; 3. The gradual blurring of the boundaries between private law and public law.

75 Forsthoff (1938).

76 Osterhammel (2009).

77 Forsthoff (1971b).

they can manage autonomously is continuously shrinking: "Forsthoff's methodological programme goes far beyond the ultimately banal postulate that the juristic discourse has to take 'social realities' into account. He wanted to rethink the ordering structures of law from the perspective of social realities *in order to adapt juristic forms to a changed reality from within*, to conceptualize this changed reality in legal-dogmatic terms. For Forsthoff, all juristic endeavours to capture reality were solely in the interest of this *dialectical return* to legal concepts."[78]

Summing up Forsthoff's analysis, Florian Meinel explains how we are to understand this dependence of this individual on the state as service provider:[79]

> "Forsthoff illustrates his hypothesis with the graphic distinction between 'effective' and the 'controlled' life space.[80] In agrarian society and still in the bourgeois age, people from the classes that shaped political life lived in an environment they could 'regard as their own': 'The farm, the field belonging to them, the house they lived in;' that is to say, their life basis was assured by property rights: their 'controlled life space'. The goods of the controlled life space could ensure 'a comparatively secure living', because in their subjective sphere people could dispose freely over them.
>
> With the transition to a modern economy and a way of life rooted in the division of labour, people had to range far beyond the life space they controlled in order to provide themselves with the necessities of life. Forsthoff calls the sphere in which people move but which does not 'belong' to them personally their 'effective life space.' We could also speak of socialized or social life space. The necessities of life that people can avail themselves of in their effective life space differ from those available in their own life space in that they are typically not the product of people's own work but of a specialized production process based on the division of labour. ... As Forsthoff puts it, citing Max Weber, people have to 'appropriate' them. ... Where 'smooth appropriation' through the free circulation of goods no longer functions, the state itself takes over distribution. Individuals then depend essentially on the complex administrative system and its services. They use public transport and communication facilities, purchase gas and energy, use public health services and social security institutions. The state does not, of course, provide all such services itself. But it becomes the omnipresent guarantor of 'appropriation'. In Enst Jünger's *Der Arbeiter* we read that 'nine tenths of everything the modern human being has would immediately become worthless if they were to be abstracted from the existence of the state'."[81]

78 Meinel (2011) 133.
79 Meinel (2011) 154–155.
80 The following brief quotes are all from Forsthoff (1938).
81 Jünger (1981) 292.

Because of these processes, the administrative authorities gain enormous power potential, which, following Michel Foucault, is nowadays generally referred to as "organic power" or Giorgio Agamben as sovereign power over "naked life".[82]

> "Already under the sway of liberal ideas and constitutional orders, the state had experienced an extraordinary growth in power. It gained control over the essential prerequisites for the life of the individual to a degree surely quite alien to the absolute police state. This absolute police state could supervise professional life, rebuke Kant, censure Schiller, and prohibit the spread of deterministic theories; it could certainly determine the very details of how people ought to live. But it was far from exercising the same responsibility for ensuring that life was possible at all as does the state today."[83]

Meinel outlines just how comprehensively the administrative authorities as service providers affect the realities of life for every individual:

> "For Forsthoff, this power over the basics of life manifested itself not only in the form of direct or indirect public services with regard to which the *administrative authorities* acted chiefly as *providers of services of general interest*. … In a 1950 lecture, he stated: 'The provision of essential public services is thus no longer only a matter of satisfying community needs at the local level. It means rather the organization of large economic and social spaces.'[84] In the first place, this certainly includes public utility services, infrastructure management, and public health, hence soft power through benefits of all sorts ('the carer also rules!'[85]). But, for Forsthoff, services of general interest included developmental administration in the broadest sense – not concerned with individual intervention in subjective rights: economic planning; managing the labour market; spatial planning; influencing the population ideologically through propaganda and the mass media; 'harnessing and steering the emotional energies of the modern masses'.[86] And the whole field of psychological (and some day genetic) influence and prevention, which the state cannot forgo, not least *because, presiding over industrial society, it is obliged to generate growth* and must therefore ensure that the population can optimally serve the industrial employment regime."[87]

One last sociological observation important for the conception of administrative law and the functional logic of the modern administrative state: the

82 See Foucault (1978–79); Agamben (1995).
83 Forsthoff (1938) 8.
84 Forsthoff (1950) 6.
85 Forsthoff (1964) 65.
86 Forsthoff (1942) 69.
87 Meinel (2011) 164–165.

replacement of the ideal of equality held high by the liberal state governed by the rule of law by concentration on the differing needs of various social groups:

> "The ideal of civil liberty was at the same time an ideal of civil equality, and society based on equality before the law was the 'object' of administrative action. ... This notion, too, was incompatible with the provision of services of general interest. If the separation of society and the state is eliminated and hence – from the point of view of the state – the nature of society as a unitary object, the formal basis for societal equality is also lost. In modern administration, eligibility is based ... not on civil equality but on inequality among social groups. Social groups depend in various ways on the state machinery for service provision, distribution, and legalization and for this very reason have to act collectively in order to effectively assert their claims of access vis-à-vis the state. The provision of services of general interest thus cancels out the status of civil equality. The fundamental normative category is not the citizen but the 'beneficiary', whose existence is registered in terms of entitlement: as consumer or as entrepreneur, as country or city dweller, as traffic participant, as tenant, patient, worker, employee, and so on. The state as provider of services of general interest is no longer the state of a given society but a state of social groups."[88]

So much for the *resonant actor* Ernst Forsthoff's analysis and responses.[89]

II. The preventive state and "its" preventive security law

Rereading my 2001 essay on regulated self-regulation, which addresses the relationship between the preventive state and its security law in some depth,[90] I was struck by how, in concept formation and semantic shifts, the authors cited capture a development whose functional logic has become fully apparent only through the scourge of terrorism since 9/11. We cast only a brief glance at this development, not only flanked but also exacerbated by abandonment of the classical concept of 'warding off danger' in favour of suppressing it by 'ensuring security'.[91]

88 Meinel (2011) 169.
89 See Badura (1966); Badura (1967).
90 Schuppert, G. F. (2001) 210 ff.
91 On the failure of the proportionality principle to develop a disciplinary effect in crime prevention see Schuppert, G. F. (1996).

III. The concept and workings of the preventive state

The preventive state[92] undertakes to prevent dangers, not to ward them off. Dieter Grimm: "In contrast to a state that sees itself primarily as a repressive authority, and which can accordingly wait for socially detrimental events to occur before reacting, a prevention-oriented state has to detect potential crises at the very onset and try to nip them in the bud. The state comes into play not only when concrete danger threatens but already when abstract risks are identified."[93]

Particularly interesting is how the preventive state comes into action, what tools and procedures it uses. Grimm has this to say about the liberal repressive state governed by the rule of law: "State repression finds expression in intervention against manifest disturbance of a legally established normal state of affairs with the aim of restoring this state of affairs. It thus acts reactively and selectively. ... Preventive action by the state, in contrast, takes the form of avoiding undesirable developments and events. It is therefore prospective and comprehensive."[94]

This is precisely the point. The prospective and comprehensive preventive state has been provided with an appropriate toolbox in the form of the Prevention of Trafficking in Illegal Drugs and Other Manifestations of Organized Crime Act (OrgKG) and the later Fight against Crime Act (VerbrBekG). These acts legalize precisely what the preventive state has to rely on: the preventive and comprehensive fight against crime.

* *The preventive state as a security state*

In analogy to 'welfare state', a term that stresses the provision of social security and the establishment of social justice as key functions of the state in industrial society, we can call the preventive state a 'security state' to stress the central function of the state in providing security through evolving security law and through administration adequate to the task. Indeed, *changing terminology* manifestly indicates shifts in the sense of a functional change in administration and administrative law in the field of "providing security and order."[95] This can be outlined under two headings:

92 Grimm (1986) 38–54; also published in Grimm (1991); see also Denninger (1988).
93 Grimm (1991) 198.
94 Grimm (1991) 199.
95 On the provision of security and order within the structure of state responsibilities see the typology of Rose, R. (1975); see also Schuppert, G. F. (1980).

* *The provision of security by the state as a basic right*

There has been broad consensus that the provision of security is a central function of the state and that the basic duty of the citizen to renounce force corresponds to the state monopoly of the use of force and the state's duty to enforce the law. Gusy rightly comments: "Today, security is recognized as a task of the state. It covers not only sanctioning breaches of the law that have already occurred but also putting a stop to ongoing attacks against the legal order and warding off future attacks. This makes the enforcement of the legal order a public good. In the risk society, security is a public good."[96]

Recent discussion has emphasized the constitutional rank of security as a task of the state. For Volkmar Götz, the constitutional-law quality of the "internal security" mandate of the state is an expression of the "*constitutional-law dimension of demands on the state.*"[97] Josef Isensee writes of a "basic right to security".[98]

In brief, this terminology provides "flanking conceptual protection" for the natural logical tendency of the preventive state to go beyond the constraints on police action that the traditional concept of danger imposes and, in the name of countering risks, to progressively waive the domesticizing impact of the proportionality principle.

* *From police law to security law*

This title of Christoph Gusy's[99] Bielefeld inaugural lecture captures the functional change in law following the advent of the preventive state as security state. The substantive shift came on tiptoe in the guise of a terminological change with the inexorable career of the concept "internal security". Whereas Götz's entry in the "Manual of German Constitutional Law" (Drews / Wacke / Vogel / Martens: "Handbuch des Deutschen Staatsrechts") would once perhaps have appeared under the headword "Gefahrenabwehr" ("averting danger")[100] it is now to be found under "Innere Sicherheit" ("internal security"). This concept not only dedifferentiates branches of security, bringing them together under a general heading but, as Götz him-

96 Gusy (1994) 192.
97 Götz (1988) 1007 f.
98 Isensee (1983).
99 Gusy (1994).
100 Drews et al. (1986).

self puts it, it expresses a demand on the state lending argumentative weight to a policy for combating crime that presents itself as a security package. Under the heading "internal security – promise and real possibility; Alfred Dietel rightly remarks:

> "The concept 'internal security' has become a subject in its own right. As political promise, 'internal security' has more positive connotations than the more juristically neutral term 'public security'. A political capacity to act and determination are better signalled by measures to improve 'internal security' because this can always give the impression that major and important matters are at issue."[101]

"Security law", the matching concept to "internal security" as a task of the state therefore goes beyond classical police law. This development merely obeys the logic of the preventive state. It is therefore not a question of halting this logic but of not allowing the *logic of substantive demands on the state* to blur the distinction between police and justice, repression and prevention, police service and intelligence service, etc. In this field, jurisprudence faces a new challenge in finding a balance that both works and secures freedom.

> Security is a state that, under the modern conditions of the risk society increasingly reaches beyond the domain of police and traditional police law. If, in establishing and maintaining security, the state and the police are only two factors among many, the interests that have to be taken into legal account, too, become more numerous and more complex. This is where security law begins. It is, however, also evident that the real problems that present themselves are less and less accessible from the beaten paths of police-law dogmatics. Many questions arise off the beaten track, but, so far, few answers have been found. In this regard jurisprudence is almost everywhere in its infancy."[102]

Here too, as we shall see, the function of the legal system and legal science is clearly to react to changes in the actual state of affairs not only by echoing them but also by addressing them and by amplifying them through linguistic change – so-called semantic shifts[103] – and thus responsively impacting reality.

101 Dietel (1987) 57.
102 Gusy (1994) 207–208.
103 On changes in statehood reflected by "semantic shifts" see Schuppert, G. F. (2010) 116 ff.

C. From the private law of the constitution to the constitution of private law: the necessary correspondence between the conceptual models of jurisprudence and social and economic conditions

I. The necessary correspondence between law and social reality or why legal concepts can not only age but also lose their function

In 1960, one of the giants of German jurisprudence, Franz Wieacker,[104] addressed the German Association of Jurists on the occasion of its centenary,[105] an institution whose task it is to periodically check the 'reality adequacy' of the law in place and, where needful, to recommend reforms. We could thus speak of an institutionalized attempt to ensure the resonance capacity of the legal system and its jurisprudence through a sort of constant monitoring.

Wieacker paid tribute to the founding of association, which took place against the backdrop of a "fraternity of jurists" determined to reform the legal order through national codification:

> "Since the professors of law, the high judges, the leading attorneys, and the experts from the ministries of justice and legislation were of one mind, idea and reality, theory and practice, legal policy, and application of the law came ever closer in the manner characteristic of the heyday of a legal culture.
>
> This favourable constellation at the hour of birth of the German Association of Jurists was no accident. It was grounded in the intellectual, political, and economic actuality of civil jurisprudence at that time. Public prestige for scholarly jurisprudence is possible only if it is able to *express vital demands of the society of its time*; the *curious interaction between intellectual and social forces* then sets in that is one of the existential conditions of law. For this reason, determining the 'social model' of codification (attempted elsewhere[106]) is a precondition for understanding the functions, victories, and decline of the great legal codes."[107]

Because of this *necessary interdependence between the legal order and society*, it is not only likely but normal for a certain conceptualization of law to age when this correspondence between law and societal reality erodes: "If there

104 Wieacker's best-known work, which now enjoys canonical status, is "A History of Private Law in Europe" (1996).
105 Wieacker (1960).
106 Wieacker (1953).
107 Wieacker (1960).

really is interdependence between the spirit of a legal order and the structure of its society – what we call the 'social model' – there will also have to be structural shifts in modern economic society supplanting the classical dogmatic context of general private law by once marginal areas. In short, classical private law started to age because the free, pioneering society of the nineteenth century, whose social and economic conditions were reflected in its dogmatics, no longer exists."[108]

Writing on the constitutionalization of private law as a development process Felix Maultzsch[109] argues in similar vein. He comments on the drifting apart of the classical civil law model prior to the introduction of the Civil Code and the reality of the modern administrative state:

> "This system with its cornerstones of civil equality, and freedom of contract and property provided a formally oriented framework that was also binding on lawmakers and therefore constitutional to the extent that any legal-policy/purposive reshaping of private-law conditions did not lie within its competence. Against this backdrop, basic rights, too, could only offer defence against state interference. Extending their application to relations between private persons would have run counter to the fundamental parameters of the nineteenth century legal structures. However, there were already signs that this conception of civil law was on the wane, witness the growing discussion on the social function of private law. It was *Otto Gierke* who famously proposed that a 'drop of socialist oil' should be infused into the coming Civil Code.[110] In his view, civil law ought not to persist in a purely liberal basic attitude but embrace higher, social objectives if it wished to survive in the emerging modern administrative state and industrial society."[111]

A third author should be cited on the correspondence between legal and social orders: from a systems theoretical perspective legal, Dan Wielsch points to the need for *societal adequacy of law*, which requires at least that the order be *adequately complex*:

> "In minimalistic intent, we translate the concept as adequate complexity. In a broad sense, this means that the law has institutions at its disposal that are compatible with the levels of abstraction demanded by society. The necessary categorial reductions of law should not be allowed to hinder an increase in societal complexity but, on the contrary, enable it. What is necessary are selectors that, despite a high level of societal complexity, enable relatively simple decisions to be made without these

108 Wieacker (1960) 6.

109 Maultzsch (2012).

110 Gierke (1889) 3.

111 Maultzsch (2012) 1041–1042.

> decisions reducing societal complexity through their binding effect.[112] This is also likely to be true for the implementation of collectively defined control plans entrusted and credited to law, such as are generated in and through the political system. The focus in law – at least historically – has been on providing and securing the (systemic and societal) complexity provoked by the individual seeking to realize plans of his own. One example is the figure of subjective property law, with whose aid social relations can be unravelled, spheres of interest separated and rendered variable independently of one another."[113]

Just how a lack of correspondence between legal and social order can plunge a legal model – so-called *private law society*[114] – into crisis and force it to give way to a different understanding of law is shown by the shift from private law as constitution to the constitution of private law.

II. From private law as constitution to the constitution of private law

The development process is described by Dan Wielsh in an essay on "Basic Rights as Justificatory Rules in Private Law."[115] He begins by outlining the ambitious self-conception of a civil jurisprudence as a societal order:[116]

> "However, the self-awareness of this society that defines itself as civil cannot be fully explained in terms of the liberation of individuals from the estate-based, feudal order so that they now stand atomized vis-à-vis the state they themselves have authorized. It can be understood only if a further assumption is taken into account: that society has at its disposal 'institutions with the innate capability to coordinate and thus *directly steer and influence* the plans and actions of free, autonomous people[117] in such a way that society is able in itself to attain prosperity and justice. Only because civil society has at its disposal a non-hierarchical ordering mechanism in the shape of the free transaction economy and competition can it emancipate itself from substantive provisions pertaining to the public good in the state and limit itself to enabling free self-determination. The overall societal and constitutional policy status of this regulatory process arises only from the link between private law and this ordering process, from its relationship with an economic system that provides market access, that leaves the beneficial use of resources and participation in the work process to the free decision of economic operators, and which knows

112 Luhmann (1970) 175–202.
113 Wielsch (2001) 36.
114 See Riesenhuber (ed.) 2007.
115 Wielsch (2013).
116 Wielsch (2013) 721–722.
117 Böhm (1966) 88 (highlighting in original).

> only one legal basis for the resulting system of communication and cooperation: private law."[118]

In brief, this means: "Private law is raised to the status of a societal order and the – decentralized – 'steering' of a society is entrusted to free and autonomously planning individuals."[119]

According to Wielsch, however, private law cannot satisfy the macro-societal regulatory demands made of it, chiefly for *methodological reasons*:

> "Adoption of the constitutional-law promise of equal freedom through private law lends this law macro-societal status. This alone explains and justifies the nineteenth century notion of the priority of private law over constitutional law. Methodologically, however, private law is inadequately equipped for the task. The public-law perspective on subjective rights and private-law institutions adopted by ordoliberal legal theory remains marginal. The prevailing view is that of an 'unpolitical' private law whose task it is to establish a bilateral balance of interests. ... Because the prevailing methodological understanding lacks any sense for a constitutional view of subjective rights and private autonomy, the societal function that private law has assumed is not adequately perceived. ... On the other hand, ... law fails to honour its own promise of equal freedom because it ignores the actual preconditions for claiming civil liberties. It is a hallmark of formal liberal law that it throws no light on its own functional conditions."[120]

With the enactment of the Basic Law and, in particular, with the rulings of the Federal Constitutional Court that define this basic order, the sceptre has passed to *constitutional law*. Wielsch notes:[121]

> "The promise of equal freedom passes from the private-law constitution and private law to the democratic constitution and the basic rights, albeit without competition losing its quality as an institution under constitutional law. Basic rights assume a socially constitutive function, but in so doing can build on the regulatory function of social institutions and private law.
>
> The precondition is that basic rights – as well as the political system – are also binding on society itself. For this purpose, their dogmatic interpretation as bans on interference, requiring the state to refrain from action, does not suffice. Basic rights must be able to *change* society. This is achieved if they are understood as precepts for shaping the law that are implemented by the branches of government (legislature, executive, and judicature) within the specific framework of their functions and responsibilities. What decisively sets the course is that constitutional jurisdiction also qualifies basic rights as objective fundamental norms that present decisions on

118 Mestmäcker (2007) 41.
119 Wielsch (2013) 722.
120 Wielsch (2013) 728 f.
121 Wielsch (2013) 731 f.

values for all areas of simple law.[122] Over and beyond the interpretation of individual basic norms, the basic law catalogue as a whole is treated as an objective order and system of values."[123]

In brief, the establishment of the necessary correspondence between the legal and social orders is primarily a task for the – reflexive – legal order[124] itself. This can require law to develop suitable methods for adequately discharging its controlling function;[125] but, as we have seen, it can also prove necessary to change the relationship between entire fields of law, as has been done with probably irrevocable effect by the constitutionalization of the whole legal order.[126]

D. The multiple life worlds of the law: the helpful perspective of legal pluralism

I. The societies of law

In his seminal work on the law of legal pluralism,[127] Ralf Seinecke posits that all communities tend to give themselves regulatory regimes of their own: "Every society, community, or association finds (at least theoretically) the normative force to establish its own law. Communities themselves recognize their given order as law. This insight has been formulated under wide-ranging epistemological conditions; nevertheless, all legal theoreticians of 'societal law' in the modern age have faced the same difficulty: the 'Malinowski problem', i.e., the distinction between law and other social norms."[128]

This is exactly what we mean when, in the "language of governance", we say that every governance collective tends to organize itself as a regulatory

122 First: BVerfGE 6, 55 (72) – Income splitting: Article 6 I of the Basic Law is not only an institutional guarantee but a fundamental norm (Grundsatznorm), "that is to say, a binding decision on values for private and public law pertaining to the entire field of marriage and family."
123 A year later, BVerfGE 7, 198 (205) – Lüth.
124 See the reflections of the present author in: Schuppert, G. F. (2016a).
125 See Schuppert, G. F. (2017c).
126 See Schuppert, G. F./Bumke (2000).
127 Seinecke (2015).
128 Seinecke (2015) 157.

collective in order to stabilize itself internally and differentiate itself from the environment;[129] it is another question whether – as a second step – we speak of law or reserve this honorific for state-made law. If, as we suggest,[130] we operate with a broad concept of law, we will doubtless end up with a *broad concept of legal pluralism*, which Seinecke "provisionally" defines as follows:

> "Legal pluralism covers all legal or social constellations, circumstances, and situations in which various types of legal rules, legal orders, or legal sources can be subscribed to from a normative, descriptive, or world-view perspective. This plurality of law can be described politically, sociologically, or juristically, as well as historically narrated. It concerns individual subjects, small communities, entire societies, social fields, and communicative social systems alike. To the extent that this normative diversity is understood to be juristic, legal pluralism is always a critical normative concept. In every legal pluralism, the word law constitutes an episteme or weltanschauung in its own right, thus structuring the normative, political, and social perception of the world.
>
> In brief, legal pluralism means all socio-legal constellations in which different sorts of legal rules, legal principles, legal orders, legal sources, legal history, and legal views interact or collide and which can be distinguished from one another in normative, descriptive, empirical, or world-view terms."[131]

We are thus dealing with different worlds of law, which – and this is the essential point – reflect different *views of the world* in the sense of Rosa's sphere of resonance, a phenomenon we shall be looking at in brief in concluding this second part.

II. Communities of law and their specific world-views

With the help of Ralf Seinecke, we can best understand what is meant by citing two legal pluralists. A number of general remarks will then conclude this section.

- The first author is Robert Cover from the world of Jewish law, where no clearly marked boundary is drawn between life-world and law. He employs the metaphor of a bridge:

129 In extenso in Schuppert, G. F. (2016b) 63 ff.
130 Schuppert, G. F. (2016b) 251–291.
131 Seinecke (2015) 8.

> "Law ... is a bridge in normative space connecting ... the 'world-that-is' ... with our projections of alternative 'worlds-that-might-be' .... In this theory, law is neither to be wholly identified with the understanding of the present state of affairs nor with the imagined alternatives. It *is* the bridge – the committed social behavior which constitutes the way a group of people will attempt to get from here to there. Law connects 'reality' to alternity constituting a new reality with a bridge built out of committed social behavior. Thus, visions of the future are more or less strongly determinative of the bridge which is 'law' depending upon the commitment and social organization of the people who hold them."[132]

Seinecke notes that, for Cover, law is always "embedded law," embedded in the life-world of the given community:[133]

> "This conception of law runs contrary to classical concepts. It refers not to institutionalized coercion, not to a ruling state, not to good old justice, not to community recognition and not to a communicative code. Cover has a quite different law in mind. The question 'What is law?' takes on a quite different meaning for him. Cover embeds the law of a community in its life-world. Law constitutes the world in which we live, our nomos:
>
> 'We inhabit a *nomos* – a normative universe. We constantly create and maintain a world of right and wrong, of lawful and unlawful, of valid and void. ... No set of legal institutions or prescriptions exists apart from the narratives that locate it and give it meaning. For every constitution there is an epic, for each decalogue a scripture. Once understood in the context of the narratives that give it meaning, law becomes not merely a system of rules to be observed, but a world in which we live.'"[134]

We add a further comment by Seinecke, in which he speaks of the *sounding board of law*:

> "Cover strongly attacks the project of legal positivism. He confronts the notion of functional or instrumental law with the eternal stories from the world of law and justice. They still resonate against the sounding board of law to disclose the deficient perspective of juristic positivism. Cover deliberately describes his law not in an analytic study: he presents it in a story of its own. In this narrative, law draws its strength not only from normative postulates but also from the history and myths of law. Cover understands the two elements law and narrative as "inseparable": every rule needs history and fate, beginning and end, explanation and goal. Similarly, every narrative relies on a normative standpoint. It needs the moral of the story."[135]

132 Cover (1993) 176–203, here 176.

133 Seinecke (2015) 263.

134 Cover (1983) 4.

135 Seinecke (2015) 265.

- The second author to be considered is the legal pluralist Boaventura de Sousa Santos, whom we have already mentioned in the first part of this book. Seinecke sums up his *world-view legal pluralism*:

> "This link between law and life world also shapes the political and postmodern legal pluralism of Boaventura de Sousa Santos.[136] As in Jewish law, he combines the topoi of law and life, knowledge and action, theory and practice; of emancipation and politics, of truth and activism. This political law is part of many worlds and is to be found in all "structural spaces" of the world. The law of the household, work, community, market, state, and world together form the interlegal space of law. But Santos does not limit his legal pluralism to legal orders in the modern sense of the term. He associates it closely with the world-view demands and perspectives of international leftwing politics. For law as a "map of misreading" always provides information about the truth of the world – who deserves law and who has no right to it."[137]

- We bring the second part of this book to an end with the apt concluding remarks of Ralf Seinecke:

> "Legal pluralism is characterized by the diversity of perspectives. It lacks an imperial nomos that establishes the sovereignty and dominance of a first legal order. Only thus can legal pluralism guarantee a space of their own to the alternative ways of life and life-worlds of law. For this reason, the nomos of legal pluralism is fundamentally controversial: interaction between legal orders brings together the various alternative legal orders with their bridges to other world-orders in a nomos of legal pluralism, and hence introduces chaos into the order of law – legal pluralism is pictured as a nomos of nomoi.
>
> In legal pluralism, different legal and world orders are superimposed. While interaction at the level of law can in one sense still be contained by a certain order of law, it gets out of control in the nomoi of legal orders. For legal pluralism lacks a prevailing and sovereign perspective. In the nomos of legal pluralism, no primary law dominates. The concept of legal pluralism encompasses first, second, third, many legal orders without bringing them under the control of any one order. In the nomos of legal pluralism, the disorder of orders prevails. For this reason, legal pluralism is the nomos of nomoi."[138]

136 See, above all, de Sousa Santos (1987).

137 Seinecke (2015) 299.

138 Seinecke (2015) 373.

Part 3
Role of Legal Regimes and Concepts

In examining the role of various legal concepts and regimes, we shall consider four equipped with a marked *globalization gene* that predestines them to play a major part in the global history of ideas. Each concept or regime is to be understood only in the given context:

- Worldwide Enlightenment and universal natural law
- The history of international law as a political history of ideas
- The invention of human rights
- The dynamics of rule-of-law principles

We begin with the Enlightenment and "its" natural law. The Age of the Enlightenment is not only an interesting epoch in the history of ideas: a somewhat more comprehensive consideration of this period can also throw light on the legal concept and regime of natural law, notably with respect to the Enlightenment in the history of communication, institutions, and power. These three aspects also prove fruitful in examining natural law as a "language of politics."

7

A Comprehensive Study of Natural Law and Enlightenment

The particularly interesting legal concept of natural law can be understood only against the backdrop of the Enlightenment – a key epoch in the history of ideas.[1] A closer look at this phenomenon is therefore called for.[2] To avoid drowning in the ocean of literature on the subject, we limit our analysis to *five disciplinary approaches*:

- The Enlightenment as global history
- The Enlightenment as history of communication and media
- The Enlightenment as history of institutions
- The Enlightenment as the history of power
- The Enlightenment as legal history, namely the history of natural law

We begin with the history of the Enlightenment as global history.

A. The Enlightenment as global history

The Enlightenment clearly had a worldwide impact. Wolfgang Hardtwig divides his book on the Enlightenment and its impact on the world into three parts. The first deals with Germany, the second with Europe and the third with the USA, China, and the Ottoman Empire.[3] However, this territorializing approach misses the most important point, namely the globality of the Enlightenment as a *worldwide communicative exchange of ideas and knowledge*.

Steffen Martus describes an occurrence in 1721 that illustrates what is meant. The enlightener Christian Wolff – who held a chair in mathematics at the University of Halle, but also taught agronomy, metaphysics, ethics, and politics – held a lecture on the political wisdom of the Chinese:

> "Wolff snubbed his theological audience at a solemn meeting of the Prorektorat in July 1721 when he *globalized the claim of philosophy to validity*. Only at first glance was the subject he had chosen – the 'practical philosophy of the Chinese' – exotic and remote: by that time Europeans were already well acquainted with China. Since

1 See Haakonssen (2012).

2 For a useful overview see Stollberg-Rilinger (2016); a comprehensive and pleasurable read is provided by Martus (2015).

3 Hardtwig (ed.) (2010).

the Jesuit mission in the sixteenth century, the Middle Kingdom had been a challenge to Christian thought."[4]

Since European enlighteners were bothered above all by the high cultural level of China, which, as travellers reported, managed "without an extensive religious, metaphysical superstructure, relying solely on the secular wisdom of Confucianism,"[5] there was lively interest in the teachings of Confucius, which – as Martus recounts – were soon known throughout Europe:

> "The Latin translation of Confucian writings, which the Jesuit missionary Philippe Couplet had published in 1687 under the title *Confusius Sinarum Philosophus* and dedicated to Louis XIV, was read everywhere in Europe. ... In 1711, the Belgian Jesuit François Noël brought back from his twenty years in China an extended and amended translation of Confucian writings (*Sinesis Imperii libri classici sex*). Wolff reviewed this edition for, among other publications, the Leipzig *Acta Eruditorium* and the Jesuit *Journal de Trévaux*. Chinese philosophy clearly had something to say to all Christian confessions. The fact that Wolff read Noël and initially did not know Couplet's edition was not without consequences. One of his main arguments was that the Chinese had no concept of God at all and therefore could not be branded as atheists, as 'deniers of God'. The older edition by Couplet, however, placed the greatest value on the fact that the Chinese had originally known and honoured the true Deity. This was one of the Jesuit strategies to defuse the problem of how such an advanced civilization could manage without Christianity: the Chinese were really Christians but simply didn't realize it."[6]

Sebastian Conrad has examined the "*Enlightenment without frontiers*"[7] in great depth and intensity.[8] He sees the Enlightenment also and primarily as a response to the global challenges that European expansion inevitably engendered.[9] In his view, the resulting globalization affected the *global market of knowledge* more than that of ideas. The Enlightenment mindset is hence "*world making*:"

> "In many regards, key elements of the intellectual sea change of the Enlightenment can be understood as reaction to the broadening of Europe's horizons. It began with the 'discovery' of the New World and came to a climax in the late eighteenth century with the maritime exploration of the Pacific through the voyages of James Cook and Louis-Antoine de Bougainville. Many of the key categories for the devel-

4 Martus (2015) 265.
5 Martus (2015)
6 Martus (2015) 266.
7 This is the title of the second part of Martus's (2015) work, 263–462.
8 Conrad/Osterhammel (eds.) (2016) 412–626.
9 Reinhard (2016).

> opment of modern sciences were systematically addressed in awareness of growing global interconnectivity and in terms of *assimilating the 'world' into the European repertoire of knowledge*."[10]

Conrad sees the *modern human sciences* as playing a central role in this "world making":

> "The *modern human sciences*, in particular, were a medium for ordering the global reality of the age. Other examples are debates on the nature of 'man' beginning with Bartolomé de las Casas and later in fascination with the 'noble savages' of North America or the Pacific; the work done on international law and the international order since Hugo Grotius – his *Mare liberum* was a chapter in a legal opinion written for the Dutch East India Company; the ethnological and geographical survey of the globe in the course of the major voyages of discovery; comparative linguistics and religious studies; theories of free trade and its civilisational impact; the concept of race and debates on mono- or polygenesis (Are humans all descended from one race, or does humanity have more than one origin?); discussions on the concept of cosmopolitanism; and, finally the dichotomy of civilization and barbarism, and the discovery of a progressing and progressive time regime. The spatial expansion of Europe posed a cognitive challenge that triggered a fundamental reorganization of knowledge and the ordering of scholarly disciplines."[11]

Although a lot more could be said about the Enlightenment as global history, this brief glance must suffice to show what is meant and to demonstrate that a global history of ideas and knowledge would have to be written above all as *entangled history*.

B. The Enlightenment as a history of institutions

My study of "political culture" includes a chapter entitled "political culture as institutional culture,"[12] positing that every epoch produces characteristic institutions:[13] in the Middle Ages, for instance, the feudal system as a mode of personal rule; in early modern times the territorial state with its bureaucratic administration; in early financial capitalism the East India trading companies; and in the nineteenth century the institution of local self-government.

10 Conrad/Osterhammel (eds.) (2016) 483.
11 Conrad/Osterhammel (eds.) (2016).
12 Conrad/Osterhammel (eds.) (2016) 343 ff.
13 Schuppert, G. F. (2008b).

The same applies for the Age of the Enlightenment with its universities as new state institutions, its academies of the sciences, and innumerable salons, societies, and fraternal organizations. We begin with the Berlin Academy of the Sciences. The universities are an interesting case as part of the modernization programme of the territorial state. We shall take a brief look at them:

I. Functional diversity of the typical Enlightenment institution university

Earlier in this book, the Gelehrtenrepublik, Republic of Letters, or République des lettres has been discussed as a virtual republic with networklike structures.[14] But the institution of the university increasingly became a welcome and necessary *institutionalized rallying point* for this republic. This function changed the nature of the university. We look first to the *university as locus of institutional power*:

> "Although scholars inhabited a relatively halcyon republic and had none of the trappings of a sovereign state: no territory, no tax system, no administration, no diplomatic representation, no standing army, they used institutionalized power in the form of the university, settled themselves into state structures, and made common cause with their courtly patrons. *The university was thus the most important locus where the Republic of Letters took shape as governance structure*. There were other institutions, too: high schools, academies, libraries, societies, salons; and there were many forms of private scholarship, as well as various professions with a learned background, whose representatives pursued scholarly interests more or less casually. However, the university remained a beloved and hated, willingly despised, and almost obligatory organization through which almost all enlighteners passed."[15]

In simplified, 'from-to' terms, the evolution of the university can be described in its development from Medieval corporation to the "early modern university in the context of territorialization and state formation":[16] "The history of the early modern university is marked by emancipation from the ecclesiastical-religious environment and embedding in the early modern

14 Part One, Chapter 3 of this book, B. I.

15 Schuppert, G. F. (2008b) 94.

16 See Füssel (2006) 63.

territorial state. Early modernity has thus been described as the "territorial age" (Moraw) of the university. Initially, the Reformation brought a massive drop in enrolment. Only with the reform of Wittenberg University, which provided a broad model for other Protestant universities, did the situation return to normal. The decoupling of educational elites from the ecclesiastical sphere of influence was accompanied by a shift from a "clerically determined 'strangers university' to a politically integrated 'family university'."[17] The decline in the proportion of clerics on the teaching staff and the abolition of celibacy for professors were necessary preconditions for the formation of such an educational oligarchy."[18]

The function and development of the early modern university can perhaps be best explicated by looking at a particular place and person. Steffen Martus has chosen the reformational University of Halle and its founding vice-chancellor Christian Thomasius. The epochal figure of Thomasius, like all enlighteners a "highly gifted copywriter and strategist in self-marketing"[19] gives concrete shape, as it were, to the Enlightenment.

Thomasius pursued a policy of *alliance between court and university*, and demanded that students be taught social, communicative, and moral skills.

> "The Enlightenment was to grow out of the alliance between court and university, politics and scholarship.
>
> The accord between the two worlds provided 'useful and pleasant' training. The university was to teach the basic knowledge and skills needed for autonomous learning. The learned bookworm was replaced by the worldly-wise man of the new age, who feared no international competition and availed himself of the state machinery of government and civil service. This was how Thomasius – like his contemporary Christian Weide – defined a 'political' concept of scholarship that valued sophistication, astuteness, and practical experience, which stressed judgement and the faculty of critical thought ('iudicium') over the preservation and administration of knowledge ('memoria'), and which cleared away barriers to useful scholarly knowledge."[20]

In the pursuit of his goals, Thomasius was none too gentle and beat the drum for himself and his projects. Steffen Martus describes this "Enlightenment style":

17 See Asche (1998).
18 Füssel (2006) 63–64.
19 Martus (2015) 98.
20 Martus (2015) 98–99.

> "Christian Thomasius's combative Enlightenment led historians to posit a historical schism, making Halle the first university of the Enlightenment. Before Halle, darkness or at best twilight had prevailed; with Halle, the light of reason began to shine. Where scholasticism had once tyrannized philosophy, wisdom now ruled with the gentle hand of better arguments; before Halle, authority and sectarianization had stifled thought; the new university cleared the path for reason and critique.
>
> Christian Thomasius varied this message. In 1696, for example, he declared with biblical pathos: 'All my teachings seek only to convince scholars and students of how prevailing scholarship is full of tripe and hogwash, and how this can be disposed of.' Thomasius clearly did not lack self-confidence. In the name of the Enlightenment he succeeded not only in making his opponent look bad but also like reactionary die-hards."[21]

II. The language of jurisprudence as increasingly important language of politics in the early modern principality

In his seminal study on rank, ritual, and conflict in the early modern university, Marian Füssel[22] describes not only the struggle of scholars to gain appropriate rank in a society still based on estates, but also the university as a communicative microcosm[23] marked by bitter contests for rank and reputation within the institutional governance structure "university." One element in this battle for first place in the university hierarchy[24] was the dispute between faculties on which could claim first place for itself. While theology was accustomed to being regarded as the meaning-giving lead discipline, the jurists gained increasing favour with rulers as the holders of useful knowledge on governance and administration. Marian Füssel describes this shift of power within universities:

> "… the ruler needed above all legally trained civil servants to develop territorial statehood. The law faculty was often better endowed than others, evidencing the growing influence of the ruling prince. The conversion of the jurist into court official was part of the development of a bureaucratic administrative apparatus whose immediate social consequence was the differentiation of a court-centred civil

21 Martus (2015) 97.

22 Füssel (2006).

23 Füssel (2006) 3: On the "communication space university", in which symbolic praxis plays a key role.

24 Füssel (2006) 2: "The struggle for the church pew, rank in processions, or seating arrangements at university festivities was less a matter of 'vanity fair' than an essential element in the social existence of *homo hierarchicus*."

> service hierarchy, a process that led, for example in sixteenth century Bavaria, to numerous precedence conflicts between 'Hofrat' and 'Kammerrat'. Until the end of the seventeenth century, noble birth and academic qualifications were apparently treated as 'functional equivalents', as the example of Württemberg shows. The 'dynamization of the social order' then also depended less on a strong economic middle class than on the increasing bureaucratization of the princely state."[25]

This is, so to speak, the common reading. We choose to dig a little deeper, with the aid of Rudolf Sichweh's impressive study on the early modern state and the European university.[26] In three steps, he offers interesting comments on the general topic of a global history of ideas and knowledge in the language of law.

He starts by outlining the development of juristic activity from the role of clerical jurist to what could be called "all-round" jurists of great utility in shaping the emerging early modern state:

> "Increasingly important fields of activity such as advocacy and the administration of justice play a role, which distinguished themselves more and more from ecclesiastical and state administration. The new role of the jurist was, however, not yet professional in the modern sense of having a frame of reference in the legal system as a functional system differentiated out in society. It is defined rather in close relation to two key determinants: *estate structures* and the *emergence of the early modern state*, which remained relevant until the progressive differentiation of the legal system in the nineteenth century produced a new type of juristic profession, which, while monopolizing responsibilities in the legal system, could no longer claim importance in society as a whole comparable to that of early modern jurists."[27]

Second, Stichweh shows that the language of legal science and the jurists who engage in it *was regarded as a language for speaking of the body politic*, and thus as a "language of politics":

> "In describing the importance of early modern legal studies and early modern jurists for society as a whole, contemporaries frequently posited a direct connection between knowledge of the law and the polity that was independent of any specific legal subject matter. In a certain regard, legal knowledge functioned as knowledge of a class of texts: texts about the body politic. The prevailing conviction in early modernity of the central importance of the ancient languages, embodied in classical and imitable texts, very probably facilitated and plausibilized the reception of the ancient legal texts. This link between rhetoric, texts, knowledge of law that was also open to other types of text, and direct reference to the polity is clearly expressed in a

25 Füssel (2006) 67–68.
26 Stichweh (1991).
27 Stichweh (1991) 352.

> paraphrasing comment by Wilfried Prest on Thomas Elyot's 'The Boke Named the Govenor' from 1531. 'Elyot maintained that the classical Roman jurisprudent, exemplified by Cicero, Quintilian, Servus Sulpitius and Tacitus – gentlemen *whose learning was not confined to the law* and whose involvement with the law was undertaken as a part of public duty [...]'.[28] In this sense, knowledge of the law is a specialization (in the polity) that is no specialization."[29]

This is the critical point, namely the "*generalist nature of juristic competence*,"[30] which makes the species of jurists into all-rounders and thus indispensable to the early modern state as a *governance type.*[31]

For an estates-based society, however, it was also indispensable to integrate jurists, to fit them into the estates system. Stichweh argues, thirdly, that the holders of legal knowledge were *under obligation to the polity* on account of this knowledge:

> "Knowledge of the law in early modernity ... either *generates standing* (for commoner jurists) or *validates status* (for the nobility). The link between achieving or validating status and law is also about the legitimation of status. Obtaining social position through legal knowledge is a legitimate aspiration because, by assuming this position, one also assumes the obligations to the polity inherent in legal knowledge."[32]

So much on the multifunctionality of university, notably legal training in the early modern territorial state.

C. Enlightenment as the history of power

In his global history of the Enlightenment, Sebastian Conrad warned against any, necessarily vain, attempt to find a clear and all-embracing definition of the phenomenon Enlightenment. One should instead look to see who uses the concept and to what end:[33]

> "It is more interesting to ask what historical actors did with the concept and what their interest was in referring to it. One should not mistake "Enlightenment" for an analytic category. It was primarily a concept one could point to in order to assert

28 Prest (1984) 315.

29 Stichweh (1991) 353.

30 Stichweh (1991) 356.

31 On the governance perspective for the analysis of different governance regimes, see Esders / Schuppert, G. F. (2015).

32 Stichweh (1991) 354.

33 Conrad (2016) 478.

> claims or legitimate demands. 'Scholars ought not to search feverishly for a still better definition', was the suggestion of Frederick Cooper with reference to the 'modernity' concept. 'They ought rather to listen to what is said in the world. For our purposes, this would mean, that when speaking of the Enlightenment, scholars ought to ask how the concept is used and why'."[34]

We are happy to follow this advice and explore from this perspective why princely rulers such as the Elector Frederick III founded universities to disseminate the teachings of the Enlightenment and natural law. Steffen Martus offers a highly plausible explanation for such "top-down Enlightenment":

> "It was increasingly about setting landmarks. Court and university, politics and scholarship cooperated to give the principality an interesting image. For the new policy for attaining enlightenment, attractiveness was a decisive factor: the 'subject' was to be made an inviting status, not one submitted to by order. So how could the country be made so attractive that people would willingly bow to the rule of a monarch? In early modernity and especially during the Enlightenment, the authorities found an answer to such questions in the university. It *was expected to 'enhance the political power of the territorial state'*.[35] With universities, rulers pursued confessional politics; they used them for prestige purposes, and had their subjects trained to become functionaries. Universities served as elements in projects that reached far beyond the lecture hall. This was true of Halle and of the fourteen other universities founded between 1648 (Bamberg) and 1786 (Bonn)."[36]

The university was thus "part of a whole reform package,"[37] and the inaugural festivities upon the founding of the University of Halle were designed to demonstrate the alliance between politics and scholarship:

> "It was a state ceremony, staging the university as a symbol of the governmental competence of Frederic III – thus the name; thus the link with the elector's birthday; thus the highly symbolic ceremony in Halle, which was located in the virtual centre of the scattered territories of the principality. Even the weather played along: during the night it rained repeatedly, but in the morning when the elector had his first appearance, the heavens had 'cleared up again' and 'stayed clear until the end of the projected ceremony'. The heavens sent signs of the times."[38]

This brings our brief survey of the Enlightenment to an end, so that we can now turn to the interesting topic of "natural law as a 'language of politics'."

34 Cooper (ed.) (2005) 115.

35 Martus (2015) quoted here Kittsteiner (2010) 322.

36 Martus (2015) 110–111.

37 Martus (2015) 111.

38 Martus (2015) 113.

D. The Enlightenment as legal history: the epochal importance of natural law

So-called natural law can be looked at under two epistemological headings: the multifunctionality of natural law in the process of the early modern Enlightenment, and especially whether the language of natural law can and ought to be understood as a language of politics. But these issues can be discussed only if we have some idea about what natural law actually is.

I. What exactly is natural law?

Perhaps the best approach to this question is to look for common ground among the various natural law theories. In her study of natural law theories, Barbara Stollberg-Rilinger[39] has found such commonalities, which are usually not seen as such. She identifies first a common method and second shared key concepts.

On the common methodological basis of natural law theories, she notes:

> "The major systematic natural law theories come from the seventeenth century, from Hugo Grotius, Thomas Hobbes, Baruch Spinoza, John Locke, and Samuel Pufendorf. They revolutionized juridical and political thought and supplanted the traditional practical philosophy of the Aristotelian tradition. Like the natural scientists of the seventeenth century, natural law theoreticians were intent on leaving the tangle of authorities behind them and determining the immutable regularities of human co-existence with the aid of a precise method. To achieve cognitive certainty in the field of practical philosophy, i e., ethics, economics, and politics, theoreticians therefore emulated the 'geometrical', *analytic-deductive method of the natural sciences*: they reduce the polity, as it were, to its smallest components in order to reassemble it systematically. Setting out from certain premises about the 'nature of man', they claimed that a binding system of norms could be derived by cogent logic through methodologically regulated reasoning"[40]

Barbara Stollberg-Rilinger has this to say about interaction between key concepts of natural law, the *state of nature and contract*:

> "Of central importance were … first the fiction of a *state of nature* and second the legal figure of the *contract*. Unlike all earlier natural law theories, the point of departure was the individual, completely unconnected human being in a fictive 'state of nature', and the question was how in this situation rights and duties could

39 Stollberg-Rilinger (2016) 204 ff.

40 Stollberg-Rilinger (2016) 204.

be grounded at all. In this state of original freedom from all ties, no bond connecting people and engaging them mutually was found other than free contractual agreement. All forms of lawful community – from marriage to family and the state, the *societas civilis* – were thus attributed to the voluntary (whether explicit or tacit) conclusion of a contract by all individuals. One hence abstracted from all historical power relations in order to reestablish them on the basis of the will of the individual. On the assumption of unfettered freedom of contract of the individual in a state of nature, every form of exercising power, from slavery to absolute monarchy could be justified – by asserting that subjects, serfs, and slaves had voluntarily (explicitly or tacitly) submitted to the rule of their lords. But on this basis, every form of rule can just as well be called into question – by arguing that the rights of the individual in a state of nature are fundamentally inalienable and that the founding of the state can serve only to preserve these rights."[41]

This shows that the contract argument can be used both to legitimate and to criticize power relations. But before taking a closer look at this multifunctionality, this Janus-facedness of natural law, we consider what one of the greatest experts on the subject, Knud Haakonssen, has to say about "the unifying ideas of early modern natural law – taken as a whole":

"First, there was the idea of a basic rule of law of nature that, if followed, will relate individuals to the natural world and to each other in some sort of community. There was also consistently reference to some sort of divinity, but this varied so much that neither the divine character in question nor the human relationship thereto can be captured in one simple formulation to cover all.

Secondly, it was proposed that this natural law could be comprehended by our natural cognitive powers – often called reason – as distinct from revelation. What humanity could understand in this way was the point or rationale of the natural law, (but by no means all natural lawyers thought that this sufficed to make the law a prescriptive or obligatory norm).

Thirdly, it was a shared idea that this understanding arose from a common human appreciation of our condition in the world, provided we abstract from all specific attempts to live by the law of nature. In other words, if we consider ourselves to be in a state of nature. Integral to this procedure was that, considered as purely natural beings, we were thought to be in *some* sense equal.

Fourthly, the means of living by the law of nature and thus relating to each other in common – or, in the process-language generally used, the means of getting out of the pure state of nature – were contracts, in *some* sense of this troublesome term.

Fifthly, once communities, especially political communities, exist, their rules, especially civil laws, replace the law of nature."[42]

41 Stollberg-Rilinger (2016) 204–205.
42 Haakonssen (2012) 52–53.

Having gained some idea about what natural law and natural law thought is, we now turn to its multifunctionality and double-facedness.

II. The multifunctionality and two faces of natural law

The first author to be cited on this point is Steffen Martus. Although he has little to say about natural law in his fascinating book on the Enlightenment, he does offer a very cogent description of its multifunctionality and of its two faces.

> "Natural law combined concepts of legal policy with forward-looking propositions. It cultivated the scholarly ideal of the mathematical method, witness René Descartes, Thomas Hobbes, and Baruch Spinoza. It formulated answers to the 'religious crises of Europe', by providing a profane basis for society embracing people of all faiths. And it drew on absolutist visions of government. Its cognitive business included fundamental reflection on human nature and speculation about the historical origins and development of the human species Above all, however, natural law provided very pragmatic recommendations on everyday conduct.
>
> The first step was made by the *Legal Enlightenment*, which separated sacred from profane interests: what was of advantage for life after death was not to be recommended without further ado for life on earth. The second step taken by the Legal Enlightenment was to draw a distinction between law and morality. These two distinctions had a purpose, namely, to bring notions and fantasies of the right and good life down to a level compatible with humanity, to reduce theological, political, and legal impositions – and at the same time *make access to religion, morality, politics, and law more effective*."[43]

In "Early Modern Natural Law Theories"[44] Knud Haakonssen provides a formidable and convincing overview of the functions of natural law. He identifies the following three main functions of natural law in early modernity:

- *A new legitimation basis for political authority*

> "Above all else, the ever deepening territorialisation of political authority demanded *a source of political legitimacy* that was independent of the metaphysically based hierarchy of authority in the universal Church. This was the root cause of the institutionalisation of natural law that took place first in Protestant countries. There had of course been an intensive cultivation of natural law in the institutions of the

43 Martus (2015) 74–75.

44 Haakonssen (2016).

Catholic Church of the Middle Ages, and this continued to be the case also after the Reformation. However, scholastic natural law was philosophically embedded in a religious metaphysics that was anathema to much – though by no means all – Protestant natural law. And, more importantly, scholastic natural law was academically and institutionally part of the traditional philosophy curriculum and of theology (eventually moral theology). *Protestant natural law was made an independent discipline* through the establishment of professorial chairs devoted to the subject, and a great deal of the history of early modern natural law is concerned with the conflicts over the control of the subject through these positions. Within the universities it was a triangular *contest between philosophy, law and theology*, while externally it was a matter of the influence of political and religious authorities. In short, natural law had functions within a wide spectrum of contexts, ranging from the geo-political and pan-European to domestic politics and institution building, and this lent the subject an indisputable identity as an historical phenomenon of considerable importance."[45]

We will be coming back to this important function of natural law as a concept of political authority legitimation.

- *Grounding a civic ethics*

"As a course in the 'lower' philosophical faculty, natural law had *a basic pedagogical task*, namely, to instruct young men in elementary social ideas, a kind of pre-modern 'civics'. This accounts for the fact that we find natural law ideas in all kinds of intellectual endeavor in the Enlightenment, for so to speak everyone who had even the rudiments of advanced education would have been exposed to it in some form. In the hands of the 'higher' faculty of law (and in some cases still theology) and in university consistoria it was a distinct legal doctrine and hence a juridical resource separate from the multitude of domestic laws. But first of all natural law was politically important by *supplying a systematic theory of social and political life*. These functions as a *civic ethics*, a legal doctrine and juridical reserve power and a socio-political theory were not, however, united by one particular philosophical theory. To the contrary, the intellectual rationale for how to fulfil the functions was an object of intense contestation. The institutional and functional identity of early modern natural law must not mislead us to believe that it was also an intellectually coherent movement or school. It was not, for there were a multitude of theoretical endeavours going on within the institutional set-up. In fact, natural law in this period may usefully be characterized as 'a clearing house … for a wide array of theological, jurisprudential and philosophical disciplines'."[46]

45 Haakonssen (2016) 77.
46 Haakonssen (2016) 78.

In addition to this multidisciplinarity of natural law, a third function needs to be stressed, namely that it can be used a *distinctive language* in different contexts:

- *Natural law as a "distinctive language" to be used in different contexts*

> "In sum, early modern natural law was first of all an academic discipline institutionalised for political reasons to discharge social, juridical and political functions. It commanded a *distinctive language*, a literary style or genre, a canon of defining works, and it had a clear conception of its own history as something new and in that sense modern. ... The challenge is to understand why more or less everyone at the time, irrespective of philosophical or confessional standpoint, thought that something new and distinctively modern had been introduced that was worth fighting over from quite different points of view and for widely different purposes. The scholarly confusion over this *theoretical and practical pluralism* has been increased by the fact that *some of the main natural law thinkers in our period were not philosophers* in anything like the modern sense of the term."[47]

According to Knud Haakonssen, the multidisciplinarity and multifunctionality of natural law is particularly well illustrated by Hugo Grotius:

> "Considered in a philosophical light Hugo Grotius (1583–1645) has often been seen as an epigone, if not simply a plagiarist, of leading scholastic natural lawyers. However, if we take up the task not of tracing original formulations of, or contributions to ideas considered trans-historically but of understanding what Grotius was trying to do in his time and place with whatever ideas he had available, then his historical standing becomes intelligible. In this respect, Grotius must be acknowledged as the defining initiator of modern natural law, for that was how he was viewed during most of the seventeenth and eighteenth centuries. He was not a philosopher, nor did he claim to be one. He was *primarily a humanist scholar, a lawyer and legal and political advisor*, and his basic consideration in his writings was how to make cases for individuals, whether natural persons maintaining rights of private belief against religious authority or corporate persons, such as the Dutch East-India Company, asserting rights to the open sea. Of course Grotius also presented philosophical ideas, but these were materials for the making of arguments, not building blocks for scholastic and similar philosophical constructions."[48]

It is a short step from "distinctive language" to the language of natural law as a "language of politics."

47 Haakonssen (2016) 79.
48 Haakonssen (2016) 80.

III. The language of natural law as a language of politics

It is obvious that the language of early modern natural law functioned as a language of politics, but because this is a very important point, as we shall demonstrate this under three headings:

- *The language of natural law as the language of legal policy*

Barbara Stollberg-Rilinger has shown that natural law could be used both to *justify and criticize law*. On natural law as *method for justifying law* she has this to say:

> "Whatever sort of reforms were demanded in the eighteenth century – whether designed to strengthen central authority or to permit general participation therein – they had to be justified and legitimated in a new way. The traditional sorts of legitimation were no longer suitable because they pleaded either divine lawmaking or time immemorial or consensus of the estates. Now, however, what was at issue was to create something new in opposition to the old; possibly against resistance from the privileged. A new authority was therefore needed to legitimate intervention in extant law. The new method of justifying law that made this possible was modern natural law or the law of reason. Essentially it did two things: it responded to the confessional schism and the loss of the Christian world order and placed the norms of human co-existence on a new theoretical basis independent of competing religious claims to truth. Second, it reacted to the new needs for political action (in whoever's interest) and offered a new legitimation basis for such action. Natural law was a *method* of justifying law; it cannot be pinned down to specific *substantive* positions. Indeed, it could be used both to legitimate absolute power and to establish universal human rights."[49]

Our author comments on the *critical potential of natural law* in providing a yardstick for extant law:

> "Natural law theories thus provided a method both for justifying law and for criticizing existing law. Fundamental, modern, and new was that it provided a standard competing with the conventional, religious-traditional legitimation of power and legal relations. The People as a sum of individuals, not old-established, estate-based corporations and office holders were now regarded as the source of governmental authority, as the original sovereign. The critical potential this concept offered could be used for two opposing purposes: in the interest of unified state authority against noble privileges, or in the interest of the individual citizen against the authority of the state; in brief, it was a very flexible tool in the struggle about what law was."[50]

49 Stollberg-Rilinger (2016) 203.
50 Stollberg-Rilinger (2016) 207.

Michael Stolleis sets a somewhat different accent in discussing the *driving force of early modern natural law in legal policy*, identifying four key function of natural law:

> "The natural law of early modernity performed four essential functions: it supplied the key provisions of emerging international law, which, as Europe expanded in Asia and America, needed a new rational conceptual apparatus applicable for 'all humanity'. It constituted a rational legal theory (broadly independent of Roman law) and thus provided a critical yardstick for labyrinthine extant law. It prepared the national codifications absolutism sought by promoting the development of general legal concepts and designing an (abstract) order. Finally, it supported the establishment of a neutral legal basis on which the feuding religious parties of 'Old Europe' could meet while factoring out the issue of truth, an early form of later tolerance and protection of the freedom of religion as a basic right."[51]

* *The political fungibility of natural law: harmonious political developments and shifts of emphasis*

In his major history of public law in Germany, Michael Stolleis identifies *four phases in the development of natural law*, each of which he attributes to specific authors:

> "1. The natural law of the sixteenth and early seventeenth centuries integrated into the theological context of late medieval scholasticism (J. Oldendorp, F. Vitoria, F. Vasquez, B. de Ayala, F. Suarez, P. Ramus, J. Althusius, H. Grotius); 2. The 'classical' natural law systems or state constructions largely emancipated from moral theology developed *more geometrico* (Hobbes, Spinoza, Pufendorf, Wolff); 3. The natural law theories of the High Enlightenment, in which the moral and legal regulatory systems (*honestum, decorum, iustum*) are separated from the sake of individual freedom of action and which deploy natural law chiefly as systematic-critical benchmark vis-à-vis antiquated legal states of affairs (Thomaisus, Wolff); and 4. The liberal and individualistic natural law systems emerging in the aftermath of the Revolution, whose demands for fundamental rights and the separation of powers constituted a transition to the catalogue of German early constitutionalism from 1800."[52]

According to Stolleis, political developments match these four phases:

> "Natural law systems respond to the times; their full significance is to be understood only from the double perspective of the link between individual thought and historico-situational dependence. The veil of abstract phrasing conceals passionately experienced practical problems. In the age of the wars of religion, early absolutism, and the imperialist ventures of the Spanish, Dutch, and English to acquire colonial

51 Stolleis (2014) 148.

52 Stolleis (1988) 269.

> empires, natural law could achieve three things: it provided an interconfessional theoretical level at which the religious conflict could be neutralized by elaborating universally binding legal bases. It offered an opportunity to give timelessly valid form to the political pressure of the princely state and to support the estates-based state in the struggle against absolutism through the natural-law grounding of international and estate sovereignty. And, finally, drawing on the ancient dualism of *jus naturale et gentium* and *jus civile*, natural law transcending all nations and positive international law brought forth jointly by the nations could be developed to regulate and attenuated war."[53]

He describes the *political embeddedness* of phases two to four in the development of natural law as follows:

> "In the second phase, which coincided with 'high' absolutism, the estate-based state suffered defeat or was at least rolled back; the religious question had become less urgent and the European states had agreed on procedures for limiting conflict. All efforts now concentrated on internally enforcing the state's monopoly of force and preventing revolutions, civil wars, and local uprisings, on rationally constructing the machinery of government, notably through legislation, and on subjugating the remaining intermediary powers in a united territorial entity.
>
> In the third phase, in which state, society, and individual begin to differentiate, in which religiousness and happiness take an individualistic turn towards the 'private', natural law offers protective arguments against tutelage by Church and state, it limits state interference by abolishing 'irrational' proceedings, offences, and punishments; i e., it also has a practical and reformatory impact on the constituent society through 'enlightened' state lawmaking.
>
> Finally, in the fourth phase, the always inherent revolutionary components in natural law developed when, in the late eighteenth century, it supported critique of the Ancien Régime. By demonstrating that estate-based restrictions and discrimination run counter to 'natural rights', it justified changes to the status quo; it becomes the 'natural law of the revolutionary' who evoked the inalienable right to protection against human oppression in legal form."[54]

* *Natural law as political theory: changes in the political thrust of natural law*

As we have seen, natural law is multifunctional and highly fungible from a political point of view: in brief, "there is scarcely any philosophical or political standpoint that has not been justified by natural law in the course of the centuries."[55] Despite the seemingly arbitrary deployment of the "all-purpose weapon natural law," it is nevertheless useful to clarify the political thrust of natural law, as Diethelm Klippel has done in his seminal study on the

53 Stolleis (1988) 269–270.
54 Stolleis (1988) 270.
55 Klippel (1987) 267.

political importance of German natural law in the eighteenth and nineteenth centuries.[56]

As far as natural law in early modernity is concerned – associated with the names Pufendorf, Thomasius, and Wolff – he and many others posit that *natural law operated as a political theory of absolutism*:

> "... older German natural law ... is ruler's law and a tool for stabilizing monarchic absolutism. Pronouncing on the relationship between ruler and subject, the subfield of natural law *ius publicum universale* opts clearly in favour of the ruler: '*Regere Rempublicam Principibus prorium;quare et ius publicum universale Principibus proprium*'.[57] This is the case for many natural law theories. The subject in the state, for instance, unlike man in a state of nature (and thus also the ruler) is described not in terms of *libertas* but of *subiectio*. He is due at most factual freedom. The turning point from *libertas naturalis* to obedience by the subject is the social contract, which cannot always be understood as an 'emancipatory category' but is used in masterly fashion, especially by older German natural law, to justify absolutism. This is achieved with the figure of the 'tacit social contract'. The *patientia* or *taciturnitas* of subjects is taken to mean their consent to the conclusion and the terms of the contract, up to and including unbounded power for the ruler. Thus, natural law systems not only fail to run counter to absolutism but use the contract model to shield and enforce it theoretically."[58]

Similarly, Michael Stolleis has this to say under the heading "*natural law and absolutism*":

> "The theory of natural law in the phase of the power struggle between the absolute monarchical state and its opponents (estates, nobility, and cities) performed an essentially practical function of promoting the concentration of state authority in the hands of an individual. Because it was able to show that the succession God-ruler-paterfamilias corresponded to the natural hierarchy of the patriarchy and that the vesting of sovereign rights in one person best served the need of the weak individual for protection, natural law proved a suitable tool for justifying and securing princely rule. Since it went beyond extant positive law, it served especially to modernize the legal order. Owing to its symmetry and external calculability, it could be used to smooth down or eliminate medieval legal conditions. To impose itself, the emerging territorial state needed to abolish a multiplicity of traditional special rights. Rights were now no longer to be granted to an individual or to individual special-right communities as *privilegium* but to be enforced as objective norms applicable for all. Variously structured special-right groups were gradually superseded by the unitary body of subjects; the modern use of the word *suiectus* (subject) marked the demand to this effect clearly enough. The associated concen-

56 Klippel (1987).
57 Fritsch (1734) 5.
58 Klippel (1987) 271.

> tration of power was at the same time the precondition for unitary legislation that at least aspired to equality among subjects. The hope that the traditional addition of special rights could be replaced by *uniformes leges*[59] encouraged the codification efforts of the eighteenth century inspired by natural law."[60]

Stolleis sums up the function of the language of natural law as a language of politics in relation to absolutism: "Natural law has therefore served both to establish and to juridify the modern state intent on uniformity and the rational pursuit of ends. Both absolutism and its opponents in the estates, the cities, and the confessions helped themselves to its tools, legitimizing and criticizing government each on the basis of what, from their particular perspective, constituted "natural law." Neither ideology nor the critique of ideology could do without the evocative topos "nature.""[61]

Only from about 1790, as Klippel shows, did a distinct, truly radical change occur in the political thrust of natural law: towards liberal political theory:[62]

> "A glance at the natural law theory literature quickly reveals the change in direction: the focus is on 'humanity', the personal nature of the human being, which is an end in itself and a basis for copious catalogues of human rights. They include, albeit with differing frequency, almost all such rights that have become an integral part of liberal political theory, especially since the American *Bill of Rights* and the French *Déclaration des droits de l'homme et du citoyen*, such as the freedom to engage in a trade or industry, property, freedom of opinion and the press, and the freedom of religion. Furthermore, these rights are understood as directed against the state and feed into an incipient conceptual separation of state and civil society.
>
> These demands would have come to nothing had natural law not changed its frame of reference. The older conception of any form of pre-state state of nature was therefore abandoned. 'To be exact, the true state of nature, i e., the condition appropriate to the nature of man, is none other than the state.'[63] Consequently, natural law now formulated its demands – notably the catalogues of human rights – no longer for the state of nature in the sense of older theory and hence for sovereign rulers and their families, but for every human being and for realization in the state. If we regard the essence of man in the state – immutable in all conditions – as a state of nature, we (and what more do we want) arrive at natural and proven rights that

59 Ickstatt (1747) 792.
60 Stolleis (1988) 276–277.
61 Stolleis (1988) 277.
62 Klippel (1987) 273–274.
63 Schaumann (1792) 149.

> are subject to no change or contradiction and which can and must be a valid norm for all courts and a reliable touchstone for all proposed rights and demands'."[64]

If, as Klippel shows at length, natural law carved out its political riverbed in the late eighteenth century, this does not invalidate our finding that the language of natural law has always operated as a language of politics. On the contrary, this is demonstrated particularly clearly by the so-called renaissance of natural-law thinking after the collapse of the Nazi regime, a phase of German history in which – as the post-1945 literature shows[65] – was to enable a political re-orientation evoking natural law.

Before bringing our reflections on Enlightenment and natural law to a close and embarking on an excursus on the global history of knowledge in the eighteenth century, we shall take a brief look at the link between natural law and globalization – still under the guidance of Michael Stolleis.[66]

IV. Natural law as a phenomenon concomitant with globalization?

In an essay on "Naturgesetz und Naturrecht," Michael Stolleis posits that the first wave of globalization promoted the development of universal natural law. As he (and we[67]) understand it, the period concerned in the discovery of the world in the fifteenth century:[68]

> "If by globalization we mean a special expansion of communication and commodity flows around the world and a specific perception of world society as 'a whole', this development begins in human history in 1492. The circumnavigation of the globe and the discovery of America by the Portuguese and Spanish in the late fifteenth and sixteenth centuries enormously broadened experience of the world, and were very likely the necessary run-up to the 'Copernican revolution' of 1543. The earth was now definitively grasped as a spherical planet in orbit around the sun, which could be circumnavigated, explored, and taken possession of. As everyone knows, this took place during the centuries of European expansion from the sixteenth to the nineteenth century."[69]

64 Klippel (1987).
65 See, for example, the collections of essays by Maihofer (ed.) (1966).
66 Stolleis (1988).
67 Schuppert, G. F. (2014).
68 Stolleis (1988) 140.
69 Reinhard (1983, 1985, 1988, 1990); Fisch (1984).

This exploration, surveying, and appropriation of the world, he claims, saw the birth of universal natural law in the form of *international law claiming universal validity.*

> "The entire process, I posit, was the essential driving force for the development of a universal natural law. Since the earth had now become finite and accessible through the circumnavigation of Africa to the east and the crossing of the Atlantic to the west, the leap could now be made from geographical unity to universal legal unity. The heyday of the School of Salamanca, for example with the relecciones *De Indis* and *De iure belli* by Francisco de Vitoria, the writings of Hugo Grotius 'Mare liberum, sive de iure quod Batavis competit ad Indicana commercia dissertatio' (1609) and 'De iure belli ac pacis' (1625), John Selden's 'Mare clausum seu de dominio maris' (1635) are patently shaped by the expansive activities of the great colonial nations. Now that the western European monarchies found themselves in competition with one another in their forays on the high seas and in strategically important trading posts, they needed an international legal basis. Even though emerging international law developed at an early date as a special area of natural law, both were generally applicable. They were to apply for Christians and heathens, and if not for all heathens then at least for those who lived in advanced civilizations and with whom, from the European point of view, one could negotiate 'on equal terms'. In this sense, traditional *ius gentium* developed into law *inter gentes*."[70]

However, Stolleis goes still further, speculating on the role of universal natural law in current globalization:

> "If one of the essential causes of the rise of natural law in early modern times was the first wave of globalization, how does it stand with second-wave, present-day globalization? Since the nineteenth century, it encompasses all means of communication and transport and at the turn of the twentieth to the twenty-first century it has expanded into a factually global society. There is intensive discussion in modern international law about whether this will lead to constitutionalization of the new world order. The universal catalogue of human rights (perhaps also modified from culture to culture), emerging international criminal law, and worldwide networks of transnational law and non-state law all point in this direction. The law that holds together or overarches this new 'multinormativity' would have to be a new natural law. A 'natural law without God', nurtured by the thinking of early modernity, modernized for modern world society, held together by consensus, what else? Even the Roman law notion that natural law applies equally to humans, animals on the face of the earth, birds in the air, and everything that swims in water (D. 1,1,3) could, in the light of ecological dangers come back into favour."[71]

70 Stolleis (1988) 141.
71 Stolleis (1988) 148–149.

8

Rethinking International Law and its Language

Before considering a number of paradigmatic cases to demonstrate that the language of international law[72] provides innumerable examples of use as a language of politics, we take an overall look at the central role that language plays in the discourses of international law, at who uses it and how as a "language of politics."

A. Some particularities of the language of international law

I. The key role of language in a legal regime between ideas and facts

The deontological order proposed by international law has always been suspected of fragility because a central enforcement authority[73] is lacking and pure political power prevails because, "in individual cases," dominant states tend to exploit international law when it serves their political objectives while ignoring it or interpreting it to suit their purposes when it runs counter to their interests.[74]

With Martti Koskenniemi one could say that international law is at home in two worlds: the world of ideas – so that the history of international law would also have to be written as a political history of ideas[75] – and the world of power – so that the history of international law would have to be presented as a history of power.[76,77] In "From Apology to Utopia," Koskenniemi describes how international law sits on the fence:

72 Both "Völkerrecht" (literally "law of nations") and "internationales Recht" translate as "international law," the more current term in German being "Völkerrecht."
73 On the key importance of different norm enforcement regimes see Schuppert, G. F. (2016b) Chapter 4: "From the Plurality of Normative Orders to the Plurality of Norm Enforcement Regimes: Jurisdictional Communities and their Specific Jurisdictional Cultures," 188–250.
74 Outstanding among the critics of international law are protagonists of the "rational choice" approach; see, for instance, Goldsmith / Posner (2003).
75 See Grewe (1984).
76 On history as the history of power see Mann (1994, 2001).
77 Deitelhoff / Zürn (2016).

> "According to one view, international law is a set of ideas, manifested in the form of rules. This is followed by an epistemology according to which to know international law objectively is to grasp those rules in their authenticity. State behaviour, will or interest are sociological facts which may have had an effect on the law but which are external to its present content. To concentrate on facts is both an epistemological error (as it fails to notice that facts appear through conceptual apparatuses) and loses the law's normativity, its capacity of being opposed to naked power.
>
> According to another view, international law is a fact. This is accompanied by an epistemology according to which rules are only 'transcendental nonsense'. To make sense of them, they must be referred back to the (social, biological, economic, power-based etc.) facts (needs, interests) to which they give more or less adequate expression. To stare at the abstract formulations of rules is doctrinal subjectivism. A concrete study of law needs to relate rules to their social context."[78]

However, we would not be taken in by a fruitless dichotomy if ideas and facts were played off against one another. We fully agree with Koskenniemi that we perceive and order the world of facts with the help of ideas and conceptual schemes, so that, armed with a "cognitive map,"[79] we can find some sort of orientation: "... [O]ur perception of facts is always conditioned by conceptual schemes which have already organized the world in some intelligible fashion ... all knowledge about facts is interpreting knowledge, ... the 'real world cannot be grasped in its purity but only in its reflection in a conceptual scheme. These conceptual schemes – social theories, scientific paradigms, assumptions, psychological predispositions etc. – 'fabricate' what we feel as neutral facts."[80]

Language now comes into play, for with its help we structure the infinity of random facts.

> "The most obvious conceptual scheme which controls our perception is language. As Roland Barthes points out, reality is divided by language, not by itself.[81] Contrary to the common-sensical view, language does not reflect the world but interprets it, carves it up, makes sense of the amorphous mass of things and events in it. In this sense, facts are constructed as they are perceived though language. Just as language is conventional, so is the world it mediates. There is no necessary, 'objective' reason why some aspects of the world are categorized while some are not. The feeling of sense and relevance which we relate to the world is not the reason but the effect of language. ... [T]here is no such pure observation of international reality as

78 Koskenniemi (2005) 520.
79 See Rosa (1999).
80 Koskenniemi (2005) 524–525.
81 Barthes (1983).

> law-as-fact lawyers assume. In some way or other, our conventional ways of speaking about international relations and international law seem to determine what we can believe to take place in international life."[82]

Such concepts include not only 'the State' but also 'contract', 'intervention', and 'owner':

> "... [L]egal terms such as 'owner', 'contract', 'corporation' or 'intervention', 'treaty', 'government' appear not to mirror social reality but constitute what can be seen in it. It is simply impossible to think of a political balance of power, for example, without having internalized a legal-formal concept of the State and some idea of binding contract whereby alliances can be formed. Though it would be incorrect to say that the 19th century system of Great Power primacy was legal construction, its functioning presupposed legally formulated agreement on European matters and the principal method of maintaining the system – collective intervention – was a legal construction. Similarly, when American and Soviet leaders meet today, the context of their discussion is structured and the choices delimited by the goal of reaching legally formulated agreement."[83]

If this is indeed the case, jurists – in all fields and not only in international law – must be able above all to handle language. Years of legal socialization have convinced the author that it is not a matter of amassing legal knowledge (even though this has its uses) but of mastering legal argument, that is to say, learning what is called "legal reasoning." Not only a certain vocabulary must be mastered but also the grammar of a language. A lawyer proficient in the language of law in this sense can argue for and against any issue. This has earned the profession the reputation of perverting the course of justice; in fact the capability is proof of competence in the law. In the epilogue to "From Apology to Utopia," Martti Koskenniemi comments:

> "[This book] seeks to articulate the *competence* of native language-speakers of international law. It starts from the uncontroversial assumption that international law is not just some haphazard collection of rules and principles. Instead, it is about their use in the context of legal work. The standard view that international law is a 'common language' transcending political and cultural differences grasps something of this intuition. So do accounts of the experience that even in the midst of political conflict, international lawyers are able to engage in professional conversation in which none of the participants' competence is put to question by the fact that they support opposite positions. On the contrary, *lawyers may even recognize that their ability to use rules in contrasting ways is a key aspect of their competence* – reflected in popular caricatures of lawyers as professional cynics. Whatever our view about the

82 Koskenniemi (2005) 525.

83 Koskenniemi (2005) 526.

> moral status of the profession, however, that status is not an aspect of a person's quality as a 'native language-speaker of international law'. Or to put this in another vocabulary, international law is not necessarily representative of what is 'good' in this world. This is why the linguistic analogy seems so tempting. Native language-speakers of, say, Finnish, are also able to support contrasting political agendas without the question of the genuineness of their *linguistic* competence ever arising. *From Apology to Utopia* seeks, however, to go beyond metaphor. Instead of examining international law *like* a language it treats it *as* a language. This is not as exotic as it may seem. No more is involved than taking seriously the views that, *whatever else international law might be, at least it is how international lawyers argue*, that how they argue can be explained in terms of their specific 'competence' and that this can be articulated in a *limited number of rules that constitute the 'grammar' – the system of production of good legal arguments*."[84]

If language is so important for the resonance capacity of actors in the world of law, we must sit up and take notice when language usage changes whether suddenly or gradually. We now turn to this question.

II. The importance and function of "semantic shifts" in the field of international law

Martti Koskenniemi is an author particularly interested in the vocabularies of international law discourses, and who accordingly registers every change in language usage. In "Legitimacy, Rights, and Ideology"[85] he identifies what we have called "semantic shifts," even discovering a *new language*, the "*language of legitimacy*."

We turn first to "*change of vocabularies*":

> "'We need to treat our normative concepts less as statements about the world than as tools and weapons of ideological debate.'[86] As Quentin Skinner has shown us, tracing the lineaments of the change of political concepts works from ideological description to critique. When vocabularies – especially normative vocabularies – change, at issue is also a shift in the way the social world is being understood: some ways of describing the world begin to seem *passé* or inappropriate, old positive words transform into names for negative stereotypes. Terms such as 'manliness' or 'virtue' that we remember from nineteenth century politics and the classical tradition, for example, have turned into negative or ironic markers, carrying fragments of meaning from past vocabularies that make them inappropriate for use in contemporary politics. Such changes are not only about political correctness. *They reflect*

84 Koskenniemi (2005) 567–568.
85 Koskenniemi (2003).
86 Skinner (2002) 177.

> *transformations in seeing the social world*, highlighting some of its aspects, downplaying others. As critique, conceptual study draws attention to the blindspots and biases of such markers, and of those that have replaced them, thus enquiring into the way *language enacts politics*."[87]

Such a change in language usage occurred after the Cold War.

> "The transformations in the international world that are customarily addressed as 'end of the Cold War' have likewise occasioned *a shift in diplomatic and academic vocabularies*: the languages of political realism that used to describe the international world in terms of the use of power to advance (State) interests have been supplemented and, in part, replaced by a normative vocabulary proposing what Skinner would call a 'rhetorical redescription' of the international world through normative expressions such as 'accountability', 'democracy', 'human rights', 'rule of law' and so on. Examined through the simple realist/idealist dichotomy, this shift might be seen to describe the transformation since 1989 as a return to the application of domestic categories to international affairs, advocated by the liberal legal cosmopolitanism that emerged in Europe in the 1870's and was institutionalized in and around the League of Nations. That would, however, suggest that the change would be, as it were, backwards, and perpetuate the simplistic view that international politics is 'essentially' about a more or less mindless to-and-fro between periods of heightened ('idealistic') awareness of the importance of 'law' and 'morality' and periods in which everyone's attention is focused ('realistically') on 'power' and 'interests'."[88]

But there are not only cycles of language usage focused on ideas or on power politics, but also the arrival of a new language on the stage of world politics, which Koskenniemi calls the "language of legitimacy."

> "The new normative language seeks to transcend the idealism/realism dichotomy by accommodating realist criticism. Instead of 'international law' or 'international morality' it uses the language of 'legitimacy' to grasp at the political momentum. An examination of that vocabulary – of which 'human rights' forms an inextricable part – may thus open a window on the nature of today's international political change. Unlike realist fixation on states and power, or the idealist moorings on international law and morality, 'legitimacy' possesses an elusiveness well adapted to the realities of a fluid, complex and globalizing world. Containing (unlike law) no commitment to particular institutional forms and (unlike morality) no implication of transcendental standards, as well as unburdened by the negative connotations linked to words such as 'legalism' and 'moralism' the *notion of 'legitimacy' redescribes the international world* in terms of categories whose beneficiality seems self-evident: lawfulness, fundamental values and human rights. It does this as an exercise neither in law nor

87 Koskenniemi (2003) 349.
88 Koskenniemi (2003) 349–350.

> political philosophy but in terms of an empirically oriented social science that connects popular attitudes with institutional decision-making, being itself a part of the latter."[89]

Interestingly, this new language also changes *relations between academic disciplines*:

> "The conceptual shift also marks a move in the play of authority between academic disciplines. The vocabulary of legitimacy pushes lawyers, political philosophers and realist international relations scholars all to the margin: their antics become part of the world left behind by the transformations that only become visible if articulated by the mélange of empirical sociology, psychology, and liberal political theory that is now offered by the language of legitimacy, conveniently transgressing the boundary between observation of and participation in politics."[90]

III. Power politics as "semantic imperialism"

That legal norms need to be interpreted because they take linguistic form is almost a truism and requires no further comment. Nor is there any disputing that those entitled to deliver binding interpretations of the legal concepts contained in a text are vested with considerable *interpretative authority*. As Andreas Kulick has recently shown,[91] the "vagueness and ambiguity" of legal texts has *considerable political potential*:

> "Vagueness and Ambiguity in (international) law possesses an inherently political potential. [I]f we enter the interpretation of a text with certain preconceptions, looking at it through the lens of our societal, cultural, etc. situated-ness, we inevitably will adapt the meaning to our world view as meaning exists only within our 'horizon' – which is also shaped by our political conception of the world. In many instances this may happen inadvertently, i e. non-strategically, but the political potential of Vagueness and Ambiguity may also be used deliberately, i e. strategically. This is not a new insight. As Martti Koskenniemi reminds us, it is not so much the fact that a meaning can often be twisted in several different directions but rather that classical legal thought has shrouded such subjectivity in a language and demeanour of objectivity that makes interpretation such a powerful tool.[92] Vagueness and Ambiguity are the fuel on which this engine runs. Just look at the highly

89 Koskenniemi (2003) 350–351.
90 Koskenniemi (2003) 351.
91 Kulick (2017).
92 See Koskenniemi (2004) 197, 199: "[T]he objective of the contestants is to make their partial view of that meaning appear as the total view, their preferences seem like the *universal preference*."

> vague notion of 'self-determination' in international law employed as a means for Russia to justify Crimea's secession from Ukraine[93] and incorporation into the Russian Federation."[94]

If this is the case, it would be an obvious a move to build a defined measure of vagueness and ambiguity into a legal text – such as a contract – from the outset. Inspired by Andreas Kulick, we could thus speak of the *strategic production of vagueness*:

> "VaA are being produced constantly. The lessons learned from hermeneutics and linguistics tell us that literally any use of language may produce VaA. Hence, any treaty, resolution, judgement, etc. may potentially produce VaA. What needs to be distinguished for the purposes of this study, however, is inadvertent [sic] from deliberate VaA production, i e. *strategic from non-strategic VaA production*. Non-strategic VaA production is the most common occurrence, e. g. the definition of a term in a United Nations Security Council ('UNSC') resolution laying out sanctions against a recalcitrant state. The sanctions regime is supposed to be highly specific in order to avoid loopholes as well as targeting the wrong industries or persons. If, for example, the definition of 'chemical weapons' remains ambiguous or even vague, this may seriously undermine the effect of the sanction.
>
> On the other hand, the same resolution, at least in the intention of some of its drafters, may deliberately remain vague and / or ambiguous in order to (a) reach a consensus among the required majority of the Security Council members, ...; and (b) at the same time allow for as much leeway of interpretation that some members may pursue a goal that other members sought to prevent, while not going beyond what the language of the resolution permits."[95]

What Kulick calls "constructive ambiguity" can be regarded as one form of the strategic production of vagueness:[96]

> "In this final section, I will investigate a specific strategy in the practice of the creation of international norms in relation to Vagueness and Ambiguity production and reception, the so-called 'constructive ambiguity'. In the context of international negotiations on the adoption of treaties, resolutions, etc., 'constructive ambiguity' describes the phenomenon of negotiators deliberately – i. e. usually deliberately on all sides of the negotiation table – inserting terms and phrases into the respective document that blur the meaning of the text in order to build consensus by getting all sides to commit to a final document that allows for everybody to ascribe it a

93 See address by the President of the Russian Federation of 18 March 2014, http://eng.kremlin.ru/news/6889.

94 Kulick (2017) 14.

95 Kulick (2017) 7.

96 Kulick (2017) 18–19.

> meaning suitable for his or her purposes. Differently put, 'Constructive ambiguity attempts to fashion agreement where there is none'."[97]

As Carl Schmitt would have put it, the benefits offered by a strategy of working with "dilatory formulatory compromises"[98] are obvious. Andreas Kulick:

> "What are the benefits of this strategy? The problems entailing ambiguity (or vagueness) are obvious and potentially disastrous: imagine, e. g., an armistice treaty that does not clearly define the front lines or a peace treaty that leaves vague the conditions to be fulfilled by either party in order to permanently withdraw military personnel from occupied land. 'Constructive ambiguity' push[es] fundamental disagreement from the drafting stage to the implementation stage'.[99] which with respect to *peace* agreements may result in the opposite, i. e. war.
>
> On the other hand, often – and particularly if the question of war and peace is at stake – reaching an agreement is better than none at all, whatever its flaws. In this vein, Vagueness and Ambiguity represent the solution to negotiation deadlock. Further, constructive ambiguity or vagueness make it possible for both sides to claim victory at the negotiation table without having to determine the victor in actual military confrontation. …
>
> Furthermore, Vagueness and Ambiguity mean flexibility, which is a valuable asset with regard to agreements that require a long period of implementation or in any case with 'constitutional' treaties that are supposed to establish a long-term framework. The more precise the language chosen the more specific it has to get and the more it is prone to loopholes or to leaving out the regulation of entire sets of issues that the contracting parties may not have been able to anticipate at the time of the conclusion of the agreement."[100]

If vagueness and ambiguity are not only particularly frequent in international law but are also produced with strategic intent, and if those entitled to interpret indeterminate concepts needful of definition gain considerable interpretative authority in the process, hegemonic powers will obviously use their political ascendancy to practice what we could call "semantic imperialism," for example unilaterally defining "terrorism" or "war" in the context of "war on terror" against the facts. With such practices, the hegemonic power ultimately excludes itself from the *legal discourse community*, a consequence that Martti Koskenniemi describes as follows:

97 Bell (2008) 166.
98 Schmitt (1996).
99 Bell (2008) 166.
100 Kulick (2017) 19.

> "Unlike claims of privilege or interest, claims of law constitute the claimants as members of a legal, and thus also a political community. Engaging in legal discourse, persons recognize each other as carriers of rights and duties who are entitled to benefits from or owe obligation to each other not because of charity or interest but because such rights or duties belong to every member of the community *in that position*. In law, benefits and burdens that belong to particular individuals or groups are universalized by reference to membership rules. What otherwise would be a mere private violation, a wrong done to *me*, a violation of *my interest*, is transformed by law into a violation against *everyone in my position*, a matter of concern for the political community itself. One of the striking aspects of the worldwide condemnation of aspects of the American-led 'war against terrorism' is precisely the recourse to law. Guantánamo and the war against Iraq were not just wrong, they were 'illegal'. The point of such a claim lies in its implicit suggestion that at issue are not merely specific wrongs done to some Afghani or Iraqi individuals but to everyone in their position – and most people are able to imagine themselves in such a position. Through law, the special scandal of American action may be articulated in terms of its universal nature, its being directed against the international political community itself. This is also the sense of the frequent claim that *the action appears 'imperial'*. It denies any need for the United States to take a distance from its own cultural preferences and to articulate its claims in the (legal) language of the community. It is a solipsism that resigns to the impulse of feeling threatened by 'terrorists' and those that 'harbour' them, believing they may be attacked or killed wherever and whenever it suits the empire. The action is informed only by American laws and values that exclude those who are not recognized by those laws or share those values – with them, there is neither political community nor political contestation: they are 'outlaws' against whom whatever measures may be taken."[101]

B. The language of international law as a language of justification

I. The history of international law as a history of justificatory narratives

Wilhelm G. Grewe's standard work on the epochs of the history of international law[102] reads like a history of justificatory narratives. There are two prime examples that foster this impression. The first is the struggle for legitimate "sovereignty of the sea," the second is the justification of colonialism thinly veiled as "mission civilisatrice et religieuse."[103]

101 Koskenniemi (2005) 21–22.

102 Grewe (1984).

103 See also my own reflections on globalization as "mission civilisatrice et religieuse" in: Schuppert, G. F. (2014), Chapter 4, 262–353.

Quite rightly, Grewe describes the historical importance of the civilisation concept in international law as embodying an attempt "to place the global political supremacy and colonizational function of the white race on a new legitimation basis corresponding to the changed conditions of the world in the nineteenth century."[104] In the very first issue of the "Archiv des öffentlichen Rechts" founded in 1885 – long the most prestigious public-law journal – F. von Martitz gave expression to this justificatory narrative on the occasion of the Berlin Congo Conference:

> "European governments, together with the North American Union, cognizant that dominion over the world belongs to the civilized nations and that leadership in modern world politics is in the hands of an aristocracy of nations, have taken the decisive step of bestowing on the last part of the inhabited earth, hitherto a mere geographical concept, the political organization under the protection of which human history unfolds. It is their intention to add to the European system of states, joined in the course of this century by an American and an Asian one, an African system. For this purpose they have availed themselves of the perfected forms and means that modern international law has provided for the peaceful solution of tasks that lie beyond the power and force of the single state; accordingly disposing by treaty over the vast territories of Central Africa; reconfirming the legal principle that areas in which savages and half-savages live are to be regarded and treated not as state territories but, in mutual relations between the civilized, as res nullius under international law."[105]

Grew speaks of "proud words." Anyone who has read David van Reybrouck's history of the Congo,[106] describing the cruel consequences of the "holy trinity" of state interests, commerce, and Church practices in the Congo will, however, be tempted to speak rather of cynical rhetoric.

If, in composing and enforcing a justificatory narrative, international law is, as Grewe rightly stresses, always concerned to place state actions – conquest of foreign territory, entering foreign merchant ships or whatever – on the most convincingly *legitimate footing* possible, it is not surprising that the cadence of international law's "*language of justification*" frequently echoes the related "*language of legitimacy*", which Christian Reus-Smit describes as follows:

> "We use the *language of legitimacy* in a wide range of social situations. We describe it as legitimate for parents to ask after their child's progress at school, and legitimate

104 Grewe (1984) 532–533.
105 Martitz (1885) 16f., quoted here from Grewe (1984) 533.
106 van Reybrouck (2012).

> for a tradesperson to ask for payment after work is done. In these contexts, the language of legitimacy is employed to describe not just the capacity to act, but the right or entitlement to act. Mark Suchman captures this when he defines legitimacy as 'a generalized perception or assumption that the actions of an entity are desirable, proper, appropriate within some socially constructed system of norms, values, beliefs, and definitions'.[107] It is in the political realm, though, that the original meaning of the term lies, deriving as it does from the quintessential politico-legal term 'legislate'. Here legitimacy is generally taken to mean the right to rule, or the right to govern.[108] The *Oxford English Dictionary (OED)* defines 'to rule' as to be 'in control' and 'right' *as 'justification*, fair claim, *being entitled* to privilege or immunity, thing one is entitled to'. In the political arena, broadly conceived, legitimacy thus refers to an entitlement to control, which generally means an entitlement to issue authoritative commands that require compliance from those subject to them. An actor can be said to command legitimacy, therefore, when its decisions and actions (and I would contend identities and interests) are socially sanctioned."[109]

We turn to another author who, like Grewe and others,[110] has addressed the problem of periodizing the history of international law. In "A History of International Law Histories," Martti Koskenniemi[111] presents an important example of the historical application of international-law justificatory narratives: the "*ideologies of empire*":[112]

> "'International law and empire' has now become perhaps the most popular item of international law history. When Jörg Fisch wrote *Die europäische Expansion und das Völkerrecht* in 1984, he was still a path-breaker – even as the overwhelming Anglo-centrism of the field has left this basic work relatively unread.[113] The burgeoning literature on the empire that is being produced today remains predominantly focused on the British world-system.[114] Recent writing on European penetration in North America and the Southern hemisphere has focused on the dispossession of the native populations. Regarding the Spanish empire, the works by Luciano Pereña remain largely unknown outside Spain. Though not completely free of imperial apologetics, they are, alongside the 29 volumes of the *Corpus Hispanorum de Pace (CHP)* edited by Pereña, an invaluable (though again, little known) source of materials. In Italy, Luigi Nuzzo has thrown a post-colonial eye on the legal languages of

107 Suchman (1995).
108 Coicaud (2002).
109 Reus-Smit (2007) 157 ff.
110 A useful, compact treatment of the history of international law is provided by Neff (2014).
111 Koskenniemi (2012).
112 Koskenniemi (2012) 964–965.
113 Fisch (1984).
114 See, for example, Sylvest (2008); Armitage (2000); MacMillan (2006).

colonization and conquest[115] and new works by Gozzi and Augusti deal with the encounter of non-European world with European law.[116] In Germany, older and newer historical writing covers especially the law and morality of the Spanish conquest, with emphasis often on the writings of the Spanish theologians. But Germany's own colonial period (1880–1991) is still largely untreated from the perspective of international legal history. Finally, much of the political and economic history of empire, including novel works in 'world history' is full of legal implications, though rarely treated in a systematic fashion. This applies to accounts of the 'ideologies' of empire as well as on the legal practices sustaining imperial administration."[117]

At this point we turn to a somewhat more general examination of the function of justificatory narratives.

II. The function of justificatory narratives

Wherever justificatory narratives are under discussion, Rainer Forst will inevitably be mentioned as an author who has extensively and intensively investigated the function of such narratives.[118] He shows that the function of justificatory narratives is to *establish ruling authority* and that the narratives are embedded in *specific historical situations*:[119]

> "'Normative orders' are grounded in basal justifications and serve to justify social rules, norms, and institutions; they substantiate *pretensions to power* and a specific distribution of goods and life opportunities. A normative order is hence to be seen as a *justificatory order*: it both presupposes and generates justifications. Orders of this sort are embedded in justificatory narratives that develop in historical situations and are passed down and modified over longer periods of time. We therefore use the concept as a heuristic device to combine the normative dimension of justification intent on rational persuasion with the dimension of societally effective justification found convincing and practised by the parties involved and constituted by their experience and expectations. We consider justificatory narratives to be forms of embodied rationality. In them images, sectional narratives, rituals, facts, and myths are concentrated into efficacious overall narratives lending meaning to an order. Normative orders framed in narratives – especially those that are religious in nature (divine rights versus natural rights), that go back to political achievements like revolutions or victories (e.g., in wars of liberation), or to the processing of past

115 Nuzzo (2004).
116 Gozzi/Manzini (eds.) (2008); Augusti (2009).
117 See particularly Pagden (1995); Benton (2002).
118 See, for example, Forst (1984); Forst (2007).
119 Forst (2013).

> collective injustice (e.g., crimes against humanity in the twentieth century) – have particularly strong binding force and authority; they gain historical importance, as well as emotional *identificatory force*. Historical experience with the breach of civilization caused by the Shoah, for example, determines the context of the recent conception of human dignity and human rights. Memories of the many struggles against the colonial dominance of the Europeans enhances sensitivity towards one's own right to cultural and religious identities and ways of life."[120]

As Martin Seel has shown, however, it is always about a "context of justification," about being in the right or in the wrong:

> "Whereas narratives generally place factual or fictive courses of events at various levels of complexity in a both causal and motivational context, whether transparent or opaque, justificatory narratives do more. They heighten not only *what is narrated* but also the *act of narration*. They explain or question how *right or just action in given situations has been*, how much justice or injustice has been done to those actively or passively involved. *How* they narrate (their choice of words, how they start and finish, how they stress *some* events and ignore *others*, how they ponder over or hasten through the course of events and use many other stylistic devices) throws specific light on *what* they narrate that is in one way or another evaluative. They thus articulate and modify – and occasionally transform – the *perspective* from which the normative reasons for individual and collective action that count most for the narrators or narrative authorities are to be drawn. Justificatory narratives already achieve this in everyday life – but all the more so in the form of big theological, historical, and political narratives up to and including myth and art."[121]

We now cast a brief look at the most important justificatory narratives in international law.

III. Two examples of justificatory narratives in international law

1. In search of legal title for violent Spanish expansion in South and Central America

In his work on European expansion and international law,[122] Jörg Fisch deals with the theories of the Spanish Dominican Francisco de Vitoria, whom many regard as the real father of international law:[123] "For both the sixteenth century and beyond, the teachings of the Dominican Francisco

120 Forst (2013) 13–14.
121 Seel (2013) 47–48.
122 Fisch (1984).
123 See the instructive article by Koskenniemi (2014).

de Vitoria are by far the most important. He repeatedly addressed the relevant issues. In 1539 he presented his views comprehensively and systematically in the lecture *De Indis – On the American Indians*. The entire later discussion in the sixteenth century can be seen as a commentary or debate on this lecture. And for later centuries, too, Vitoria provided almost all the points of discussion."[124]

Vitoria is concerned with finding an appropriate justificatory narrative for Spanish expansion policy in South and Central America. He starts by defining and decisively rejecting seven conceivable *titles of rule*.

> "(1.) The emperor was not master of the world by natural law, divine law, or human law. In his capacity as emperor he could therefore not dispose over the land of the American Indians. …
>
> (2.) Neither was the pope secular ruler of the entire world, and could therefore not award land in America, and if the 'barbarians' refused to recognize the pope's temporal dominion over them he was not empowered to wage just war on them. …
>
> The thrust of his argument was clear: Christian, ecclesiastical pretensions to world rule often vesting at least spiritual power over unbelievers in the pope were rejected; the power of the Church was limited to Christendom.
>
> (3.) Nor was there any legitimate title by right of discovery. Although ownerless land belonged to whoever occupied it, and the Spanish had been the first to discover and take possession of the American territories, America was not ownerless but inhabited by peoples with true public and private dominion. …
>
> (4.) Refusal to convert to Christianity is no just ground for war. The barbarians were not obliged by a simple statement or announcement to believe where there are no miraculous signs or other reasons. Otherwise they would have to believe the Saracens, too, were they to appear in the New World. No-one can be forced to believe. Unbelief is not injustice towards Christians and therefore gives them no right to conduct a just war, which can always be seen only as punishment for injustice suffered. …
>
> (5.) Nor do the sins of Indians against natural law, e. g., incest or cannibalism, provide Christians with a reason for just war. Although these are undoubtedly the gravest of sins, the pope had no jurisdiction over unbelievers. This was all the more true for the Spanish kings, whose power over the American Indians had been delegated to them by the pope. …

124 Fisch (1984) 212.

> (6.) The argument that the Indians had freely chosen the Spanish king to rule over them also gave no legitimate title in this regard. For this choice was made in fear and ignorance, factors which vitiated any freedom of election.
>
> (7.) Nor could the Spanish claim that God had made them His instrument for punishing the sins of the 'barbarians'. It was very doubtful whether this was the case, and even if it were so, it could not justify the action taken by the Spanish."[125]

Vitoria's positions with regard to *legitimate rights to rule* are less clear. The first of these legal titles that Vitoria considered legitimate belongs firmly to international law and has primarily to do with free trade:

> "The point of departure for the first legitimate title is the natural community and society of all humans. From this Vitoria derives a comprehensive right to freedom of movement and establishment, which may be restricted only if citizens of the host country suffer injustice at the hands of the foreigners. There is also a corresponding right to trade freely. No state may forbid its citizens to trade with the citizens of other states. Rights granted to some foreigners, for instance in mining, must also be equally available to all others. Finally, the children of immigrants must be granted citizenship in the host country. If the Indians refuse to grant the Spanish these rights, they may be obliged to do so by force, if need be by war."[126]

The other legitimate titles are all *religious in nature* and justify a *special right of proselytization*. They include the following:[127]

> "(2.) …
>
> (3.) If any barbarians are converted to Christ, and their princes try to call them back to their idolatry by force or fear, the Spaniards may on these grounds wage ware on them. …
>
> (4.) If a good proportion of the barbarians is converted to Christ, the pope might remove their infidel masters and give them a Christian prince if this is expedient for the preservation of the Christian faith. …
>
> (5.) The Spanish are entitled to take action against the tyranny of barbarian rulers and their tyrannical laws. This covers above all cannibalism and human sacrifice, regardless of whether the victims wish to be liberated or not. …
>
> (6.) If the 'barbarians' decided to accept the king of Spain as their prince by genuinely free choice, this might be a legitimate title, which could also be defended by force."

125 Fisch (1984) 213 f.
126 Fisch (1984) 216.
127 Fisch (1984) 219.

Vitoria's indecisive attitude is interesting towards the question of whether the Spanish crown could lay claim to *special civilizational rights* on the grounds of the mental incapacity of American Indians:

> "(8.) Finally, Vitoria raises a question that he does not venture to answer. Some claimed, he wrote, that the American Indians are 'so close to being mad, that they are unsuited to setting up or administering a commonwealth'. If this were the case, the Spanish would be bound to take charge of them as if they were simply children or animals in their own interest in order to civilize them. Vitoria made not attempt to decide whether this was really the case. Over and above the special title of tyrannical rule, he does not reject special civilizational rights but doubts whether their justification, namely the uncivilized state of American Indian society, could be substantiated. Overall, however, this title played little part in his argumentation. Other late scholastics generally gave even less space to it. They relied on religious, not on civilizational special rights."[128]

2. The "civilization and progress" project as a justificatory narrative

We return to the triad of commerce, civilizational expansion, and the Christian mission because the early phase of globalization, which is often equated with the onset of colonization, displays a tangle of *strategies for justifying European expansion*. According to Ernst Bloch, writing about travel, research, and discovery as components of cultural globalization,[129] the geographical utopias "El Dorado and Eden" are almost inextricable. Those who sailed the seven seas were in quest of both "plunder and miracles."[130]

Writing about the exploration of Central Africa under the heading *Travel, Exploration, and Occupation*,[131] Johannes Fabian cites a report by Joseph Thomson (1881) on an expedition commissioned by the Royal Geographical Society:

> „A few years ago, when Europe was stirred by the striking adventures of some of our later travellers, Livingston, Stanley, and Cameron, and united, with royalty at its head to form an International Association for the opening of Africa, a general belief arose that at last a new era of hope for the Dark Continent had been ushered in. Anticipations of civilizing centres dotted over the length and breadth of its vast area, were held by the most sanguine. Few corners were to be left unveiled. Everything

128 Fisch (1984) 222.
129 Bloch (1959) 873 ff.
130 Bloch (1959) 874 f.
131 Fabian (2000).

> that was good and great in Europe was to be transplanted to African soil, and under the nurturing care of International pioneers to be reared and developed. Travellers and other scientific men were to receive every assistance. Trade was to be introduced and developed; and of course Christianity, of whatever creed, was to be fostered and encouraged.
>
> What has really been the result? Some years have passed, and as yet we have only the sublimely ridiculous spectacle of united Europe knocking its head idiotically against a wall, betraying an utter inability to grapple with the difficulties of the case, and making itself the laughing-stock to the benighted negroes whom it undertook to enlighten."[132]

Niall Ferguson[133] addresses the triad of commerce, spread of civilization, and Christian mission with particularly intensity. On the civilizational mission as 'not-for-profit rationale for expanding British influence' he has this to say:

> "For two hundred years the Empire had engaged in trade, warfare and colonization. It had exported British goods, capital and people. Now, however, it aspired to export British culture. Africans might be backward and superstitious, but to this new generation of British Evangelicals, they also seemed capable of being 'civilized'. As Macaulay put it, the time had come to 'spread over (Africa's) gloomy surface light, liberty and civilization'. Spreading the word of God and thereby saving the souls of the benighted heathen was a new, not-for-profit rationale for expanding British influence. It was to be the defining mission of the century's most successful non-governmental organizations (NGOs)."[134]

These most successful NGOs of the century were the innumerable mission societies, which can be described as a particularly interesting species of actor in religious globalization;[135] they have been an important element is what we would now call the "voluntary sector,"[136] which played a key role in the "mission civilisatrice et religieuse":

> "Like the non-governmental aid organizations of today, Victorian missionaries believed they knew what was best for Africa. Their goal was not so much colonization as 'civilization': introducing a way of life that was first and foremost Christian, but was also distinctly North European in its reverence for industry and abstinence. The man who came to embody this new ethos of empire was David Livingstone. For Livingstone, commerce and colonization – the original foundations of the Empire –

132 Fabian (2000) 23.
133 Ferguson (2003).
134 Ferguson (2003) 119 f.
135 Greater detail in Schuppert, G. F. (2014) 339 ff.
136 See also, with further references, Schuppert, G. F. (1995c).

> were necessary, but not sufficient. In essence, he and thousands of missionaries like him wanted the Empire to be born again.
>
> This was not a government project, but the work of what we today would call the *voluntary sector.* But the Victorian aid agencies' good intentions would have unforeseen, and sometimes bloody, consequences."[137]

So far so good. We turn now to a field where justificatory narratives played a vital role during early globalization.

IV. The struggle for command of the sea in the guise of competition between sectional justificatory narratives

In Wilhelm G. Grewe's account of epochs in the history of international law, it is at first glance astonishing how much space he devotes to the "legal order of the seas." In all six parts the he addresses the maritime law problems specific to the given epoch. Listing the headings in chronological order provides a brief history of the international law of the sea:[138]

- The legal order of the seas: dominium maris – maritime dominion of the littoral powers
- The legal order of the seas: mare liberum versus mare clausum – the legal title to maritime dominion
- The legal order of the seas: the rights of neutral states in war as "liberté des mers"
- The legal order of the seas: freedom of the seas under British maritime dominion
- The legal order of the seas: the extinction of neutral rights in war
- The legal order of the seas: common heritage – the sea as common heritage of humankind

These headings alone show that a distinction must be made between the law of terra firma and the law of the sea and that "*sovereignty of the sea*" was a particularly contentious issue in the long history of European expansion. The vastness of the oceans is home not only to countless species of fish but also to the numerous justificatory narratives with which powers vying for command of the sea have armed themselves.

Before considering the most interesting of such narratives, we examine what makes the sea so fascinating to specialists in international law.

137 Ferguson (2003) 114.
138 Grewe (1984) 157 ff., 300 ff., 471 ff., 647 ff., 740 ff., 801 ff.

1. Why seas are so fascinating

- *State sovereignty and freedom of the seas*

This was the title of an essay Carl Schmitt published in 1943 on the "struggle for reorganization of the newly discovered world."[139] For Schmitt, sailing the oceans and the discovery of hitherto unknown continents led to the outbreak of a "*planetary spatial revolution*," which necessarily produced *polarized the concepts land and sea*:

> "The struggle for the oceans set in with great force already in the mid-sixteenth century when the French, Dutch, and English took up arms against the monopoly over the sea claimed by the Spanish and Portuguese. Opposing spatial concepts for land and sea developed, poles apart between closure and openness. Firm land become state territory while the sea remained free, i. e., free from the state, not part of state territory. The astonishing dualism of European international law of recent centuries took shape. The usual, unselective term "international law" is incorrect and misleading, since in reality we have two parallel, unrelated systems of international law. A Europecentric world order arose, but immediately broke down into land and sea. The land was divided into the territorially closed state territories of sovereign states while the sea remained free from the state. What does this mean for an international law regulating relations between states whose overarching concept of order is the state? The sea knows no boundaries, becomes a single, unitary space regardless of geographical location and propinquity, supposedly 'free' to all states without exception for the purposes of both peaceful trade and waging war."[140]

This freedom of the sea from state control had originally, that is to say, before the founding of the major maritime empires, also meant that it was *unregulated*. In "The Nomos of the Earth"[141] Schmitt comments:

> "Originally, before the birth of great sea powers, the axiom 'freedom of the sea' meant something very simple, That the sea was a zone free for booty. Here, the pirate could ply his wicked trade with a clear conscience. ... On the open sea, there were no limits, no boundaries, no consecrated sites, no sacred orientations, no law, and no property. ... On the sea there was no law.
>
> Only when the great sea empires, maritime nations or, to use a Greek expression, thalassocracies, arose was security and order established on the sea."[142]

Be that as it may; whether the sea is an originally law-free zone or – to be more accurate – a sparsely regulated zone, it was to become a zone of

139 SCHMITT (1943).
140 SCHMITT (1943) 86.
141 SCHMITT (2006).
142 SCHMITT (2006) 43 f.

competing legal claims at the latest with the advent of the sea-born empires competing for trade monopolies.

- *World empires and oceans*

This is the title of the third volume of the series on the "History of the World"[143] brought out byAkira Iriye and Jürgen Osterhammel. This volume, edited by Wolfgang Reinhard, is concerned not only with world empires, their rise and fall[144] – the usual topic of historians – but explicitly with the oceans as spaces of historical interest. The contribution by Stephan Conermann addresses the history of the Indian Ocean,[145] and Wolfgang Reinhard, writing about an Atlantic world[146] classified primarily in terms of seafaring nations competing for trade monopolies, identifies the following:

- the Spanish Atlantic[147]
- the Portuguese Atlantic[148]
- the Dutch Atlantic[149]
- the Jewish Atlantic[150]
- the African Atlantic[151] and
- the French and British Atlantic[152]

Wolfgang Reinhard explains the clearly burgeoning interest of historians in the oceans:

> "Long before the 'spatial turn' in the social sciences and humanities, Fernand Braudel had in 1949 discussed the Mediterranean as historical space, identifying lasting geohistorical structures and long temporal waves of socio-economic cycles.[153] His influence proved so great that practically every larger stretch of sea

143 See six volumes of "Geschichte der Welt": Gehrke (ed.) (2017); Kafadar (ed.) (2014); Reinhard (ed.) (2014); Conrad / Osterhammel (eds.) (2016); Rosenberg, E. (ed.) (2014); Iriye (ed.) (2013).

144 See also, with further references, Schuppert, G. F. (2014) Chapter 2: "Imperien und Netzwerke als globalisierungstypische Governancestrukturen", 101 ff.

145 Conermann (2014).

146 Reinhard (ed.) (2014) 670–831.

147 Reinhard (ed.) (2014) 778 ff.

148 Reinhard (ed.) (2014) 789 ff.

149 Reinhard (ed.) (2014) 792 ff.

150 Reinhard (ed.) (2014) 795 ff.

151 Reinhard (ed.) (2014) 796 ff.

152 Reinhard (ed.) (2014) 809 ff.

153 Braudel (1992).

is now likely to have found its historian. Several volumes of a new series *Seas in History* have appeared.[154] Why the maritime perspective is successful is meanwhile clear. The 'spatial turn' having taught us to see *space as a communication medium*, the seas prove particularly interesting from this point of view. Lacking a stable human population and because of their remoteness from regulation, the seas lack the surplus qualitative 'tenacity' that enables places and countries to resist reduction to communication. Chapter three is therefore concerned not only with the Indian subcontinent but also with 'the world of the Indian Ocean', with East Africa, the Red Sea, the Persian Gulf and its littoral countries, and to the East at least the Gulf of Bengal. The final chapter addresses the 'Atlantic world', the communication space forming and formed by the inhabitants of three continents. However, in both cases, Braudel's socio-economic perspective is broadened to include cultural history, and the human capacity for action he so misprized is once again taken seriously."[155]

In similar vein Stephan Conermann writes about the Indian Ocean:

> "Long before the fourteenth century, sailors, merchants, pious men, and migrants crossed the Indian Ocean in search of merchandise, new territories, and land for settling. Over the centuries, these constant activities transformed the Indian Ocean into an *interactional space covered by many networks*. The prime focus was on commerce, especially the transport, purchase, and sale of goods over great distances. But trade also included the *exchange of knowledge, forms of faith, and values*. The Indian Ocean thus developed into a complex field for economic, social, and political action directly or indirectly linked to the whole of Europe, Africa, and Asia.
>
> The history of South Asia and the Indian Ocean can thus still best be understood as *economic history*. Other analytic approaches are of course conceivable, for instance environmental history in the framework of 'travelling concepts' or against the backdrop of migration, mobility, or conflicts. But so far, no substantial studies of this sort have addressed the region. We shall therefore concentrate on trade."[156]

Our concern, however, is not economic history and the oceans – Wolfgang Reinhard's key concepts – as contact zones, communication and interactional spaces, but the *history of power as legal history* and the role justificatory narratives play in this context.

154 See Kirby/Hinkkannen (2000); Freeman (2010); Pearson (2003).
155 Introduction: Reinhard (ed.) (2014) 36.
156 Conermann (2014) 505.

2. The sea as a space of competing legal claims

If, in principle, the sea was open to all nations for local and long-distance trade[157] and they predictably got in each others' way, the "high seas" were more or less predestined to be an *arena for transnational conflicts*. Since disputes were about economically vital rights of use and monopolies, they obviously *had to be fought out in the language of law*. Writing about the "curse of the oceans," Michael Kempe comments:[158]

> "If we look at European relations in the Atlantic against the backdrop of the vicious circle of piracy, reprisal voyages, and the fight against piracy, it is obvious that the newly discovered maritime zones were by no means outside the law or subject only to the law of the jungle. Arguments always took legal form, *accusations were always formulated as legal complaints*. Although the sea was always a contentious issue at international law, it was not without law; it was a *space of divergent legal claims*. For one sovereign power, the letter of marque and the letter of reprisal served as legal remedies in the extraterritorial pursuit of economic, political, and also religious interests, as spatial extension of these interests beyond its own territory – up to the shores of newly discovered lands and continents. For another, the legal right to treat all voyages it did not approve as acts of piracy served to enforce claims to dominion and monopolies over maritime areas outside Europe. The 'politicization of the oceanic space'[159] between America and Europe took place primarily in juridical guise. The sea thus became a space of opposing legal strategies covering it like vectors – not as a mere receptacle of such strategies but as a vector field shaped by them. However, such an understanding of the law was purely instrumental on all sides, making the high seas an arena for transnational conflict in which contradictory, mutually exclusive legal postulates met, competed, and collided. In the course of their discovery by the Europeans, the seas spanning the globe thus became a *legal space of fragmented globality and global fragmentation*,[160] which sharpened awareness of the need to create an international order."[161]

157 See NAGEL, J. (2007).
158 KEMPE (2010).
159 See MANCKE (1999).
160 In similar vein: BENTON (2003).
161 KEMPE (2010) 71.

3. Two justificatory narratives at work

- *Mare liberum versus mare clausum*

This fundamental politico-conceptual dispute brought the established maritime empires, above all Spain and Portugal into conflict with nations aspiring to this status, notably the Netherlands. The conflict was not fought out in open naval battles but, as Carl Schmitt puts it, in a "hundred-year book war,"[162] in which many renowned authors participated.[163] "However, one should not allow the concrete significance of the publications to be submerged in the plethora of titles with such catchwords as "freedom" or "exclusiveness" of the sea. Vitoria had in mind the freedom of overseas missions and propagation of the Catholic faith; others thought only in terms of breaking the Spanish and Portuguese monopolies on overseas trade; still others thought in terms of regional or local disputes about European ports or the question of fisheries …."[164]

So it was really a *war of expert opinions* with probably the most famous expert in legal history, Hugo Grotius, on the one side, who in an opinion for the Dutch East India Company (VOC) pleaded for the freedom of the seas in the interest of this "statehood entrepreneur"[165] and John Selden, from whom the English crown had commissioned a report published under the heading "Mare clausum," but which never achieved the explosive force of Grotius' paper.[166] So much has been written about this[167] that we can forego the role of war correspondent.

Instead, we leave the floor to Michael Kempe, who is quite clear that abstract legal principles were not the issue but purely and simply the promotion of trade interests – the language of international law as a language of politics : "The noble dictum 'freedom of the seas' should not obscure the fact that international law was practised not primarily in pursuit of some international legal ideal but to enforce trade interests. Northern Europeans were intent on undermining the trade monopoly of the Iberian powers overseas

162 Schmitt (2006) 178 f.

163 An overview of the authors involved is provided by Kempe (2010) 96–97.

164 Schmitt (2006) 179.

165 On what we have called statehood entrepreneurs as globalization pioneers, see Schuppert, G. F. (2014) 36 ff.

166 Schmitt (1943) 151–152.

167 See, for example, Klee (1946).

in order to develop their own monopolies. The call for freedom of trade and navigation fell silent as soon as these countries had themselves gained the status of maritime trading powers."[168]

The trade interests at issue were *trade monopolies* and the states involved were well advised to mutually respect the monopolistic situation:

> "Despite all rhetoric to the contrary, both Southern and Northern Europeans fundamentally agreed on the monopolistic nature of trade with their own colonies or overseas partners. When the principle of freedom of the seas began to impose itself in state practice and in international-law theory in the late seventeenth century,[169] for international relations at sea – dominated by the Europeans – this meant in concrete terms the mutual recognition of each others' monopoly claims. Above all non-European countries, not being "full subjects" of international law were excluded from this closed circle of staked out spheres of interest. Disregarding what really lay behind the slogan, the tenet that ships on the high seas were inviolable, deriving from the principle of 'freedom of the seas', became the key precept of international navigation."[170]

The only actors to trouble the waters were the pirates.

- *Piracy as effective other-ascription*

Pirates as miscreants disrupting trade had to be combated and it was therefore legitimate to confiscate their ships and booty. In this, all important seafaring nations were agreed. The vital question – as today with the concept of terrorism – was who was *entitled to define* piracy or, to be more precise, who sought to claim this right in an act of "semantic imperialism." Quite rightly, Michael Kempe therefore describes the concept of pirate as one of *other-ascription*: "Significant from the viewpoint of international law were above all the denunciations of many inhabitants of the Arabian Peninsula or the Malay Archipelago as pirates and robbers under the mantle of British imperialism in the course of the nineteenth century. This shows particularly clearly what appellations such as 'freebooter', 'buccaneer', and 'pirate' always amounted to, namely terms of other-ascription to delegitimize the action and violence of the opponent and hence to justify one's own, for instance with such self-descriptions as 'pirate hunter' or 'maritime police'."[171]

168 Kempe (2010) 97.
169 Greater detail in Graf Vitzthum (ed.) (2006) 1–61.
170 Kempe (2010) 98.
171 Kempe (2010) 21.

In the contest for control of sea routes, piracy thus became a reproach all parties levelled at one another, leading to the resourceful device of providing one's own people with so-called "lettres de marque" or powers of reprisal to protect them against accusations of piracy.[172] On the logic of what could be called a "blame game," Michael Kempe comments:

> "Meanwhile, the Spanish and Portuguese treated all seafarers who entered their sphere of influence as 'piratas' or – which was the same for them – 'corsarios', regardless of whether they carried any sort of official document or not. What for the one was regular seizure was for the other merely piracy. This shows what 'pirate' or 'freebooter' had always been: terms of other-ascription. With all sides permanently accusing each other of piracy while adhering to the legal device of reprisal or marque to justify their own use of violence, all parties accepted that there was a difference between lawful and unlawful forms of appropriation. With the aid of letters of marque and reprisal, this distinction was also transferred to the sea as unity of the difference between right and wrong. The slowly dawning awareness of maritime spaces of hitherto unknown dimensions did nothing to change this. By provided seafarers entering distant worlds with such licences, the legal practices of European waters were extended to maritime regions outside Europe, as well."[173]

How the piracy issue could be instrumentalized in the context of legitimizing the conduct of the opponent is clearly illustrated by England's strategy to use it to *legitimate worldwide jurisdictional claims*. Kempe comments on this variety of the language of international law as a language of justification:

> "... The international piracy question pointed to the lack of a superior authority as a fundamental dilemma for legal relations between equal sovereign powers. Even the top English admiralty judges were forced to admit that disputes such as that about the Scottish privateer mentioned could never be decided unequivocally 'because here is no third Power that can give a Law that shall be decisive or binding between two independent Princes'.[174] The international piracy problem thus drew attention to a basic problem concerning legal relations between sovereign power that has remained virulent to this day.
>
> Jenkins used the universality of criminal law pertaining to piracy to advance universal claims for English admiralty jurisdiction. Not only were the immediate coastal waters of the kingdom subject to the sovereignty of the English crown. In order to protect the public peace, the freedom and safety of navigation throughout the world, the king had, by virtue of his 'imperial crown', the authority and right to prosecute piracy and other crimes at sea. This right extended to the remote coasts of the Atlantic, into the hidden nooks of the Mediterranean, and to every part of the

172 Greater detail in Kempe (2010) 46ff.

173 Kempe (2010) 46.

174 Quoted from Kempe (2010) 177.

> Pacific and every other sea, 'even in the remotest corners of the world'. In keeping with the universality principle, Jenkins admitted, all other nations also had this legal right. As the admiralty judge knew all too well, this meant that international conflicts in dealing with privateering and piracy were pre-programmed. But he also knew that England as a proud sea power could afford to claim such authority in the hope that, with the help of universal piracy law, the English crown could further extend its claims to power and dominion."[175]

V. Dominion over justificatory narratives as truly hegemonic power

When embarking on our exploration of the language of international law, we had mentioned the phenomenon of "semantic imperialism." Defining it in somewhat modified and simplistic form, we could say the "the hegemon is whoever possesses interpretative authority over justificatory narratives."

Writing about the concept of justificatory narrative, Rainer Forst describes the connection between power and the binding determination of the content of justificatory narratives:

> "To have power means to influence, determine, occupy, or even close the space of other subjects' reasons and justifications – and the degree to which this is done is important. It can take place in isolated cases – through a good speech or a deception – but it can also have its place in a societal structure that is based on certain justifications or consolidated justificatory narratives. Accordingly, a justificatory order is always a power order, which says nothing about either the justification or the constellation of power. Justifications can be imposed or freely shared, and there are many modes between these poles. Power thus always unfolds in the communication space, but this does not mean that it is well grounded. It is always discursive in nature, and the struggle for power is the struggle for the possibility of structuring or even controlling the justification resources of others."[176]

Instead of "semantic imperialism" we could also speak of *narrative power* and, as the following quotation suggests, of the *international legal order as a justificatory order:*

> "Justificatory narratives unfold normative power to the extent that they throw a certain light on the political and social world; the past, present, and future; on reality and ideals, connecting individuals with a collectivity and forming an accepted justificatory order. This normative power or force says nothing about the normative quality of the justifications proferred and the historical correctness of the narratives; they can also be ideological in nature. But in this case, too, the force of a

175 Kempe (2010) 177–178.

176 Forst (1984) 22–23.

narrative feeds not only on the collective perception of its cogency but on the acceptance of the superordinate principles and values that express the justifications generated. The power of a justificatory narrative arises from its historical exercise of power and its normative acceptance: *power is the ability to bind*."[177]

C. The history of international relations as a history of juridification

For the past some ninety years, the jurisprudential discipline of international law has been flanked by "international relations"[178] (IR), a subdiscipline of political science. A brief glance at the subject suggests that the history of international relations can be addressed as a history of juridification. This is to our purpose, since we wish to show that the language of law also plays an important role on such eminently political terrain as international relations.

I. Four stages in the juridification of international politics

Martin List and Bernhard Zangl note four *surges in the juridification* of international politics,[179] which are also reflected in developments in the language of law, notably international law.

- *The first stage: recognition as formally equal legal regimes*

  "The modern international system of states was normatively construed in categories of international law as an initially minimal order under public law that, at the latest from the seventeenth century, was to become more than a material power structure. This could be described as the first stage in the juridification of the modern system of states – initially limited to Europe. This legal order is more than a mere fact of power because states *recognize* one another as formally equal. This self-description of states as elements in a system of mutual recognition is, as it were, a whole new ball game: the language game of international law."[180]

177 FORST (1984) 24.
178 SPINDLER/SCHIEDER (eds.) (2006) 9, date the emergence of international relations as a subdiscipline of political science from 1919, the year in which the first professorships were established.
179 LIST/ZANGL (2003).
180 LIST/ZANGL (2003) 365.

* *The second stage: the universalization of international law*

"Naturally, recognition of formal equality is not the same as factual equality. The inferior party ignores factually superior power only at the peril of punishment – in the last resort – of demise. However, willingness to recognize the other is a sovereign decision. Nevertheless, recognition among states still depends decisively on factual power considerations (for instance, on the power actually exercised in a given area). No state is easily admitted to the language game of international law. The universalization of international law, too, followed on the factual increase in the importance of non-European powers and on their formal recognition, lastly in the major round of decolonization in the second half of the twentieth century. The outcome was the division of the world into some 190 sovereign states and thus the universalization of international law under the UN Charter."[181]

* *The third stage: from the law of coexistence to the law of cooperation*

"Among the specific aspects of constituting the modern system of states in the categories of international law was its indispensable relationship with morality. The pretensions of the law to validity ultimately draw on extra-legal, ethical grounds. The *language game of law* has its own rules for determining validity, but the law as a whole lives not only from this formal validity – legality – decided by its own rules, but by reference to ultimately extra-legal legitimacy. Of course, the *out-differentiation of law as a language game of its own* concomitant with modernity should not be ignored. Legal argument is a different exercise from arguing in ethical-moral terms. And law, including valid international law is not in every specific case ethically correct. Law, notably international law, tends rather to react to the plurality of diverging values shaped by morality and religion by providing rules for coexistence, which can be converted only very cautiously and slowly into rules of cooperation on the basis of common interests, and, even more prudently, on the basis of common values."[182]

* *The fourth stage: institutional consolidation of juridification processes*

"The impressive proliferation of international agreements alone would scarcely justify speaking of a fourth stage of international juridification. Current literature – in both jurisprudence and political science – on international juridification processes therefore focuses not so much on the quantitative increase in international treaties and the legal norms they lay down: it tends rather to stress the qualitative developments that have occurred since the 1980s. These new developments can be understood as a fourth stage on international juridification. They are marked by the *institutional intensification of the juridification process*, which supports the *language game of international law* through appropriate procedures.

181 List/Zangl (2003) 366.
182 List/Zangl (2003) 367.

According to the literature, current developments therefore consist less in international law producing new substantive (primary) rules than in setting new sorts of procedural (secondary) rules. The international law infrastructure has accordingly advanced considerably through agreed procedures for making, implementing, applying, and enforcing law."[183]

II. From war and peace to cooperation on questions of political order

Under this heading, Nicole Deitelhoff and Michael Zürn in their recent "Textbook on International Relations"[184] address the development of theories of international relations as a sequence of three paradigms:

> "The beginnings of the IR Galaxy were … superimposed by the question of war and peace and by the question of how wars can be prevented. These questions drive all 'paradigms' in the sense of IR theory. Ultimately, a changing world political situation cancelled out the *peace paradigm,* and specific theoretical problems were supplanted by a cooperation paradigm addressing addressed the conditions under which states cooperate, what it involves, and what the consequences are … The cooperation paradigm finally weakened as – in the view of scholars – anarchy became less pronounced in the international system. An essential condition for this was the enormous institutional dynamic that developed after the end of confrontation between the blocs. Already since the 1980s, the intensity of exchanges between societies had increased and with it the pressure of problems, requiring more and different international institutions. Not only has the number of international institutions risen tremendously since the 1990s; their form has also changed. They have intervened more and more drastically in national societies, also without the direct consent of the states involved. With these changes, the cooperative approaches, which had concentrated primarily on the act of cooperation, had less and less weight. Instead, a systemic perspective came to the fore that analysed the interplay between particular regulatory arrangements and institutions in terms of *global governance*. This placed the international system as political order centre stage, focusing on the structure of this order, on authority, and on rule, as well as resistance … The *order paradigm*, as Google Ngram Viewer data show, has been the dominant paradigm for some time in the German-speaking IR galaxy, but this development is also apparent in the English-speaking galaxy, which, owing to the predominance of the USA in world politics, has traditionally focused strongly on realistic theories."[185]

183 List/Zangl (2003) 371.
184 Deitelhoff/Zürn (2016).
185 Deitelhoff/Zürn (2016) 294–295.

This sequence of three paradigms – the peace paradigm, the cooperation paradigm, and the order paradigm – can be read not only as a sequence of bodies of theory but also as a *sequence of growing juridification* in international politics. From this point of view, the so-called cooperation paradigm is merely an abbreviation for *cooperative structures* needed to realize cooperative gains, that is to say, the necessary provision of – as governance studies puts it – appropriate *regulatory structures* and *regulatory regimes*.[186] And the *order paradigm*, which Nicole Deitelhoff and Michael Zürn rightly translate by "global governance," is clearly a paradigm to be expressed in the language of law.

This is apparent if one takes a somewhat closer look at what is really meant by "*global governance*." Like the present author,[187] Deitelhoff and Zürn understand governance not as a primarily normative concept in the sense of "good global governance" but as an "analytical construct that encompasses the overall arrangement of different forms of control at various levels of decision-making."[188] As the passage points out, it is about *regulatory arrangements* of all sorts – a particularly useful insight for anyone like ourselves who propagates an understanding of jurisprudence as a *science of regulation*:[189]

> "Governance in this second sense means the totality of collective *regulatory arrangements* addressing a particular problem or a particular societal state of affairs, and which are justified by reference to the collective interests of the group affected. Thus 'governance' refers not to isolated rules, such as the imposition of customs duties but to the *sum of rules* pertaining to a matter, such as international trade policy, and their interaction. It covers both the *content of regulation* and the norms that determine the coming into being and enforcement of the regulatory content. The *problems and matters concerned* – the second element of the definition – can be, for example climate issues, trade relations, financial relations, or human rights. But they could also be *collisions between such regulatory arrangements* or questions of *secondary rules*."[190]

Interestingly, however, this analytic approach, too – which we consider to be the right one – cannot quite manage without *normative grounding*: global

186 On governance as governance in and through regulatory structures see Schuppert, G. F. (ed.) (2005) 371–469.

187 See Schuppert, G. F. (2011a).

188 Deitelhoff / Zürn (2016) 204.

189 Schuppert, G. F. (2019).

190 Deitelhoff / Zürn (2016) 205.

governance, as the following passage shows, speaks not only in the language of analytical analysis but also in the *language of justification*;

> "Third, we can speak of governance only if the actors involved assert that it is their *intention* to promote the *common interest of a collectivity* or, even more strongly, the *common good of society*. The postulated goal must therefore be to deal with a societal problem through regulation. What is explicitly at issue is the *justification* of action, not necessarily the actual motivation behind it. Global governance as an overall arrangement accordingly includes all rules for the regulation of societal relations whose *justification* is oriented on fundamental social values and which have transnational effects, regardless of whether such rules achieve or block attainment of the postulated goals, and quite regardless of whether they are hierarchically organized or have arisen in a context without a superior, central authority."[191]

We bring this section to an end with a passage in which our authors point once again to the lasting dynamics in the development of global governance structures, identifying five stages or levels of international politics that clearly cannot be described without recourse to the *regulation concept*.

> "Apart from quantitative growth and spread, the second measure of dynamism is a new quality of international and transnational institutions establishing authority through all stages of political developments. In political science, the stages of political development are often described in terms of the political cycle model. In simple terms, five stages can be distinguished at the international level: making decisions on rules – supervising compliance with them – arbitrating disputes on compliance – enforcing rules – assessing results and thus setting agendas."[192]

191 Deitelhoff / Zürn (2016) 205.
192 Deitelhoff / Zürn (2016) 211.

9

Human Rights and Language: A Political Perspective

A. Human rights as the political creed of modernity

No-one will deny that there are many facets to the idea of human rights.[193] This idea, however, has, above all, been one thing: a *political project* seeking in all historical contexts to change the world. The language of human rights is primarily a *language of political change*.[194]

We call three authors to the witness box to testify on the *symbiotic relationship between law and politics* conveyed by the concept of human rights. The first is Ben Golder. He describes human rights as grounding and restricting politics, as *the political credo of modernity*: "Human rights in this very familiar guise represent the preeminent universalist political credo of late modernity: idealist, foundationalist, metaphysical, irreducible to calculation. Indeed to call them a political credo is not quite to do them justice – human rights, according to this reckoning, are both pre- and supra-political, providing the moral foundation and limits to politics itself."[195]

Our second witness is Makau Wa Mutua, who, writing about the symbiotic relationship between politics and human rights, rightly points out that we are well advised not to take the often unpolitical rhetoric of many human rights actors at face value: "Since the Second World War, international human rights law has become one of the most pre-eminent doctrines of our time. Diverse groups from sexual minorities to environmentalists now invoke the *power of human rights language*. But this universal reliance on the language of human rights has failed to create agreement on the scope and content of the human rights corpus. Debates rage over its cultural relevance, ideological and political orientation, and thematic incompleteness. What these debates obscure is the fact that *the human rights corpus is a political ideology*, although its major authors present it as non-ideological."[196]

193 See the overview in Mutua (2000).

194 On the political history of ideas in a "language of political change" see the introduction to this book, 1–31.

195 Golder (2016) 684–685.

196 Mutua (2000) 149.

The third author is Samuel Moyn, who begins his impressive book on the history of human rights as follows:

> *"When people hear the phrase 'human rights', they think of the highest moral precepts and political ideals.* And they are right to do so. They have in mind a familiar set of indispensable liberal freedoms, and sometimes more expansive principles of social protection. But they also mean something more. *The phrase implies an agenda for improving the world,* and bringing about a new one in which the dignity of each individual will enjoy secure international protection. *It is a recognizably utopian program*: for the political standards it champions and the emotional passion it inspires, this program draws on the image of a place that has not yet been called into being. It promises to penetrate the impregnability of state borders, slowly replacing them with the authority of international law. It prides itself on offering victims the world over the possibility of a better life. It pledges to do so by working in alliance with states when possible, but naming and shaming them when they violate the most basic norms. Human rights in this sense have come to define the most elevated aspirations of both social movements and political entities – state and interstate. They evoke hope *and provoke action*."[197]

This passage stresses what is characteristic of the *human rights project*: first, it is a *utopian project* that goes beyond "pure" politics, calling to mind a favourite book, Ernst Bloch's "The Principle of Hope."[198] Second, it is a *genuinely political project* because inspired by the will "to improve the world." And, third, it is consequently a *project intended to be realized*, driven by a dynamic almost impossible to check, which is accordingly a thorn in the flesh of politics.

B. The idea of human rights at the interface between ethics, politics, and law

I. The life of the human rights concept in overlapping normative worlds

In the realm of administrative organizational law, some organizations or institutional arrangements are often found to be at home in two normative worlds, private law (most frequently) and public law. In the age of the "cooperative state" and "private-public partnerships,"[199] there is hence a trend towards *hybridizing administrative structures*,[200] which has led to the creation of hybrid types of organization, half enterprise, half public author-

197 Moyn (2012) 1.
198 Bloch (1959).
199 See Schuppert, G. F. (2011b).
200 See Schuppert, G. F. (2012b).

ity.[201] A prime example in Germany is the defunct "Treuhandanstalt" – the federal trustee agency that administered the property of the former German Democratic Republic – for historical reasons a cross between government agency and liquidation management – which led a life between different jurisdictions: company law (in its capacity as "controlling enterprise") and public law (as "Anstalt des öffentlichen Rechts – "institution under public law").[202] But human rights are not about life in various jurisdictions but about life in various normative worlds. With the aid of three authors we cast a brief glance at this special situatedness of the human rights project. Writing about modern human rights as a task for Christians and Muslims, Heiner Bielefeldt rightly places the human-rights understanding of freedom at the "*focus of ethics, politics, and law*":

> "However wrong it would be to monopolize human rights as a simple progress ideology of the modern age, it would be just as wrong and one-sided to treat it only as a sort of emergency brake against a general 'decline narrative' of modernity. In modern crises of traditional, ethical consensus grounded directly in religion and of traditional legal institutions, a new conceptualization of freedom has asserted itself. With hitherto unheard of conviction, the moral subject position of the human being, his/her responsibility and self-determinacy has been made the *focus of ethics, politics, and law*. This modern view of freedom has also become definitive for human rights. Human rights differ from premodern conceptions of law essentially in their pursuit of *politico-legal* recognition for equal freedom and participation for the individual. The guiding human-rights principle of equal, solidary freedom finds exemplary expression in Article I of the Universal Declaration of Human Rights: 'All human beings are born free and equal in dignity and rights. They are endowed with reason and conscience and should act towards one another in a spirit of brotherhood. They are endowed with reason and conscience and should act towards one another in a spirit of brotherhood.'"[203]

In similar vein, our second author Winfried Brugger has this to say about the position of human rights between morality, law, and politics under the heading "*positivity and suprapositivity of human rights*":

> "The demands of human rights express protest against conditions and modes of action that those affected regard as political and social oppression. The acts criticized can often be attributed to state-made laws and regulations adopted by political

201 On this phenomenon of hybrid organizational forms in the modern administrative state, see Schuppert, G. F. (2000), recital 120 ff.

202 See my contribution to "Treuhandanstalt": Schuppert, G. F. (1992).

203 Bielefeldt (1996).

> majorities or dominant minorities. Nor can it be excluded that political power holders have acted in line with prevailing social morality.[204] For minorities who feel they are oppressed, this means that, if their situation cannot be improved within the framework of the social and political system, they will have to assert and justify their demands for justice at levels of argument that go beyond *enacted and enforced law* and prevailing positive social morality. The demands of human rights operate at this level. Human rights claim to be 'law of the law', 'higher', 'pre-state', 'natural' law of the individual or humanity as such, a normative yardstick against which extant positive law is to be measured. Such higher law can clearly not be validated by state legislation or by social acceptance: its validity needs to be derived from bodies of norms of *enlightened, critical morality*."[205]

If human rights are grounded above all in enlightened, critical morality, this does not mean that they are not part and parcel of the world of law and politics. As far as the world of law is concerned, Brugger[206] comments:

> "[Human rights] always have a *tendency towards juridification*. The champions of human rights want to see them incorporated into the existing legal system (or if this is not possible into a new legal system) and integrated under constitutional law so that political rule can be transformed from a coercive system into a true 'Rechts-Ordnung' – a true order of law and rights.[207] As the 'basis of freedom, justice, and

204 An example illustrates this. After the drafting of the American constitution in 1787, discrimination against people of colour in the United States was long endorsed by both enacted law and prevailing social morality. The United State Supreme Court described the position in *Dred Scott v. Sandford*, 60 U.S. (19 How.) 393, 405 f. (1857) as follows: Afro-Americans "were at that time considered as a subordinate and inferior class of beings ... They had for more than a century before been regarded as beings of an inferior order, and altogether unfit to associate with the white race, either in social or political relations; and so far inferior, that they had no rights which the white man was bound to respect; and that the negro might justly and lawfully be reduced to slavery for his benefit. He was bought and sold, and treated as an ordinary article of merchandise or traffic, whenever a profit could be made by it. This opinion was at that time fixed and universal in the civilized portion of the white race. It was regarded as an axiom in morals as well as in politics, which no one thought of disputing, or supposed to be open to dispute; and men in every grade and position in society daily and habitually acted upon it in their private pursuits, as well as in matters of public policy, without doubting for a moment the correctness of this opinion."

205 Brugger (1989) 559.

206 Brugger (1989) 559–560.

207 This was fully evident in the American Revolution. The colonists had long sought to combat certain interventions and discrimination by the Crown, evoking traditional English rights. When this proved to be of no avail, they necessarily fell back on a "higher" law than the positive English law in force, namely on innate, natural, inalienable human rights – which they claimed the Crown had violated. See the impressive Declaration of

> peace in the world' human rights are intended to prevent injustice, so that people are not obliged to rise against tyranny and oppression as the last resort."[208]

As far as belonging to the world of politics is concerned, Bruggers shows that it is ultimately impossible to make a fine distinction between morality, law, and politics in the field of human rights. They are inseparably interwoven:

> "There is ... no *naive anti-politics attitude* underlying the human rights issue. Human rights thinking recognizes that political disputation is justified and necessary not only between competing interests but also between different conceptions of justice. It is not by chance that the guarantee of democratic participatory rights is a vital line of development in the history of human rights. However, human rights thinking also posits limiting the legitimation of political decision-making through state authority, even by majority decision. Political decisions can find greater or less acceptance, generating different degrees of consensus and dissent. From the perspective of basic and human rights, this produces an important substantive and ultimately institutional distinction: decisions are made in every polity that the parties affected, whether they agree with them or not, can no longer accept as having been reached in keeping with the relevant criteria for justice and legitimacy but must consider *unacceptable, unjust, and arbitrary.* There would then be no more *contentious legal cases* that could be sufficiently legitimated by majority decision. Prima facie they would them be indisputable cases of injustice, to be prevented wherever possible. To dispel any suspicion of a violation of justice, political (and in the given case, democratic) legitimation is then not enough. To secure justice and realize the common good in such cases, political power would have to be subject to substantive limitation through suitable precautions and more thoroughgoing examination of the public interests driving state intervention, above all the separation of powers, the entrenchment of fundamental rights, and their safeguarding by constitutional courts."[209]

Our third author in Wolfgang Schluchter, who shall have the last word on the subject:

> "The legal principles of human rights *bridge the gap* between the ethic of responsibility and positive law. ... They are a 'component' of both ethics and law. ... From the point of view of ethics, they are legal to the extent that they mean an institutional guarantee; and from the perspective of law they are ethical to the extent that they are inalienable and therefore vested with supra-empirical dignity ...."[210]

Independence on 1776, which enumerates and deplores the "long train of abuses and usurpations," the "absolute despotism," and the "absolute tyranny" of the Crown.

208 Preamble to the Universal Declaration of Human Rights. See also Article 1 (2) of the Basic Law.

209 Brugger (1989) 560–561.

210 Schluchter (1979) 155.

As interim appraisal we offer an observation and two conclusions. The *observation* is concerned with the parallelism of the human rights concept and notions about justice and the common good. The duty of all state power to further the common good is – as we have seen in the case of human rights – both supra-positive guiding principle and legal concept,[211] as Bardo Fassbender shows:

> "The notions of 'common good', 'common weal', 'public interest', and 'public spirit' born in antiquity have in modern times become politico-social guiding concepts – precisely by virtue of their substantive vagueness, their shifting meaning, the changes in their orientational function, and finally because of the various political options associated with them'.[212] Over the past two decades, the conceptuality of the common good has gained new momentum in political theory and social philosophy – against the backdrop of the state losing its long defended monopoly as guardian, interpreter, and enforcement agent of the common good, while a pronounced societal pluralism has made agreement increasingly difficult on a universally binding, substantive exposition of the common good as identity-forming definition of the characteristics of the 'polity'. ... The common good is also a legal concept. Peter Häberle has even spoken of 'jurisprudence as a science of the common good'.[213] ... In the legal order of the Federal Republic of Germany, the 'common good' or 'public interest' serve to justify authority under public law and – limiting fundamental rights and imposing obligations – as legal title and basic rule for resolving disputes where interests collide (principally in relations between the individual and the state, but also between different statutory bodies)."[214]

The first conclusion is that the human rights project would not be beneficial were the triad of morality, law, and politics to be dissolved, leaving only one of the three to carry the load. This could be a real danger if reliance were to be placed solely on *juridification of the human rights idea*,[215] virtually "filing it away." Without constant input from morality and ethics it would not only lose its *bridging function*: the language of human rights would surely lose its

211 On this use of the common good as "value-related formula" on the one hand and legal yardstick on the other, see Stolleis (1987) col. 1061.

212 See Münkler/Bluhm (eds.) (2001) 9.

213 See Häberle (1976) 292.

214 Fassbender (2003) 1.

215 As per 13 November 2014, the two most important agreements, the International Covenant on Civil and Political Rights (ICCPR) and the International Covenant on Economic, Social and Cultural Rights (ICESCR) have been ratified by 168 and 162 states respectively (overview in the United Nations Treaty Collection 2014). This has induced me to speak of the enforcement of human rights as a "juridified revolution" (See Schuppert, G. F. (2015) 247 ff.)

force as a "language of political change." If this is the case, our second conclusion must be that the *language of human rights has to be a multilingual language*, which can enter the debate on the good and just order of a society as a language of morality, law, and politics. Only then can the human rights project successfully *bridge* ethics, law and politics.

II. The standard-setting force of human rights

In the face of unacceptable rules of positive law, as Winfried Brugger has shown, "an opposing 'higher', 'pre-state', 'natural' law of the individual or humanity as such" is needed as a "*normative yardstick*."[216] The search for such a supra-positive standard is particularly incontestable when – as under the Nazi regime – "unacceptable laws" claimed validity as positive state-made law and were accordingly implemented, or should one rather say "executed." In the Federal Republic of Germany, this search for touchstones in coming to terms with Nazi injustice after the Second World War led to a renaissance of natural law. Under the heading "Natural Law or Legal Positivism,"[217] a collection of essays edited by Werner Maihofer addresses the subject.[218] But this natural law renaissance was short-lived, producing a subjective "criterion gap" in the country, which not only encouraged receptiveness towards human rights but also resulted in their being incorporated in the constitution, the "Basic Law."

As Samuel Moyn has described at length,[219] the triumphant progress of human rights as normative yardstick began with the "Universal Declaration of Human Rights" in 1948 – slowly at first, but picking up speed from the 1970s. Every form of political rule in the world was now inexorably measured against the yardstick of human rights. We can therefore speak of the standard-setting force of human rights.

Dieter Gosewinkel has discussed this standard-setting force of the language of human rights in a recent publication on citizenship in Europe in

216 Brugger (1989) 559.
217 Maihofer (ed.) (1966).
218 It is striking what a high proportion of these contributions have appeared in Church publications; see, in the order of the list of contents: Süsterhenn (1947); Wolf (1947/48); Weinkauff (1951/52); Utz (1951); Dombois (1955); David (1956).
219 Moyn (2012).

the twentieth and twenty-first centuries.[220] He notes the "breakthrough of a political movement for human rights," also substantially borne by international organizations such as the "International Labour Organization" (ILO):

> "The instrumentalization of human rights in the turmoil of the Cold War and their violation in the state-building process in decolonized regions did not prevent the new universal legal standards from attaining independent status as an effective global measure of equality and justice, and in the 1950s and 1960s, to win a great deal of support in Europe, notably on the anti-imperialist left. This involved highly heterogeneous motives and tendencies. For example, the protest of the European and American left against the Vietnam War and the Russell Tribunals of the 1960s cited the violations of human rights laid down in international treaties and codifications. The cultural upheaval, symbolized as international event by 1968, brought forth new social movements. They justified their demands, more radical than those of the established movements, on grounds of new human rights standards, whose universalism was above state-made law and, so to speak, put this law under 'top-down' political pressure for change."[221]

He has this to say on the rise of human rights as *guiding political idea* in the United States of the 1970s:

> "All these phenomena, which in the late sixties and early seventies consolidated into an international human rights discourse and a global politics of human rights, displayed strong differences – up to and including manifest contradictions – with respect to strength, motivation, and geographical orientation. But they also shared characteristics that proved decisive for the rise of human rights politics in the decades that followed: evocation of legal standards that ranked both legally and morally above the state and put pressure on the state, *the claim of global validity for these standards* and the transnational organization of the enforcement of human-rights norms."[222]

In Europe, too, human rights unfolded their full force only in the seventies:

> "However, it was only in the 1970s that they became an effective political weapon in Europe in the struggle for individual rights, which gradually began to change political systems themselves. This had been preceded by two United Nations human rights covenants concluded in 1966 on civil and political rights and on economic, social and cultural rights. The Soviet Union had joined in 1973 and Poland in 1977. But the *political dynamite* developed only in the mid-1970s through a particular constellation in which an intergovernmental agreement on human rights standards had been taken up by civil-society groupings and used effectively in opposing their own governments. In Helsinki in 1975, the Conference for Security and Coopera-

220 Gosewinkel (2016).
221 Gosewinkel (2016) 471–472.
222 Gosewinkel (2016) 473.

> tion (CSCE) concluded an agreement between 35 European countries with a highly contested agreement on human rights at its heart."[223]

Taking the example of Poland, Gosewinkel discusses the impact of the "Helsinki effect" on political practice:

> "When – after the opposition movement had invoked the constitution – the Polish government in 1976 envisaged an amendment to confirm the 'unwavering and fraternal ties with the Soviet Union', the dissident movement, which was rapidly winning support in society, veered to international law: it now argued that every constitutional amendment should be in keeping with the CSCE agreement. The opposition to the communist regime had thus established *a new legal hierarchy*: national guarantees of civil rights in the constitutions of socialist countries had to meet the international standard of human rights and were subject to corresponding scrutiny."[224]

So much on the standard-setting force of human rights.

C. The idea and history of human rights reflected in three major narratives

I. The narrative of Paul Gordon Lauren: the triad of visions, visionaries, and dramatic events

Writing about "visions seen"[225] in his history of human rights, Lauren describes the idea of human rights as one of the most influential visions of our time:

> "Among all … visions, perhaps none have had impact across the globe more profound than those of international human rights advocates. Thoughtful and insightful visionaries in many different times and diverse locations have seen in their mind's eye a world in which all people might enjoy certain basic and inherent rights simply by virtue of being human. They have viewed these rights or fundamental claims by persons to obtain just treatment as stemming from nature itself and thus inherited by all men, women, and children on earth as members born into the same human family entitled to be accorded worth and dignity. Moreover, with this premise they have envisioned a world without borders or other distinctions that divide people from one another in gender, race, caste or class, religion, political belief, ethnicity, or nationality. Such visions of human rights have contributed to the long struggle for the worth and dignity of the human person throughout history. More recently, they have heavily shaped the entire discussion about the meaning of

223 Gosewinkel (2016) 474.
224 Gosewinkel (2016) 479.
225 Lauren (1998).

> modern politics and society around the world, and in the process provided perhaps the most revolutionary concept of our own time."[226]

However, changing the world requires not only visions but also a *type of actor* that Lauren call a *visionary*:

> "The evolution of international human rights, ... has required in the first instance *people serving as visionaries*. There must be thoughtful men and women not only capable of imagining possibilities beyond existing experience themselves, but also of conveying these visions to others. They may do this through their teachings, as in the messages of the prophets Isaiah and Muhammed, the parables of Jesus, the instructions of Kong Qiu, or the lessons of Siddhartha Gautama and Chaitanya. They may achieve this through other forms of communication that infuse dreams such as the speeches of Cicero or Franklin Roosevelt, the poetry of Sultan Farrukh Hablul Matin or Ziya Gokalp, the letters of Abigail Adams, *the manifestos of Karl Marx*, the journals of Hideko Fukuda, the pamphlets of H. G. Wells, the decisions of the judges presiding over the International Military Tribunal at Nuremberg, the encyclicals of Pope John XXIII, or the songs of the civil rights movement such as 'We Shall Overcome'. These visionaries may transmit their ideas to others by means of lengthy treatises such as the published writings of Bartholomé de Las Casas, John Locke, Mary Wollstonecraft, or Kang Youwei. Or, they may convey visions through *resolutions or proclamations* such as the Universal Declaration of Human Rights."[227]

Interesting in this passage is not only the list of visionaries from Muhammad to Pope John XXIII but also the catalogue of media visionaries have used to spread their message, with particular stress on "*manifestos, resolutions and proclamations*." The *declaration* could be described as a specific form of the language of human rights, if not *the* specific form of this language.

Paul Gordon Lauren sees a third necessary element apart from visions and visionaries as "conditions for change": "events of consequence",[228] by which he means historical events generally described as revolutions: "One of the reasons why these cause-and-effect relationships occur is that events such as revolutions and wars destroy existing structures of authority, privilege, and vested interests, thus making change possible. Violence and upheaval – whether they occur in Europa, North America, Latin America, Asia, Africa, the Middle East, or islands of the Pacific – result in a transformation of established institutions of control."[229]

So much for the first narrative.

226 Lauren (1998) 1.
227 Lauren (1998) 285.
228 Lauren (1998) 290.
229 Lauren (1998) 291.

II. The narrative of Lynn Hunt: reading novels and declaring rights

1. Reading novels

In this chapter we have already made acquaintance with Lynn Hunt's "Inventing Human Rights"[230] when explaining human rights not only as a reaction to the experience of injustice but also as a consequence of people's growing awareness of their own autonomy. Hunt points out that autonomy and empathy belong together, and that it is empathy that comes into play when reading novels; not just any sort, but the "epistolary novels" so popular in the eighteenth century. This literary genre invited the reader, especially the female reader, to identify with the correspondents and to share their joys and sorrows:

> "Novels made the point that all people are fundamentally similar because of their inner feelings, and many novels showcased in particular the desire for autonomy. In this way, *reading novels created a sense of equality and empathy* through passionate involvement in the narrative. Can it be coincidental that the three greatest novels of psychological identification of the eighteenth century – Richardson's *Pamela* (1740) and *Clarissa* (1747–48) and Rousseau's *Julie* (17619 – were all published in the period that immediately preceded the appearance of the concept of 'the rights of man'?"[231]

Hunt's argument is convincing. Our brief look at the history of globalization as communication history has shown, more or less in passing, that the eighteenth century was the century of correspondence,[232] not primarily business correspondence, but that between people with ties of friendship who used letters as a medium for the free expression of feelings and sensibility:

> "The eighteenth century was the golden age of friendship and therefore it was the golden age of the letter. The enthusiasm of friendship could be given free and uninhibited expression in letters; the letter could be called 'the bulletin of sensibility and friendship'; lively correspondence was the criterion of friendship. ... The craving for friendship necessarily entailed a craving for letters. 'Let us rather exchange amicable letters', Luise Gottsched wrote to a friend. 'This is and remains our most delightful occupation for as long as we must be apart'. To write to friends was 'the most agreeable, enjoyable occupation' and one knew no greater 'pleasure' than to receive letters from friends. With what jubilation they are greeted! They are awaited

230 Hunt (2007).
231 Hunt (2007) 39.
232 See Steinhausen (1968).

'like the Messiah! With what yearning they are awaited! – 'I languish, my dearest friend', wrote Nicolai to Merck, 'for a letter from you'."[233]

If letters were thus the form of expression for feelings and sensibility, the epistolary novel, according to Lynn Hunt, was the appropriate medium for engendering awareness of one's own *interiority*, communicable to others.

"By its very form, then, the epistolary novel was able to demonstrate that selfhood depended on qualities of 'interiority' (having an inner core), for the characters express their inner feelings in their letters. In addition, the epistolary novel showed that all selves had this interiority (many of the characters write), and consequently *that all selves were in some sense equal because all were alike in their possession of interiority.* The exchange of letters turns the servant girl Pamela, for example, into a model of proud autonomy and individuality rather than a stereotype of the downtrodden. Like Pamela, Clarissa and Julie come to stand for individuality itself. Readers become more aware of their own and every other individual's capacity for interiority."[234]

2. Declaring rights

Just as letters and novels in epistolary form were the appropriate medium in the eighteenth century for gaining awareness of one's own personality, "declarations" seemed to be the obvious medium for communicating that one had become aware of one's own rights, of rights rooted in one's own person. This was the case with the declaration of the American colonies in which they expressed their political will to free themselves from the British Crown in the language of a "declaration of rights":

"The events of 1774–76 thus temporarily fused particularistic and universalistic thinking about rights in the insurgent colonies. In response to Great Britain, the colonists could cite their already existing rights as British subjects and at the same time claim the universal right as equal men. Yet, since the latter in effect abrogated the former, as the Americans moved more decisively toward independence *they felt the need to declare their rights as part of the transition from a state of nature back into civil government* – or from a state of subjection to George III forward into a new republican polity. Universalistic rights would never have been declared in the American colonies without the revolutionary moment created by the resistance to British authority. Although everyone did not agree on the importance of declaring rights

233 Steinhausen (1968) 307 f.

234 Steinhausen (1968) 48.

> or on the content of the rights to be declared, *independence opened the door to the declaration of rights*."[235]

This "*rights talk*", as Lynn Hunt calls it, spread like an epidemic: "Despite its critics, rights talk was gathering momentum after the 1760s. 'Natural rights', now supplemented by 'the rights of mankind', 'the rights of humanity', and 'the rights of man', became common currency. Its political potential vastly enhanced by the American conflicts of the 1760s and 1770s, talk of universal rights shifted back across the Atlantic to Great Britain, the Dutch Republic, and France."[236]

The most important destination of this "travelling rights talk" was naturally France, where the "language of rights" finally imposed itself:

> "The American precedents became all the more compelling as the French entered a state of constitutional emergency. In 1788, facing a bankruptcy caused in large measure by French participation in the American War of Independence, Louis XVI agreed to convoke the Estates-General, which had last met in 1614. As elections of delegates began, declaratory rumbles could already be heard. In January 1789, Jefferson's friend Lafayette prepared a draft declaration and in the weeks that followed Condorcet quietly formulated his own. The king had asked the clergy (the Frist Estate), the nobles (the Second Estate), and ordinary people (the Third Estate) not only to elect delegates but also to write up lists of their grievances. A number of the lists drawn up in February, March, and April 1798 referred to 'the inalienable rights of man', 'the imprescriptible rights of free men', 'the rights and the dignity of man and the citizen', or 'the rights of enlightened and free men', but 'rights of man' predominated. *The language of rights was now diffusion rapidly in the atmosphere of growing crisis*."[237]

This spreading "language of rights", as Hunt shows, had an internal logic, what we could call a logic of *ongoing expansion*, embracing first religious minorities, then slaves, and finally women, as well. Hunt therefore speaks of the "*bulldozer force of the revolutionary logic of rights*".[238]

235 Hunt (2007) 121–122.
236 Hunt (2007) 125.
237 Hunt (2007) 127–128.
238 Hunt (2007) 160.

III. The narrative of Samuel Moyn: a political history of the reception of human rights

In "The Last Utopia,"[239] Samuel Moyn presents a quite different narrative from those of Lauren and Hunt. For him the real story of human rights after decades of political insignificance begins with their "explosion" in the 1970s. It is worthwhile considering this story, albeit in much abbreviated form, because it shows what a *key role certain actors* play in the diffusion of ideas, whether we call them in general terms "transfer agents" or specifically "human rights activists." Moyn highlights three such "diffusion agents."

- *Social movements and NGOs*

The role of NGOs in promoting human rights has been described ad nauseam.[240] We limit ourselves to Moyn's comments on the role of social movements:

> "*Most of all, social movements adopted human rights as a slogan for the first time*. As the 1970s continued, the identification of such causes as human rights struggles snowballed, continuing across the world throughout the decade (indeed through the present). This serial amplification occurred even as states negotiated the Helsinki Final Act, signed in 1975, that inadvertently provided a new forum for North Atlantic rights activists. And then came 1977, a year of shocking and altogether unpredictable prominence of human rights. One of the most fascinating lessons of the period is how little known were the Universal Declaration and the project of international human rights when it began, and how these earlier 'sources' were discovered only after *the movements that claimed them got going*."[241]

- *The prominent role of Amnesty International*

Samuel Moyn is clearly fascinated by the pioneering role of Amnesty International (AI). He has this to say about the organization's modus operandi:

> "Indeed almost alone, Amnesty International *invented grassroots human rights advocacy*, and through it drove public awareness of human rights generally. Its contribution would reach its highest visibility when it received the Nobel Peace Prize in 1977, the breakthrough year for human rights as a whole, though it began its work years earlier. Unlike the earlier NGOs that invoked human rights occasionally or often, AI opened itself to mass participation through its framework of local chap-

239 Moyn (2012).
240 See, for example, Bianchi (1997).
241 Moyn (2012) 121.

> ters, each acting in support of specific, personalized victims of persecution. And unlike the earliest human rights groups, it did not take the UN to be the primary locale of advocacy. Skirting the reform of international governance, it sought a direct and public connection with suffering, through lighting candles in a show of solidarity and writing letters to governments pleading for mercy and release. These practical innovations depended in equal parts on a brilliant reading of the fortunes of idealism in the postwar world and a *profound understanding of the importance of symbolic gestures*."[242]

One particularly successful method employed by Amnesty International has been the collection and dissemination of information about unacceptable conditions and practices:

> "Amnesty International's novel methods of information gathering went in the 1970s far beyond its original methods of forming adoption groups to write pleas for individual release. And these methods were also critical to how it came to be (and, soon enough, were copied by other organizations). Even before the very early translation of dissident texts provided by AI's London-based research bureau, the organization had begun to focus its attention on torture in the later 1960s. It pioneered the gathering of information about depredations under Greek military rule from 1967–1974. Providentially, in 1972 the organization opened a Campaign against Torture, published a global analysis of the problem, and initiated a petition drive (the first signatory being Joan Baez, who opened it at an April 1973 concert). Seán MacBride, for his contribution to the campaign, won the Nobel Peace Prize in 1974, thereby raising the profile of human rights and broadcasting the very idea that social movements could coalesce around them. After the political coups in Chile and Uruguay, Amnesty International and other NGOs were active in gathering information and raising consciousness about infractions in those two countries. The information they gathered was spread most notably at the United Nations and in Washington, D.C., where AI opened an office in 1976. Such activities prompted some of the first analyses of AI's campaigns for wider publics, both in the academy and at large."[243]

- *Jimmy Carter Superstar*

Samuel Moyn identifies President Jimmy Carter as an absolute star in the popularization of the human rights idea. "Coming out of nowhere," he was the right man with his deep-rooted morality in the right place and at the right time to spread the message of human rights: "In the right place at the

242 Moyn (2012) 129–130.
243 Moyn (2012) 147–148.

right time, Carter moved 'human rights' from grassroot mobilization to the center of global rhetoric."[244]

Jimmy Carter's inaugural address on 20 January 1977, which focused on commitment to the message of human rights, dramatically enhanced the standing of the human rights idea. This is particularly worth noting, because, as the phenomenon of American "civil religion" shows,[245] each newly elected president of the United States quite deliberately takes the opportunity of the inaugural address to stress the unity of the profoundly American civil religion and the policy he intends to pursue. Jimmy Carter did just this:

> "The year of human rights, 1977, began with Carter's January 20 inauguration, which put 'human rights' in front of the viewing public for the first time in American history. This year of breakthrough would culminate in Amnesty International's receipt of the Nobel Peace Prize on December 10. Carter's inaugural address on January 20 made 'human rights' a publicly acknowledged buzzword. 'Because we are free we can never be indifferent to the fate of freedom elsewhere', Carter announced on the Capitol steps. 'Our commitment to human rights must be absolute'. The symbolic novelty and resonance of the phrase in Carter's policy is what mattered most of all, since he embedded it for the first time in popular consciousness and ordinary language. Arthur Schlesinger, Jr. once called on the 'future historian' to 'trace the internal discussions ... that culminated in the striking words of the inaugural address'. No one, however, yet knows exactly how they got there. But soon after, the term was being interpreted as 'almost a theological point for Carter. He can't stamp out sin, but he keeps on praying'."[246]

But that was not all: in a speech at a ceremony at Notre Dame University, Jimmy Carter even declared human rights to be the *basis for the future foreign policy of the United States*:

> "But by spring, Carter gave a programmatic address at Notre Dame's commencement, laying out a full-scale foreign policy philosophy based on human rights, while Secretary of State Cyrus Vance offered some specifics at the University of Georgia Law School. Even as Carter's subordinates 'groped' to define policy, American elites embarked on an extended discussion of human rights, from their historical origins, to their contemporary meaning, to their case-by-case implications. *The issue had become relevant and even 'chic'*, Roberta Cohen, executive director of the International League (who would shortly join the Carter human rights bureau), told the *New York Times*. 'For years we were preachers, cockeyed idealists, or busybodies and now we are respectable. ... Everybody wants to get into human rights. That's fine,

244 Moyn (2012) 155.
245 See my little book: Schuppert, G. F. (2012c) 67 ff.
246 Moyn (2012) 155.

> but what happens if they get bored?' This upsurge in interest could not compare to that of the 1940s, when even the highest officials did not use the language of human rights (except Winston Churchill once out of office), and internationalists were concerned with the UN alone. In the 1970s, by contrast, popular mobilization and then Carter's interest kicked off a much larger and more public discussion that continues in the present."[247]

So much to the narrative of Samuel Moyn.

IV. What the three narratives teach us

All three narratives deal with the "big idea" of human rights, an idea that is so influential that Marcus Llanque in his history of political ideas has no hesitation in calling present times the "age of human rights."[248] This idea of human rights has gone through a long juridification process, and now finds expression largely in the *language of law*, to be precise, in the language of law as a *language of politics*. Despite the depressing stories of growing violations of human rights in the most recent Report of Amnesty International,[249] it can be said that the human rights idea has now imposed itself.[250]

This, however, is only one side of the coin. As the book titles "Visions Seen" and "The Last Utopia" suggest, the idea of human rights cannot be fully juridified. It can remain effective only if it keeps its visionary and utopian roots and continues to draw inspiration from them. If these roots are severed with the stamp "dealt with" as in the human rights conventions, the triad of morality, law, and politics would crumble. The human rights idea would lose its specific role as a morally grounded normative yardstick of politics. In attaining the goal of improving the world it would accordingly still be necessary to read novels and declare rights.

As "rights talk" pertinently indicates, the global dissemination of the the human rights idea has always been an ongoing *communication process*.[251] To succeed, talking about rights has always needed more than a globally comprehensible language. As a result, globalization of the human rights message

247 Moyn (2012) 157.
248 Llanque (2016) 114 ff.
249 Shetty (2017) 38 f.
250 Llanque (2016) 115.
251 See my reflections on "Global Communication about Ideas and Law" in: Schuppert, G. F. (2015) 209 ff.

necessarily poses a permanent translation problem.[252] As far as the problem of a common language is concerned, Samuel Moyn rightly stresses that the language of human rights – which also became the language of dissidence in the Soviet Union and the Eastern Bloc and of resistance against Latin American military dictatorships – could became a a "lingua franca": "It was the decision of a sector of the Latin American left to resist the regional repression in human rights terms that helped make the fortune of the concept in that region and beyond. As in the Soviet Union before, it also mattered that the language proved to be highly coalitional and ecumenical in providing a *lingua franca* for diverse voices."[253] And it is convincing that Moyn so strongly emphasizes the importance of Jimmy Carter as a human rights activist. Not in his role as successfully human rights politician but as a president of the United States who spoke the language of human rights – as "plain language." Marcus Lanque is therefore quite right to regard it as an essential function of human rights to provide a common language spanning cultural boundaries:

> "One can really make politics with human rights and not only set political goals.[254] This points to greater potential for interpreting human rights than the assumption of hegemonic liberalism will have us believe. The human rights idea had already embarked on different paths in the Universal Declaration of Human Rights. The declaration is based not only on a liberal-individualistic understanding of law but also takes account of social and political contexts. It was therefore no systemic inconsistency when in the course of decolonization the collective dimension of human rights was more strongly stressed, along with the self-determination of nations, sovereignty over natural resources, and the protection of indigenous peoples. Humanity, too, can be addressed as a subject of rights, rights to collective goods such as biodiversity, nature, water, the sea, and the atmosphere. Human rights thus provide a language at least for conceptualizing basal conflicts across all cultural differences, hence *paving the way to universal communication and cooperation*."[255]

If this is the case, it is only logical to follow Florian Hoffmann[256] in understanding the discursive nature of human rights as the key aspect. Ben Golder summarizes the argument as follows, bringing us back to the parallels with the concept of the common good:

252 See Bachmann-Medick (2012).
253 Bachmann-Medick (2012) 144.
254 Hoffmann, S. (ed.) (2010).
255 Hoffmann, S. (ed.) (2010) 122.
256 Hoffmann, F. (2006).

> "… for Hoffmann it is precisely this discursive character of human rights (human rights 'talk') that 'secures' their democratic open-endedness and incipient plurality. … Neither the 'objective' discursive meanings of human rights nor their unofficial 'subjective' articulations by individual speakers can ever finally be determined or delimited, and for him the very meaning of human rights only emerges fleetingly and from time to time when different discourses and subjective understandings of human rights encounter, affect and modify each other in 'a dynamic process of mutual feedback loops'. For Hoffmann, this 'pragmatic perspective aims to comprehend human rights discourse, not in terms of what it could be, or ought to be, but in terms of what it arguably is, namely a *plural, polycentric, and ultimately indeterminate discourse* amenable to use by nearly everybody everywhere', which is consequently 'beyond the control of those creating them, and is ultimately uncertain. There is no single correct signification and thus use of human rights'."[257]

In other words, if a global history of ideas and knowledge is to be written, the career of the language of human rights as a "language of rights" and a "language of political change" would be an essential element in the project. This being the case, we conclude this chapter with a glance at the various ways in which the language of human rights has been used in various historical contexts and by various actors.

D. The language of human rights as the language of politics at work

I. The myth of a "pure" history of ideas

Writing about human rights between politics and religion, Wolfgang Reinhard reflects on an aspect that naturally captures our attention: the history of ideas and human rights. He posits that there are no free-floating, ready-to-use ideas: they are always born and used in *an interest-driven context*:

> "Pallas Athene, the combative goddess of wisdom, is believed to have emerged fully armed from the head of Zeus. Thus the Greek myth. Ideas are similarly considered to emerge ready-to-use from the brains of geniuses. Thus the myth espoused by the history of ideas. When demythologized, the process looks more modest and more complex. Often enough, a genius merely formulates a long overdue concept. Although a cultural repository of thought provides the raw material for new ideas, these ideas first have to be formulated as they come into being. Often enough, what is new about them is that they establish and conceptualize hitherto incommunicable, perhaps even inconceivable states of affairs, even though with hindsight we can identify their beginnings and roots in the history of ideas. The new is produced by

257 Golder (2016) 694.

> certain interests under certain underlying conditions, often enough by the need *to legitimate* the outcome of a development in a changing or in an unchanged environment."[258]

This need to legitimate certain developments brings us to our next topic.

II. Two notable contexts of application for the language of human rights

1. The language of human rights as a language of legitimacy

There is no disputing that the protection of human rights is of crucial importance for the *legitimacy of the secular state*. Winfried Brugger:

> "Throughout history, the question of [the legitimation of political power] has found a variety of answers. From antiquity until well into the Middle Ages, power relations were mostly based on descent and tradition. This traditional justification of governmental power was flanked by religious justification, which until well into modern times was an essential support for secular and spiritual rule in the Western hemisphere, and in some non-Western cultures such as Islam is still so today. In the modern age, however, a third line of justification for the state has come to the fore, which, from a global point of view, must now be considered dominant. Only a state that respects human rights can count on acceptance by its citizens and describe itself as a state governed by the rule of law.
>
> The 1789 French Declaration of the Rights of Man and the Citizen states this succinctly in Article 2: 'The goal of any political association is the conservation of the natural and imprescriptible rights of man', and in Article 16: 'Any society in which the guarantee of rights is not assured, nor the separation of powers determined, has no Constitution.'
>
> Developments over the past 200 years can thus be summed up as follows: the justification of the modern state depends essentially (if not exclusively) on respect for human rights."[259]

Although it is not fully clear what finally moved the deputies of the French National Assembly to draft the Declaration of the Rights of Man and of the Citizen, they were obviously aware that the special revolutionary situation called for a fundamentally *different basis for the legitimacy of political power* than in the past:

258 Reinhard (2014) 313.
259 Brugger (1989) 538–539.

> "The Assembly finally voted on August 4 to draw up a declaration of rights without duties. No one then or since has adequately explained how opinion finally shifted in favor of drafting such a declaration, in large part because the deputies were so busy confronting day-to-day issues that they did not grasp the larger import of each of their decisions. As a result, their letters and even later memoirs proved tantalizingly vague about the shifting tides of opinion. We do know that the majority had come to believe that an *entirely new groundwork* was required. The rights of man provided the principles for *an alternative vision of government*. As the Americans had before them, the French declared rights as part of a growing rupture with established authority. Deputy Rabaut Saint-Etienne remarked on the parallel on August 18: 'like the Americans, we want to regenerate ourselves, and therefore the declaration of rights is essentially necessary'."[260]

With regard to the function of human rights as *fundamentally new legitimation concept for state power*, Hunt adds:

> "In one document, therefore, the French deputies tried to encapsulate both legal protections of individual rights *and a new grounds for governmental legitimacy*. Sovereignty rested exclusively in the nation (Article 3), and 'society' had the right to hold every public agent accountable (Article 15). No mention was made of the king, French tradition, history or custom or the Catholic Church. Rights were declared 'in the presence and under the auspices of the Supreme Being', but however 'sacred', they were not traced back to that supernatural origin. Jefferson had felt the need to assert that all men were 'endowed by their Creator' with rights; the French deduced the rights from the entirely secular sources of nature, reason, and society. During the debates, Mathieu de Montmorency had affirmed that 'the rights of man in society are eternal' and 'no sanction is needed to recognize them'. The *challenge to the old order* in Europe could not have been more forthright."[261]

2. The llanguage of human rights as the language of justification

As far as the language of law as a language of justification is concerned, we have become well acquainted with this phenomenon in connection with the language of international law. The language of human rights as – to quote Bardo Fassbender – key element of the common good under international law[262] – is clearly well suited for deployment in political controversies and conflicts, as the following examples show.

260 HUNT (2007) 130.
261 HUNT (2007) 132.
262 FASSBENDER (2003) 1 ff.

- *The suitability of the language of human rights as an element in political justificatory rhetoric.*

Samuel Moyn offers numerous examples of this suitability in his book on the history of human rights.[263] The first example concerns justification of the entry of the United States into the Second World War particularly its involvement in the struggle against Nazi Germany. The authoritative grounds were stated by Roosevelt and Churchill in the so-called Atlantic Charter. Moyn has this to say:

> "The declaration proclaimed the Allies, convinced that complete victory over their enemies is essential to defend life, liberty, independence and religious freedom, and to preserve human rights and justice in their own lands as well as in other lands'. *Human rights began first of all as a war slogan, to justify* why the Allies had to be 'now engaged in a common struggle against savage and brutal forces seeking to subjugate the world'. But no one could have said what the slogan implied."[264]

The "justificatory language"[265] of human rights, as our second example shows, proved extremely useful in justifying the founding of the United Nations, for which good reasons had be found in the light of the failure of the League of Nations: "To the extent that [the American internationalists] remained in the negotiations, human rights and other idealistic formulations *reflected a need for public acceptance and legitimacy*, as part of the rhetorical drive to distinguish the organization from prior instances of great power balance. It was a narrow portal to offer morality to enter the world, and a far cry from a utopian multilateralism based on human rights."[266]

Now to the third example: the language of human rights has played a crucial role in the political rhetoric of *anti-communism and anti-totalitarianism.* Samuel Moyn:

> "By the later 1930s, however, a dominant understanding began to crystallize in this prewar struggle over the phrase's implications: it came to *be antitotalitarian*, a meaning codified most clearly by the most prominent world figure ever to use the phrase before FDR [Frank Delano Roosevelt, G.F.S.], Pope Pius XI, in largely neglected references dating from 1973. 'Man, as a person', Pius declared in *Mit brennender*

263 Moyn (2012).
264 Moyn (2012) 49.
265 Concept in Moyn (2012) 57.
266 Moyn (2012) 59.

> *Sorge*, his famous encyclical decrying the fate of religion under the Nazis, 'possesses rights that he holds from God and which must remain, with regard to the collectivity, beyond the reach of anything that would tend to deny them, to abolish them, are to neglect them'. The pope was on his own journey, having discovered only in these years that the 'totalitarian' regimes were hostile to Christianity, after a period of judicious waiting and alliance seeking."[267]

This example is important because, especially after the Second World War, the *Christianization of human rights* was to be observed.[268] Writing about modern human rights as a task for Christians and Muslims, Heiner Bielefeldt[269] describes how, in the light of the success of the human rights idea, both Christianity and Islam have sought to claim this idea for themselves as home grown.

Very prominent was naturally the omnipresent anti-communist thrust of the language of human rights. Samuel Moyn comments:

> "Then, by 1947–48 and the crystallization of the Cold War, the West succeeded in capturing the language of human rights for *the crusade against the Soviet Union*; the language's main promoters ended up being conservatives on the European continent. Having failed to carve out a new option in the mid-1940s, human rights proved soon after to be just another way of arguing for one side in the Cold War struggle.[270] … human rights became almost immediately *associated with anticommunism*. Besides an international controversy around discrimination against South Asians in South Africa, the two major *cause célèbres* in which human rights were invoked at the United Nations and in international fora generally were *anticommunist in spirit*. In one, the Soviet Union was criticized on human rights grounds for prohibiting women who were Soviet citizens from migrating to join their foreign husbands abroad; the second, and most visible of all, revolved around the internment and trial of Cardinal József Mindszenty, The Primate of Hungary, in 1948–1949, and related abuses of Christians in Eastern Europe like the house arrest of Cardinal Josef Beran in Czechoslovakia – both campaigns occurring so quickly after the Universal Declaration as to help define its bearing."[271]

267 Moyn (2012) 50.
268 Moyn (2012) 74 ff.
269 Bielefeldt (1996).
270 Moyn (2012) 45.
271 Moyn (2012) 71.

* *The invention of responsibility to protect*

On this prominent *justification*,[272] Andreas Rödder[273] has this to say, under the heading "between human rights imperialism and indifference: responsibility to protect and humanitarian intervention":

> "The sovereignty of states and universal human rights have repeatedly been evoked as basis and ideals for the international order, especially after 1990 – and have often been at odds. The concept of *responsibility to protect*,[274] formulated in 2005 by the United Nations and adopted by 192 countries, provided a theoretical loophole. If a state failed to meet its responsibility to protect its population, the protection of people against serious violations of human rights justified armed intervention from outside and against the sovereignty of the state in question."[275]

We now make a sweeping turn to the "dynamics of the rule of law."

272 The Global Centre for the Responsibility to Protect (https://www.globalr2p.org/) summarizes this responsibility to protect by sovereign states as follows:
The R2P Concept
The Responsibility to Protect – known as R2P – refers to the obligation of states toward their populations and toward all populations at risk of genocide and other large-scale atrocities. This new international norm sets forth that:
- The primary responsibility to populations from human-made catastrophe lies with the state itself.
- When a state fails to meet that responsibility, either through incapacity or ill-will, then the responsibility to protect shifts to the international community.
- This responsibility must be exercised by diplomatic, legal, and other peaceful measures and, as a last resort, through military force.

These principles in a 2011 report of the *International Commission on Intervention and State Sovereignty* and were endorsed by the United Nations General Assembly in the *2005 World Summit Outcome Document* paragraphs 138 and 139.

273 Rödder (2015).

274 See Cohen (2012).

275 Rödder (2015) 346.

10

History of Political Ideas: Significance of Language of the Rule of Law

In concluding the third part of this book, we examine the role of the language of the rule of law[276] in the history of political ideas. The aim is not to give a detailed description of what are generally considered the elements of the rule of law[277] nor to decline the functions of rule-of-law principles.[278] We have already looked at them briefly under the heading "legal certainty as the "idée directrice" of law"[279] and in connection with the "invention of public office,"[280] so important for the rule of law. Nor will various conceptualizations be weighed up, notably whether a "thinner conception" that addresses the formal virtues of the rule of law is to be preferred over a "thicker conception" that firmly posits human rights as a crucial component thereof.[281] A great deal has been written about all these aspects (not least by the present author) and the state of discussion is relatively easy to access.[282]

Our approach is a different one. Certain key topoi of the political history of ideas are addressed to discover whether and, if so, how intensively these central topics in the history of political ideas have been discussed in the language of the rule of law or – to include the potential of the language of law – could or ought to be discussed.

The first concept to consider is the legitimacy of political authority.

276 Although there are differences between "Rechtsstaatlichkeit" and "rule of law," they do not warrant treatment as separate concepts.
277 See, for example, the treatment of the "essential elements of the rule of law principle" in: Benda (1995); on the components of the "rule of law" see Tamanaha (2007).
278 See Schuppert, G. F. (2007d).
279 Part Two, Chapter Two of this volume.
280 Part Two, Chapter One of this volume.
281 In detail, see Schuppert, G. F. (2009).
282 On the various conceptualizations of the rule of law see Schuppert, G. F. (2008b) 683–745.

A. Legitimate authority: authority based on and limited by law

The legitimacy of authority has always been a central topic in the political history of ideas and philosophy of the state.[283] Under the conditions of globalization and transnationalization, it has experienced an impressive renaissance;[284] Michael Zürn has spoken of the role of *political science as a science of legitimation*.[285] As we have seen in the preceding section on the language of human rights, invoking law and its protection has always been among the most important resources for legitimizing the authority of the state. Jean Bodin took the view that only sovereign power exercised in accordance with the law and limited by the law could claim to differ from the practices of robbers or pirates.[286] Arther Benz is probably right to assert "that limitation of state power by law and constitution is a fundamental precondition for legitimate, state authority."[287] But the relationship between power and the law, as we shall see, is somewhat more complicated.

I. The dialectical relationship between power and law: law as the basis and limitation of power

According to Hermann Heller,[288] law not only limits but also *shapes power*. This "fundamental insight into the power-shaping nature of law" means that the relationship between power and law must be seen as *dialectical*:

> "As long as law and the volitional power of the state are addressed without considering dialectical aspects, neither the particularity of law nor that of the state can be properly understood, let alone the relationship between the two. Both the validity and the positivity of law are incomprehensible without correlative mapping of state and law. Law must be recognized as the necessary condition for the modern state, and the state as the necessary condition for modern law. Without the power-shaping character of law, there is neither normative legal validity nor state power; without the law-shaping character of state power there is neither legal positivity nor state. The relationship between state and law is possible neither as undiscriminating unity nor as unbridgeable contrariety. The relationship between law and state is therefore a

283 Hofmann (2000).

284 See Nullmeier et al. (2010); Nullmeier et al. (eds.) (2012).

285 Zürn (2011a) 629.

286 Bodin (1961), I: 1–3, 128–132.

287 Benz (2006) 143.

288 Heller (1970).

> dialectical one, namely, a necessary relationship between separate spheres and inclusion of each pole in its opposite (Cohn, Theorie der Dialektik, p. 52 ff., 264 f., 287)."[289]

Marin Kriele describes this dialectical relationship between power and law in similar vein: "Power derives from law, and the law derives from power. The two seemingly exclusive propositions are nevertheless both right. Institutions of the state decide what the law is, but they decide by virtue of competence assigned to them: the organizational norms that decide on the assignment of competence can also be amended, but only by the competent institutions and through the procedures provided for this purpose."[290]

Using a somewhat different terminology, one can speak with Arthur Benz of a *duality of legitimation and limitation*, a relationship that has found its currently valid form in the idea of the *constitutional state*. According to Benz, the modern state developed as a legal order, as an institution that justifies and limits power. This duality of legitimation and limitation was based on the existence of law prescribed for the state,"[291] namely by tradition or religion. Once tradition and religion were no longer able to justify law, the institution "state" logically needed to be reinvented:

> "The legal order that constituted the state needed to be derived from sources other than tradition and religion. The history of ideas offers various approaches to solving this problem. What finally made the grade was the concept of the democratic constitutional state in which the tensions between law and state are integrated not abolished."[292]

To sum up, the language of law and its hard core, the rule-of-law principle, could with respect to the state be seen as two languages: a language of justification and a language of limitation. Arthur Benz's conclusion is that these two languages come together in the language of constitutionalism.

289 Heller (1970) 191–192.

290 Kriele (1990) 23.

291 Benz (2006) 147.

292 Benz (2006) 147.

II. The language of the rule-of-law constitution as a language of rules and procedures

If the relationship between power and law is dialectical, the question is how this relationship actually "works," how this interplay operates. The answer is in principle quite simple: certain *rules* are needed to *organize* these dialectical relations:

> "The concept of law ... points to specific characteristics of institutions and processes of institutional politics: if the state is institutionalized as a legal order, the political processes that constitute and change this order must also operate in accordance with *rules* and must not be subject to the arbitrariness of individuals or powerful groups. *Democratic processes, too, must obey rules* – by which the multitude of individual wills is transformed into a collective will. This raises the question of what rules apply for the political procedures by which the legal order of the state is established. What legitimates these rules and by what processes are they made and put into effect?"[293]

The task of providing theses indispensable *procedural rules* is given to the *constitution – understood as both institution and process*, and hence to a constitutional language that as language of rules and procedures frames the political process and thus limits it:

> "From a formal point of view, the modern state is an institution grounded in law. The law defines the functions and powers of the state, its authority. Assuming office in the state involves a limitation on the exercise of power, of power conferred under the rules of state institutions. Unlike societal organizations, the state is characterized by specific functions and competences: it alone is entitled to set universally valid and binding norms (lawmaking) and to enforce them by coercive means. But this does not vest it with boundless sovereignty. Both the content of the rules and the exercise of force are limited by law.[294] This law goes back to *procedures*, which have in turn to be set and guaranteed by the state. The limitation of power by law therefore also requires power limited by law."[295]

This view of the *state as an institution*[296] that operates by defined rules and in defined organizational forms brings us to the next point.

293 Benz (2006) 144.
294 Benz (2008) 97–109.
295 Benz (2006) 152.
296 See Anter/Bleek (2013) 89 ff.: "Der Staat als Institution."

B. The state: the organized unity of decision-making and action. The language of organizational and procedural law

I. Statehood requires organization

In his constitutional law theory, which characteristically combines legal and sociological perspectives, Hermann Heller has coined a particularly apt and hence often quoted term to describe the particularity of the institution "state" as the *"organized unity of decision-making and action"*.[297]

This definition indicates that such unity does not appear out of the blue: it *has to be organized*. Heller's key concepts are therefore *organization* and *organize*.

He has this to say about the *state as organization*:

> "In fact, the entity 'state' exists as a neither 'organic' nor fictitious human action-entity (Wirkungseinheit); it is a special type of organized action-entity. *The law of organization is the most fundamental constitutive law of the state.*[298] Its unity is true unity in an operational structure whose existence in the form of human collaboration is enabled by the action of special 'organs' consciously directed towards effective entity formation. Never ... does the relative natural or cultural uniformity of the local inhabitants in itself produce the entity state. Ultimately, this is always and only to be understood as the outcome of conscious human action, of conscious entity formation, of *organization*."[299]

Activity intent on building an organization is called *organization*, and can be described as follows:

> "*Organizing* is an activity directed towards instigating and realizing such actions (and omissions) as are necessary for the present and constantly regenerated *existence of an*

297 Heller (1970) 228 ff.

298 Heller is referring here to his preceding reflections on – to use the language of governance theory – "institution building." He notes (p. 88):
"All societal coexistence is ordered coexistence. In the merely factual, i. e., rule-driven regularities of societal action, too, societal orders find expression that lend consistency to human coexistence and the possibility of concerted collective collaboration. But it is still a big step from order to organization, from coherent societal conduct to relatively enduring unity of action ...
Collective action in manifold centres of action is integrated only where the performance of the many is – possibly compulsorily – unified and uniformly put into effect through action consciously directed towards the unity of action. This form of activity concerned with the mode and order of connecting and effectively upgrading performance can be called conscious entity building or organization."

299 Heller (1970) 230.

> *ordered structure for action* (organization). From a phenomenological standpoint there are three mutually exacting 'elements' in every organization: societal action by a number of people in cooperation; whose collaboration 2. is regularly oriented on a rule-driven order, whose setting and safeguarding is in the hands of 3. special institutions. Every group capable of deciding and acting, every collective action-entity is an organized action structure consciously constituted by institutions to achieve unity of decision and effect. The extent to which organized members are themselves also institutions depends on how cooperative or hierarchical the structure of the organization is. At any rate, every extensive organization, notably the state, is always based on the societal division of labour. The action structure we call 'state' has autonomized itself above all by assigning particular governmental functions to *special institutions*."[300]

But the production of a collective capacity for decision-making and action requires not only a certain measure of institutional concentration[301] but also, for purposes of institutional will-formation, certain *procedural rules*. Writing about premodern political procedures, Barbara Stollberg-Rilinger stresses the importance of procedural autonomy for the "*formation of a body politic with a consistent will*":

> "To distinguish between and explain various types of procedure, I propose (with reference to Luhmann) procedural autonomy as a criterion. The *need for collective political action* (for instance, warding off external enemies, dealing with public order problems, providing funding, etc.) can call for procedures to be developed that enable collective decision making and conflict management (in the language of early modernity: *procedures for building a body politic with united purpose*). If political procedures are to produce decisions accepted as binding by all those affected, and thus – even without the executive having any or only inadequate means of enforcing them – producing a collective capacity to act, if political procedures are to acquire such authority, they will require, among other things, a degree of structural autonomy from the (estates-based, hierarchical, corporative) environment."[302]

A particularly instructive example of the connection between procedural law and institutionalization are the procedural rules for the election of bishops. On the importance of this for the institution "Church", Andreas Thier remarks in his book on "Hierarchy and Autonomy":[303]

300 HELLER (1970) 231.

301 On state formation as the outcome of process on institutional agglomeration see ROKKAN (1975).

302 STOLLBERG-RILINGER (ed.) (2001) 9 f.

303 THIER (2011).

> "In late antiquity and the Middle Ages, hierarchical order and then institutional autonomy became the determining characteristics of institutional Church identity. This is particularly apparent with regard to rule-setting for the appointment of bishops. Hierarchical elements grew in importance as did the question of subject matter and reach of the autonomous decision-making powers of those involved. Decisive for these developments was the procedural manner in which bishops were appointed jointly by clergy, laymen, crown province bishops or metropolitans. Elaborated above all in the ecclesiology of Cyprian of Carthage, the notion of ordered procedure became the key guiding principle in conciliar and papal rule-setting. In such transitions from ecclesiological concepts of order to concrete arrangements, enduring regulatory traditions developed, which, especially in the eleventh century, were to gain particular normative authority. As far as media are concerned, the precondition for this tradition formation was the embedding of ecclesiastical legal culture in the written word, notably in Church canon collections. These repositories of Church legal culture ensured that the rules passed down were available. They were to become important for the further development of normative knowledge in the Church."[304]

He later adds:

> "The gradual development of rules for filling leading positions in the Church was reflected in the institutional consolidation of the Church from about the first century and in the consequent development of a structure of ecclesiastical offices."[305]

Pausing to take stock, we note that, as far as the state is concerned as decision-making and action entity, two types of law are involved whose importance is often underestimated: *organizational law* and the *law of procedure*.[306] It would be doing injustice to these two varieties of law to see them only from a practical, instrumental point of view, as elements in advanced administrative studies. Organizational and procedural law offer a great deal more. As we have seen, they are *important control parameters* in governmental and administrative action,[307] and thus – in our terminology – two highly important languages of politics. We consider two examples.

304 Thier (2011) XI.

305 Thier (2011) 15.

306 From the public administration perspective on organization and procedure as control level of administrative action, see Schuppert, G. F. (2000) 544 ff., 772 ff.

307 For a detailed treatment of organizational law, see Schuppert, G. F. (2012b).

II. Organizational and procedural law as manifestations of law relevant to the history of ideas: two examples

1. The example of the separation of powers

The organizational principle of the separation of powers clearly has a fascination for exponents of constitutional law theory. It is treated at length in every "theory of the state", perhaps not least because it offers an opportunity to honour one of the heroes of the political history of ideas, Charles de Secondat Baron de la Brède et de Montesquieu.[308] The "idée directrice" of the separation of powers principle is to *prevent the abuse of power* through an institutional arrangement of mutual constraints[309] constituting a system of "checks and balances."[310] Roman Herzog, for example comments as follows on this broadly accepted understanding of separation of powers theory:

> "... Since it first found literary expression in the eighteenth century, separation of powers theory has posited that the institutions of the limited power complex that results from the separation of powers ought not to encounter one another with indifference but *check* one another; i. e., impel each other to exercise power correctly and *restrain one another from abusing power*. If one is not prepared to accept that loyal holders of power do this in violation of the fundamental limits to their responsibilities, it will be necessary to conceive of the separation of powers not as the assignment of responsibilities that leads to hermetic closure but as *a system of mutually overlapping jurisdictions* within which each power is tied to concurrent acts of will by different office holders. Historically, separation of powers theory has consequently never led to clean-cut divisions between different branches of government but always to a more or less stable, extremely complicated system of mutually overlapping powers and participatory rights. To be exact, such overlap does not, as is often assumed, violate the principle: it necessarily arises from it in the pursuit of mutual constraint."[311]

We do not really need to know more about the organizational principle of the separation of powers, nor to ascertain whether, in party-state democracy, we are perhaps dealing with interlocking or even entangled powers.[312] Our sole concern is to show that a principle of the law pertaining to the organization of the state has operated since the eighteenth century as a language of politics.

308 On Montesquieu's separation of powers theory see Imboden (1959); Kägi (1961).

309 See Fleiner/Basta Fleiner (2004) 236 ff.

310 Benz (2008) 151 f.

311 Herzog (1971) 229–230.

312 Herzog (1971) 235.

2. The example of bureaucracy

Particularly from the perspective of the history of ideas, bureaucracy is especially interesting because – almost more than separation of powers theory – it reveals the close links between seemingly technico-institutional organizational arrangements and notions about the *legitimacy of state power*. Our concern is not the efficiency of bureaucratic administration or adding to the ever popular, trite criticism of bureaucracy so rife since Franz Kafka and Heimito von Doderer,[313,314] but with bureaucracy as the embodiment of an – extremely successful[315] – type of modern "domination." Predictably and inevitably this places us in the company of Max Weber.

Weber identifies various types of domination defined in terms of legitimation basis. He distinguishes three pure types: charismatic, traditional, and the legal, rational domination characteristic of the modern state. The last is based on belief in the legality of the set order and the right of those called upon to exercise such power to issue commands. Weber's basic thesis[316] is that the last type of domination requires exercise of a specific type, namely administration that implements the set order and applies rules; that, being rule-bound, acts in accordance with learnable routines, which convey predictable and rational decision-making behaviour. *This type of domination is called bureaucracy.*

According to Maximilian Wallerath, the function ascribed to it was "to ensure the ousting of absolutist and feudal regimes by legal-rational governance structures. Personal, patriarchal power and subjective arbitrariness was to be replaced by rational rule on the basis of law and superior purposiveness."[317]

The rule-boundedness that Max Weber repeatedly emphasises gives a hierarchically organized bureaucratic administration, as Horst Dreier point

313 One of my favourite books deserves a mention here: Doderer (1951) [engl. transl. (2000)].

314 See Seibel (2016) 132 ff.

315 On bureaucratic administration as model for success in modern administrative culture, see Schuppert, G. F. (2006).

316 Good accounts of Weberian bureaucracy in Albrow (1972) and in Mayntz (ed.) (1968) 27 ff.: Max Webers Idealtypus der Bürokratie und die Organisationssoziologie.

317 Wallerath (2000) 363.

out,[318] doubly *grounding in constitutional law*: as legal domination it is rooted in the rule-of-law principle and in the democracy principle as authority implementing democratically produced policy programmes cast in the form of enacted law.

> "With regard to democracy, the *binding nature of enacted law and checks on the executive branch* are of crucial importance for politics. Bureaucratic administration is nothing other than an instrument for enforcing laws and programmes that have been produced by democratic procedures. No considerations other that compliance with the law should feed into decisions. Formality and the written form permit the lawfulness of administrative action to be examined and to correct unlawful decisions. Hierarchical organization ensures the accountability of administrative authorities to parliament: the responsible minister must be able to rely on his instructions, for which he is accountable to parliament, being carried out by even by the lowest-ranking officers in his department."[319]

And this bureaucratic administration has not only been grounded in the rule of law and democracy but is also the key agent in *dealing with societal modernization processes in society*, as Lutz Raphael rightly stresses:

> "Administrative authorities in the nineteenth century had to cope with unheard of *acceleration in economic and social processes*; indeed, at times the administration itself sought to trigger or accelerate this dynamic. The administrative state under the rule of law was a regulatory side effect of far-reaching social, cultural, and above all economic mobilization processes. Whatever labels are attached to these critical junctures in the development of European history – whether modernization, modernity, onset of the capitalist world order, or whatever – the *services and functions of bureaucracy have always been an indispensable element of this transition*, and are among the formative bases if our current world, however sceptical and suspicious one might be about their future."[320]

In all, the example of bureaucracy shows that both the language of state organization and the language of administrative organization operate not primarily as the languages of a technico-instrumental organization theory but as languages of politics, as the political debates and disputes of the nineteenth century impressively demonstrate.

318 Dreier, H. (1991) 125 ff.
319 Benz (2001) 131–132.
320 Raphael (2000) 12.

C. Justice through the rule of law? The idea of institutional justice

I. Buon governo e giustizia[321]

It is doubtless part and parcel of the political history of ideas and the philosophy of the state that good government has above all to be just government. For example, Philippe Mastronardi's work on constitutional theory bears the revealing subtitle "general constitutional law as theory of the good and just state";[322] and Arthur Benz, writing on the state as legal order, notes that: "Even before the state appeared on the stage of history, political theoreticians had recognized that good government obtains only if it *serves the common good and justice*. Greek and Roman antiquity sought guarantees for good government in the constitutional order. By this they understood the division of responsibilities and governmental functions in the hope that this would either produce *just holders of power* or restrain the exercise of power and prevent it from going against the common good and justice. Constitutional theory with its distinction between good and degenerate constitutions systematized the possibilities of separating governmental functions."[323]

As this passage shows, there are basically two ways to ensure just rule: training power holders to become *just ruler personalities* or creating *power structures that guarantee justice*.

As far as justice personified in the just prince was concerned, it was thought in the seventeenth and eighteenth centuries that it could be fostered by "manuals on good government",[324] a widespread literary genre that went by the name of "Fürstenspiegel".[325] Foremost among the virtues of the Christian prince was justice, as Hans-Otto Mühleisen notes with reference to Erasmus of Rotterdam:

> "The Christian prince can rightly claim that his subjects know and respect the law if he himself knows and obeys the laws of the Supreme Ruler Christ, i. e., if he

321 As the knowledgeable reader will immediately recognize, this title refers to Lorenzetti's famous Siennese allegory of good government, in which the figure of Giustizia plays a central role. For a comprehensive interpretation of the allegory see the superb book by Heyen (2013) 53 ff.

322 Mastronardi (2007).

323 Benz (2006) 144–145.

324 Müller (1985) 594.

325 Greater detail in Skallweit (1957).

> commits himself to justice. As a Christian, the prince can propitiate God best through a caring attitude towards his people in government'. The cross is laid upon him, which from an Erasmian point of view is equivalent to justice: 'If you do what is right; if you do violence to no man; if you sell no office and accept no bribe, even if your purse suffers harm. Be steadfast and take care above all that you *gain the prize of justice*'."[326]

The mists of time have veiled this variant on securing the just exercise of power through personalization, despite Pierre Rosanvallon's return to the literary tradition in a recent book.[327] The notion of promoting justice through just institutions has gained more and more ground. Discussing current theories of justice, Bernd Ladwig notes:

> "Whoever acts justly contributes directly or indirectly to just conditions. If everyone treated everyone with respect, the direct result would be a state of all-round mutual respect. If more people donate to OXFAM than before, the indirect result would probably be that more would be done to combat hunger in the world. Perhaps the most important thing, however, that anyone can do for justice is to *support just institutions*. Institutions are the focus of judgments about justice that seek its realization. There are good reasons for this. Institutions and institutional orders play an essential role in whether and how justice imprints itself on our world. Modern philosophers and economists have therefore placed greater value on institutions and societal structures as opposed to individuals and their virtues. The expectations of justice have since weighed less heavily on the shoulders of the individual. Most theories of justice now focus not on the qualities of the individual but the *properties of institutions*."[328]

This invites us to take a brief look at the idea of institutional justice.

II. The idea of institutional justice

Rainer Forst presents highly interesting thoughts on the idea of institutional justice[329] in his consideration of transnational justice and democracy.[330] First he joins us in rejecting the *dominance of distributive justice*, above all because it neglects the question of who makes decisions on distributing goods, by what procedures, and in what institutional contexts: "These recipient-oriented perspectives centred on goods and distribution hide essential

326 Mühleisen (1999).
327 Rosanvallon (2018).
328 Ladwig (2011) 47 f.
329 See, above all, Rawls (1979) and Höffe (2010).
330 Forst (2012).

aspects of justice. First, the question of how the goods to be distributed come into being, and hence the question of production and its just organization. But still more important, the political question is disregarded of who decides on the structures of production and distribution and how – as if there were a vast distribution engine that only needs to be correctly programmed."[331]

However, if the main concern is who, by what procedures, and in what institutional contexts decides the distribution of generally scarce goods, institutions need to be developed that can be expected to promote justice. Justitia is "a goddess created by humanity who comes into the world to banish arbitrariness; she is therefore present wherever arbitrariness prevails (or threatens). *She therefore demands specific institutions* – for instance, a *legitimate legal situation* in the place of the "natural state" of arbitrariness; but she cannot presuppose what she demands."[332]

We agree with Forst that, from this point of view, justice is an institutional virtue: "*Justice* is a relational, as well as an *institutional virtue*; it does not refer to all asymmetrical relations between human beings without discrimination, but it does refer to those which exhibit forms of rule or domination and social arbitrariness – wither in contexts involving only sparse legal regulation or in thicker institutional contexts, within and beyond the state."[333]

This is only a short step away from identifying *two types of justice-related institutions*: "It is also important to distinguish between institutions necessary for realizing justice and institutions or (more or less institutionalized) conditions that make justice necessary and 'promote' it. We can call these practices *promoting justice* or *requiring justice*."[334]

Modifying Forst's terminology and with reference to the institutional economics work of Douglass North, John Joseph Wallis, and Barry R. Weingast on the one hand [335] and Daron Acemoglu and James A. Robinson on the other,[336] we propose to speak of institutions *inhibitive of justice* – that

331 Forst (2012) 31.
332 Forst (2012) 37.
333 Forst (2012) 38–39.
334 Forst (2012) 41.
335 North et al. (2009).
336 Acemoglu/Robinson (2013).

favour arbitrariness – and institutions *conducive to justice*, drawing a distinction between these two types of institution.[337]

As regards justice, we now turn to the *substance* of the rule of law – a principle that is a pillar of our body politic.

III. The justice genes of the rule of law

When considering institutions conducive to justice, the institution of the rule of law cannot be left aside: it is regarded as a bulwark against injustice and arbitrariness. Michael Stolleis has this to say:[338] "Throughout the First World War and the Weimar Republic, 'Rechtsstaat', 'l'état de droit', 'rule of law' stood for state action bounded by law and accountable to the courts, for an independent judiciary, and, in a broader sense, also for an incorruptible public service committed to the public good: all in all, for protection of the individual against arbitrariness";[339] We begin with this bulwark function of the rule of law.

1. Law and arbitrariness

Horst Dreier[340] addresses the opposition between law and arbitrariness that Rainer Forst has described:

> "Little seems to be so clear and undeniable as the irreconcilable opposition between law and arbitrariness; at any rate, if we take arbitrariness in the now current sense of the term to mean erratic, indiscriminate, high-handed action without apparent rational motivation or understandable grounds. *The term wears, so to speak, reproval on its sleeve.* Arbitrariness thus seems to be more or less the quintessence of flouting the notion of law and the central functions of every legal order. This explains such widespread assertions as 'arbitrariness and law are in principle opposites', or, even stronger, arbitrariness is the '*counter-concept to justice*' or 'blatant injustice'. And, indeed, where law is to serve as a conflict resolution tool, to guarantee expectational security, and to enable people to live together in freedom and equality, it can

337 North et al. (2009), Acemoglu/Robinson (2013) explain the difference between these two types of institutions, taking the example of institutions with restricted access (inhibitive of justice) and institutions with unrestricted access (conducive to justice).

338 Stolleis (2012).

339 Stolleis (2012) 49.

340 Dreier, H. (2012).

> perform these fundamental tasks only if laws and their application are seen to further not arbitrariness but reliability and predictability, not to be playing a game of blind man's buff."[341]

The ideational value of law in relation to justice derives chiefly from the control function of law in modern societies:

> "If, as a specific social technique, law is to steer human co-existence, arbitrariness has no place. In 'The Concept of Law', first published in 1961, H.L.A. Hart posits that universal, general and binding norms are at the very core of justice. It would be a contradiction in terms when setting norms to apply arbitrariness as a principle."[342]

So far so good.

But this undoubted inclination of law towards justice tells us nothing about whether the institution of the rule of law deserves to be called conducive to justice. A look at the institutional virtues of the rule of law will help justify the epithet.

2. The institutional virtues of the rule of law conducive to justice

In addressing the institutional virtues of the rule of law, we are referring to the rule of law that developed in the course of the nineteenth century as a "political programme"[343] directed towards protecting civil liberties through the legal limitation and disciplining of state authority.[344] In what follows, we are concerned not with a *material concept of the rule of law* – predominant after 1945 in response to the abuse of law under the Nazi regime – aiming to "*produce a materially just legal state of affairs.*"[345] What is at issue is a rule of law not confined to formal guarantees – and which can therefore be dismissed as unpolitical – but an institution whose components – the separation of powers, an independent judiciary, lawful administration, and the guarantee of comprehensive legal protection – are committed to the material goal of a just order of the body politic, with an unassailable hard core[346] that

341 Dreier, H. (2012) 1–2.

342 Dreier, H. (2012) 2–3.

343 Stolleis (2012) 47.

344 Instructive on the civic rule of law programme: Raphael (2000) 26 ff.

345 Böckenförde (1976) 65–92, here 81.

346 The Bertelsmann Transformation Index 2003, Gütersloh 2004, for instance, counts the following four elements as belonging to the basal architecture of the rule of law: 1. To what extent are the branches of government independent and interdependent? 2. Is there

enhances the chances of (as Höffe would have put it) things being just in the world.

It is therefore not about playing off the material rule of law against the formal rule of law but about assessing the intrinsic value of formal legal guarantees and ordered procedures and their contribution to realizing a just order of the state and society. Ernst-Wolfgang Böckenförde describes the *indivisible unity* of the formal and material aspects of the institution of the rule of law:

> "The call for the material rule of law overlooks or underestimates the intrinsic importance, *the material intrinsic importance of formal legal guarantees and ordered procedures*. It is precisely formal guarantees and procedures that shield and protect individual and societal freedom by warding off direct action against individuals or societal groups in the name of absolute enacted or believed material content or so-called values; in this they prove to be institutions of freedom; they have little to do with formalism, let alone positivism. This dismantling of freedom by totalitarian regimes never begins with the exploitation of formal guarantees and procedures but always with them being disregarded in the name of a higher, material, and pre-positive law, be it the 'true religion', the 'homogeneous national community' or the 'proletariat'. Only at the second stage, when the new law has been installed as a means of revolutionary change, does the positivism and legalism of totalitarian regimes arise."[347]

To sum up, it is the institutional virtues of the rule of law that are directed towards enabling and promoting justice as an institutional virtue. We can therefore speak of the rule of law as an institution that promotes justice. This brings us to our next topic.

D. How much rule of law is there in good governance?[348]

A great deal. A glance at the elements generally considered to constitute the core of this worldwide, globally operative "guiding principle of state-

an independent judiciary? 3. Is the abuse of power by representatives legally or politically sanctioned? And 4. To what extent are civil liberties (human rights, judicial rights, anti-discrimination laws, freedom of religion) in place and to what extent is violation actionable?

347 Böckenförde (1976) 82–83.

348 With reference to Kötter (2013).

hood"[349] shows why this is so. Franz Nuscheler offers a catalogue of the most current good governance criteria:[350]

- "Establishment of functioning administrative structures and / or administrative reforms for improved management of the public sector;
- Accountability of the rulers to the ruled and their elected representatives;
- Transparent governmental and administrative action, especially in the use of financial resources, which also require independent auditing;
- The rule of law, i. e., the binding effect of law and institutionalized law enforcement, which provide legal certainty for investors and safeguard property rights;
- And combating corruption."

This catalogue alone shows that, almost without exception, the criteria listed come under the broad rubric of what we have called the "*institutional virtues of the rule of law*." At the latest, however, the high rule-of-law content of good governance becomes fully clear when we consider "combating corruption"; after all, corruption is the paramount example of "bad governance."[351] This also explains why fighting corruption ranks so high on the agenda of exponents of the good governance concept. It is therefore all the more worth noting that the distinguished Romanian corruption scholar Alina Mungiu-Pippidi declares that only an "*institutional approach*" can succeed in the battle against corruption. In "Corruption: Diagnosis and Treatment"[352] she proposes distinguishing between two fundamentally different "rules of the game" practised in a society: "*particularism*" and "*universalism*." By "particularism" she means a culture of privileges,[353] whereas "universalism" de-

349 Dolzer (2004).

350 Nuscheler (2009) 13 f.

351 See Mungiu-Pippidi (2006) 86: "Political corruption poses a serious threat to democracy and its consolidation. One year after the widely acclaimed Orange Revolution in Ukraine, one could already buy, though not very cheaply, a seat in the Ukrainian parliament. The lack of success in curbing corruption, combined with ever more widespread discussion of the issue, renders voters extremely cynical and threatens to subvert public trust in emerging democracies." On the phenomenon of "bad governance", especially in developing countries, Moore, M. (2001).

352 Mungiu-Pippidi (2006).

353 Mungiu-Pippidi (2006) 88: "A culture of privilege reigns in societies based on particularism, making *unequal treatment the accepted norm in society*. Individuals struggle *to belong to the privileged group* rather than to change the rules of the game. … Influence, not money, is the main currency, and the benefits to an individual anywhere in the chain are hard to measure: Favors are distributed or denied as part of a customary exchange with rules of its own, sometimes not involving direct personal gain for the 'gatekeeper'."

scribes an attitude prevailing in society "where equal treatment applies to everyone regardless of the group to which one belongs."[354] To behave "particularistically", however – it should be realized – is in keeping with the "human nature" and is therefore so widespread:

> "Particularism is not a social 'malady', as corruption is usually described, but rather a default, natural state, and therefore arises frequently. Social psychology provides considerable evidence that the nature of man is sectarian, and that social identity results from biased intergroup comparison and self-enhancing behaviour. Humans naturally favor their own family, clan, race, or ethnic group – what Edward C. Banfield[355] called 'amoral familism'. Treating the rest of the world fairly seems to be a matter of extensive social learning and sufficient resources. Societies which have travelled furthest from that natural state of affairs and have produced a state which treats everyone equally and fairly are exceptions and products of a long historical evolution. Such evolution should not be taken for granted; indeed, as James Q. Wilson[356] argues, universalism and individualism, which spread in the West after the Enlightenment to become generally agreed norms, are neither natural nor necessarily and invariably good principles. To understand individual behavioural choice, an understanding of governance context is therefore indispensable, and anticorruption strategies created in disregard to this are predetermined to fail."[357]

If this is the case, then fighting against corruption is not a problem of combating individual misconduct. What is needed is to *change the "rules of the game"* and thus – if sets of rules in the social-science sense are understood as institutions[358] – to take an *institutional approach*:

> "Corruption in society is therefore not conceptualized in this book as an aggregate of individual corruption. The non-corrupt countries at the top of Transparency International's Corruption Perception Index (CPI) do not differ from countries on the bottom simply by the number of individuals engaged in corrupt acts, *but by their institutions*; in other words, by *the rules of the game* influencing power distribution and the shaping of the allocation of public resources. The countries at the top of the Control of Corruption scale managed *to institutionalize* open and nondiscriminative access at some point in their past, and so their institutions differ substantially from the ones at the bottom. … Many countries in the middle struggle between two worlds, for in them both universalistic and particularistic practices coexist, more or less competitively. … But regardless of how wide the variation might be, some sort of invisible threshold exists between a society where ethical

354 Mungiu-Pippidi (2006) 88.
355 Banfield (1958).
356 Wilson, J. (1993).
357 Mungiu-Pippidi (2015) 23–24.
358 Good overview in Immergut/Jäger (2008).

> universalism is the norm and one where the norm is particularism – and one can predict fairly well what treatment and what share of public resources to expect from the state if one knows where one stands in the status ranks."[359]

Given her "institutional approach", it is not surprising that Alina Mungiu-Pippidi has adopted the institutional economics distinction between institutions *with and without restricted access*, integrating it in the following overview[360] of four different governance regimes. The table, which can be read as a scale of the rule-of-law content of various governance regimes, brings this section to a close.

Governance Regimes and their Main Features

Governance regimes	Limited access order			Open access order (Universalism)
	Patrimonialism	Competitive particularism	Borderline	
Power distribution	Hierarchical with monopoly of central power	Stratified with power disputed competitively	Competitive with less stratification	Citizenship. Equality
State autonomy	State captured by ruler	State captured in turn by winners of elections	Archipelago of autonomy and captured 'islands'	State autonomous from private interest (legal lobby, etc)
Public resources	Particular and predictable	Particular but unpredictable	Particular and universal	Ethical universalism
Separation public-private	No	No	Poor	Sharp
Relation formal/informal institutions	Informal institutions substitutive of formal ones	Informal institutions substitutive of formal ones	Competitive and substitutive	Complementary
Mentality	Collectivistic	Collectivistic	Mixed	Individualistic
Government accountability	No	Only when no longer in power	Occasional	Permanent
Rule of law	No; sometimes 'thin'	No	Elites only	General; 'thick'

359 Mungiu-Pippidi (2015) 23.
360 Mungiu-Pippidi (2015) 29.

E. Rule of law promotion and rule of law control as policy instruments

I. Panacea: the rule of law?

Promotion of the rule of law is among the favourite projects of the Western world, notably in the Federal Republic of Germany.[361] The present author contributed to conceptualizing a major conference devoted to this subject, held in Berlin on 15th January 2009 under the heading "The Rule of Law – Patent Recipe for All the World? Promoting the Rule of Law in Foreign Policy".[362]

The popularity of "rule of law promotion" has not declined, rather the opposite. In "Rule of Law Dynamics",[363] published in 2012, no fewer than five contributions are devoted to rule of law promotion:

- A Comparison of the Rule of Law Policies of Major Western Powers[364]
- Rule of Law Promotion through International Organization and NGOs[365]
- Civil Military Cooperation in Building the Rule of Law[366]
- Developing a Theoretical Framework for Evaluating Rule of Law Promotion in Developing Countries[367] and
- Rule of Law Promotion after Conflict: Experimenting in the Kosovo Laboratory[368]

The array of rule of law activities, their intensity and financial scale have given occasion to speak of a "rule of law promotion industry."[369] Particularly interesting about the phenomenon[370] is the interrelatedness of this actor constellation, since it clearly reveals the *genuinely political nature of rule of law promotion*. Jane Stromseth, David Wippman, and Rosa Brooks have identified three groups of actor:

361 See – somewhat at random – Konrad Adenauer Stiftung (ed.) (2009); Federal Foreign Office (ed.) (2007).
362 Auswärtiges Amt (ed.) (2009).
363 Zürn et al. (eds.) (2012).
364 Schimmelpfennig (2012) 111 ff.
365 Heupel (2012) 133 ff.
366 Röder (2012) 206 ff.
367 Gillespie (2012) 233 ff.
368 Zajac-Sannerholm (2012) 252 ff.
369 See Carothers (ed.) (2006).
370 See "The Rule of Law Revival", in: Schuppert, G. F. (2008b) 683 ff.

> "The *World Bank and multinational corporations* want the rule of law, because the sanctity of private property and the enforcement of contracts are critical to modern conceptions of the free market. ... *Human rights advocates*, though not typically allies of multinational corporations, business interests, or international financial institutions, are similarly enthusiastic about the rule of law. ... The human rights-oriented conception of the rule of law involves, at a minimum, due process, equality before the law, and judicial checks on executive power, for most human rights advocates regard these as essential prerequisites to the protection of substantive human rights. ... Increasingly, international and national *security experts* also want to promote the rule of law, seeing it as a key aspect of preventing terrorism. Especially since September 11, 2001, military and intelligence analysts have drawn attention to the ways in which the absence of the rule of law can lead to instability and violence and create fertile recruiting grounds for terrorist organizations. ..."[371]

The point to be made here is that the language of rule of law promotion in its most advanced form is a language of politics.

II. The new EU framework to strengthen the rule of law

The European Union sees itself not only as an economic community, a community of law, and a political community, but also as a community of values.[372] This conception is expressed in Article 2 of the Treaty on European Union, as amended by the Treaty of Lisbon:

> "The Union is founded on the values of respect for human dignity, liberty, democracy, equality, the rule of law and respect for human rights, including the rights of persons belonging to minorities. These values are common to the Member States in a society in which pluralism, non-discrimination, tolerance, justice, solidarity and equality between women and men prevail."

In order to maintain the cohesion of this community of values, Article 7 of the EUT introduces a special procedure to be applied if a Member State infringes fundamental principles. Since this is indeed bringing up the big guns, the definition of such infringement and the conceivable consequences are set out as follows (Article 7 paras. 1 and 3 of the EUT in excerpt):

> "On a reasoned proposal by one third of the Member States, by the European Parliament or by the European Commission, the Council, acting by a majority of four fifths of its members after obtaining the consent of the European Parliament, may determine that there is a clear risk of a serious breach by a Member State of the

371 Stromseth et al. (2006) 58 f.
372 See Joas/Mandry (2005).

> values referred to in Article 2. Before making such a determination, the Council shall hear the Member State in question and may address recommendations to it, acting in accordance with the same procedure.
>
> Where a determination under paragraph 2 has been made, the Council, acting by a qualified majority, may decide to suspend certain of the rights deriving from the application of this Treaty to the Member State in question, including the voting rights of the representative of the government of that Member State in the Council."

In March 2014, the Commission published a communication presenting a "framework to safeguard the rule of law in the European Union":[373] "Although it does not permit new types of legally binding measure, it does substantially strengthen the role of the Union in this field. The Communication establishes a pre-Article 7 procedure and thus introduces general and continuous monitoring. Such a framework to safeguard the rule of law is per se a new tool and also a major step in integration policy."[374]

Three characteristics mark this *genuinely political* tool offered by the rule of law framework. Armin von Bogdandy and Michael Ioannidis:

> "The first characteristic is specific reference to the rule of law. It can therefore not be used to protect all the fundamental values listen in Article 2 TEU but only to uphold the – broadly defined – principle of the rule of law, that is regarded as the 'foundation of all values upon which the Union is based'.
>
> A second characteristic of the rule of law framework is the assumption that the rule of law is upheld in Member States of the Union. Isolated cases of breaches of fundamental rights or miscarriages of justice are not sufficient grounds to activate the framework. It can be activated only in extreme situations that adversely affect 'the integrity, stability and proper functioning of the institutions and mechanisms established at national level to secure the rule of law'. The Commission terms such situations 'systemic breakdown'.
>
> A third characteristic is that, under the framework, the Commission assumes a stronger role in safeguarding the rule of law than is assigned to it under Article 7 TEU: the framework is triggered solely by the Commission, and it makes all decisions without the collaboration of other institutions. This does not prevent it from drawing on the expertise of other EU institutions and international organizations, such as the Venice Commission of the Council of Europe."[375]

373 Communication from European Commission (2014).

374 Bogdandy/Ioannidis (2014).

375 Bogdandy/Ioannidis (2014) 39.

* *Concluding remarks*

Looking back over the reflections on the "language of the rule of law" presented in this chapter, it is clear that it is not only an important language of the political history of ideas but that has also shaped the latter since antiquity. This has not only been so with regard to the "obvious cases" of the legitimacy of political authority, good government as the just exercise of power, and equal application of the law; it also holds true for two more specific variants of the language of law: organizational law – viz "separation of powers" – and procedural law – viz rule-bound bureaucratic administration. Finally, the thoughts on the rule-of-law content of "good governance" and the EU Rule of Law Framework have shown that arguing in the "language of the rule of law" can be of considerable practical political importance.

Part 4
Global History of Political Ideas: Major Legal Concepts

The third part of this book addressed the role of various legal regimes and legal principles in a global history of ideas and knowledge: natural law, international law, human rights, and the rule of law. We turn now to the importance of key legal concepts in the global history of political ideas. Such a project necessarily requires a choice to be made from among the concepts that play a significant role in more than one discipline. We have opted for the following four:[1]

- *State, state authority*
- *Sovereignty*
- *Constitution*
- *Contract*

These are all concepts that play a crucial role not only in the home disciplines of the present author – constitutional law and theory of the state (*Staatsrecht* and *Staatslehre*) – but also in other academic disciplines such as political science, historiography (witness Reinhard's "Geschichte der Staatsgewalt"[2]), sociology, political philosophy, and public administration. However, since we are particularly interested in the *role of the language of law*, in discussing these four concepts we shall be focusing on how much *legal content* they have. Only then can we decide how important the language of law is in a global history of ideas and knowledge.

We begin our conceptual expedition with the concept of state.

1 A fifth would be property, but this concept is addressed in separate study, already completed in manuscript form, to be published under the title "Property – Intellectual and Social History of a Legal Institution" ("Eigentum – Ideen- und Sozialgeschichte eines Rechtsinstituts").

2 Reinhard (1999).

11

The Concept of State and its Authority

A good place to start finding out about the concept of state is to consult an encyclopedia of the state[3] or politics,[4] a manual of political philosophy and social philosophy,[5] or the now standard work on the modern state by Arthur Benz.[6] The information they offer is discouraging: there appears to be consensus that it is difficult if not impossible to define the state. Arthur Benz quotes Raymond Boudon and Francois Bourricaud to the effect that "defining the state is an almost hopeless task".[7] With almost moving intensity, Josef Isensee, a leading German teacher of constitutional law, describes the inevitable *"relativity of all concepts of the state"*:

> "What the *state* is cannot be reduced to a single concept or captured by a scholastic definition. This is in the nature of the subject: the complexity and spatio-temporal mutability of state phenomena. A concept can capture only one of countless aspects of 'the state'. Consequently, all concepts of the state are necessarily relative, and many such concepts are accordingly needed. An approximative picture can emerge only from the multitude of aspects that come into view in circumnavigating the topic. The state as the subject matter of scholarly research requires both normative and empirical methods. It is addressed by many disciplines: legal, philosophical, historical, economic, political and other 'social-scientific' fields of study: all that traditionally constitute the → '*Staatswissenschaften*' ('sciences of the state') in the broadest sense of the term. → *Staatslehre* ('theory of the state)."[8]

Given these difficulties, various strategies can be considered. Christoph Möller suggests following the Anglo-American pattern of simply doing without a definition;[9] or one could ask whether a concept of state is really necessary.[10]

3 In Germany, encyclopaedias of the state (Staatslexika) traditionally have a denominational orientation. Apart from the Catholic "Staatslexikon in fünf Bänden" by the Görres-Gesellschaft (ed.) (1989), there is the Protestant "Evangelisches Staatslexikon" by Heun et al. (eds.) (2006).

4 See, for example, Fuchs / Roller (2007).

5 Gosepath et al. (eds.) (2008).

6 Benz (2008).

7 Boudon / Bourricaud (1992) 540–549, here 540.

8 Isensee (1989) col. 134.

9 Möllers (2006).

10 Benz (2008) is convinced that it is necessary (6): "We need the concept of state to describe an institution of modern societies performing important services indispensable for the continued existence and quality of society. This is where a substantial part of politics takes

We are firmly convinced that such *avoidance strategies* are not the solution: the manifest, enduring role of the state as key governance actor[11] makes it more necessary than ever to map out the contours of the concept.[12] Our strategy is to circle the object "state" to gain a closer view from three different angles – in the hope that the intersections will throw the "nature" of the state into relief, teaching us something about the role of the language of law in the process. The itinerary proceeds under three headings:

- *Functions of the state and the role of law*
- *The state as form of rule and the role of law*
- *State semantics and the role of the language of law*

A. Functions of the state and the role of law

In his key article on the state in the Görres Society dictionary, Josef Isensee lists six *functional characteristics of the modern state* (for which he reserves the term "state").[13]

- The modern state as an *entity of peace*
- The modern state as a *decision-making entity*
- The modern state as an *action entity*
- The modern state as a *legal entity*
- The modern state as a *power entity*
- The modern state as a *solidarity association*

The following samples all show that these various entities cannot be described without the help of law and its language. This hold true in the first place for the modern state as peace entity: "The modern state … has brought peace to society, disarmed the citizenry, and replaced self-justice *by*

place and will do so for the foreseeable future." Unlike concepts such as government, administration, governance, etc., "state" captures the specific *form of authority* that has developed in modern society. The concept also helps us understand changes in politics and society. We may be experiencing a fundamental shift towards a system of rule that can be clearly distinguished from what we call the state. But it is perhaps not the form but only the content and procedures of state authority that are changing, which does not necessarily mean that the challenges facing government and administration are any less daunting.

11 See, in substantive agreement, Anter (2013) 17 ff.; and Schuppert, G. F. (2013a) 29 ff.

12 See Schuppert, G. F. (2018a).

13 Isensee (1989) col. 136.

procedure … This *obligation* of the citizen *to keep the peace*is the counterpart of the state's *monopoly of force*."[14] Still more evident is the situation with the state as decision-making entity: "In accordance with a given *division of powers and rules of procedure*, the state deals with disputes that affect public welfare and whose settlement cannot be left to societal self-regulation."[15]

We have already discussed the modern state as an *action entity* (Hermann Heller: *Handlungs- und Wirkungseinheit*) at some length: it is the law as *organizational and procedural law* that produces this entity and renders it viable. And the state as a *legal entity* requires no further comment. With regard to the state as a *power entity*, power, too, is organization through law: "The basis is the monopoly of legitimate physical violence (Max Weber). Only the state has the right to use coercion and to maintain organized coercive potential: police, army, administrative or judicial execution and enforcement. *By virtue of these tools*, it differs from non-state associations. Indeed, the means, not the ends constitute its particularity."[16] Finally, the state as a *solidarity association* is also constituted legally: "State solidarity is legally constituted and organized as a (territorial) body corporate, and thus as a legal person that lends the association legal identity regardless of shifting membership. Membership of the corporate association of the state, of the nation arises from citizenship."[17]

In brief, the state as a viable actor is constituted by law, above all by organizational and procedural law. If we add what we have learned in discussing rule-of-law principles about the function of law in establishing and limiting power, we can join Arthur Benz in describing the "*authority of the state under the rule of law*" as follows:

> "Sovereignty and the authority of the state as integral part of the institutional order of the state are limited by law. Only to the extent that they serve to realize the law are they considered legitimate power. This does nothing to lessen their coercive nature for those affected. But they find recognition only in conjunction with the structures of a democratic state under the rule of law. Their exercise is entrusted to special institutions of democratic lawmaking, bureaucratic administration, and the judiciary. The coercive power of the modern state is therefore necessarily tied to the form of enacted law and the structure of a democratic state under the rule of law."[18]

14 Isensee (1989) col. 136.
15 Isensee (1989) col. 136.
16 Isensee (1989) col. 137.
17 Isensee (1989) col. 138.
18 Benz (2008) 133.

B. The state as a form of authority and the role of law

According to Christoph Möllers, "The state is a central category in the Western tradition for describing a highly aggregated *system of authority* distinct from others (→ Herrschaft). The concept combines institutional development, political theory, and legal dogmatics in a *mix* often difficult to clarify."[19] A look at what booming empire research calls *imperial rule* reveals that law plays a particularly important role in this mix. Jane Burbank and Frederick Cooper have addressed the manifestations of imperial rule with particular intensity,[20] examining what actually goes to make up the repertoire of imperial rule. As they show for the Roman and Chinese empires – their favourite examples – law is one of the most important elements in this repertoire.

Burbank and Cooper speak of the Roman Empire as a *republic built on war and law*,[21] where we encounter law in three guises, first accompanying Roman (state)[22] institution-building in developing the structures of republican governance:

> "The radical move from kingship to republic was accompanied by measures designed to prevent a return to one-man rule. Personal authority in the republic was constrained by a strict term limit on magistracies, by the electoral power of the people's assemblies, and by the authority of the senate – a council of serving or former magistrates and other men of high office. Underlying these institutions and giving them force was a commitment to legal procedures for *defining and enforcing rules* and for changing them. The historian Livy described Rome as 'a free nation, governed by annually elected officers of state and subject not to the caprice of individual men, but to the overriding authority of the law' (History of Rome)."[23]

Secondly, law acts as the unifying bond of the Roman Republic, constituting what Burbank and Cooper describe as an important element in the "*seductive culture*" of Rome:

> "Law was part of this Roman civilization, both a *means of governance* and a *support for the social order*. … What was Roman about Roman law from republican times, and

19 Möllers (2006) col. 2272.

20 Burbank/Cooper (2010).

21 Burbank/Cooper (2010) 44.

22 Whether we can speak of "state" rule in "ancient Rome" in connection with governance structures is a controversial subject among historians; see Wiemer (ed.) (2006); and Lundgren (ed.) (2014).

23 Burbank/Cooper (2010) 25 f.

what became a powerful historical precedent, was *professional interpretation*, operating in a polity where the manner of making law was itself an ongoing and legitimate political concern. Rulers had issued laws in much earlier times; the Babylonian king Hammurabi who ruled from 1792 to 1750 BCE had a law code inscribed in stone. The Greeks had laws and theories of the state and the good, but they did not create a legal profession. From the mid-second century BCE, just as the republic was expanding most aggressively in space and institutions, jurists appeared in Rome, drawing up legal documents, advising magistrates, litigants, and judges, and passing on their learning to their students."[24]

What proved to be particularly important, however, was the *granting of Roman citizenship as an element in the Roman expansion strategy*:

> "To govern outside their capital, Romans developed strategies that would enter the repertoires of later empire-builders. One of these was the enlargement of the sphere of Roman rights. … [Of] particular import for Rome's future was that its citizenship came to be desired by non-Romans, and was preferable to substantive autonomy in allied cities or colonies. From 91 to 88 BCE, Rome's Italian allies rebelled against their lack of full Roman rights and fought Rome to attain them. After much debate, the senate made the momentous decision to grant citizenship to all Latins. Extending citizenship became both a *reward for service* and a means to *enlarge the realm of loyalty*."[25]

Burbank and Cooper describe this *unifying function* of Roman citizenship as follows:

> "Citizenship, as we have seen, had been central to Roman politics from republican days, a means to draw loyal servitors into the empire's regime of rights, a status so advantageous that Latins had fought for the privilege of becoming Romans in the first century BCE. The institution of citizenship was also connected to the most basic mechanism of imperial rule – military service, law, and, providing for them both, taxes. The emperor Caracalla's enlargement of citizenship in 212 CE has been interpreted as a measure of necessity: if all free males in the empire were made citizens, they could be called to serve in the army, to submit compensation if they did not serve, and to pay inheritance taxes imposed on citizens. But Caracalla's declaration focused on religious cohesion: with citizenship, the worship of Roman gods would be extended throughout the empire. An incorporating and unifying impulse was at the core of the new policy. Through military service, taxation, legal protections, and common deities, ten of millions of people – free men with their families – would be connected more directly to the empire's projects and to a Roman way of life."[26]

24 Burbank/Cooper (2010) 36.
25 Burbank/Cooper (2010) 30 f.
26 Burbank/Cooper (2010) 39.

With regard to the *Chinese Empire*, Burbank and Cooper also delve deep into the "*toolkit for Empire*", especially during the *Qin dynasty* in the third century BCE and the following *Han dynasty*. Over this period, what we would now call a *regulatory and administrative state* developed:

> "If the Qin empire was to last, the emperor's claim to universal power had to be recognized throughout his enlarged realm The empire was divided into command areas, and further into counties; these were administered by officials appointed from the center and subject to recall at any time. Three different officials – a governor, a military commander, and an imperial inspector – supervised each commandery. Qin governance by centrally appointed officials contrasts with Rome's empowerment of local elites and senators to exploit distant territories on their own."[27]

Burbank and Cooper describe this rule-bound civil service machinery:

> "For the Han, unlike the Romans, a large and intricately organized body of officials was critical to imperial power. The tradition of learned advisors offered rewards and pitfalls both to ambitious councillors and to the emperor, who benefited from multiple sources of advice but could also succumb to flattery and intrigue. The capital city, with its dominating and off-bounds imperial palace, teemed with officials and their staffs and servants. Officials served on a scale of ranks – 18 in 23 BCE – with a sliding scale of remuneration. The Grand Tutor, three grand ministers (of finance, of works, and the commander in chief of the military), and nine lesser ministers, as well as a powerful secretariat, could influence, guide, or obstruct the emperor's will. So, too, could the emperor's family, including the emperor's mother, whose powers were enhanced by the seclusion of the imperial court. These competing networks diversified the information, goals, and capacities of the centralized administration.
>
> Government by officials was invigorated by meritocratic selection. The emperor recruited not from an aristocracy but from the sons of landowners, and in 124 BCE he created an imperial academy – some call it a university – to train them in techniques of rule, record keeping, and Confucian ideals. By 1 CE a hundred men a year were passing examinations by scholars and entering the bureaucracy. Young men from the provinces, usually nominated by officials, were brought to the capital to study and be evaluated. Candidates were placed in service throughout the empire; the most highly appreciated served in the capital."[28]

To sum up: both the Roman and the Chinese Empires show how important law was as a pillar of the state repertoire of rule.[29] Whereas the issues in

27 Burbank/Cooper (2010) 48.

28 Burbank/Cooper (2010) 51.

29 See also our reflections on: Geschichte des modernen Staates als Geschichte des Rechts, in: Schuppert, G. F. (2003) 77 ff.

Rome were institution-building through law and the institution of citizenship as a tool for the "governance of diversity", in China the chief concern was the crucial importance of a professionalized body of officials – i.e., bureaucracy – for the efficient administration of a gigantic imperial space. We turn now from these old empires to the third variant of our unity strategy.

C. State semantics and the role of law

I. Jurists as strongly committed trustees of the concept of state

The search for a manageable definition of state will almost inevitably take us to the famous three elements theory of jurist Georg Jellinek,[30] who posits that the architecture of the state comprises territory, nation, and authority:

> "German jurists perfected the theory of the state, in 1837 declared the state to be a legal entity, and finally developed an authoritative definition of the state. The following features or claims accordingly characterize the modern state: 1. A state territory as exclusive area of authority, 2. A national people as sedentary association of persons with permanent membership, 3. A sovereign state authority, which means (a) internally a monopoly of the legitimate use of physical violence, (b) externally legal independence from other authorities. Strict unity of territory, people, and authority are a sort of common denominator. There is only one state authority, and the constitutive people (Staatsvolk) composed of legal individuals speaks only one language."[31]

Although there can be objections to Jellinek's successful definition, the historian Wolfgang Reinhard, writing under the heading "modern state-building – an infectious disease?" has not hesitated to use it as a working definition.[32] And the very plausible thumbnail portrait of the modern state provided by Arthur Benz clearly betrays the influence of Jellinek's three element theory. Benz's "approach to the concept of state" reads as follows:

> - "The modern state is a *territorial state*; its power extends over an area where it exercises exclusive supreme authority and is formally subject to no external influences.

30 Jellinek (1966).

31 Reinhard (1999) 16.

32 In: Reinhard / Müller-Luckner (eds.) (1999) VIII.

- The state is the body of the citizens of its territory, which constitutes itself as national people (*Staatsvolk*) or political nation (*Staatsbürgernation*).
- The state is an *organized decision-making and action entity* (Heller [1934] 1983: 259) of a society. It is empowered – as minimum competence – to make law and exercise legitimate coercion (*monopoly of domination*, Weber [1921] 1967: 29), and, moreover, it has the function of providing public goods and services – however defined in the political process.
- The state is grounded institutionally in the *constitution*, which provides the legal basis for its action.
- The political structure of the modern state is *democracy*: decisions by institutions of the state must derive from the will of the united people.
- The activities of the state include implementing the will of the people, determined in democratic procedures, through a governmental and administrative organization that has developed from the administrative staff of the absolute monarch. The form of organization designed to ensure predictability and controllability is *bureaucracy*."[33]

The dominance of jurists in developing and administering the concept of state is certainly to be explained by the fact that the discipline of jurisprudence has to operate more than any other with this concept. This is particularly apparent in the subdiscipline *international law*: "States constitute the international legal community as original and regular members. International law depends on defining the state. The status of a polity as a state decides whether it is recognized as a subject of international law and a member of the system of rights and obligations under international law. The 'three elements' the necessary and sufficient preconditions under international law are state territory, state people, state authority (*Staatsgebiet, Staatsvolk, Staatsgewalt*) (G. Jellinek)."[34]

But constitutional law, too, needs the state – as *assignee of legal responsibilities*: "In law, 'state' refers to a normatively defined organizational form of sovereign power to which only certain rules of constitutional and international law apply. To this extent, the concept describes a *legal attribution construction*, a legal subject to which certain actions can be attributed.[35] However, the legal status of 'state' presupposes the existence of an order defined in terms of territory and personnel such as that expressed and

33 Benz (2008) 38.
34 Isensee (1989) col. 135.
35 Kelsen (1993) 264 f.: Österreichische Staatsdenker.

applied in Georg Jellinek's three element theory (state authority, state territory, state people)."[36]

The concept of state is thus at home in the discipline of jurisprudence, and there are no signs of it being evicted.

German political science, by contrast, has expended much effort on *avoiding* the concept of state, a *strategy* Arthur Benz explains as follows:

> "In avoiding the concept of state, political science not only distanced itself from the older *Staatslehre* (theory of the state) but also reacted to the fact that, in modern societies, politics also takes place outside the state and that the boundaries between state and society are becoming increasingly blurred. Attention turned first to associations that represent societal interests and seek to promote them in competition and cooperation with one another. Later one discovered the outsourcing of public sector functions to non-state organizations. … moreover, politics and the state are even farther apart for those who discover politics outside established institutions, 'beyond formal responsibilities and hierarchies' and who accuse experts that 'equate politics with the state, with the political system, with formal responsibilities and advertised political careers' of misunderstanding the concept of politics.[37] At any rate, there is no denying that, empirically, politics is not limited to the framework of the state. Changes in statehood – which some equate with the decline of the state – that clearly lead to state activities 'fraying' in the course of internationalization and privatization,[38] seem to corroborate the view of those who deny the state concept its central importance in political science."[39]

In actual fact, however, the concept of state is not only experiencing a renaissance in political science; empirical observation in recent years suggest it is in the best of health and shows no signs of expiring as predicted.[40]

36 Möllers (2008) 1272.
37 Beck (1993) 156.
38 Leibfried/Zürn (eds.) (2005) 17–27.
39 Leibfried/Zürn (eds.) (2005) 4–5.
40 See Vosskuhle et al. (eds.) (2013); see also Anter (2016), which, incidentally, strongly stresses the contribution of jurists to current state theory: "Among the authors who currently represent a realistic theory of the state are notably Gunnar Folke Schuppert, Josef Isensee, and Dieter Grimm. Interestingly, all three are jurists, albeit with a strong inclination towards the social sciences."

II. The meteoric career of the state concept in the guise of the "reason of state"

There seems to be broad agreement that the real career of the state concept really took off only when it came to be linked with the 'reason of state' notion: "The origins of the concept [of state] appear to lie in the political prudential literature of early modern Italy ... It served as a terminological means of differentiating between innerwordly political organization and transcendental claims to rightness, thus describing precisely the function of substantive autonomization of the political order from material demands on its content. However, the Italian authors tended to make topical rather than systemic use of the idea. The topos is the *reason of state* (Staatsräson, ragione dello stato, raison d`état) as a passpartout argument for enforcing order against moral or religious objections."[41]

According to Herfried Münkler, reason of state is a "*tendentious term* used in the building of the early modern state, steering its internal consolidation and external expansion."[42] In similar vein, Paul-L. Weinacht speaks of the double thrust of reason of state: inwards and outwards:

> "The advance of thinking in terms of the state that accompanied the transformation of overall conditions – grounded in estates and princely rule – in the absolute princely state (Fürstenstaat) is evident on a number of fronts: 'ratio status', the politico-juridical concept of the new princely regime, had many adversaries: within, the estates, without, the emperor and the empire; both within and without: the churches; and not least of all the concrete interests of external competitors and rivals (i.e., their reason of state). The reason of state had its profile sharpened by these conflicts: as legal doctrine of the absolute regime internally, as political doctrine of prudence (new politics) externally."[43]

In parallel to the two chief aspects of the reason of state concepts – internal stabilization of rule and building an external carapace, the passage shows that reason of state also gained the quality of a legal concept. Herfried Münkler comments on this interdependence between the internal and external aspects of the associated *juridification of the reason of state*:

> "With the development of the European system of states, interest grew among kings and princes to centralize rule within their states ... Central authorities tend above all

41 Möllers (2008) 1271.
42 Münkler (1987) 169.
43 Weinacht (1975) 70–71.

> to concentrate legal and fiscal powers to enable the state to focus all its energy outwards in the event of political and military conflict. The question of the religious unity of the state is also important in this context, which – in conflict with the 'liberty' of the estates – joins forces with the idea of the reason of state ... What in Machiavelli and Guiccardini was justified only on grounds of utility, was in the confessional disputes in the second half of the sixteenth and the first half of the seventeenth centuries legally underpinned by the evocation of emergency. Thomas Aquinas had already advanced the notion of 'derogatio legis' (derogation from the law) for purposes of 'utilitas multorum'; this was supplemented by Seneca's maxim: 'Necessitas omnen legem frangit' – necessity breaks every law. This formula was taken over by Justus Lipsius (Politicorum libri sex, IV, 14; 1589) and Hippolithus a Lapide (Diss. de ratione status, Prol., Sect. V; 1640); Jean Bodin (République, IV, 3; 1576) reworded it as: 'Nulla igitur tam sancta lex est, quam non oporteat urgente necessitate mutari' – no law is so sacrosanct that it cannot be changed in an emergency. The reason of state idea thus begins to assume legal character."[44]

The development of the reason of state concept has been described in similar vein by Michael Stolleis:

> "The more territories formed themselves into 'states' by developing their own administration, educational facilities, and armies, the more plausible it seemed to assert their own 'raison territoriale'. With the almost unconstrained sovereignty brought by the Peace of Westphalia, this fact also gained legal recognition. Not only the renaissance of the universities after the war but also the removal of this legal obstacle probably explain the broad wave of legal dissertations on the 'ratio status' from 1650 on. While setting external bounds to the reason of state of the given sovereign, these treatises also discussed the internal possibilities and limits of legitimation vis-à-vis the estates and subjects. The latter aspect is particularly important; for the right of expropriation, contract termination, the levy of special taxes, and the revocation of old privileges and other special legal titles needed legal justification. It was supplied not only by the well established devices of necessitas, notturft, bonum commune and utilitas publica but also by the *reason of state as a legal concept*. The jurist Besold was clearly aware of this shift in categories: 'Ratio politica, quam nunc vocant de Statu (olim aequitas & epieikeia) transgreditur legibus, scripto vel voce promulgatae; literam, sed non sensum & finem'. This is the early, moderate level at which, although breaching the letter of the law, the reason of state fulfilled its 'spirit'. Later, the reason of state was to change into a unilateral governmental *legal title justifying interventions* of all sorts, while its parallel limiting function weakened as absolutism consolidated."[45]

44 Münkler (1985) 23 ff., 27 f.

45 Stolleis (1990) 37 ff., 68 f.

These two passages lend support to Münkler's definition, encompassing as it does the *content and thrust of the reason of state*. Summarizing early modern reason-of-state and arcana literature, he seeks to concentrate the central elements of the reason of state:

> "The common denominator of all reason-of-state theories is the power to contravene traditional and positive law internally and the authority to terminate contracts externally; but in both cases with the objective interests of the state strictly in mind. The reason of state accordingly means rejecting all concepts of politics committed to universal norms and values, the triumph of the particular in the sphere of the political."[46]

What is striking about this definition is that *dealing with law* constitutes the core of the reason of state – and of sovereignty. If the essence of sovereignty is the justification and *institutionalization of the lawmaking monopoly*, the core of the reason of state lies in the authority to contravene the law. This recalls the role of the language of international law as a language of justification discussed above in the context of international law.

III. A remarkable semantic shift: from state to statehood

If the "state" is not disappearing but is clearly more and more in its element in times of crisis – financial, monetary, European, or whatever – as an entity with an effective executive, this indicates that it is the *concept* of state that is in retreat.[47] Over recent decades, the discussion on the state has revealed a conspicuous shift in usage from *state* to *statehood*. Talk is now almost only about statehood, not only in the two collaborative research centers "Changing Statehood" ("Staatlichkeit im Wandel", University of Bremen, until 31/12/2015) and "Governance in Spaces of Limited Statehood" ("Governance in Räumen begrenzter Staatlichkeit" FU Berlin until 31/12/2015), but in almost all more recent publications. Note what a student advisory service brochure at the University of Passau has to say about a study programme: "The bachelor's programme 'Governance and Public Policy – Staatswissenshaften' is grounded in disciplines that classically address the relationship between the state, society, and the economy. This programme combines political science,

46 Münkler (1987) 269.
47 On the inappropriateness of the retreat metaphor for the development of the modern state, see Schuppert, G. F. (1995b).

historical, economic, philosophical, (international) law, and sociological aspects. *'Statehood' as the subject and focus of the programme* encompasses both the nation-state perspective and the various forms of political activity (domestic, international, supranational), that are examined at multi-disciplinary and interdisciplinary levels."

Since, in our experience, semantic shift is less a fashionable label than (like the shifts from third sector to civil society and from control to governance) an expression of more profound processes of change, or at least of a more or less radical change in perspective,[48] this shift from state to statehood deserves our attention; there must be particular grounds for this change in terminology. Three can be identified:

- One decisive advantage of the statehood concept is that it imposes no categorization and thus helps avoid unease about assessing the extent to which the EU has a state-like quality. Hans-Jürgen Bieling and Martin Große-Hüttmann comment: "In this connection we speak explicitly of 'statehood' and not of 'state' because the concept of statehood is more open and adaptable from an analytical point of view … Especially in the debate on the state-like nature of the European Union there is a 'wide conceptual mantel of statehood',[49] since the EU is a specific, historically contingent, institutionally and dynamically shifting form of a model for political order, which is not to be understood as a deficient or underdeveloped form of a 'state' on the model of OECD states.[50]
- Historians who are concerned with "statehood" in antiquity or the Middle Ages[51] also appreciate the concept: it can, for example, prove helpful in answering the question of whether the governmental practices of the Roman Empire can be described as a "state". Under the heading "statehood as analytic category", Christoph Lundgreen explains: "Statehood should … first … be understood as ongoing process rather than state. Movement within this process should, second, not be coupled with the figure of thought of rise and fall or other teleological concepts but be treated analytically as weaker or more intensive statehood. If, moreover, political science sees *varying statehood* as characteristic of the present day and comparative history as typical of the nineteenth century, the strict "state / non-state" dichotomy ought to be abandoned in analysing antiquity, as well[52] Writing about "statehood and political action in imperial Rome", Hans-Ulrich Wiemer remarks in similar vein: "Whenever it is a question of the action patterns and spaces of political actors, it is also question of what forms of state-

48 See Schuppert, G. F. (2018b).
49 Ref. Schuppert, G. F. (2010) 129.
50 Bieling / Grosse-Hüttmann (eds.) (2016) 11–30, here 15.
51 See Esders / Schuppert, G. F. (2015).
52 Lundgren (2014) 34–35.

hood determine how they act … What is decisive is institutionalization, i. e., objectivization and stabilization, the performance of joint responsibilities, so that there are necessarily varying degrees of 'statehood'."[53]

- Governance studies, too, prefer to work with the concept of statehood, because it can capture entities – 'étatique ou non étatique' – that are either not states in the legal sense of the term or only partly or deficiently provide what is normally associated with the concept and expected of the modern, Western type of state. What the statehood concept thus permits is to enter the whole motley world of "varieties of statehood", to study the various "configurations of statehood",[54] and not to limit oneself to the narrow perspective of statehood as defined by the OECD.

What does the semantic shift from state to statehood mean for the language of law? This massive change in language use can be understood as a call for jurisprudence to overcome its fixation on an essentialist and supposedly exactly defined concept of the state, which had developed in the course of the nineteenth century and encouraged the dominance of thinking in terms of the nation-state,[55] by doing two things: first to address the *state as a process*[56] and thus avoid having to write its history as a narrative of either rise or fall (the latter being the more popular option);[57] and second to take up the analytical potential of classical "Staatswissenschaft", ("science of the state") and apply it anew under the conditions of Europeanization, transnationalization, and globalization. In what could be called *"Staatlichkeitswissenschaft"* ("science of statehood"), the language of law would retain its legitimate place.

It will be no surprise that we now turn to the concept of sovereignty, generally considered the central characteristic of the modern state.

53 Wiemer (ed.) (2006) 1–2.

54 Zürcher (2005) 13–22.

55 On these isolation tendencies, see Glenn (2013).

56 Schuppert, G. F. (2010).

57 See my controversy with the Bremen Collaborative Research Centre "Staatlichkeit im Wandel" in my article, Schuppert, G. F. (2008c) with the response by Genschel/Leibfried (2008).

12

Sovereignty and the Modern State: Legal and Political Perspectives

A. The triad of state, reason of state, and sovereignty as basic chord of the modern state

There is broad agreement that the concepts state, sovereignty, and reason of state are closely related and that it is the theories of sovereignty and reason of state that spelled out the developmental and functional logic of the emerging early modern state. That a state conceived of as sovereign – once it was in existence – would have to have the power to act in accordance with its "raison" has been plausibly argued by Joseph R. Strayer, who correctly stresses the functional link between recognizing sovereignty and accepting the orientation of state action on the reason of state:

> "Recognition of the theory of the divine right of kings makes resistance a wrong and thus strengthens the state. For those sceptical about the divine right of kings, there was the theory that the state was indispensable for human welfare and that the concentration of power that we call sovereignty was essential for the continued existence of the state. People could not lead a decent life – according to Hobbes they could not live at all – unless they lived in a sovereign state and obeyed its commands. To weaken or destroy the state meant to threaten the future of the human race. A state was therefore empowered to take all conceivable steps to ensure its own survival, even if its action seemed unjust or cruel."[58]

Michael Stolleis, too, writing about the idea of the sovereign state, mentions sovereignty and reason of state in one breath, as if they were identical twins:

> "The theory of sovereignty is a consequence of the autonomization of politics in the sixteenth century. The politico-administrative apparatus was to be granted a monopoly of decision-making and the use of force, it was to be separate from rival societal powers and to control them. Acting in accordance with the reason of state, asserting the status of subject under international law, and eliminating (weakening) intermediary powers are aspects of the fundamental political needs of early modernity. They are responses to the gradual collapse of the structures of the medieval order, including the feudal system; to the end of the dualistic overarching of Europe by Church and Empire; to schism and religious wars, and, not least, to fundamental changes in economic conditions with tremendous growth in financial requirements."[59]

58 Strayer (1975) 99–100.
59 Stolleis (1996) 63 ff., 82 f.

A third voice in this chorus points out that the two theories or concepts marking the functional logic of the modern state are – a rather rare case – clearly associated with two names: Jean Bodin and Niccolo Macchiavelli, recognized as the godfathers of the modern state. Dieter Wyduckel comments:

> "The theories of reason of state and sovereignty that took shape in the course of the sixteenth century reveal an – often overestimated – change in the conception of law and state, reflecting not only the trend towards detheologization of the medieval view of the polity but also the notion of subordinating political rule to rational considerations. Whereas Niccolo Macchiavelli saw the reason of state as grounded in the necessity of state, Jean Bodin declared sovereignty to be the decisive criterion of the polity, defining it as supreme, legally unbounded power over citizens and subjects (summe in cives ac subditos legibusque soluta potestas)."[60]

This should sufficiently indicate that the concept of sovereignty is crucial for all concern with the political history of ideas. We, however, are primarily interested in whether sovereignty is really a legal concept, a political concept, or both at the same time.

B. Sovereignty – legal concept, political concept, or both?

Sovereignty is undoubtedly a *political concept*, since it is about fundamental questions of institutionalized human sociation. Ulrich K. Preuß therefore sees it as a *key concept of the political*:

> "There are basic concepts for understanding the social world that are so general that they develop varying but essentially identical meanings in wide ranging spheres of life. We speak of the individual, the human being, of contract, of power, or of country in describing very general social states of affairs. But if we instead of individual we say citizen; instead of contract, alliance; instead of power, rule; instead of land, territory, we have entered the realm of the political. Concepts that are constitutive for the sphere of the political and originally have meaning only in this sphere, I call key concepts of the political. Thus 'citizen' does not mean only human being, individual, or person, but the individual as member of a political community. The concept 'alliance' describes a contractual relationship in the sphere of the political; 'territory' is not simply a defined piece of the earth's surface but a politico-geographical space. In this sense, I speak of sovereignty as a key concept of the political: it unfolds its meaning only in the context of the political. Indeed, we can

60 Wyduckel (1979) 12–13.

> say that the modern concept of the political constitutes itself as an independent sphere of human associations only through the category of sovereignty."[61]

But the concept of sovereignty is also without a doubt a *legal concept*. This is apparent not only when one looks at international law as a legal regime for relations between sovereign states but is also shown also by the fact that the heart of sovereignty is a set of rights. Thomas Fleiner and Lidija R. Basta Fleiner[62] are our witnesses on the content of sovereignty:

> "BODIN showed almost statesmanlike far-sightedness in discussing the attributes of sovereignty. What powers and competencies does a state or a prince have to have to be described as sovereign? Sovereignty includes above all the right to issue laws for every individual. This right includes the power to amend customary law and grant new privileges. 'All the other attributes and rights of sovereignty are included in this power of making and unmaking law.' BODIN, Book I, Chapter 10, p. 83). Among the other attributes of sovereignty BODIN lists are the right of making peace and war, of hearing appeals from the sentences of all courts whatsoever, of appointing and dismissing the great officers of state, of taxing, or granting privileges of exemption to all subjects, of appreciating or depreciating the value and weight of the coinage, of receiving oaths of fealty from subjects and liege-vassals alike."[63]

If this is so, both political science and jurisprudence can legitimately claim the sovereignty concept for themselves – and they are at liberty to do so. The real charm of the concept, however, lies precisely in the fact that it cannot be neatly divided up between politics and law. As Dieter Grimm has noted, it is a "*basic legalo-political concept*".[64] Matthias Mahlmann remarks: "The concept of sovereignty is a basic concept of law and of politics."[65]

We take a similar view, but add two justifications that clarify the matter. The first quote is from a dictionary entry on sovereignty by Peter Nieson, which sums up the indivisible link between the political and legal content of the concept: "Sovereignty means the capability to make collectively binding decisions autonomously for a number of persons. In the history of political thought, sovereignty is therefore primarily identified with the legislature as the supreme state authority. This underlines that sovereign power is exercised by means of positive law."[66] Although Matthias Mahlmann, too, primarily

61 PREUSS (2007) 313.
62 FLEINER/BASTA FLEINER (2004).
63 FLEINER/BASTA FLEINER (2004) 321.
64 GRIMM (2007) 304–310.
65 MAHLMANN (2007) 270.
66 NIESEN (2008) 1205.

stresses the eminently political importance of the sovereignty concept,[67] in the same breath he emphasizes the crucial role of law in making the autonomy of political self-determination possible in the first place under the carapace of sovereignty: "Self-determination requires social organization, tempered in essence by institutions and law. The sovereignty of the organizational entity thus formed, traditionally a state, is in the political sphere the equivalent of the individual self-determination of the subject."[68]

C. The political dimension of the sovereignty concept

The political dimension of the sovereignty concept becomes particularly clear when one considers the functions attributed to it. From this historical perspective two are especially prominent: to eliminate all intermediary claims to power and to establish a unitary power centre:

> "The historical function of the sovereignty concept is to establish a power centre for binding decision-making and to emancipate it from all claims of supranational and subnational actors to participate in government. This also announced the modern autonomy of politics from other functional areas of society. However, the political system reserved to itself not only regulatory power over all other functional areas in society such as religion, science, and the economy – even if it did not necessarily intervene – it also switched the polycratic structures of the Middle Ages to a new, strictly hierarchical mode of control."[69]

The second, just as important historical function was to overcome civil war-like religious conflicts:

> "'Sovereignty' was the answer, proposed in 1576 by Jean Bodin, to the crisis of the medieval order, which arose in the aftermath of the sixteenth century schism and which culminated in the religious civil wars. Bodin saw the only hope for peaceful co-existence between the confessions at loggerheads about religious truth was to create an institution raised above the warring parties that imposed an independent secular order and enforced it of its own authority. However, this required all sover-

67 Mahlmann (2007) 278–279: "It is an eminently political concept, not only because it raises fundamental questions of law and political organization but also because, within its framework, concrete political disputes are fought out about the distribution of power in a society and its relationship to other organizational entities – from the theory of political absolutism to the limits of the powers of the individual state in the light of modern human rights."

68 Mahlmann (2007) 279.

69 Niesen (2008) 1206.

> eign rights – including the right to use force – distributed substantively and territorially among many independent wielders of power under the medieval order to be concentrated in one pair of hands to constitute an all-inclusive power centre. The downside was the corresponding complete disempowerment of societal forces."[70]

Dieter Grimm therefore rightly stresses that the *political unity formula of sovereignty serves also as a legitimation formula clad in the language of law*:

> "Bodin called this new sort of overall authority sovereignty, which he defined as supreme and unrestricted governmental power. For those who wielded it, it meant the power to legally bind everyone in their area of authority without themselves being legally bound. For Bodin, sovereignty in this sense was indivisible. Shared sovereignty was not sovereignty. Sovereignty was therefore not a collective term or generic concept for single sovereign rights but a unitary concept describing a new quality of rule and which thus marked the passage from the Middle Ages to modern times. Under these circumstances, it corresponded to nothing in the real world at the time of its development. 'Sovereignty' was a theoretical construct, not a theory conceptualizing reality but one that anticipated reality, *that guided and legitimated changes* to it."[71]

The key tool in implementing what was attributed to the sovereignty concept is, however, law. Law – and this means above all enacted law – occupies first place in the governmental repertoire of the sovereign state; Ulrich K. Preuß:

> "Whoever has the authority to make law with unilateral sovereignty is sovereign. This means two things: first, the institutionalized supremacy of rule and second its expression in the form of enacted law. Bodin put it with the greatest clarity when he contrasted sovereignty with the traditional mode of lawmaking by contract or 'covenant': 'A law and a covenant must … not be confused. A law proceeds from him who has sovereign power, and by it he binds the subject to obedience, but cannot bind himself. A covenant is a mutual undertaking between a prince and his subjects, equally binding on both parties, and neither can contravene it to the prejudice of the other, without his consent (Bodin 1576/1981: chap. 8: 70). *Law and contract are different manifestations of law*, so that only the contract but also the law emanating from sovereign rule is therefore a mode of political integration – a novel one that Bodin was the first to explicate."[72]

Since, however, law is always involved, we ought to take a brief look at the juridical construction of sovereignty.

70 Grimm (2007) 304.

71 Grimm (2007) 304–305.

72 Preuss (2007) 314.

D. The juridical construction of sovereign state authority

In his impressive work on state and sovereignty, Helmut Quaritsch[73] addresses the juridical construction for concentrating public authority envisaged in Bodin's sovereignty theory. *He identifies three elements of sovereign state authority: unity, singularity, and unilaterality.*

The *singularity of state authority* in the hands of the sovereign is effected by *monopolizing lawmaking power*, that is, by monopolizing the competence that is the core of sovereignty: "donner loy á tous en general, et á chacun en particulier". Quaritsch:

> "Vesting 'donner-loy' competence with its deduced powers exclusively in the sovereign meant that, in this monopolized domain, to raise an objection to a sovereign, irreversible ('absolute') decision was, ipso jure, unlawful; denial of obedience was resistance, which could and had to be broken by physical force. The primacy of the lawmaking institutions and the normative complex created by them was thus established in the most important field of domestic action by the sovereign: setting generally applicable rules of behaviour."[74]

The *unity of state authority* is established and ensured by means of an organizational construction, which we shall be examining below: *public office*, that is to say, the *understanding of rule as the exercise of a public office entrusted to the holder*. Under Bodin's conception of sovereignty, the authority entrusting an office to someone, supervising his exercise thereof, and dismissing the holder, can perforce be only the sovereign himself. Helmut Quaritsch:

> "Public authority takes ... only two forms: the sovereign and the holder of public office. Someone who exercises public authority as officeholder is among the 'governmental' institutions appointed by the sovereign; his area of responsibility is assigned to him, he himself is an agent. It was therefore possible for the holder of sovereignty to withdraw the powers entrusted to the current officeholder at any time, to assign them to another or exercise them himself. This established not only the primacy but also the substantial unity of the power existing in a 'ŕepublique'. The concentration and categorization of all powers – including those of the sovereign – of command and coercion under the heading of 'puissance publique' excluded any thought of sovereignty and public authority being independent of one another. The sovereign's power of disposition over his subjects and the exercise of public authority brought together all non-sovereign authorities with powers of command and coercion in a single entity."[75]

73 Quaritsch (1970).
74 Quaritsch (1970) 267.
75 Quaritsch (1970) 268 f.

Finally, with regard to the *unilaterality of state authority*, the requirement of sovereign rule for *unilateral decision making* follows from the nature of sovereignty itself as a concept for ensuring the capacity of the state to act, also and particularly where antagonistic interest structures and confessional schism prevail. Having defined the first characteristic of sovereignty ("The first attribute of the sovereign prince is ... the power to make law binding on all his subjects in general and on each in particular."), Bodin immediately adds: "But to avoid any ambiguity one must add that he does so without the consent of any superior, equal, of inferior being necessary. If the prince can only make law with the consent of a superior he is a subject; if of an equal he shares his sovereignty; if of an inferior, whether it be a council of magnates or the people, it is not he who is sovereign."[76]

This strong emphasis on the need for unilateral decision-making authority is a logical consequence of the function Bodin attributed to his sovereignty theory as a reaction to the civil war in France "by establishing the legal basis for powerful kingship to ensure peace between the confessions and to reconstruct the broken order of the commonwealth in stability"[77] Quaritsch:

> "The background to the demand for unilateral decision-making was the experience of the later Middle Ages and the civil wars of the sixteenth century. The harmony of values and interests presupposed by the dualistic conception had fallen victim to 'growing social differentiation' (Luhmann) and confessional dissension. The conflicts resulting from this disintegration had reached dimensions and intensity such that the hitherto recognized authorities were no longer able to handle them through consensus. Bodin's solution was to exclude the representatives of disintegration from conflict management decisions: 'Tous les états demeurent en pleine subiection du Roy, qui n'est aucunement tenu de suyvre leur advis, ny accorder leur requestes'. This posited a system that, in social-scientific terms, transferred societal conflicts to the environment of the state machinery of government and thus made them solvable. The estates were thus deprived of the opportunity to continue pursuing their views, interests, and objectives as binding elements of the action programme of their organizations and to lay legal claim to them before the royal leadership of the association. The realization of this principle put control in the organization on a completely different footing completely alien to that which had prevailed throughout the thousand years of the Middle Ages:

76 Bodin (1955); quoted from the English edition, 82.
77 Bodin (1955).

> the plurality of ruling powers was revoked and replaced by a relationship of protection and obedience applicable to and binding on all members of the order."[78]

So much on the legal construction elements of Bodin's sovereignty theory.

E. On balance

When sovereignty is discussed or written about today, what is generally at issue is "whether the concept of sovereignty still corresponds to something real and is therefore suitable for describing current conditions",[79] whether it has not long since eroded,[80] and how it is to be understood in political multi-level systems such as the European Union.[81] We have not addressed all this,[82] because our focus is solely on the *role that the language of law plays* when it comes to describing and understanding one of the *key concepts in the political history of ideas*.

The result is clear. As the *semantic mix* of the state concept has shown, the state cannot be adequately described without the vocabulary of law. When dealing with the politically momentous and successful concept of sovereignty, we find that law and politics cannot be kept apart. The recipe is primarily political, even though the necessary ingredients have always been of legal provenance. Things might be no different with the key concept of 'constitution.'

78 Quaritsch (1970) 271 f.
79 Grimm (2007) 304.
80 See, for example, van Staden / Vollaard (2002).
81 See Grimm (2012) 275–292.
82 See our own contribution: Schuppert, G. F. (2007b).

13

Diverse Perspectives on the Constitution

What we have learned about the concepts of state and sovereignty repeats itself when we come to the constitution. Whereas "state" proved to be a semantic mix, and "sovereignty" a "legalo-political" concept, "constitution" appears to be a halfway-house concept between law and politics, since *constitutions* – to quote Günter Frankenberg – *"give societies politico-legal form"*:

> "Constitutions give societies politico-legal form as an entity – state, nation, people, federation, or union. They lay down the principles, institutional arrangements, and decision-making procedures by which societies go about governing themselves and by which they seek to safeguard their cohesion. At the same time, constitutions betray the hopes and fears of their authors about the two main problems: justifying legitimate authority and establishing societal integration. The essential character of constitutions – both functions and content – finds legal expression in their primacy over all other legal rules of national law. As a sort of 'normative nobility' they form the apex of the normative pyramid, after having come into being in some special way such as by referendum. Once in place, they can be amended only by a special procedure, generally by a qualified majority vote – if revision by lawmakers duly empowered to this effect is not entirely excluded."[83]

If constitutions are therefore a *both political and legal form* societies give themselves to organize the life of the polity, the *language of constitutionalism* is both a political and legal language. This self-evidence invites a number of additional comments to throw light from various angles on the interlocking of law and politics apparent in the *constitution as an institution*.[84]

A. The constitution as an institution between the politicization of law and the juridification of politics

In premodern societies, law was deemed valid by virtue of immemorial tradition or by divine institution: the notion that law could be made was alien to them. When tradition and religion lost their power to validate law, Dieter Grimm argues, the relationship between law and politics changed fundamentally – with the emergence of the early modern territorial state and the positivization of law: "Law had become makeable and could be deployed

83 Frankenberg, G. (2008) 1411.

84 See North (1990) [transl. 1992] on the stabilization function of institutions, taking the example of the constitution.

as a tool for political purposes. This reversed the old primacy. Politics now ranked higher than law and lent it content and validity."[85]

This absolutist period of *politicization of law* was brought to an end by the burgeoning power of the bourgeoisie and their ultimately incontestable demand for the lawmaking powers of the monarchical sovereign to be abolished, once again reversing the relationship between politics and law. The politicization of law was succeeded by the *juridification of politics*. As Grimm shows, the vehicle for this reversal was the constitution:

> "The desired limitation of political disposition over law could … itself be achieved only through law. Although this law then had to be superior to enacted law, it could not be supra-positive. *The solution to this problem was the constitution*. Unlike natural law, it was positive law. However, *introducing the constitution made positive law reflexive*: it was divided into two different normative complexes, the first laying down the conditions for making and validating the second. Normsetting was thus itself normativized. Although politics retained its power to make law for society, it no longer enjoyed the freedom of the absolute monarch: it was itself subject to the binding force of law. First of all, this involved procedural rules that had to be respected if a political decision was to be accepted as a collectively binding norm. Second, however, substantive demands were made of enacted law in the shape of basic rights, flouting which could nullify it."[86]

So much on Dieter Grimm's outline of historical developments.

B. The constitution as the order of the political

In our "Staatswissenschaft"[87] we had posited that the complicated categorization of the worlds of law and politics through the hybrid institution of the constitution can succeed only if both worlds are catered for, resulting neither in total politicization of law nor in total juridification of politics.

Nowhere do we find this thesis better formulated than by Ulrich K. Preuß, who has this to say about the *constitution as the interface of law and politics*:

> "*In the constitution, law meets politics*. But this is not the place for a rerun of the drama – particularly popular in Germany – of irreconcilable opposition between, on the one hand, the legal neutrality, objectivity, reason, justice, procedural orientation,

85 Grimm (2001) 13–32, here 18.
86 Grimm (2001) 20.
87 Schuppert, G. F. (2003) 743 ff.

discursivity, and protective quality of law and, on the other, the political partisanship, fixation on power and will, irrationality, strategic orientation on success, unobjectiveness, and decisionism of politics. This would contribute little to understanding the concept of constitution. What goes to make up the constitution concept is not the fact that it connects law with politics but the difficulty of developing a *concept of constitution in which the creative force of politics can unfold.*

The heart of the current international debate on the concept of constitution thus lies in the search for institutional conditions under which democratic politics can be rediscovered in its creative importance as a medium of human problem resolution and given its rightful place."[88]

If, as we agree, a concept of constitution needs to be developed in which the creative force of politics can unfold, but within the *framework of the constitution*, thinking in dichotomies – the world of law versus the world of politics – will not be very helpful:

"The constitution as the 'order of the political' would be very inadequately defined were we to understand it as the embodiment of an ultimately insoluble tension between the irrational abyss of politics and the rationalization achievements of law, especially its formality and its bent for systematic consistency. *Splitting the constitution into a rule-of-law logic and an opposing political logic*, or the assertion – typical of anti-liberal constitutional critics – that the liberal and democratic elements of modern civil constitutions contradict one another exemplify a basic current of theory that claims the constitution can at best curb the incomprehensible force of the political from without, but can never tame and reform its inherent wildness."[89]

An adequate understanding of the constitution can therefore be gained only by avoiding thinking in terms of any *essential opposition* between law and politics, cancelling out this opposition in the *function the constitution* performs in *ordering the political*. Preuß:

"This is clearly much more and much more demanding than erecting barriers against absolutist political authority with its proclivity for the arbitrary. 'A constitution is that which results from an effort to constitute' – this simple sentence resumes the entire complexity of the constitutional programme. *A constitution constitutes a political community.* What seem to be purely negative provisions, such as defensive rights or the separation of powers and mutual checks and balances also *constitute an order*, not by eliminating politics but rather by channelling its energies in a manner that enables it to establish the framework conditions for societal liberty. The programme of traditional constitutionalism, too, whose concise message can be expressed in two words: 'limited government', thus contains no less than the high-flying goal of *establishing a political order.* But it is a concept in which the political

88 Preuss (ed.) (1994) 7–36, here 7 ff., 8 f.

89 Preuss (1994) 9.

(the quintessence of the aspirations to unity and identity at large in a society) is constituted as a medium of societal self-government, i. e., in which the political is set at liberty in civilized form. It faces the seeming chaos of societal multiplicity and diversity not as an unfathomable, uncomprehended and redeeming 'Other', as a promise of salvation, and thus as an ever-looming threat. As an ordering force itself, it is subject to the necessity of form, of limitation, and of *mediating between opposites*."[90]

C. Constitutional law as political law

There is broad agreement that constitutional law is close to politics, is "politics-related law" – as Böckenförde puts it,[91] "political law", as Isensee calls it, albeit in inverted commas. On the literary topos of "political law", Isensee is therefore probably safe in asserting that:

> "Constitutional law is 'political law' – that is the usual topos, if not commonplace, of the literature on constitutional law and theory. Whoever avails themselves of it can expect broad agreement. But they cannot rely on everyone who agrees meaning the same thing. The statement is unclear and ambiguous. What is clear, however, in speaking of 'political law' is the intention to attribute a special quality to constitutional law that distinguishes it from other law, whatever this distinction might be."[92]

What, then, is this special quality of constitutional law that makes of it a sort of hybrid type of law rooted in both the world of law and the world of politics? Ernst-Wolfgang Böckenförde:

> "In a specific sense, constitutional law is *politics-related law*. This is because it is the *field of law* closest to *politics* and which *directly interlocks* with it. It regulates access to the political decision-making power concentrated in the state, determines the procedures by which it is exercised, and sets limits to it. It accordingly regulates and distributes positions of power and decision-making with regard to shaping and ordering life in society, sets the possibilities and limits of determining the future, orders and channels the process of political will-formation. Regardless of their content, the provisions of the constitution are related per se to politics, act as structuring and regulative factor in the political life of the state polity. This politics-relatedness also means that constitutional law repeatedly switches to the modality, the aggregate state of the political, which is characterized by specific tensions. It cannot be detached from this context because it always relates to the ordering and regu-

90 Preuss (1994) 11 f.
91 Böckenförde (1969).
92 Isensee (1992) 103 ff., 104.

> lation of political power, and thus to the central domain of constant political disputation."[93]

Even if constitutional law disputes never cease to be *legal disputes*, they are often *also in the aggregate state of political controversies*:

> "The provisions and principles of constitutional law are far more direct that those in other fields of law, an expression of political notions of order, political decisions, or of compromises; with respect to the subject of regulation, they address a specific politics-related content. The fundamental concepts of constitutional law such as democracy, the rule of law, the federal state, the free democratic basic order, are not by chance but necessarily politico-ideological concepts. As a consequence, disputes under constitutional law also display a specific politics-related content and therefore easily, if not necessarily end up in the aggregate state of political controversy. This does not mean that they cease to be legal disputes."[94]

The *simultaneity of the political and legal aggregate state* of constitutional law disputes suggests that we can indeed speak of constitutional law as a *hybrid type of law*.

D. The constitution as key element of a polity's political culture

However difficult it may be to define political culture with any precision[95] – some describe it as trying to nail jello to the wall[96] – there can be no doubt that the constitution is a key element in the political culture of a polity and that *constitutional culture*[97] and *administrative culture*[98] are important elements in the overarching political culture of a country. Jürgen Gebhardt[99] posits that, in the medium of political culture, the constitution unfolds its *symbolic and instrumental functions* in two ways: "In fulfilling its *symbolic function*, it explicates the guiding regulatory principle of political society, thus normativizing the regulatory and meaning content of political culture. In fulfilling its *instrumental function*, it regulates the political process, thus supplying the rules of the game for the political system."[100]

93 Böckenförde (1969) 320 f.
94 Böckenförde (1969) 321.
95 For a comprehensive description see Schuppert, G. F. (2008).
96 Kaase (eds.) (1983) 144–171.
97 See Gebhardt (ed.) (1999).
98 For informative overviews see Jann (2000); Wallerath (2000) and Priebe (2000).
99 Gebhardt (ed.) (1999) 7–14.
100 Gebhardt (ed.) (1999) 8.

Of decisive importance is the *function of the constitution as rallying point for the politico-cultural self-understanding of a society.* Hans Vorländer:

> "Constitutions are not only part of a specific political culture, they are also an important rallying point for a society's politico-cultural self-understanding. Constitutions perform a *communal service* towards determining how a society sees itself as a political community. In the first place, rules that constitute the political order lay down procedural and institutional arrangements on the political process and political behaviour. From the multitude of contingent rules, those are selected that are to apply for the order being constituted.[101] At the same time, however, *these rules stake out the communicative and deliberative space of a political community.* Constitutional disputes are therefore always about the rules by which a political community forms, changes, and maintains itself. *Constitutional discussions are societal discourses about self-understanding.* They shape the forums in which disputation about norms and thus about the community's constitutive values and obligations takes place. A dispute about the constitutionality of placing crucifixes in school classrooms by order of the state is primarily a dispute about the status of religion and its symbolic representation in the public life of a political community. That such a dispute, like many in the past, is fought out by political forces and societal actors around and about the constitution and not infrequently on the back of the constitutional court can, in "judicial-state" intensification, be criticized as a weakness of parliamentary democracy; on the other hand, it impressively demonstrates that the constitution has become the footing for political disputation. Where the constitution becomes the vanishing point of politics and society, things may look bad for the democratic culture of debate, but the constitution is accepted as the highest authority."[102]

Vorländer describes what he calls the *communal services* of the constitution:

> "These disputes about the constitution can themselves become tradition. They integrate a society by conducting conflicts on the basis of the constitution: 'The Constitution is best understood as an historically rooted tradition of theory and practice – an evolving language of politics through which Americans have learned to talk to one another in the course of their centuries-long struggle over the national identity.' As American constitutional history shows, the constitution becomes a *narrative of societal self-understanding*. Constitutional development reflects great societal conflicts, historical turning points, phases of change and watersheds in the values held by the polity, and relations between political and societal institutions. The history of the constitution and its interpretation become a *mirror of* the *societal and cultural development* of a political community, it can *reflect the historical learning processes of a democratic society.* Interpretation of the constitution by the – far from exclusive – circle of interpreters reveals shared meanings, as well as temporary or lasting cleavages. If it is true that the great metanarrative of liberal democracies has come to an

101 See Luhmann (1973).
102 Vorländer (1999).

> end (Richard Rorty), the constitution can stop the gap in the expectation or at least hope that the controversy about it and its fundamental institutions, procedures, and values will lead to habitual appropriation of the democratic and liberal principles characteristic of a constitutional community. This is ultimately the essence of talk about 'constitutional patriotism', whose civil-religious overstatement is the 'constitutional cult.' The constitution then becomes a bible or prayerbook of societal self-reassurance."[103]

So much on some of the views we have collected on mutual relations between law and politics. Before concluding, we will cast take a glance at the juristic construction of the institution "constitution."

E. Construction plan and key juristic elements of the institution "constitution"

As far as the construction plan of modern constitutions is concerned, Günter Frankenberg identifies four regulatory fields that practically all constitutions address:

- "On questions of *justice*, catalogues of basic rights flanked by rule-of-law principles and procedures provide essentially identical answers throughout the world: with the protection of equal freedom, constitutions guarantee all liberty for individual and collective self-determination, they institutionalize and limit the legitimate power of all state and public authorities.
- With respect to the *the good life* or the common good, constitutions affirm values to be translated into state objectives and constitutional missions – such as solidarity, keeping of the peace, public welfare, or the advancement of women; or into obligations of the state such as protecting life and health, or the family and child education; or which are realized in civic obligations such as military service or tax liability.
- Constitutions devote most space to *rules organizing the state*. They answer the questions informed by historical experience about political prudence with institutions and procedures for political decision-making and by assigning and distributing authority among organs of the state and ensuring mutual checks and balances.
- The fourth element concerns the *validity, amendment, and protection of a constitution*. These meta-rules shape the self-reflexivity and modernity of constitutions in the narrow sense of the term. They ensure that these constitutions draw their legitimacy from within themselves and exclude transcendental sources of legitimacy by regularly honouring the people as sovereign, tying any change to a decision by this sovereign or their representatives."[104]

103 Vorländer (1999) 82–83.

104 Frankenberg, G. (2008) 1413.

After this, as far as we can judge, correct list of contents, we need only name the *three juridical elements* on which the well-functioning of the *constitutional state*[105] depends:

Rainer Wahl has resumed these three basic elements of constitutional statehood with exemplary clarity and concision:

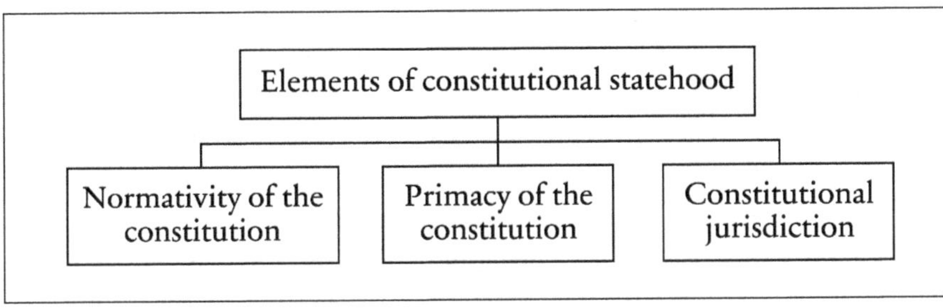

> "The constitutional state is based on the understanding that the written constitution is the basic law and the *highest authority in the legal order*. This general idea is given precise legal substance through the formulation and recognition of two legal principles: normativity of the constitution and primacy of the constitution. The first and logically superior principle, *normativity of the constitution*, states that the written constitution is not merely declamation, declaration, or political programme but *itself binding law*. The second principle, *primacy of the constitution*, is based in legal theoretical terms on the concept of the *hierarchical structure of the legal order*: the constitution is at the apex of the hierarchy of legal norms; subordinate to it is the 'simple' statute and the statutory instrument based on special legal empowerment. The primacy of the constitution finds expression in the principle of the constitutionality of all law (Article 20 III of the Basic Law). At the same time, the primacy of the constitution means that the lawmaker is subordinate to it.
>
> In a third important step, this substantive superiority of the constitution to all other law is joined by the implementation and effectuation of this primacy by an *elaborate system of constitutional jurisdiction*. The possibility of court supervision secures substantive material superiority by sanctioning violation of the constitution through statutory law by nullification. Disputes on constitutional law are fought out before the courts, ending with a binding ruling by the highest court.
>
> Taken together, these three elements, the normativity of the constitution, the primacy of the constitution, and constitutional jurisdiction form the legal heart of the (developed) constitutional state in the second half of the twentieth century."[106]

105 On the constitutional state as state type see Schuppert, G. F. (2003) 743–834.

106 Wahl (2001) 1041.

Having explored what constitutions generally regulate and the basis of their – also political – impact and authority, we conclude the chapter with a look at how constitutions actually come about.

F. How constitutions come about

All our reflections from various perspectives on the concept of constitution and constitutional functions have shown that the institution of the constitution is at home in the border country between law and politics and the language of constitutionalism is accordingly also a language of politics and a language of law. A last and particularly weighty argument should convince any reader not yet persuaded that law and politics are inseparably entwined in the institution of the constitution. It is the concept of "*constituent power*", which clearly straddles law and politics.

The constituent power of the people – a boundary concept between law and politics

As constitutional history shows, constitutions are produced in specific historico-political situations, mostly in the throes of radical change by which one political order is replaced by another. Since the French Revolution, what "erupts" under these circumstances has been called "*pouvoir constituant*", "*constituent power*", which, according to the democratic theory of government, can lie only with the people.[107] Although "constituent power" has the air of a concept of legal competence, there are no legal rules determining that, when, and how this constitution-making authority of the people comes into its own: *the politico-legal "big bang" of making a constitution* occurs in the absence of a constitution as binding normative order and without a set of rules providing instructions for drawing up a constitution as binding legal regime: "As the *pouvoir constituant* that *antecedes* the legal constitution, the constituent power of the people cannot be legally established by the constitution itself, nor can the forms in which it expresses itself be fixed. It has

107 This was clearly the assumption of the fathers and mothers of the Basic Law for the Federal Republic of Germany: in the preamble we find: "The German people have adopted, by virtue of their constituent power, this Basic Law." On the whole complex see Schuppert, G. F. (1984) 37 ff.

and retains an original, direct, as well as elemental quality. Accordingly, it is in a position – *precisely as a political factor* – to seek out and create forms of expression on its own."[108]

However, if the constituent power cannot be legally domesticated, the process of producing a constitution can be understood only as a political act. In the demanding diction of constitutional theory, Ernst-Wolfgang Böckenförde comments on this simple conclusion:

> "The constitution does not derive normative stabilization and regulatory force from a legal norm that stands above it or from a special sanction, which does not exist. Instead, it derives it from an idea of order established once, sustained, and normatively solidified by *political decision* borne by the people or by the crucial groups and powers within society. The power that brings forth and legitimizes the constitution must consequently present itself – also – as a *political entity*. Notions of what is just and right, ideas of political order attain formative and legitimatory force for human coexistence only when affirmed by people or groups of people as living conviction and embodied in an upholding *political force or authority*. Thus, the constituent power – as a concept of constitutional theory and constitutional doctrine – cannot be defined either as a merely hypothetical or a purely natural law basic norm. It must be understood as a real political factor that establishes the normative validity of the constitution. Of course, as such it cannot exist within or on the basis of the constitution, for example as an 'organ' created by the constitution; it must precede the constitution and the *pouvoirs constitués* established and limited by it. Precisely this precedence and superiority vis-à-vis the pouvoirs constitués represent the characteristic nature of the constituent power.[109]

This also means that constituent power is always latently present; at any time it can actualize itself or remain dormant for a longer period if the constitution it has created proves to be both stable and adaptable[110] and – ideally – even borne by a living *constitutional patriotism*:[111]

> "If the constituent power of the people is (also) a *real political factor* and force necessary to legitimize the constitution and its claim to validity, it cannot be juristically relegated to oblivion once it has fulfilled this function; it is and remains this factor and force. It would be curious to imagine that the necessary legitimation of the constitution could be reduced to the single point in time of its (revolutionary) creation, after which it would retain validity by a virtually self-sustaining process, independent of the continued existence of this legitimation. If the fundamental decisions of the constitution lack an enduring or self-renewing existential grounding

108 Böckenförde (2011) 105.
109 Böckenförde (2011) 100.
110 See my reflections on the subject in: Schuppert, G. F. (1995a).
111 See Gebhardt (1993) 31 ff.

> through the political and legal convictions that are alive in the concrete community united in the state, the constitution itself would inevitably erode. Its normativity would either trickle away between competing basic constitutional conceptions in search of a different order, or it would fall victim to general apathy."[112]

Even if – as we have seen – the constituent power cannot be domesticated legally, the process of making a constitution must be organized in one way or another. Böckenförde:

> "It is a priori impossible to separate a fundamental, boundary concept of constitutional law *from its entanglement with politics*. What is possible, however, and what constitutes an important task of constitutional law, is this: (1) the actions of the constituent power of the people, which can never be shut out, can be somehow circumscribed; (2) suitable measures can ensure that its expression triggers *procedures provided for the purpose*, thus cushioning and channelling it, but also allowing for actualization."[113]

As far as the practice of constitution-making is concerned, there are various procedures that come into question, two in particular: *convoking a constituent national assembly*, and appointing an *assembly to draft a constitution* followed by a plebiscite.

First procedure: a *constituent* national assembly that has arisen from democratic elections, and which itself decides on and positivizes constitutional law (in its more detailed version in basic decisions already rendered). A confirmation or decision by the people in the sense of citizens eligible to vote does not take place. This is how the Weimar constitution came about in 1919. It was agreed upon and enacted by the Weimar National Assembly, which had been elected on the basis of universal and equal suffrage. …

Second procedure: a *constitution-making assembly*, a 'convention', which is summoned or democratically elected. It submits the text of the constitution as a proposal to the people, which itself decides to accept or reject it. The constitutions of the southern German Länder after 1945 (Bavaria, Württemberg-Baden, Hesse, Rhineland-Palatinate) as well as those of Bremen and North Rhine-Westphalia, were deliberated and agreed upon by popularly elected Landtage (state parliaments), which doubled up as constitution-making conventions, and were subsequently adopted by referendum."[114]

112 Böckenförde (2011) 106.
113 Böckenförde (2011) 107.
114 Böckenförde (2011) 108–109.

But constitutions come into being not only through quasi "eruption" of the constituent power of the people; another case, no less frequent in constitutional history, is *constitution-making by contract*. The most recent example of contractualist constitution making[115] is the contractual network of the 'union of states' that goes by the name European Union, an act of constituting a transnational basic order that has provoked intensive discussion on whether constitution is a suitable descriptor;[116] we shall not be going into this controversy here. In constitutional history, at any rate, *contracted constitutions* are to be regarded as a separate type of constitution-making. Under the heading "*consociational systems of governance*", Arthur Benz has this to say:[117]

> "The forms of authority that developed here [what is meant is in deviation from the dominant model of the sovereign territorial state] did not initially point in the direction of the modern state that established itself only later in these areas. It was characterized by a mixture of estate-based separation of powers and federal union, which is also referred to as consociational governance. However, this rough description hides considerable differences. The Swiss federation of rural communities had little in common with the alliances between Italian city republics secured only through diplomacy or with the more strongly institutionalized association of Hanseatic cities, in which the patrician class of merchants ruled, or the Republic of the United Netherlands with its estate-based institutions. The German Reich, which since 1648 had developed more and more into a union of states, comprised principalities under absolute monarchs and free cities with estate-based systems of government and free cities under the paramountcy of an increasingly weak emperor. But all these structures differed significantly from the model of the emerging territorial state. Its existence posed a challenge for the political theory of the time. What had to be clarified was whether these forms of rule were deviations from the normal development model, that is to say, forms that would not survive the conflicts of the modern age, or whether they were closer to a natural, just, and stable government than the emerging absolutist state. The former view was that taken by theoreticians such as Bodin and Pufendorf, the latter that adopted by a group of theoreticians long forgotten or neglected by the history of ideas who were inspired by Calvinist or Jewish thought, but who also drew on Aristotle and the humanism of antiquity."[118]

We can let this intellectual dissension be, but the encounter with the constitution as contract gives occasion to take a brief glance at the concept of contract with regard to its importance in the history of ideas.

115 See Frankenberg, G. (2008) 1412.
116 See Grimm (2005).
117 Benz (2008) 24.
118 Benz (2008) 24.

14

Contract as a Legal Concept

The reader can rest assured that we plan no juridical lecture on the concept and function of the contract. Keeping in mind our fundamental objective of examining the importance of the language of law in the context of a global history of ideas, we shall consider the concept of the contract,[119] which without a doubt belongs to the language of law, from the perspective of various disciplines. The aim is to demonstrate the eminent importance of this key legal concept in other disciplines particularly relevant to the history of ideas. However, we begin with a number of comments from the ethnology and sociology of law.

A. The contract as a tool for producing binding force

When people sociate in whatever form, social relations develop between them that, to put it in lay terms, work better if the parties are fully conscious of what is expected and what social obligations might be involved. Kiyomi von Frankenberg, writing about the "generation of obligation prior to and alongside positive law",[120] addresses the importance of *exchanges in pre-state societies.*[121] This is interesting because considering exchanges as an informal procedure for generating obligation casts particular light on the specific "institutional competence" of the contract as type of institution.

As far as the *functional logic of exchange* is concerned, the *key concept is reciprocity*:

119 In brief, there are entire areas of law in which the contract is a crucial structuring tool. This is the case for international law, which is essentially international contract law, and for used to be called public ecclesiastical law, since relations between the state and Christian confessions in Germany are organized almost exclusively by contract.

120 Frankenberg, K. (2015).

121 See Frankenberg, K. (2015) 37: "By stateless society we understand orders in which law is not exclusively legal in nature but, because of low differentiation and low professionalization, is interwoven with other (religious, moral, and political) institutions. For instance, 'judges' can also assume lawmaking or priestly functions. The law is neither differentiated in terms of fields of law nor codified in written form, and is therefore not to be distinguished from social norms."

> "The basis of exchange theory[122] is the realization that the acceptance of a gift obliges the recipient to counter-performance and that this reciprocity constitutes a 'crux of all human behaviour.'[123] The behaviours required in exchanges develop not only for reasons of expediency but on the basis of the *reciprocity norm*. It states simply that whoever gives something to another obliges this recipient to make a gift in return. Every exchange is based on three obligations: to make gifts, to accept gifts, and to return gifts. The universal, comprehensible norm of reciprocity underlying every exchange is important for maintaining social systems. The reception of advantages imposes counter-performance that confirms a social relationship. Whoever accepts a gift is under obligation to the giver. If the recipient wishes to escape possible retaliation by the giver and to maintain the possibility of further cooperation, he must return the gift. A gift is both favour and obligation because the giver gives the recipient a 'loan' in the confidence that the latter will return the gift to prove themselves worthy of trust as cooperation partner. This reciprocity in social exchange is considered a key element, indeed the 'most important basic rule'[124] for the initiation, stability, and regulation of social interaction. In its negative form, too – retaliation in accordance with the law of talion ('eye for an eye, tooth for a tooth') – the role of the reciprocity principle for the maintenance of social systems is clearly apparent."[125]

This *fundamental norm of reciprocity* is *juridified* through the institution of the contract; that is to say, the social norm becomes a legal norm:

> "Exchange theory is concerned with so-called social exchange (for instance of objects, services, or information), which differs from the economic exchange of goods in that counter-performance in social exchange is always indeterminate and not set at an exact price, so that this form of exchange can generate feelings of personal obligation, gratitude and trust. A contract, by contrast, lays down exactly what rights and duties the contracting parties have. The result is that the parties have no obligation over and above what the contract specifies. In particular, no personal gratitude is owed. … In our present-day differentiated legal system, exchange in the form of contracts is omnipresent. Synallagmatic exchange, for instance of labour for wages or goods for money has long since become so formalized that *non-compliance with its terms is actionable*. But there are also non-juridified forms of exchange, which from their structure recall those in stateless societies without centralized authority. Such exchange is resorted to in situations for which there is no (recognized) legal solution. In such situations, the parties face the problem of developing a common, effective frame of reference[126] to normatively struc-

122 A leading theoretician is Blau (1964).

123 Thurnwald (1934) 5.

124 Stegbauer (2002) 19.

125 Frankenberg, K. (2015) 35–36.

126 Goffmann (1977) 367; see also Esser (1999) 259 ff. and Hillmann (2007), headword "Bezugsrahmen" ("Frame of reference"). Frames of reference contain organizational prin-

> ture cooperation that is not legally secured, thus obviating the risk of having to rely solely on interpersonal trust and having to break off cooperation if this trust is disappointed."[127]

In brief, the contract formalizes the fundamental social norm of reciprocity and – the most important ingredient – also provides for coercive compliance. According to new institutional economics, and notably its most prominent representative – Douglass Cecil North[128] – economic prosperity requires two absolutely indispensable basic institutions: legally protected property and legally enforceable contracts:

> "Perhaps the key hypothesis of institutional economics is: growth and development depend decisively on the given valid institutions. Both the willingness and capacity to specialize and thus contribute to a stronger division of labour and to invest in durable capital goods depends essentially on the security of property rights. As we … shall see, property rights are a central component of the institutions to be economically analysed. Their content, and the costs that have to be met to impose them, and thus to obtain legal satisfaction if someone else has breached my property rights, are considered key determinants in explaining growth and development. Douglass North … points out that the inability of societies to developed effective and low-cost mechanisms for enforcing compliance with contracts is the most important reason for historical stagnation and for the current underdevelopment in the Third World."[129]

If the effectiveness of the contract lies in its potentially strong binding force and in its secured enforceability through what we have called specific "norm enforcement regimes",[130] two consequences automatically ensue: the power problem of asymmetrical contracts and the justice problem of a content acceptable to both contracting parties. Not only jurisprudence concerns itself with these problems.

ciples that determine how situations develop. They can be understood as the normative structure of a specific situation; but their normative nature is social not legal.

127 Frankenberg, K. (2015) 33–34.

128 His magnum opus of now almost canonic status is entitled "Institutions, Institutional Change, and Economic Performance", North (1990); see also North et al. (2009).

129 Voigt (2002) 1–2.

130 Schuppert, G. F. (2016b) Chapter 4: "From the Plurality of Normative Orders to the Plurality of Norm Enforcement Regimes: Jurisdictional Communities and their Specific Jurisdictional Cultures".

B. The contract as a power and justice problem

I. Contracts as a power problem: the double task of constitutional law

1. Freedom of contract and private autonomy

In liberal and particularly in market economy societies, everyone is in principle free to conclude contracts with everyone, and – within certain legal limits – on any subject. The legal terms are *freedom of contract* and *private autonomy*. Werner Flumes classical definition of private autonomy is "the principle of the self-development of legal relations by the individual in accordance with his will".[131] In constitutional law terms, private autonomy a consequence of the general freedom of action protected by Article 2 (1) of the Basic Law[132] and, at the same time – when it is a question of legal economic transactions – of the freedom of occupation protected by Article 12 (1) of the Basic Law. Private autonomy is thus another term for *self-determination*. But precisely because contracts are enforceable before the courts and can be enforced by the state, this self-determination cannot be limitless, it must be tied to constitutional law. Alexander Hellgardt:

> "To the extent that the legal system guarantees private autonomy, it recognizes the self-determination of the private sphere without this requiring further justification: stat pro ratione voluntas.[133] Private autonomy in this sense means *material self-determination*, which, owing to such a 'declaration of will' justifies recognizing a subjective right that can, where need be, be *enforced by state courts*. However, it is precisely this legal consequence – the deployment of state means of enforcement owing to the free self-determination of the private party – that reconnects material private autonomy to constitutional law: if the state attaches legal consequences up to and including coercion to private autonomous action, the basic civil liberties of the private person require a minimum of control by the state. The state is under obligation to protect; it may enforce contractual claims by sovereign means only if they can be attributed to the private autonomy of the affected party.[134] This is at any rate where an act of self-determination is *really* at issue."[135]

131 Flume (1992).
132 See BVerfGE 8, 274, 328; 89, 214, 231.
133 Flume (1992) 6: "The validity of the principle of private autonomy means recognition of the 'self-sovereignty' of the individual in the creative development of legal relations."
134 In detail, Canaris (1999) 37–51.
135 Hellgarth (2016) 69.

However, as the Federal Constitutional Court decided in its famous ruling on sureties (*Bürgschaftsentscheidung*), such *real* self-determination can be lacking if there is structural asymmetry between the contracting parties that as a rule excludes the genuine self-determination of the "weaker" party: "For the civil courts this gives rise to the duty to ensure, in interpreting and applying general clauses, that contracts do not serve as a tool for heteronomous control. If the contracting parties have agreed on a permissible arrangement, further monitoring of contractual content is generally unnecessary. If, however, the content of the contract is unusually burdensome for one party and the balance of interests is clearly unreasonable, the courts are unlikely to rule simply that 'a contract is a contract is a contract'. They must clarify whether the contractual arrangement is a consequence of structurally unequal negotiating strength, and, where necessary, intervene in the framework of the general clauses of valid civil law. How they are to proceed and what result they must come to are primarily a question of ordinary law, to which the constitution gives broad latitude. The private autonomy guaranteed by basic rights may, however, be breached if the problem of disturbed contractual parity has not been seen or its elimination attempted by unsuitable means."[136]

2. Private power in contract law

Private autonomy always brings the risk of an economically more powerful contracting party using his economic superiority to impose his own interests at the cost of the other.[137] For a realistic assessment of this danger, it is therefore useful to identify types of contract that can be considered potentially dangerous. Notable among them are long-term contracts such as[138]

- employment contracts,
- tenancy agreements,
- commercial agency contracts, and
- franchise agreements.

136 BVerfGE 89, 214 ff., 234.
137 See the interesting reflections in Franck (2016).
138 See Riesenhuber (2016).

In these fields, the courts have the task of limiting the dangers arising from actual economic asymmetry, for instance with the so-called rental brake; but as this very example shows, what is at issue is not so much controlling the content of dangerous contracts but – ultimately – regulating the housing or labour market.[139]

It is not far from dangerous contracts to unjust contracts, which we shall now look at briefly.

II. Contracts as a justice problem: the contract law literature of 16th century moral theology

The problem of the just or unjust contract was a concern not only of jurisprudence but also of – notably Spanish – moral theology, which produced a contract law literature of its own. Thomas Duve comments:

> "A few years after the conclusion of the Council of Trent, a number of works appeared in the Spanish monarchy that could be described as popular, late-scholastic contract law literature – texts addressing merchants and traders, instructing them on the principles of contract law. There had, of course, already been such *moral theological treatises on contract law* in the late Middle Ages. But then a considerable number were published and rapidly diffused outside Europe, too. Probably the best known of these works were the Tratos y contratos de mercaderes (1569, from the second edition: Summa de tratos y contratos) by Tomás de Mercado, the Arte de los contractos von Bartolomé Frías de Albornoz (1573), and the Tratado utilísmo de todos los contratos von Francisco García (1583).[140]

On the reach and importance of the moral theological contract law literature, Duve remarks:

> "Just how closely these contract law designs were associated with expansion [to India and Latin America] and how *this normative order* secured validity over long distances are shown by Tomás de Mercado's *Tratos y contratos de mercaderes*. It was dedicated to the *Consulado de Mercaderes* of Seville, the merchant guild – with jurisdictional powers – of the port city where in 1503 the *Casa de Contratación* was established and through which traffic with the New World was channelled. In his preface, Mercado states that he wrote the book at the request and for the use of these merchants, on the basis of experience that he had personally gathered in New Spain, i. e., present-day Mexico, in Seville, and Salamanca. Such a book was doubtless needed, for there was no comparable exposition, and Seville, which had

139 See Riesenhuber (2016) 199 ff.
140 Duve (2011) 147 ff., 160.

> always been a major trading city, had, since the discovery of America, lost its marginal status to become the 'centre for all merchants of the world.' Merchandise was delivered there from everywhere, even from Turkey, to be transported to America, where 'everything had such an excessive price.' The city, he remarks, had 'embraced all sorts of business', all were now merchants and traders who had once engaged in other activities. It was therefore all the more important to show 'what was allowed and what was not allowed'. For: 'in business, not to know what is just and what is not just means not to know anything, for the most important thing that every Christian must know is not to lose his eternal salvation in the attempt to amass worldly goods'."[141]

Authors like Mercado were thus ultimately concerned about the salvation of their fellow humans: "The incentive to comply with norms should be not validity prescribed by the state or by the pope, but fear for one's own salvation.[142] However, if this was not about statutory law sanctioned by the state or a particularist Spanish regulatory regime, but a contract theory as element of a "philosophical system",[143] his *demand for compliance was universal in nature*. The moral-theological contract theories were accordingly designs for a global normative order in the sense of, to quote Duve, "*global salvisic Catholicism*":

> "From the point of view of these authors, the moral-theological, philosophically grounded and canonistically furnished design for a normative order was universal because it was based on fundamental ontological assumptions independent of space and time. Precisely in this *universality* lay the resounding force of Spanish late scholastic thought, which set limits to the pope and the crown, but which ultimately provided a philosophical theoretical basis for expansion. This *universality* is evident even in contract law: where the types of contract reflect a higher order, then they *exist* throughout the world. They are reality. Law based on such fundamental ontological assumptions can abstract from particularist rights and tradition, it can permit adaptation, it is particularly suitable for reproduction in a global dimension.

This ontology with which the intellectual mobilisation of late scholastics underpinned many fields of law also meant that the new normative order, living from tradition but not bound by it, was more universalist than canon law could be: it addressed not only the baptised, as was the case with canon law, but all humanity. It was thus not limited to the *orbis christianus*. Its creators regarded it as a normative order that could claim authority through-

141 Duve (2011) 160–161.
142 Duve (2011) 162.
143 Duve (2011) 163.

out the world, as contract law and as international law, or in relation to human rights, probably the best-known historical cases of application for this universalist world-view."[144]

After this moral-theological perspective on the entire world, we conclude our excursus on the institution of contract with a look not at real but at virtual contracts, a figure of thought that also encompassed everyone in the world.

III. Contract theories as proceduralist justification theories

Contract theories, whose best known representatives are Thomas Hobbes and Jean Jacques Rousseau,[145] provide an intellectual construction by which *political authority can be justified* without reference to God or any sort of natural law. Writing about "contract law as justification theory", Wolfgang Kersting[146] explains this justificatory function of contract theories in the "Handbuch der Politischen Philosophie und Sozialphilosophie" ("Manual of Political Philosophy and Social Philosophy"):

> "'Contract theories' are conceptions in moral, social, and political philosophy that see the moral principles of human action, the rational basis for the institutional order of society and the conditions for the legitimation of political authority in a hypothetical contract concluded between free and equal individuals in a well-defined initial state, and therefore declare the general capacity for consent to be the fundamental criterion of validity. Contract theories are based on *justification-theoretical proceduralism*. The conceptual experiment on which they focus is the systematic elaboration of the conviction, typical of modernity, that society's need for justification can no longer be met by recourse to the will of God or an objective natural value order. The waning of the theological world-view, the disappearance of the traditional qualitative concept of nature in the light of modern scientific factuality, the decline of the firmly established social order with its integrated values under the growing onslaught of adaptation to civil society and the economization of societal conditions required cultural justificatory practices to be reorganized in line with the new intellectual basis of the modern world, with humankind's new conditions of self and world."[147]

144 Duve (2011) 164–165.
145 See Schaal/Heidenreich (2006) 65 ff. (Hobbes) and 139 ff. (Rousseau).
146 See Kersting (1994); also: Kersting (2004).
147 Kersting (2008) 1430.

Under contract theory, contracts were hence hypothetical, having nothing to do with the binding force of real contracts;[148] their – imaginary – conclusion was therefore not the outcome of negotiation:

> "In contractualist contracts there is no negotiating; the parties do not meet one another half way; they set out no compromises. Their function is moral-epistemological, heuristic. They are used as a means of identifying constraints on freedom that can win general recognition. Contractualist arguments are therefore always about consensus, albeit not deliberative, discursive consensus: consensus of this sort cannot prejudice the theory. *Consensus in contractualist argumentation is theoretically deduced strategic consensus*; it is based on a generalized egoism embedded in reciprocal instrumentalization. It is achieved by radically homogenizing interests; only where all parties have an interest in agreement can a representative decision be reached that is convincing for everyone, for every reader, and which is thus a generally acceptable outcome."[149]

How the concept of the social contract functioned as a *theoretical legitimation concept* is best shown by the models offered by Thomas Hobbes and Jean Jacques Rousseau. We begin with a brief explication of Hobbes' contract model by Wolfgang Kersting:

> "The contract is concluded in the state of nature, which, in the absence of valid rules and institutional structures, is a state of war where distrust and a propensity for violence prevail and everyone sees everyone as an enemy. To escape this intolerable situation, individuals conclude a contract under which they mutually promise to waive their rights and their →freedom and to found a →state, which is vested with invincible →power, ensuring a life free of violence for the community. *Hobbes' social contract is a contract that justifies authority, not a contract that limits authority.* Individuals waive their →rights unconditionally; Hobbes' contractual state therefore possesses absolute power. It is constrained neither by liberal basic rights, nor by →human rights or natural law principles. *Hobbes'* social contract presents the curious, paradoxical picture of a radical individualist justification of absolute power, a legitimation of state absolutism through the unreserved will of the individual to self-commitment."[150]

Although Rousseau, too, presupposed a humanity in a state of nature, he argues in a quite different direction:

> "Rousseau, too, attributes an inalienable right to liberty to human beings. But this requires much more than a guarantee of general freedom of action; it requires autonomy, material self-determination. But how is legitimate political →authority

148 Kersting (2001).
149 Kersting (2008) 1431–1432.
150 Kersting (2001) 82.

> possible under the conditions of inalienable self-rule? Only if, so to speak, all citizens have power in the state and make laws for themselves with one voice. Autonomy is then assured, since everyone remains subject only to their own law; then the general will, the *volonté générale*, is always the will of each individual, as well. Because it guarantees unrestricted freedom, Rousseau's social contract must necessarily lead to a republic, to direct →democracy. Any other political organization of authority is illegitimate. →Sovereignty is due only to the →people. *Rousseau's* social contract is the conceptual symbol of the political self-empowerment of the people."[151]

We conclude our excursus on the contract with another passage from Wolfgang Kersting stressing the *universal applicability of the legitimation concept of contract theory*, which explains its *central role in the political history of ideas*:

> "The contract is a highly flexible justificatory tool, which can be used in connection with a broad range of starting positions, issues, and conflict scenarios. The contractualist theory programme is therefore by no means limited to the classical issues of legitimating and limiting authority. Current practical philosophy shows that the tasks justifying moral principles and institutions, validating democracy and grounding a theory of collective action can also be tackled from a contractualist perspective. If a person concludes a contractual agreement with another, he gives his consent to the duties and correlative rights that accrue to him and the other party through this agreement. In so far as his consent is freely given and fair contractual negotiations have taken place, he has no right to complain about the normative consequences arising from this contractual agreement and must accept them as binding. The fundamental philosophical idea behind modern justice-theoretical contractualism is, in the course of appropriate generalization, to interpret the whole of society together with all its various institutional structures and arrangements as a contractual relationship and to derive the binding force of societal and political institutions, of the social and political constitution from universal consent for all members of society qua contracting parties."[152]

151 Kersting (2001) 82–83.

152 Kersting (2008) 1434–1435.

Summary

In the introduction to this book, we had asked whether and why a global history of ideas should also be written in the language of law, and came to the conclusion that the language of law – understood as a language of politics – had an essential contribution to make to any future global history of ideas.

Four observations have been central to our positive assessment of the potential the language of law offers as a language of politics.

First, discussion of the legitimacy of political authority as social-critical discourse is generally conducted as a legal discourse. This is demonstrated, above all, by the fact the revolutionary seizures of power are always legalo-semantic seizures of power, as well, which always come in the guise of a new language that requires either new concepts or reinterprets existing legal concepts.

Second, that the language of law always manages to contribute something to the global dimension of a history of ideas, as shown by the language of global constitutionalism or worldwide rule-of-law promotion. Third, this globalization "gene" of the language of law as a language of politics is also evident in the spread of justice discourses at the global level, where, as inevitable response to the ongoing globalization process, global justice is in increasing demand, thus broadening the very concept of justice (catchwords: environmental justice, climate justice).

And fourth, a future world order – however conceived – can, it would seem, not be described without the language of law. Zürn's overview[1] of the subject "speaks volumes".

Now, some 270 pages later, the critical question needs to be raised of whether the positive assessment to be found on pages 19/20 has been justified. The answer, I believe, is clear: a global history of ideas that wishes to be taken seriously cannot be written without the language of law. We shall not

1 Zürn (2011b).

repeat in detail the "evidence" we have presented in the course of this book, but the rich panorama revealed from perusing the broad field of the global history of ideas through the eyes of the law is well worth noting. We sum up under the following headings, which, having already been dealt with at length, need only brief explication without extensive references in the footnotes.

A. The statization of the world

The state is the predominant model of political authority throughout the world, regardless of periodic assertions of its demise. As Wolfgang Reinhard has commented, it is the jurists who perfected the theory of state, who in 1837 declared the state a legal person and who finally developed an authoritative definition. According to Georg Jellinek's 1900 omnipresent "general theory of the state", the modern state has three characteristics: a state territory over which it has exclusive authority, a state people as sedentary association of persons with permanent membership, and a sovereign state authority. Jurists see themselves as particularly committed trustees of the state concept, because they need it in international law, where the state is the most important subject, but also in constitutional law, where it is an entity to which legal responsibilities can be attributed.

So much for the statization of the world.

B. Four more or less successful "triumphs" under the banner of law

I. The "triumph" of natural law

The great systematic natural law theories from the seventeenth century by Hugo Grotius, Thomas Hobbes, Baruch de Spinoza, John Locke, and Samuel Pufendorf revolutionized legal and political thought and enjoyed an unprecedented triumph throughout a western world covered by a network of natural-law experts occupying chairs at universities. Michael Stolleis has pointed to the close link between the successful expansion of natural-law thought and the first wave of globalization since the discovery of America and the Copernican revolution, and speculates about the development of a future "natural law without God" under the headings "universal human rights", "emerging international criminal law", and "worldwide networks of transnational law and non-state law". Here, too, we observe the triumph of a legal idea.

II. The "triumph" of the constitutional idea and the stalling triumph of the idea of constitutional jurisdiction

Almost every modern state "affords itself" the becoming mantle of a constitution, which generally means a great deal more than a supreme organizational statute; the emphasis is on the function of a constitution as focal point of the politico-cultural self-understanding of a society. As Hans Vorländer has stressed, the rules spelled out in the constitution define the communicative and deliberative space of a political community: "Constitutional discourses are societal self-understanding discourses."[2] The role of the American constitution as the "civil religion" of the United States marking the identity of the polity is an impressive demonstration of this.

The institution of constitutional jurisdiction, too, has spread almost epidemically, albeit as an institution with varying competences. The judges of the Federal Constitutional Court have a tale to tell about the endless queue of delegations from around the world on pilgrimages to Karlsruhe – the Mecca, as it were, of the rule of law. That constitutional courts have come under massive pressure and are being politically disempowered, as currently in Poland and Hungary, is because the juridification of politics associated with the establishment of powerful constitutional jurisdiction is a thorn in the flesh of ruling authoritarian regimes – which is no argument against the idea of constitutional jurisdiction: quite the contrary.

III. The "triumph" of the idea of human rights

We deliberately speak of a triumph of the *idea* of human rights, not a triumph of human rights themselves, which in many parts of the world are not being respected or are trampled under foot. Nonetheless, they can be described as the political creed of modernity; they have standard-setting force that places semi-authoritarian and authoritarian regimes, too, in the often annoying position of having to justify themselves.

2 Vorländer (1999) 82.

But for another reason, too, the idea of human rights is an important component of any global history of ideas. As with other legal concepts and terms, concepts formulated in the form of law – like the constitution – often belong to both the sphere of law and the sphere of politics, or – like human rights – are at home in both the world of law and the world of ethics. They consequently perform a bridging function. The language of human rights has to be a multilingual language, which can enter discourses on the good and just order of a society as a language of morality, law, and politics. Only then can the human rights project successfully bridge ethics, law and politics.

IV. The "triumph" of the idea of global validity for the rule of law

The language of the rule of law does not present itself with the same moral and Christian ethical might as the language of human rights. It is more of a language of rules and procedures, which takes account of the organizational requirements of statehood, emphasizing the institutional virtues of the rule-of-law principle. For this reason, rule-of-law principles are also, on closer inspection, the hard core of good governance. This explains why the rule-of-law promotion industry operating worldwide finds it so attractive to draw on all forms of rule-of-law organizational and procedural law – catchwords: separation of powers, independent judiciary.

Then there is what we call the justice gene of the rule of law, which manifests itself above all in the idea of institutional justice: "buon governo e giustizia" – as depicted in the Lorenzetti's famous allegory of good government – are inseparable.

So much for the four "triumphs" under the banner of law. Finally, we cast a brief glance at a number of key concepts originating from the world of law without which no history of political ideas is conceivable.

C. Three key concepts from the world of law intrinsic to the global history of ideas

I. Sovereignty

The idea of the sovereign state, too, clearly demonstrates that concepts of the political history of ideas belong both to the world of politics and to that of law. For some authors, sovereignty is a key concept in politics, for others a central concept of international and constitutional law. Dieter Grimm gives what is possibly the best definition when he calls sovereignty a "basic legal-political concept."[3] He describes the political unity formula of sovereignty as a legitimation formula couched in the language of law, aptly capturing sovereignty's belonging to two worlds.

II. Contract

The situation with the concept of contract is quite similar to that of sovereignty. On the one hand, the contract is a legal tool for generating obligation; on the other, in the form of social contract, it play a crucial role in the political philosophy of early modernity. Without the figure of thought of the hypothetical social contract, as we have known since Hobbes, Locke, and Rousseau, there is no escape from the "state of nature" or justification for a civil society of property owners. Political philosophy's "social contract theories" operate as proceduralist theories to justify political authority,[4] and as such are a legitimation concept based on consensus indispensable for modern constitutional law.

III. Property

We had not yet addressed property, an obvious gap when it comes to providing a concluding overview and one we shall seek to close to at least some extent, stressing once again, quite simply, that concepts are not always at home in only one language: they may be used in the languages of more than one discipline. As Hannes Siegrist and David Sugarman have convincingly shown,[5] several scholarly disciplines can be described as "property sciences", each with its own language of property. Five can be identified:

- The language of law; property is above all a legal institution that attributes certain rights to a given owner – rights of use, rights of disposal, rights of exclusion – and which requires non-owners to respect these ownership rights.

3 Grimm (2007).
4 Kersting (2004).
5 Siegrist/Sugarman (ed.) (1999) 1 ff.

- The language of theology, which understands property as an element of the divine order of creation, where God is and remains the primal owner but entrusts the legal organization of property to man-made law.
- The language of political philosophy, which has developed a basic narrative to justify and legitimize private property – differing only in nuances – in which the concepts "state of nature" and "social contract" play a central role.
- The language of institutional economics, which treats property as a conglomerate of property rights that are precisely defined by the legal system and have above all to be guaranteed, in order to minimize economic transaction costs and make effective economic activity possible in the first place; this also requires contracts to be enforceable.
- The language of anthropology, which treats property as a form of relationship with the world and the establishment of property as an act of appropriating the world, and which posits a basic anthropological need to have something of one's own.

These comments should suffice to demonstrate the multilinguality of the language of property. We finish with a few remarks on the language of law as a language of political authority.

D. The language of law as the language of political authority

We begin with the observation – which has run through the entire book – that law, politics, and power are clearly inseparable. The often cited "final proof" is constitutional jurisdiction. We have discussed this in connection with the constitutional court's control over foreign policy,[6] but this is not our concern here. We are interested not in whether politics is made in Karlsruhe – perhaps even in excess – but in the *function of law for the operation of all political sociation*.

This fits in neatly with the Hans Mohr's succinct statement "political culture is unthinkable without law";[7] which we can only confirm from our experience in studying the difficult to define phenomenon of "political culture."[8]

But it goes beyond the link between law and the values and political culture of a polity – which alone would justify writing a history of political ideas in the language of law, too. It has to do with the history of the modern

6 See my dissertation: Schuppert, G. F. (1973).

7 Mohr (1999) 109.

8 Schuppert, G. F. (2008) 659 ff.: "Politische Kultur als Strukturierungsaufgabe des Rechts".

state as a history not only of power but also of law. That this is so is more than apparent when we recall that the hard core of Bodin's sovereignty theory consists precisely in claiming the monopoly of lawmaking for the absolutist territorial ruler; we have discussed this in detail in the section on the concept of sovereignty. Nor should we forget the historically well-founded observation that seizures of power generally take the form of seizures of law; witness the notorious example of National Socialism.

Rather than listing further proofs for the entanglement of law, politics, and power, we conclude by giving the floor to Martti Koskenniemi, a specialist in international law we have often cited, who calls on us to shake off our inability "*to recognize law as a central element of authority*". In the same discussion, he added: "The second point – and this has long been my concern – is to demonstrate the central role of law in constellations of power and dominance – in everything we do ... It is not about getting rid of law but of better understanding and applying it."[9]

In precisely this sense, we are also concerned to understand law as a central element of authority and give it its due place in a global history of ideas. It is our firm conviction that a history of political ideas would not only be incomplete but also deficient if law were not to be taken into sufficient account as one of the pillars of political authority and political culture. We believe that the reflections and findings presented in this book more than justify writing a history of political ideas also in the language of law. In brief, the language of law is – from A to Z – also and above all a language of politics and therefore necessarily a subject for the political history of ideas.

9 Kemmerer (2015, German ed.) 46.

Bibliography

Acemoglu, Daron, James A. Robinson (2013), Warum Nationen scheitern. Die Ursprünge von Macht, Wohlstand und Armut, Frankfurt am Main

Agamben, Giorgio (1995), Homo sacer: Die souveräne Macht und das nackte Leben, Frankfurt am Main

Albrow, Martin (1972), Bürokratie, Munich

Anderson, Elizabeth (1999), What is the Point of Equality?, in: Ethics 109, 287–337, https://doi.org/10.1086/233897

Anderson, Elizabeth (2012), Equality, in: Estlund, David (ed.), The Oxford Handbook of Political Philosophy, Oxford / New York, 40–57, https://doi.org/10.1093/oxfordhb/9780195376692.013.0002

Anter, Andreas (2004), Die Macht der Ordnung. Aspekte einer Grundkategorie des Politischen, Tübingen

Anter, Andreas (2013), Der Staat als Beobachtungsobjekt der Sozialwissenschaften. Das Trugbild vom verschwindenden Staat und die Normativität des Gegenstandes, in: Bach, Maurizio (ed.), Der entmachtete Leviathan. Löst sich der souveräne Staat auf?, Zeitschrift für Politik, Sonderband 5, 17–27, https://doi.org/10.5771/9783845244273-15

Anter, Andreas (2016), Die Staatstheorie der Gegenwart. Ein Forschungsbericht, in: Zeitschrift für Politische Theorie 7, 239–247, https://doi.org/10.3224/zpth.v7i2.08

Anter, Andreas / Wilhelm Bleek (2013), Staatskonzepte. Die Theorien der bundesdeutschen Politikwissenschaft, Frankfurt am Main

Armitage, David (2000), The Ideological Origin of the British Empire, Cambridge

Armitage, David (2012), What's the Big Idea? Intellectual History and the Longue Durée, in: History of European Ideas 38, 493–507

Arnauld, Andreas von (2006), Rechtssicherheit. Perspektivische Annäherungen an eine 'idée directrice' des Rechts, Tübingen

Asche, Matthias (1998), Über den Nutzen von Landesuniversitäten in der Frühen Neuzeit – Leistungen und Grenzen der protestantischen "Familienuniversität", in: Herde, Peter, Anton Schindling (eds.), Universität Würzburg und Wissenschaft in der Frühen Neuzeit, Würzburg, 133–149

Assmann, Aleida (2011), Einführung in die Kulturwissenschaft, Berlin

Assmann, Jan (2000), Religion und kulturelles Gedächtnis. Zehn Studien, Munich

Augusti, Eliana (2009), The Ottoman Empire at the Congress of Paris: Between New Declensions and Old Prejudices, in: Beck Varela, Laura et al. (eds.), Crossing Legal Cultures, Munich, 503–519

Austin, John L. (1962), How to do Things with Words, Oxford

Auswärtiges Amt (ed.) (2009), Der Rechtsstaat – Patentrezept für alle Welt?, Berlin

BACHMANN-MEDICK, DORIS (2009), Cultural Turns. Neuorientierungen in den Kulturwissenschaften, 3rd ed., Reinbek bei Hamburg

BACHMANN-MEDICK, DORIS (2012), Menschenrechte als Übersetzungsproblem, in: Geschichte und Gesellschaft 38/2, 331–359, https://doi.org/10.13109/gege.2012.38.2.331

BADURA, PETER (1966), Verwaltungsrecht im liberalen und im sozialen Rechtsstaat, Tübingen

BADURA, PETER (1967), Das Verwaltungsrecht des liberalen Rechtsstaats. Überlegungen zur Entstehung des wissenschaftlichen Verwaltungsrechts, Göttingen

BADURA, PETER (1987), Verfassung, in: HERZOG, ROMAN et al. (eds.), Evangelisches Staatslexikon, 3rd. ed., Stuttgart, cl. 3757–3760

BAECKER, DIRK (2013), Beobachter unter sich. Eine Kulturtheorie, Berlin

BAER, SUSANNE (2004), Schlüsselbegriffe, Typen und Leitbilder als Erkenntnismittel und ihr Verhältnis zur Rechtsdogmatik, in: SCHMIDT-ASSMANN, EBERHARD, WOLFGANG HOFFMANN-RIEM (eds.), Methoden der Verwaltungsrechtswissenschaft, Baden-Baden, 225–251

BANFIELD, EDWARD C. (1958), The Moral Basis of a Backward Society, Glencoe, IL

BARTHES, ROLAND (1983), Elements of Semiology, New York

BAYLY, CHRISTOPHER ALAN (2006), Die Geburt der modernen Welt. Eine Globalgeschichte 1780–1914, Frankfurt am Main

BECK, ULRICH (1993), Die Erfindung des Politischen, Frankfurt am Main

BECKERT, SVEN KING (2014), Cotton. Eine Geschichte des globalen Kapitalismus, Munich

BEIERGRÖSSLEIN, KATHARINA et al. (2013), Das Naturrecht an den Universitäten Würzburg und Bamberg im 18. Jahrhundert, in: Zeitschrift für Neuere Rechtsgeschichte 35, 172–192

BELL, CHRISTINE (2008), On the Law of Peace: Peace Agreements and the Lex Pacificatoria, Oxford, https://doi.org/10.1093/acprof:oso/9780199226832.001.0001

BELLOMO, MANLIO (2005), Europäische Rechtseinheit. Grundlagen und System des Ius Commune, Munich

BENDA, ERNST (1995), Der soziale Rechtsstaat; in: BENDA, ERNST et al. (eds.), Handbuch des Verfassungsrechts (1), 2nd ed. (student ed.), Berlin, 719–798

BENTON, LAUREN (2002), Law and Colonial Cultures. Legal Regimes in World History 1450–1900, Cambridge

BENTON, LAUREN (2003), Oceans of Law: The Legal Geography of the Seventeenth-Century Seas, in: DOYLE, DEBBIE ANN, BRANDON SCHNEIDER (eds.), Seascapes, Littoral Cultures, and Trans-Oceanic Exchange, Conference Proceedings, Washington, D.C., http://webdoc.sub.gwdg.de/ebook/p/2005/history_cooperative/www.historycooperative.org/proceedings/seascapes/benton.html

BENZ, ARTHUR (2001), Der moderne Staat. Grundlagen einer politologischen Analyse, Munich, https://doi.org/10.3790/978-3-428-51004-7

BENZ, ARTHUR (2004), Institutionentheorie und Institutionenpolitik, in: KÖNIG, KLAUS et al. (eds.), Institutionenwandel in Regierung und Verwaltung. Festschrift für Klaus König zum 70. Geburtstag, Berlin, 19–20

BENZ, ARTHUR (2006), Selbstbeschränkung des Souverän: Der Staat als Rechtsordnung, in: BECKER, MICHAEL, RUTH ZIMMERLING (eds.), Politik und Recht, Wiesbaden, 143–163

BENZ, ARTHUR (2008), Der moderne Staat. Grundlagen einer politologischen Analyse, Munich, https://doi.org/10.1524/9783486711202

BENZ, ARTHUR (ed.) (2004), Governance. Regieren in komplexen Regelsystemen. Eine Einführung, Munich, https://doi.org/10.1007/978-3-531-90171-8

BENZ, ARTHUR et al. (ed.) (2007), Handbuch Governance. Theoretische Grundlagen und empirische Anwendungsfelder, Wiesbaden

BERTRAND, NICOLAS (2012), Das Regelwerk der Lagerhaft in den nationalsozialistischen Konzentrationslagern, in: Journal der Juristischen Zeitgeschichte 6, 1–12, https://doi.org/10.1515/jjzg.2012.1

BIANCHI, ANDREA (1997), Globalization of Human Rights: The Role of Non-state Actors, in: TEUBNER, GUNTHER (ed.), Global Law Without a State, Dartmouth, 179–212

BIELEFELDT, HEINER (1996), Moderne Menschenrechte als Aufgabe für Christen und Muslime, in: MISSIONSWISSENSCHAFTLICHES INSTITUT MISSIO e.V. (ed.), Ein Glaube in vielen Kulturen. Theologische und sozialpastorale Perspektiven für ein neues Miteinander von Kirche und Gesellschaft in der einen Welt, Frankfurt am Main, 361–373

BIELING, HANS-JÜRGEN, MARTIN GROSSE-HÜTTMANN (eds.) (2016), Europäische Staatlichkeit. Zwischen Krise und Integration, Wiesbaden, https://doi.org/10.1007/978-3-658-03790-1

BLAU, PETER MICHAEL (1964), Exchange and Power in Social Life, New York

BLOCH, ERNST (1959), Das Prinzip Hoffnung, 2 vols., Frankfurt am Main

BLOCKMANS, WIM (1997), A History of Power in Europe: Peoples, Markets, State, Brussels

BLUMENTHAL, JULIA VON (2005), Governance: eine kritische Zwischenbilanz, in: Zeitschrift für Politikwissenschaft 15, 1149–1180

BOBZIN, HARTMUT (2007), Der Koran. Eine Einführung, 7th ed., Munich

BÖCKENFÖRDE, ERNST-WOLFGANG (1969), Die Eigenart des Staatsrechts und der Staatsrechtswissenschaft, in: ACHTERBERG, NORBERT et al. (eds.), Recht und Staat im sozialen Wandel. Festschrift für Hans Ulrich Scupin zum 80. Geburtstag, Berlin, 317–331

BÖCKENFÖRDE, ERNST-WOLFGANG (1974), Grundrechtstheorie und Grundrechtsinterpretation, in: Neue Juristische Wochenschrift 27, 1529–1538

BÖCKENFÖRDE, ERNST-WOLFGANG (1976), Staat, Gesellschaft, Freiheit. Studien zur Staatstheorie und zum Verfassungsrecht, Frankfurt am Main

BÖCKENFÖRDE, ERNST-WOLFGANG (2007), Der säkularisierte Staat. Sein Charakter, seine Rechtfertigung und seine Probleme im 21. Jahrhundert, Munich

BÖCKENFÖRDE, ERNST-WOLFGANG (2011), Die verfassunggebende Gewalt des Volkes – Ein Grenzbegriff des Verfassungsrechts, in: BÖCKENFÖRDE, ERNST-WOLFGANG, DIETER GOSEWINKEL (eds.), Wissenschaft, Politik, Verfassungsgericht. Aufsätze von Ernst-Wolfgang Böckenförde. Biografisches Interview von Dieter Gosewinkel, Berlin, 97–119

BODIN, JEAN (1955), Les six livres de la République, Paris 1583 [English translation: Six Books of the Commonwealth, abridged and translated by M. J. TOOLEY, Oxford]

BODIN, JEAN (1961), Les six livres de la République (1583), Aalen, I: 1–3, 128–132

BOGDANDY, ARMIN VON, MICHAEL IOANNIDIS (2014), Das systemische Defizit. Merkmale, Instrumente und Probleme am Beispiel der Rechtsstaatlichkeit und des neuen Rechtsstaatlichkeitsaufsichtsverfahrens, in: Zeitschrift für ausländisches öffentliches Recht und Völkerrecht (ZaöRV) 74, 283–328 [English translation: Systemic deficiency in the rule of law: What it is, What has been done, what can be done, in: Common Market Law Review 51 (2014), 59–96]

BÖHM, FRANZ (1966), Privatrechtsgesellschaft und Marktwirtschaft, in: ORDO. Jahrbuch für die Ordnung von Wirtschaft und Gesellschaft 17, 75–151

BOTZEM, SEBASTIAN et al. (eds.) (2008), Governance als Prozess. Koordinationsformen im Wandel, Baden-Baden, https://doi.org/10.5771/9783845215723

BOUCHER, DAVID (1985), Texts in Context. Revisionist Methods for Studying the History of Ideas, Dordrecht, https://doi.org/10.1007/978-94-009-5075-7

BOUDON, RAYMOND, FRANCOIS BOURRICAUD (1992), Soziologische Stichworte, Opladen, https://doi.org/10.1007/978-3-322-94339-2

BRAUDEL, FERNAND (1996), The Mediterranean and the Mediterranean World in the Age of Philip II, Berkeley

BREIDECKER, VOLKER (2008), Proust Light. L. Hartleys captivating novel "The Go-Between", in: Süddeutsche Zeitung 285, 14

BROSZIES, CHRISTOPH, HENNING HAHN (eds.) (2013), Globale Gerechtigkeit. Schlüsseltexte zur Debatte zwischen Partikularismus und Kosmopolitismus, 2nd ed., Berlin

BRUGGER, WINFRIED (1989), Menschenrechte im modernen Staat, in: Archiv des öffentlichen Rechts (AöR) 114, 537–588

BUDDE, GUNILLA et al. (eds.) (2006), Transnationale Geschichte. Themen, Tendenzen und Theorien, Göttingen

BÜHLER, OTTMAR (1914), Die subjektiven öffentlichen Rechte und ihr Schutz in der deutschen Verwaltungsrechtsprechung, Leipzig

BURBANK, JANE, FREDERICK COOPER (2010), Empires in World History. Power and the Politics of Difference, Princeton

BURDEAU, GEORGES (1962), Zur Auflösung des Verfassungsbegriffs, in: Der Staat 1, 389–404

BÜRZER, MARKUS et al. (1996), Warum neue Verfahren der Konfliktregelung?, in: FEINDT, PETER HENNING et al. (eds.), Konfliktregelung in der offenen Bürgergesellschaft, Dettelbach, 13–36

CANARIS, CLAUS-WILHELM (1999), Grundrechte und Privatrecht, Berlin, https://doi.org/10.1515/9783110895773

CAROTHERS, THOMAS (ed.) (2006), Promoting the Rule of Law Abroad. In Search of Knowledge, Washington, D.C.

CHAKRABARTY, DISPESH (2013), Place and Displaced Categories. Or, How We Translate Ourselves into Global History, in: BACHMANN-MEDICK, DORIS et al. (eds.), The Trans / National Study of Culture, Berlin, 53–68

CHOW, JOHN K. (1992), Patronage and Power. A Study on Social Networks in Corinth, Sheffield

COHEN, ROBERTA (2012), From Sovereign Responsibility to R2P, in: KNIGHT, W. ANDY, FRAZER EGERTON (eds.), The Routledge Handbook of the Responsibility to Protect, London / New York, 7–21

COICAUD, JEAN-MARC (2002), Legitimacy and Politics: A Contribution to the Study of Political Right and Political Responsibility, Cambridge, https://doi.org/10.1017/CBO9780511490200

CONDORCET, JEAN-ANTOINE-NICOLAS DE CARITAT (1793), Journal d'instruction sociale (prospectus of this journal), Paris, 10–11

CONERMANN, STEPHAN (2014), Südasien und der Indische Ozean, in: REINHARD, WOLFGANG (ed.), Weltreiche und Weltmeere, Munich, 370–509

CONRAD, SEBASTIAN (2012), Enlightenment in Global History: A Historiographical Critique, in: The American Historical Review 117, 999–1027, https://doi.org/10.1093/ahr/117.4.999

CONRAD, SEBASTIAN (2013), Globalgeschichte. Eine Einführung, Munich, https://doi.org/10.17104/9783406645747

CONRAD, SEBASTIAN et al. (eds.) (2007a), Globalgeschichte. Theorien, Ansätze, Themen, Frankfurt am Main

CONRAD, SEBASTIAN et al. (eds.) (2007b), Transnationale Geschichte. Themen, Tendenzen, Theorien, Frankfurt am Main

CONRAD, SEBASTIAN, JÜRGEN OSTERHAMMEL (eds.) (2016), Geschichte der Welt. Wege zur modernen Welt 1750–1870, Munich

COOPER, FREDERICK (ed.) (2005), Colonialism in Question. Theory, Knowledge, History, Berkeley, https://doi.org/10.1525/9780520938618

COSER, LEWIS A. (1965), The Function of Social Conflict, Glencoe

COVER, ROBERT (1983), The Supreme Court 1982 Term (Foreword: Nomos and Narrative), in: Harvard Law Review 97, 4–68, https://doi.org/10.2307/1340787

COVER, ROBERT (1993), Violence, and the Law. The Essays of Robert Cover, ed. by MINOW, MARTHA et al., Ann Arbor

DAHRENDORF, RALF (1961), Gesellschaft und Freiheit. Zur soziologischen Analyse der Gegenwart, Munich

DAVID, JAKOB (1956), Wandelbares Naturrecht?, in: Orientierung. Katholische Blätter für Weltanschauliche Information 20, 171–175

DE SOUSA SANTOS, BOAVENTURA (1977), The Law of the Oppressed: The Construction and Reproduction of Legality in Pasargada, in: Law and Society 12, 5–126

DE SOUSA SANTOS, BOAVENTURA (1987), Law: A Map of Misreading. Toward a Postmodern Conception of Law, in: Journal of Law and Society 14, 279–302

DE SOUSA SANTOS, BOAVENTURA (2002), Toward a New Legal Common Sense, 2nd ed., London

Deitelhoff, Nicole, Michael Zürn (2016), Lehrbuch der Internationalen Beziehungen. Per Anhalter durch die IB-Galaxis, Munich, https://doi.org/10.17104/9783406654404

Denninger, Erhard (1988), Der Präventionsstaat, in: Kritische Justiz 21, 1–15, https://doi.org/10.5771/0023-4834-1988-1-1

Depenheuer, Otto (ed.) (2011), Erzählungen vom Staat. Ideen als Grundlage von Staatlichkeit, Wiesbaden

Dietel, Alfred (1987), "Innere Sicherheit" – Verheißung und reale Möglichkeit, in: Bull, Hans-Peter (ed.), Sicherheit durch Gesetze?, Baden-Baden, 57–82

di Fabio, Udo (2003), Die Staatsrechtslehre und der Staat, Paderborn

Doderer, Heimito von (1951), Die erleuchteten Fenster oder Die Menschwerdung des Amtsrates Julius Zihal, Munich [The Lighted Windows or the Humanization of the Bureaucrat Julius Zihale, trans. John S. Barrett, Riverside CA, 2000]

Dolzer, Rudolf (2004), Good Governance: Neues transnationales Leitbild der Staatlichkeit, in: Zeitschrift für ausländisches öffentliches Recht und Völkerrecht (ZaöRV) 64, 535–546

Dombois, Hans (1955), Das Problem des Naturrechts, Evangelisch-lutherische Kirchenzeitung 9, 199–204

Döscher, Hans-Jürgen (2005), Seilschaften. Die verdrängte Vergangenheit des Auswärtigen Amts, 2nd ed., Berlin

Dreier, Horst (1991), Hierarchische Verwaltung im demokratischen Staat. Genese, aktuelle Bedeutung und funktionelle Grenzen eines Bauprinzips der Exekutive, Tübingen

Dreier, Horst (2012), Recht und Willkür, in: Starck, Christian (ed.), Recht und Willkür, Tübingen, 1–25

Dreier, Ralf (1972), Das kirchliche Amt. Eine kirchenrechtstheoretische Studie, Munich

Drews, Bill et al. (1986), Gefahrenabwehr, 9th ed., Cologne, https://doi.org/10.1111/jopp.12053

Dryzek, John S. (2015), Democratic Agents of Justice, in: The Journal of Political Philosophy 23, 361–384

Duve, Thomas (2011), Katholisches Kirchenrecht und Moraltheologie im 16. Jahrhundert: Eine globale normative Ordnung im Schatten schwacher Staatlichkeit, in: Kadelbach, Stefan, Klaus Günther (eds.), Recht ohne Staat? Zur Normativität nichtstaatlicher Rechtsetzung, Frankfurt am Main, 147–174

Duve, Thomas (2012), Von der Europäischen Rechtsgeschichte zu einer Rechtsgeschichte Europas in globalhistorischer Perspektive, in: Rechtsgeschichte – Legal History 20, 18–71, http://dx-/doi.org/10.12946/rg20/018–071

Duve, Thomas (ed.) (2014), Entanglements in Legal History: Conceptual Approaches (Global Perspectives on Legal History 1), Frankfurt am Main, https://doi.org/10.12946/gplh1

Ebel, Wilhelm (1975), Recht und Form. Vom Stilwandel im deutschen Recht, Tübingen

ECKERT, ANDREAS (2009), Nachwort (epilogue), in: BÜSCHEL, HUBERTUS, DANIEL SPEICH (eds.), Entwicklungswelten. Globalgeschichte der Entwicklungszusammenarbeit, Frankfurt am Main, 311–319

ELLWEIN, THOMAS et al. (eds.) (1987), Jahrbuch zur Staats- und Verwaltungswissenschaft 1, Baden-Baden

EMRICH, EIKE et al. (1996), Klettertechnik für Aufsteiger. Seilschaften als soziales Phänomen, in: Kölner Zeitschrift für Soziologie und Sozialpsychologie (KZSS) 48, 144–155

ENGISH, KARL (1963), Logische Studien zur Gesetzesanwendung, 3rd ed., Heidelberg

ESDERS, STEFAN (2009), Rechtliche Grundlagen frühmittelalterlicher Staatlichkeit. Der allgemeine Treueid, in: POHL, WALTER, VERONIKA WIESER (eds.), Der frühmittelalterliche Staat. Europäische Perspektiven, Vienna, 423–432

ESDERS, STEFAN (ed.) (2007), Rechtsverständnis und Konfliktbewältigung. Gerichtliche und außergerichtliche Strategien im Mittelalter, Cologne

ESDERS, STEFAN, GUNNAR FOLKE SCHUPPERT (2015), Mittelalterliches Regieren in der Moderne oder Modernes Regieren im Mittelalter?, Baden-Baden, https://doi.org/10.5771/9783845263588

ESSER, HARTMUT (1999), Soziologie: Spezielle Grundlagen, Band 4: Opportunitäten und Restriktionen, Frankfurt am Main

EUROPEAN COMMISSION (2014), Communication from the Commission to the European Parliament and the Council: A new EU Framework to strengthen the Rule of Law, 11.3.2014, COM(2014) 158 final, Strasbourg

FABIAN, JOHANNES (2000), Out of Our Minds: Reason and Madness in the Exploration of Central Africa, Berkeley, https://doi.org/10.1525/california/9780520221222.001.0001

FAHRMEIER, ANDREAS (ed.) (2013), Rechtfertigungsnarrative. Zur Begründung normativer Ordnung durch Erzählungen, Frankfurt am Main

FASSBENDER, BARDO (2003), Der Schutz der Menschenrechte als zentraler Inhalt des völkerrechtlichen Gemeinwohls, in: Europäische Grundrechte-Zeitschrift (EuGRZ) 30, 1–16

FEDERAL FOREIGN OFFICE (ed.) (2007), Expert Conference on the Rule of Law, Conference Documentation, Berlin

FERGUSON, NIALL (2003), Empire. How Britain Made the Modern World, London

FISCH, JÖRG (1984), Die europäische Expansion und das Völkerrecht: Die Auseinandersetzungen um den Status der überseeischen Gebiete vom 15. Jahrhundert bis zur Gegenwart, Stuttgart

FISCH, JÖRG, WOLFGANG KERSTING (2004), Vertrag, Gesellschaftsvertrag, Herrschaftsvertrag, in: BRUNNER, OTTO et al. (eds.), Geschichtliche Grundbegriffe. Historisches Lexikon zur politisch-sozialen Sprache in Deutschland, vol. 1, Stuttgart, 110–128, 901–946

FLECK, LUDWIG (1980), Entstehung und Entwicklung einer wissenschaftlichen Tatsache. Einführung in die Lehre vom Denkstil und Denkkollektiv. Ed. with an introduction by LOTHAR SCHÄFER and THOMAS SCHNELL, Frankfurt am Main (first published 1935)

FLEINER, THOMAS, LIDIJA R. BASTA FLEINER (2004), Allgemeine Staatslehre. Über die konstitutionelle Demokratie in einer multikulturellen globalisierten Welt, 3rd ed., Berlin, https://doi.org/10.1007/978-3-642-18489-5

FLUME, WERNER (1992), Das Rechtsgeschäft, 4th ed., Berlin

FORST, RAINER (1984), Kontexte der Gerechtigkeit, Frankfurt am Main

FORST, RAINER (2007), Das Recht auf Rechtfertigung, Frankfurt am Main

FORST, RAINER (2012), Transnationale Gerechtigkeit und Demokratie: Zur Überwindung von drei Dogmen der politischen Theorie, in: NIESEN, PETER (ed.), Transnationale Gerechtigkeit und Demokratie, Frankfurt am Main, 29–48

FORST, RAINER (2013), Zum Begriff des Rechtfertigungsnarrativs, in: FAHRMEIER (ed.), 11–28

FORSTHOFF, ERNST (1938), Die Verwaltung als Leistungsträger, Stuttgart

FORSTHOFF, ERNST (1942), Aufgabe und Methode der Verwaltungsrechtswissenschaft, Ms., NL

FORSTHOFF, ERNST (1950), Daseinsvorsorge als Aufgabe der Sozialgestaltung in Staat und Gemeinde (Vortrag im Rahmen des 1. Staatswissenschaftlichen Fortbildungskurses der Hochschule für Verwaltungswissenschaften in Speyer), 21/10/1950, NL Forsthoff, Ts.

FORSTHOFF, ERNST (1964), Rechtsstaat im Wandel. Verfassungsrechtliche Abhandlungen 1950–1964, Stuttgart

FORSTHOFF, ERNST (1971a), Recht und Sprache. Prolegomena zu einer richterlichen Hermeneutik, 3rd ed., Halle (Saale)

FORSTHOFF, ERNST (1971b), Der Staat der Industriegesellschaft. Dargestellt am Beispiel der Bundesrepublik Deutschland, Munich

FOUCAULT, MICHEL (2008), Foucault on Governmentality and Liberalism: The Birth of Biopolitics: Lectures at the Collège de France, 1978–1979 by Michel Foucault, Basingstoke

FRANCK, JENS UWE (2016), Machtquellen: Grundlagen privater Machtpositionen, in: MÖSLEIN, FLORIAN, Private Macht, Tübingen, 529–562

FRANKENBERG, GÜNTER (2008), Verfassung, in: GOSEPATH et al. (eds.), 1411–1415

FRANKENBERG, KIYOMI VON (2015), Erzeugung von Verbindlichkeit vor und neben dem positiven Recht. Ein Erklärungsversuch zu informellen Verfahren anhand rechtsethnologischer Studien zu Tausch, in: Rechtswissenschaft (RW) 6, 27–48

FRASER, NANCY (2005), Reframing Justice in a Globalizing World, in: New Left Review 35, 69–88, https://doi.org/10.5325/editwharrevi.35.1.0088

FREEMAN, DONALD B. (2010), The Pacific, London

FRITSCH, GOTTFRIED ERNST (1734), Ius publicum universale et pragmaticum, Jena

FUCHS, DIETER, EDELTRAUD ROLLER (2007), Lexikon Politik. Hundert Grundbegriffe, Stuttgart

FÜSSEL, MARIAN (2006), Gelehrtenkultur als symbolische Praxis. Rang, Ritual und Konflikt an der Universität der Frühen Neuzeit, Darmstadt

GABRIEL, SIGMAR (2016), [Rede anlässlich der Wertekonferenz Gerechtigkeit, 9. Mai 2016], Berlin https://www.spd.de/fileadmin/Dokumente/Reden/Rede_Sigmar_Gabriel_beim_Wertekongress.pdf

GALANTER, MARC (1981), Justice in Many Rooms: Courts, Private Ordering, and Indigenous Law, in: Journal of Legal Pluralism 19, 1–47, https://doi.org/10.1080/07329113.1981.10756257

GALL, LOTHAR (1978), Zu Ausbildung und Charakter des Interventionsstaats, in: Historische Zeitschrift (HZ) 227, 552–570, https://doi.org/10.1524/hzhz.1978.227.jg.552

GAMSA, MARK (2011), Cultural Translation and the Transnational Circulation of Books, in: Journal of World History 22, 553–575, https://doi.org/10.1353/jwh.2011.0075

GEBHARDT, JÜRGEN (1993), Verfassungspatriotismus als Identitätskonzept der Nation, in: Aus Politik und Zeitgeschichte (APuZ) 14, 29–37

GEBHARDT, JÜRGEN (ed.) (1999), Verfassung und politische Kultur, Baden-Baden

GEHRKE, HANS-JOACHIM (ed.) (2017), Geschichte der Welt. Die Welt vor 600: Frühe Zivilisationen, Munich

GENSCHEL, PHILIPP, BERNHARD ZANGL (2007), Die Zerfaserung von Staatlichkeit und die Zentralität des Staates, in: Aus Politik und Zeitgeschichte 20/21, 10–17

GENSCHEL, PHILIPP, BERNHARD ZANGL (2008), Vom Herrschaftsmonopolisten zum Herrschaftsmanager, in: Leviathan 36, 430–454, https://doi.org/10.1007/s11578-008-0022-1

GENSCHEL, PHILIPP, STEPHAN LEIBFRIED (2008), Schupperts Staat. Wie beobachtet man den Wandel einer Formidee?, in: Der Staat 47, 359–380, https://doi.org/10.3790/staa.47.3.359

GIERKE, OTTO (1889), Die soziale Aufgabe des Privatrechts, Vienna, https://doi.org/10.1007/978-3-662-33115-6

GILLESPIE, JOHN (2012), Developing a Theoretical Framework for Evaluating Rule of Law Promotion in Developing Countries, in: ZÜRN et al. (eds.), 233–251

GLENN, PATRICK (2013), The Cosmopolitan State, Oxford

GNEIST, RUDOLF (1879), Der Rechtsstaat und die Verwaltungsgerichte in Deutschland, 2nd ed., Berlin

GOFFMANN, ERVIN (1977), Rahmenanalyse, Frankfurt

GOLD, THOMAS et al. (eds.) (2002), Social Connections in China. Institutions, Culture, and the Nature of Guanxi, Cambridge, https://doi.org/10.1017/CBO9780511499579

GOLDER, BEN (2016), Theorizing Human Rights, in: ORFORD, ANNE et al. (eds.), The Oxford Handbook of the Theory of International Law, Oxford, 684–685

GOLDSMITH, JACK L., ERIC A. POSNER (2003), The Limits of International Law, Oxford

GÖRRES-GESELLSCHAFT (ed.) (1989), Staatslexikon in fünf Bänden, 5th vol, 7th ed., Freiburg

GOSEPATH, STEFAN (2001), The Global Scope of Justice, in: POGGE, THOMAS (ed.), Global Justice, Oxford, 135–159

GOSEPATH, STEFAN et al. (eds.) (2008), Handbuch der Politischen Philosophie und Sozialphilosophie, 2 vols., Berlin

GOSEWINKEL, DIETER (2016), Schutz und Freiheit? Staatsbürgerschaft in Europa im 20. und 21. Jahrhundert, Berlin

GÖTZ, VOLKMAR (1988), Staatsaufgabe Sicherheit, in: ISENSEE, JOSEF, PAUL KIRCHHOF (eds.), Handbuch des deutschen Staatsrechts, vol. II, Heidelberg, 1007–1035

GOZZI, GUSTAVO, PIETRO MANZINI (eds.) (2008), L'Occidente e l'ordine internazionale, Torino

GRAF, FRIEDRICH WILHELM (2006), Moses Vermächtnis. Über göttliche und menschliche Gesetze, 3rd ed., Munich

GRAF VITZTHUM, WOLFGANG (ed.) (2006), Handbuch des Seerechts, Munich

GRAFTON, ANTHONY (2009), A Sketch Map of a Lost Continent: The Republic of Letters, in: Republic of Letters 1, 1–18

GREWE, WILHELM G. (1984), Epochen der Völkerrechtsgeschichte, Baden-Baden

GRIFFITH, JOHN (1986), What is Legal Pluralism?, in: Journal of Legal Pluralism 24, 1–55

GRIMM, DIETER (1972), Verfassungsfunktion und Grundgesetzreform, in: Archiv des öffentlichen Rechts (AöR) 97, 489–537

GRIMM, DIETER (1985), Die "Neue" Rechtswissenschaft. Über Funktion und Formation nationalsozialistischer Jurisprudenz, in: LUNDGREN, PETER (ed.), Wissenschaft im Dritten Reich, Frankfurt am Main, 31–54

GRIMM, DIETER (1986), Verfassungsrechtliche Anmerkung zum Thema Prävention, in: Kritische Vierteljahresschrift für Gesetzgebung und Rechtswissenschaft 1, 38–54; also published in: GRIMM, DIETER (1991), Die Zukunft der Verfassung, Frankfurt am Main, 197–220

GRIMM, DIETER (1990), Die Zukunft der Verfassung, in: Staatwissenschaften und Staatspraxis 1, 5–33

GRIMM, DIETER (2001), Die Verfassung und die Politik. Einsprüche in Störfällen, Munich

GRIMM, DIETER (2005), Europas Verfassung, in: SCHUPPERT, GUNNAR FOLKE et al. (eds.), Europawissenschaft, Baden-Baden, 177–200

GRIMM, DIETER (2007), Souveränität – zur aktuellen Leistungsfähigkeit eines rechtlich-politischen Grundbegriffs, in: STEIN et al. (eds.), 304–310

GRIMM, DIETER (2012) Die Zukunft der Verfassung II. Auswirkungen von Europäisierung und Globalisierung, Berlin

GROSSI, PAOLO (2010), Das Recht in der europäischen Geschichte, Munich

GUILHAUMOU, JACQUES (2002), Sieyès et l'ordre de la langue: l'invention de la politique moderne, Paris

GUSY, CHRISTOPH (1994), Vom Polizeirecht zum Sicherheitsrecht, in: Staatswissenschaften und Staatspraxis 5, 187–210

HAAKONSSEN, KNUD (2012), Enlightenment and the Ubiquity of Natural Law, in: SCHMALE, WOLFGANG (ed.), Zeit in der Aufklärung. 13. Internationaler Kongress zur Erforschung des 18. Jahrhundert, Bochum, 45–58

HAAKONSSEN, KNUD (2016), Early Modern Natural Law Theories, in: DUKE, GEORGE, ROBERT GEORGE (eds.), Cambridge Companion to Natural Law Jurisprudence, Cambridge, 76–102, https://doi.org/10.1017/9781316341544.004

Häberle, Peter (1976), Review of M. Stolleis, Gemeinwohlformeln im nationalsozialistischen Recht (1974), in: Archiv des öffentlichen Rechts (AöR) 101, 292–297

Harari, Yuval Noah (2015), Sapiens: A Brief History of Humankind, New York

Hardtwig, Wolfgang (ed.) (2010), Die Aufklärung und ihre Weltwirkung, Göttingen

Hartley, Leslie P. (2000), The Go-Between, London

Heckel, Martin (2001), Deutschland im konfessionellen Zeitalter, 2nd ed., Göttingen

Heine, Heinrich (1974), Über Frankreich (Vorrede zu "Französische Zustände"), in: Sämtliche Schriften, vol. 3, Munich, 227–235

Heinig, Hans-Michael, Christian Walter (eds.) (2007), Staatskirchenrecht oder Religionsverfassungsrecht? Ein begriffspolitischer Grundsatzstreit, Tübingen

Heller, Herrmann (1927), Die Souveränität. Ein Beitrag zur Theorie des Staats- und Völkerrechts, Berlin

Heller, Herrmann (1970), Staatslehre (1934), ed. by Gerhard Niemeyer, 4th ed., Leiden

Hellgarth, Alexander (2016), Regulierung und Privatrecht. Staatliche Verhaltenssteuerung mittels Privatrecht und ihre Bedeutung für Rechtswissenschaft, Gesetzgebung und Rechtsanwendung, Tübingen, https://doi.org/10.1628/978-3-16-154368-5

Hellmuth, Eckart, Christoph Ehrenstein (2001), Intellectual History Made in Britain: Die *Cambridge School* und ihre Kritiker, in: Geschichte und Gesellschaft 27, 149–172

Hepp, Andreas (2008), Medienwandel und die Posttraditionalisierung von translokalen Vergemeinschaftungen, in: Hitzler, Ronald et al. (eds.), Posttraditionale Gemeinschaften. Theoretische und ethnographische Bestimmungen, Wiesbaden, 132–150

Herzog, Roman (1971), Allgemeine Staatslehre, Frankfurt am Main

Heun, Werner et al. (eds.) (2006), Evangelisches Staatslexikon, 2nd ed., Stuttgart

Heupel, Monika (2012), Rule of Law Promotion through International Organization and NGOs, in: Zürn et al. (eds.), 133–152

Heyen, Erk Volkmar (2013), Verwaltete Welten. Mensch, Gemeinwesen und Amt in der Europäischen Malerei, Berlin

Hill, Christopher L. (2013), Conceptual Universalization in the Transnational Nineteenth Century, in: Moyn, Samuel, Andrew Sartori (eds.), 134–158

Hillmann, Karl H. (2007), Wörterbuch der Soziologie, 5th ed., Stuttgart

Höffe, Otfried (2010), Gerechtigkeit. Eine philosophische Einführung, 4th ed., Munich

Höffe, Otfried (2016), Geschichte des politischen Denkens, Munich, https://doi.org/10.17104/9783406697159

Hoffmann, Florian (2006), "Shooting into the Dark": Toward a Pragmatic Theory of Human Rights (Activism), in: Texas International Law Journal 41, 403–414

Hoffmann, Stefan-Ludwig (ed.) (2010), Moralpolitik. Geschichte der Menschenrechte im 20. Jahrhundert, Göttingen

HOFFMANN-RIEM, WOLFGANG (2016), Innovation und Recht – Recht und Innovation. Recht im Ensemble seiner Kontexte, Tübingen, https://doi.org/10.1628/978-3-16-154478-1

HOFMANN, HASSO (2000), Einführung in die Rechts- und Staatsphilosophie, Darmstadt

HORN, EVA (2013), The Secret War. Treason, Espionage, and Modern Fiction, Evanston, IL

HUECK, ALFRED et al. (1934), Gesetz zur Ordnung der nationalen Arbeit: Mit sämtlichen Durchführungsverordnungen, dem Gesetz zur Ordnung der Arbeit in öffentlichen Verwaltungen und Betrieben mit seinen Durchführungsverordnungen und den neuen Arbeitszeitbestimmungen: Kommentar, Munich

HUNT, LYNN (2007), Inventing Human Rights. A History, New York

ICKSTATT, JOHANN ADAM FREIHERR VON (1747), Oratio de Eurythmia politica sive pulchritudine aedificii civilis ex uniformitate firmissimo civitatis fulcro eflorescente, in: Opuscula Juridica varii Argumenti, vol. I, Ingolstadt-Augsburg

IMBODEN, MAX (1959), Montesquieu und die Lehre der Gewaltentrennung, Berlin

IMMERGUT, ELLEN M., ALEXANDER JÄGER (2008), Institution, in: GOSEPATH et al. (eds.), 547–553

IRIYE, AKIRA (ed.) (2013), Geschichte der Welt 1945 bis heute: Die globalisierte Welt, München, https://doi.org/10.17104/9783406641169

ISENSEE, JOSEF (1983), Das Grundrecht auf Sicherheit, Berlin, https://doi.org/10.1515/9783110893243

ISENSEE, JOSEF (1987), Gemeinwohl und Staatsaufgaben im Verfassungsstaat, in: ISENSEE, JOSEF, PAUL KIRCHHOF (eds.), Handbuch des Staatsrechts, vol. III, Heidelberg, 3–82

ISENSEE, JOSEF (1989), Staat, in: GÖRRES-GESELLSCHAFT (ed.), col. 133–157

ISENSEE, JOSEF (1992), Verfassungsrecht als "politisches Recht", in: ISENSEE, JOSEF, PAUL KIRCHHOF (eds.), Handbuch des Staatsrechts, vol. VII, Heidelberg, 103–164

JAMI, CATHERINE (2012), The Emperor's New Mathematics. Western Learning and Imperial Authority During the Kangxi Reign (1662–1722), Oxford, https://doi.org/10.1093/acprof:oso/9780199601400.001.0001

JANN, WERNER (2000), Verwaltungskulturen im internationalen Vergleich. Ein Überblick über den Stand der empirischen Forschung, in: Die Verwaltung 33, 351–378

JANSEN, DOROTHEA, ANDREAS WALD (2007), Netzwerktheorien, in: BENZ, ARTHUR et al. (eds.), Handbuch Governance. Theoretische Grundlagen und empirische Anwendungsfelder, Wiesbaden, 188–199, https://doi.org/10.1007/978-3-531-90407-8_14

JANSEN, DOROTHEA, KLAUS SCHUBERT (eds.) (1995), Netzwerke und Politikproduktion. Konzepte, Methoden, Perspektiven, Marburg

JARREN, OTFRIED (1987), Kommunikationsraumanalyse. Ein Beitrag zur empirischen Kommunikationsforschung?, in: BOBROWSKY, MANFRED, WOLFGANG R.

LANGENBUCHER (eds.), Wege zur Kommunikationsgeschichte, Munich, 560–588

JAUMANN, HERBERT (2011), Die europäische Gelehrtenrepublik im Zeitalter des Konfessionalismus, Wiesbaden

JELLINEK, GEORG (1919), Allgemeine Staatslehre, 2nd. ed., Freiburg i. Br.

JELLINEK, GEORG (1966), Allgemeine Staatslehre (1900), 3rd ed., Berlin

JHERING, RUDOLPH VON (1926), Geist des römischen Rechts auf den verschiedenen Stufen seiner Entwicklung, Leipzig (first edition 1852)

JOAS, HANS, CHRISTOPH MANDRY (2005), Europa als Werte- und Kulturgemeinschaft, in: SCHUPPERT, GUNNAR FOLKE et al. (eds.), Europawissenschaft, Baden-Baden, 541–574

JÜNGER, ERNST (1981), Sämtliche Werke, vol. 8, Stuttgart

KAASE, MAX, H. D. KLINGEMANN (eds.) (1983), Wahlen und politisches System, Opladen, https://doi.org/10.1007/978-3-322-86405-5

KAFADAR, CEMAL (ed.) (2014), Geschichte der Welt. Agrarische und nomadische Herausforderungen 600–1350, Munich

KÄGI, WERNER (1961), Von der klassischen Dreiteilung zur modernen Gewaltenteilung. Erstarrte Formeln - bleibende Ideen - neue Formen, Festschrift für Hans Huber, Bern

KANNOWSKI, BERND (2002), Rechtsbegriffe im Mittelalter. Stand der Diskussion, in: CORDES, ALBRECHT, BERND KANNOWSKI (eds.), Rechtsbegriffe im Mittelalter, Frankfurt am Main, 1–28

KARSTEN, ARNE, HILLARD VON THIESSEN (eds.) (2006), Nützliche Netzwerke und korrupte Seilschaften, Göttingen

KELSEN, HANS (1993), Allgemeine Staatslehre, Vienna (1st ed. 1925)

KEMMERER, ALEXANDRA (2015), "We do not need to always look to Westphalia ...". A Conversation with Martti Koskenniemi and Anne Orford, in: Journal of the History of International Law 17, 1–14; [German original: "Wir müssen nicht immer nur auf Westfalen schauen ...". Ein Gespräch mit Martti Koskenniemi und Anna Orford, in: Lange Leitung, Zeitschrift für Ideengeschichte 9 (2015), 31–46]

KEMPE, MICHAEL (2010), Fluch der Weltmeere. Piraterie, Völkerrecht und internationale Beziehungen 1500–1900, Frankfurt am Main

KENNEDY, DUNCAN (2006), Three Globalizations of Law and Legal Thought: 1850–2000, in: TRUBACK, DAVID M., ALVARO SANTOS (eds.), The New Law and Economic Development. A Critical Approach, Cambridge, 19–73

KERSTING, WOLFGANG (1994), Die politische Philosophie des Gesellschaftsvertrages, Darmstadt

KERSTING, WOLFGANG (2001), Vertragstheorien, in: HARTMANN, MARTIN, CLAUS OFFE (eds.), Politische Theorie und Politische Philosophie. Ein Handbuch, Munich, 81–84

KERSTING, WOLFGANG (2004), Vertrag, Gesellschaftsvertrag, Herrschaftsvertrag, in: BRUNNER, OTTO et. al. (eds.), Geschichtliche Grundbegriffe. Historisches Lexikon zur politisch-sozialen Sprache in Deutschland, Stuttgart, 901–946

Kersting, Wolfgang (2008), Vertragstheorie, in: Gosepath, Stefan et al. (eds.), 1430–1436

Kilian, Michael (2014), Review of *Die Diktatur der Demokratie* by Juli Zeh, in: Die Verwaltung 47, 285–311

Kipling, Rudyard (1987), Kim [1901], edited and introduced by Edward Said, London

Kirby, David, Merja-Liisa Hinkkannen (2000), The Baltic and the North Sea, London

Kittsteiner, Heinz Dieter (2010), Die Stabilisierungsmoderne. Deutschland und Europa 1618–1715, Munich

Klee, Hans (1946), Hugo Grotius und John Selden. Von den geistigen Ursprüngen des Kampfes um die Meeresfreiheit, Bern

Klippel, Diethelm (1987), Naturrecht als politische Theorie. Zur politischen Bedeutung des deutschen Naturrechts im 18. und 19. Jahrhundert, in: Bödecker, Hans-Erich, Ulrich Herrmann (eds.), Aufklärung als Politisierung – Politisierung der Aufklärung, Hamburg, 267–293

Klippel, Diethelm (2010), Staatslehre, Allgemein, in: Enzyklopädie der Neuzeit XII, 614–616

Klippel, Diethelm (2013), Die Allgemeine Staatslehre um 1800, in: Festschrift für Jan Schröder, Tübingen, 423–441

Knies, Wolfgang (1971), Grundrechte, in: Badura, Peter et al. (eds.), Recht, Fischer Lexikon, Frankfurt am Main, 49–58

Knoblauch, Hubert (2008), Kommunikationsgemeinschaften. Überlegungen zur kommunikativen Konstruktion einer Sozialform, in: Hitzler, Ronald et al. (eds.), Posttraditionale Gemeinschaften. Theoretische und ethnographische Bestimmungen, Wiesbaden, 73–88, https://doi.org/10.1007/978-3-531-91780-1_4

Kocka, Jürgen (2016), Capitalism. A Short History, Princeton

Köckert, Matthias (2007), Die Zehn Gebote, Munich, https://doi.org/10.17104/9783406622779

Kokott, Juliane, Thomas Vesting (2004), Die Staatsrechtslehre und die Veränderung ihres Gegenstandes. Konsequenzen von Europäisierung und Internationalisierung, in: Veröffentlichungen der Vereinigung der Deutschen Staatsrechtslehrer (VVDSTRL) 63, 7–100

Konrad Adenauer Stiftung (ed.) (2009), Demokratie und Rechtstaatsförderung in der Entwicklungszusammenarbeit, Berlin

Koskenniemi, Martti (2003), Legitimacy, Rights, and Ideology. Notes Towards a Critique of the New Moral Internationalism, in: Associations 7, 349–373

Koskenniemi, Martti (2004), International Law and Hegemony: A Reconfiguration, Cambridge Review of International Affairs 17, 197–218

Koskenniemi, Martti (2012), A History of International Law Histories, in: Fassbender, Bardo, Anne Peters (eds.), The Oxford Handbook of the History of International Law, Oxford, 943–971, https://doi.org/10.1093/law/9780199599752.003.0040

KOSKENNIEMI, MARTTI (2014), Vitoria and Us. Thoughts and Critical Histories of International Law, in: Rechtsgeschichte – Legal History 22, 119–138, http://dx.doi.org/10.12946/rg22/119-138

KÖTTER, MATTHIAS (2013), Wie viel Recht steckt in Good Governance? Eine Betrachtung aus juristischer Perspektive, SFB-Governance Working Paper Series, No. 58, https://doi.org/10.5771/9783845246567-553

KRAFT, INGO (2008), Die Konzeption der subjektiven öffentlichen Rechte nach deutschem Recht, in: KLUTH, WINFRIED, KLAUS RENNERT (eds.), Entwicklungen im Verwaltungsprozessrecht, Halle, 13–34

KREUZ, REINHARD G. (1978), Überleben und gutes Leben. Erläuterungen zu Begriff und Geschichte der Staatsräson, in: Deutsche Vierteljahresschrift für Literaturwissenschaft und Geistesgeschichte 2, 173–208

KRIELE, MARTIN (1990), Einführung in die Staatslehre, 4th ed., Opladen

KRÜGER, HERBERT (1964), Allgemeine Staatslehre, Stuttgart

KRÜPER, JULIAN (2015), Die Verfassung der Berliner Republik. Verfassungsrecht und Verfassungsrechtswissenschaft in zeitgeschichtlicher Perspektive, in: Rechtsgeschichte – Legal History 23, 16–51, http://dx.doi.org/10.12946/rg23/016-051

KULICK, ANDREAS (2017), Vagueness and Ambiguity in International Law, paper presented at the Colloquium at the WZB Center for Global Constitutionalism, Berlin

KUMM, MATTHIAS et al. (2014), How large is the world of Global Constitutionalism?, in: Global Constitutionalism 3, 1–8, https://doi.org/10.1017/S204538171400001X

KUNTZ, THILO (2016), Recht als Gegenstand der Rechtswissenschaft und performative Rechtserzeugung. Zugleich ein Beitrag zur Möglichkeit von Dogmatik, in: Archiv für civilistische Praxis (AcP) 216, 1–45, https://doi.org/10.1628/000389916X14752235857915

LADEUR, KARL-HEINZ (2000), Die rechtswissenschaftlichen Methodendiskussionen und die Bewältigung des gesellschaftlichen Wandels, in: RabelsZ 64, 60–103

LADEUR, KARL-HEINZ (2012), "Finding our text …": Der Aufstieg des Abwägungsdenkens als ein Phänomen "sekundärer Oralität" und die Widergewinnung der Textualität des Rechts in der Postmoderne, in: AUGSBERG, INO, SOPHIE-CHARLOTTE LENSKI (eds.), Die Innenwelt der Außenwelt der Innenwelt des Rechts, Paderborn, 173–204

LADWIG, BERND (2011), Gerechtigkeitstheorien zur Einführung, Hamburg

LAUREN, PAUL GORDON (1998), The Evolution of International Human Rights. Visions Seen, Philadelphia

LAW, DAVID S., MILA VERSTEEG (2011), The Evolution and Ideology of Global Constitutionalism, in: California Law Review 99, 1163–1257

LEIBFRIED, STEPHAN, MICHAEL ZÜRN (eds.) (2005), The Transformation of the State?, Cambridge, https://doi.org/10.1017/CBO9780511752193

LEIBFRIED, STEFAN, MICHAEL ZÜRN (eds.) (2006), Transformationen des Staates?, Frankfurt am Main

LIST, MARTIN, BERNHARD ZANGL (2003), Verrechtlichung internationaler Politik, in: HELLMANN, GUNTHER et al. (eds.), Die neuen Internationalen Beziehungen. Forschungsstand und Perspektiven in Deutschland, Baden-Baden, 361–400

LLANQUE, MARCUS (2016), Geschichte der politischen Ideen. Von der Antike bis zur Gegenwart, 2nd ed., Munich

LOVEJOY, ARTHUR O. (1936), The Great Chain of Being. A Study in the History of an Idea, Cambridge, MA

LOVEJOY, ARTHUR O. (1940), Reflections on the History of Ideas, in: Journal of the History of Ideas 1, 3–23, https://doi.org/10.2307/2707007

LÖW, MARTINA (2001), Raumsoziologie, Frankfurt am Main

LUHMANN, NIKLAS (1970), Positivität des Rechts als Voraussetzung einer modernen Gesellschaft, in: Jahrbuch für Rechtssoziologie und Rechtstheorie 1, 175–202

LUHMANN, NIKLAS (1973), Politische Verfassungen im Kontext des Gesellschaftssystems, in: Der Staat 12, 1–22, 165–182

LUHMANN, NIKLAS (1993), Das Recht der Gesellschaft, Frankfurt am Main

LUHMANN, NIKLAS (1995), Social Systems, Stanford

LUNDGREN, CHRISTOPH (2014), Staatlichkeit in Rom? Diskurse und Praxis (in) der römischen Republik, Stuttgart

MACMILLAN, KEN (2006), Sovereignty and Possession in the English New World. The Legal Foundations of Empire 1576–1640, Cambridge

MAETSCHKE, MATTHIAS et al. (eds.) (2013), Das Recht der Industriellen Revolution, Tübingen

MAHLMANN, MATTHIAS (2007), Gründungsmythos und Autonomie – Aspekte der Souveränität, in: STEIN et al. (eds.), 270–279

MAIHOFER, WERNER (ed.) (1966), Naturrecht oder Rechtspositivismus?, Darmstadt

MANCKE, ELIZABETH (1999), Early Modern Expansion and the Politicization of Ocean Space, in: The Geographical Review 89, 225–236

MANN, MICHAEL (1994), Geschichte der Macht, vols. I and II, Frankfurt am Main

MANN, MICHAEL (2001), Geschichte der Macht, vol. III, Part 1, Frankfurt am Main

MANSFELD, WERNER et al. (1934), Die Ordnung der nationalen Arbeit. Kommentar zum Gesetz zur Ordnung der nationalen Arbeit, Berlin

MARSHALL, TIM (2015), Die Macht der Geographie. Wie sich Weltpolitik anhand von 10 Karten erklären lässt, Munich

MARTITZ, FERDINAND VON (1885), Das Internationale System zur Unterdrückung des Afrikanischen Sklavenhandels in seinem heutigen Bestande, in: Archiv für öffentiches Recht (AöR) 1/1, 3–107

MARTUS, STEFFEN (2015), Aufklärung. Das deutsche 18. Jahrhundert – ein Epochenbild, Berlin

MASTRONARDI, PHILIPPE (2007), Verfassungslehre, Bern

MAULTZSCH, FELIX (2012), Vergleichende Betrachtungen zum deutschen und amerikanischen Recht, in: Juristenzeitung 67, 1040–1050, https://doi.org/10.1628/002268812803757704

MAUS, INGEBORG (1980), Bürgerliche Rechtstheorie und Faschismus. Zur sozialen Funktion und aktuellen Wirkung der Theorie Carl Schmitts, Munich

MAYNTZ, RENATE (2005), Governance-Theory als fortentwickelte Steuerungstheorie?, in: SCHUPPERT, GUNNAR FOLKE (ed.), 11–20

MAYNTZ, RENATE (ed.) (1968), Bürokratische Organisation, Cologne

MCCARTY, PHILIP (2014), Globalizing Legal History, in: Rechtsgeschichte – Legal History 22, 283–291, http://dx.doi.org/10.12946/rg22/283-291

MEINEL, FLORIAN (2011), Der Jurist in der industriellen Gesellschaft. Ernst Forsthoff und seine Zeit, Berlin, https://doi.org/10.1524/9783050056395

MENCHÚ, RIGOBERTA (2010), I, Rigoberta Menchú. An Indian Woman in Guatemala, 2nd ed., London (1st ed. 1984)

MESTMÄCKER, ERNST-JOACHIM (2007), Franz Böhm und die Lehre von der Privatrechtsgesellschaft, in: RIESENHUBER, KARL (ed.), Privatrechtsgesellschaft. Entwicklung, Stand und Verfassung des Privatrechts, Tübingen, 35–52, https://doi.org/10.1515/9783110977721.31

MEYER, BERTHOLD (ed.) (1997), Formen der Konfliktregelung. Eine Einführung mit Quellen, Opladen

MEYER, CHRISTOPH H. (2010), Europa lernt eine neue Sprache. Das Römische Recht im 12. Jahrhundert, in: SCHNEIDMÜLLER, BERND et al. (eds.), Verwandlungen des Stauferreichs. Drei Innovationsregionen im mittelalterlichen Europa, Darmstadt, 321–335

MINTZ, SIDNEY W. (2007), Die süße Macht. Kulturgeschichte des Zuckers, 2nd ed., Frankfurt am Main

MITCHELL, DAVID (2011), The Thousand Autumns of Jacob de Zoet, New York

MOHR, HANS (1999), Wissen. Prinzip und Ressource, Berlin

MÖLLERS, CHRISTOPH (2006), Staat, in: HEUN et al. (eds.), col. 2272–2274

MÖLLERS, CHRISTOPH (2008), Staat, in: GOSEPATH et al. (eds.), 1270–1275

MOORE, MICK (2001), Political Underdevelopment: What Causes Bad Governance'?, in: Public Management Review 1, 385–418, https://doi.org/10.1080/14616670110050020

MOORE, SALLY FALK (1973), Law and Social Change: The Semi-Autonomous Social Field as an Appropriate Subject of Study, in: Law and Society Review 7, 719–746

MÖSTL, MARKUS (2002), Die staatliche Garantie für die öffentliche Sicherheit und Ordnung, Munich

MOYN, SAMUEL (2012), The Last Utopia. Human Rights in History, Cambridge, MA

MOYN, SAMUEL, ANDREW SARTORI (eds.) (2013), Global Intellectual History, New York

MÜHLEISEN, HANS-OTTO (1999), Gerechtigkeitsvorstellungen in "Fürstenspiegeln" der frühen Neuzeit, in: MÜNKLER, HERFRIED, MARCUS LLANQUE (eds.), Konzeptionen der Gerechtigkeit. Kulturvergleich – Ideengeschichte – Moderne Debatte, Baden-Baden, 81–99

MÜLLER, RAINER A. (1985), Die deutschen Fürstenspiegel des 17. Jahrhunderts. Regierungslehren und politische Pädagogik, in: Historische Zeitschrift (HZ) 240, 571–597, https://doi.org/10.1524/hzhz.1985.240.3.571

MÜLLER-MALL, SABINE (2012), Performative Rechtserzeugung, Weilerswist

Mulsow, Martin (2015), Ideengeschichte als Verflechtungsgeschichte. Impulse für eine "Global Intellectual History", Werkstattbericht, Max-Weber-Kolleg Erfurt

Mulsow, Martin (2016), Elemente einer globalisierten Ideengeschichte der Vormoderne, unpublished manuscript, Erfurt / Gotha

Mulsow, Martin, Andreas Mahler (eds.) (2010), Die Cambridge School der politischen Ideengeschichte, Berlin

Münkler, Herfried (1985), Staatsräson und politische Klugheitslehre, in: Fetscher, Iring, Herfried Münkler (eds.), Pipers Handbuch der Politischen Ideen, vol. III: Neuzeit: Von den Konfessionskriegen bis zur Aufklärung, Munich, 23–72

Münkler, Herfried (1987), Im Namen des Staates. Die Begründung der Staatsraison in der Frühen Neuzeit, Frankfurt am Main

Münkler, Herfried, Harald Bluhm (eds.) (2001), Gemeinwohl und Gemeinsinn. Historische Semantiken politischer Leitbegriffe, Berlin, https://doi.org/10.1515/9783050079639

Mungiu-Pippidi, Alina (2006), Corruption: Diagnosis and Treatment, in: Journal of Democracy 17, 86–99

Mungiu-Pippidi, Alina (2015), The Quest for good Governance. How Societies Develop Control of Corruption, Cambridge, https://doi.org/10.1017/CBO9781316286937

Mutua, Makau Wa (2000), Politics and Human Rights: An Essential Symbiosis, in: Byers, Michael (ed.), The Role of Law in International Politics. Essays in International Relations and International Law, Oxford, 149–176, https://doi.org/10.1093/acprof:oso/9780199244027.003.0009

Nagel, Jürgen G. (2007), Abenteuer Fernhandel. Die Ostindienkompanien, Darmstadt

Nagel, Thomas (2013), Das Problem globaler Gerechtigkeit, in: Broszies / Hahn (eds.), 104–145

Neff, Stephen C. (2014), A Short History of International Law, in: Evans, Malcolm D. (ed.), International Law, 4th ed., Oxford, 3–28, https://doi.org/10.1093/he/9780199654673.003.0001

Neyer, Jürgen (2004), Postnationale politische Herrschaft: Verrechtlichung und Vergesellschaftung jenseits des Staates, Baden-Baden

Nicklas, Thomas (2010), Völkerrecht für die Satteltasche? Fragen nach Macht und Recht an das grotianische Jus gentium, in: Lappenküper, Ulrich, Reiner Marcowitz (eds.), Macht und Recht. Völkerrecht in den internationalen Beziehungen, Paderborn, 53–69

Niesen, Peter (2008), Souveränität, in: Gosepath, Stefan et al. (eds.), Handbuch der Politischen Philosophie und Sozialphilosophie, 2 vols., Berlin, 1205–1211

Nollmann, Gerd (1997), Konflikt in Interaktion, Gruppe und Organisation. Zur Konfliktsoziologie der modernen Gesellschaft, Opladen

North, Douglass C. (1990), Institutions, Institutional Change, and Economic Performance, Cambridge; [German translation: Institutionen, institutioneller Wandel und Wirtschaftsleistung, Tübingen 1992]

North, Douglass C. et al. (2009), Violence and Social Orders: A Conceptual Framework for Interpreting Recorded Human History, Cambridge; [German translation: Gewalt und Gesellschaftsordnungen. Eine Neudeutung der Staats- und Wirtschaftsgeschichte, Tübingen 2011]

Nullmeier, Frank et al. (2010), Prekäre Legitimitäten. Rechtfertigung von Herrschaft in der postnationalen Konstellation, Frankfurt am Main, https://doi.org/10.5771/9783845245072-9

Nullmeier, Frank et al. (eds.) (2012), Der Aufstieg der Legitimitätspolitik. Rechtfertigung und Kritik politisch-ökonomischer Ordnungen (Leviathan Sonderheft 27), Baden-Baden

Nuscheler, Franz (2009), Good Governance. Ein universelles Leitbild von Staatlichkeit und Entwicklung? INEF-Report 96, Duisburg

Nussbaum, Martha C. (2006), Frontiers of Justice. Disability, Nationality, Species Membership, Cambridge, MA

Nuzzo, Luigi (2004), Il linguaggio giuridico della conquista, Strategie di controllo nelle Indie spagnole, Naples

O'Neill, Martin (2008), What Should Egalitarians Believe?, in: Philosophy and Public Affairs 36, 119–156, https://doi.org/10.1111/j.1088-4963.2008.00130.x

O'Neill, Onora (2001), Agents of Justice, in: Metaphilosophy 32, 180–195, https://doi.org/10.1111/1467-9973.00181

Osterhammel, Jürgen (2003), Kolonialismus, 4th ed., Munich

Osterhammel, Jürgen (2005), Weltgeschichte: Ein Propädeutikum, in: Geschichte in Wissenschaft und Unterricht 56, 452–479

Osterhammel, Jürgen (2009), Die Verwandlung der Welt. Eine Geschichte des 19. Jahrhunderts, Munich

Osterhammel, Jürgen (2011), Globalization, in: Bentley, Jerry H. (ed.), The Oxford Handbook of World History, Oxford University Press, 89–104

Osterhammel, Jürgen (2015), Globalifizierung. Denkfiguren der neuen Welt, in: Lange Leitung. Zeitschrift für Ideengeschichte 9, 5–16

Osterhammel, Jürgen (ed.) (2008), Weltgeschichte, Stuttgart

Oxfam International (2008), Oxfam Briefing Paper 117, Climate Wrongs and Human Rights. Putting people at the heart of climate-change policy, Oxford, https://oi-files-d8-prod.s3.eu-west-2.amazonaws.com/s3fs-public/file_attachments/bp117-climate-wrongs-and-human-rights-0809_9.pdf

Pace, Enzo (2009), Religion as communication, in: International Review of Sociology 21, 205–229, https://doi.org/10.1080/03906701.2011.544201

Pagden, Anthony (1995), Lords of all the World. Ideologies of Empire in Spain, Britain and France c. 1500-c. 1800, New Haven

Pauly, Walter, Martin Sielinger (1999), Der deutsche Verfassungsstaat, in: Ellwein, Thomas, Everhard Holtmann (eds.), 50 Jahre Bundesrepublik Deutschland. Rahmenbedingungen – Entwicklungen – Perspektiven, Politische Vierteljahreszeitschrift – Sonderheft 30, Opladen, 79–90, https://doi.org/10.1007/978-3-322-80357-3_5

PEARSON, MICHAEL N. (2003), The Indian Ocean, London, https://doi.org/10.4324/9780203414132

PETERS, ANNE (2015), Global Constitutionalism, in: GIBBONS, MICHAEL T. (ed.), The Encyclopedia of Political Thought, London, 1484–1487

PIEROTH, BODO, BERNHARD SCHLINK (2010), Grundrechte. Staatsrecht II, 26th ed., Heidelberg

POCOCK, JOHN G.A. (1962), The History of Political Thought: A Methodological Enquiry, in: LASLETT, PETER, WALTER GARRISON RUNCIMAN (eds.), Philosophy, Politics and Society. Second Series, Oxford, 183–202

POCOCK, JOHN G. A. (1973), Politics, Language and Time. Essays on Political Thought and History (Studies in Political Theory), New York

POLLAK, MICHAEL (1990), Rassenwahn und Wissenschaft. Anthropologie, Biologie, Justiz und die nationalsozialistische Bevölkerungspolitik, Frankfurt am Main

POPITZ, HEINRICH (1992), Phänomene der Macht, 2nd ed., Tübingen

PRANTL, HERIBERT (2016), Staatlicher Liebesbrief, Süddeutsche Zeitung 280, 3–4, 49

PRATT, MARY LOUISE (1992), Imperial Eyes. Travel Writing and Transculturation, London

PREST, WILFRIED R. (1984), Why the History of the Professions Is Not Written, in: RUBIN, GERRY R., DAVID SUGARMAN (eds.), Law, Economy and Society, 1750–1914: Essays in the History of English Law, Abingdon/Oxon, 300–320

PREUSS, ULRICH K. (1994), Revolution, Fortschritt und Verfassung, new ed., Frankfurt am Main

PREUSS, ULRICH K. (2007), Souveränität – Zwischenbemerkungen zu einem Schlüsselbegriff des Politischen, in: STEIN et al. (eds.), 313–335

PREUSS, ULRICH K. (ed.) (1994), Zum Begriff der Verfassung. Die Ordnung des Politischen, Frankfurt am Main

PRIEBE, REINHARD (2000), Anmerkungen zur Verwaltungskultur der Europäischen Kommission, in: Die Verwaltung 33, 379–413

PUHLE, HANS-JÜRGEN (1973), Vom Wohlfahrtsausschuß zum Wohlfahrtsstaat. Entwicklungstendenzen staatlicher Aufgabenstellungen und Verwaltungsprobleme im Zeichen von Industrialisierung und Demokratisierung, in: RITTER, GERHARD A. (ed.), Vom Wohlfahrtsausschuß zum Wohlfahrtsstaat. Der Staat in der modernen Industriegesellschaft, Cologne, 29–68

PUTIN, VLADIMIR (2014), Address by President of the Russian Federation, http://eng.kremlin.ru/news/6889

QUARITSCH, HELMUT (1970), Staat und Souveränität, vol. 1: Die Grundlagen, Bad Honnef

RAJ, KAPIL (2000), Mapping Knowledge Go-Betweens in Calcutta, 1770–1880, in: SCHAFFER et al. (eds.), 105–150

RAPHAEL, LUTZ (2000), Recht und Ordnung. Herrschaft durch Verwaltung im 19. Jahrhundert, Frankfurt am Main

RAPHAEL, LUTZ (2001), Radikales Ordnungsdenken und die Organisation totalitärer Herrschaft: Weltanschauungseliten und Humanwissenschaftler im NS-Regime, in: Geschichte und Gesellschaft 27, 5–40

RAWLS, JOHN (1979), Eine Theorie der Gerechtigkeit, Frankfurt am Main

RAWLS, JOHN (1999), A Theory of Justice, 2nd ed., Cambridge, MA

REINHARD, WOLFGANG (1977), Gegenreformation als Modernisierung? Prolegomena zu einer Theorie des konfessionellen Zeitalters, in: Archiv für Reformationsgeschichte 68, 226–252, https://doi.org/10.14315/arg-1977-jg13

REINHARD, WOLFGANG (1983, 1985, 1988, 1990), Geschichte der europäischen Expansion 1415–2015, 4 vols., Stuttgart

REINHARD, WOLFGANG (1995), Was ist katholische Konfessionalisierung?, in: REINHARD, WOLFGANG, HEINZ SCHILLING (eds.), Die katholische Konfessionalisierung, Münster, 419–452

REINHARD, WOLFGANG (1999), Geschichte der Staatsgewalt. Eine vergleichende Verfassungsgeschichte Europas von den Anfängen bis zur Gegenwart, Munich

REINHARD, WOLFGANG (2011), Die Nase der Kleopatra. Geschichte im Lichte mikropolitischer Forschung. Ein Versuch, in: Historische Zeitschrift 293, 631–666, https://doi.org/10.1524/hzhz.2011.0057

REINHARD, WOLFGANG (2016), Die Unterwerfung der Welt. Globalgeschichte der europäischen Expansion 1415–2015, Munich, https://doi.org/10.17104/9783406687198

REINHARD, WOLFGANG (ed.) (2014), Geschichte der Welt. Weltreiche und Weltmeere 1350–1750, Munich , https://doi.org/10.17104/9783406641138-18

REINHARD, WOLFGANG, ELISABETH MÜLLER-LUCKNER (eds.) (1999), Verstaatlichung der Welt? Europäische Staatsmodelle und außereuropäische Machtprozesse, München, https://doi.org/10.1524/9783486594447

RENN, JÜRGEN, MALCOLM D. HYMAN (2012), The Globalization of Knowledge in History: An Introduction, in: RENN, JÜRGEN (ed.), The Globalization of Knowledge in History, Berlin, 27–51

REUS-SMIT, CHRISTIAN (2007), International Crisis of Legitimacy, in: International Politics 44, 157–174, https://doi.org/10.1057/palgrave.ip.8800182

RICHARDS, THOMAS (1993), An Imperial Archive. Knowledge and the Fantasy of Empire, London

RIESENHUBER, KARL (2016), Private Macht im Vertragsrecht – Langzeitverträge, in: MÖSLEIN, FLORIAN, Private Macht, Tübingen, 193–212

RIESENHUBER, KARL (ed.) (2007), Privatrechtsgesellschaft. Entwicklung, Stand und Verfassung des Privatrechts, Tübingen

RÖDDER, ANDREAS (2015), 21.0. Eine kurze Geschichte der Gegenwart, Munich, https://doi.org/10.17104/9783406682476-11

RÖDER, TILMAN J. (2012), Civil Military Cooperation in Building the Rule of Law, in: ZÜRN et al. (eds.), 206–232

ROKKAN, STEIN (1975), Dimensions of State Formation and Nation-Building: A Possible Paradigm for Research on Variations within Europe, in: TILLY, CHARLES (ed.), The Formation of Nation States in Western Europe, Princeton NJ, 562–599

ROSA, HARTMUT (1994), Ideengeschichte und Gesellschaftstheorie: Der Beitrag der "Cambridge School" zur Metatheorie, in: Politische Vierteljahresschrift (PVS) 35, 197–223

ROSA, HARTMUT (1999), Die prozedurale Gesellschaft und die Idee starker politischer Wertungen. Zur moralischen Landkarte der Gerechtigkeit, in: MÜNKLER, HERFRIED, MARCUS LLANQUE (eds.), Konzeptionen der Gerechtigkeit: Kulturvergleich – Ideengeschichte – Moderne Debatte, Baden-Baden, 395–423

ROSA, HARTMUT (2016), Resonanz. Eine Soziologie der Weltbeziehung, Berlin

ROSANVALLON, PIERRE (2018), Good Government, Cambridge, MA

ROSE, JONATHAN (1998), The History of Books: Revised and Enlarged, in: MASON, HAYDN T. (ed.), The Darnton Debate: Books and Revolution in the Eighteenth Century, Oxford, 83–104

ROSE, RICHARD (1975), On the Properties of Government: A Developmental Analysis of Public Policies, in: European Journal of Political Research 4, 247–289

ROSENBERG, DANIEL (2003), Early Modern Information Overload, in: Journal of the History of Ideas 64, 1–9

ROSENBERG, EMILY S. (ed.) (2014), Geschichte der Welt 1870–1945. Weltmärkte und Weltkriege, Munich

ROY, ARUNDHATI (1999), Das Ende der Illusion, Munich

RUDLOFF, WILFRIED (2003), Das Wissen der kommunalen Sozialverwaltung in Deutschland: Diffusion, Formen und Konflikte 1900–1933, in: Formation und Transfer städtischen Verwaltungswissens, Jahrbuch für Europäische Verwaltungsgeschichte 15, 59–88

RÜTHERS, BERND (1970), Institutionelles Rechtsdenken im Wandel der Verfassungsepochen. Ein Beitrag zur politisch-kritischen Funktion der Rechtswissenschaft, Bad Homburg v.d.H.

RÜTHERS, BERND (1992), Ideologie und Recht im Systemwechsel. Ein Beitrag zur Ideologieanfälligkeit geistiger Berufe, Munich

RÜTHERS, BERND et al. (2010), Rechtstheorie. Begriff, Geltung und Anwendung des Rechts, 5th ed., Munich

SACHS, WOLFGANG (2003), Environment and Human Rights, Wuppertal Institute Papers 137, Wuppertal

SACHSENMAIER, DOMINIK (2011), Global Perspectives on Global History: Theories and Approaches in a Connected World, Cambridge, https://doi.org/10.1017/CBO9780511736544

SCHAAL, GARY S., FELIX HEIDENREICH (2006), Einführung in die Politischen Theorien der Moderne, Opladen

SCHAFFER, KAY, SIDONIE SMITH (2004), Human Rights and Narrated Lives. The Ethics of Recognition, New York, https://doi.org/10.1057/9781403973665

SCHAFFER, SIMON et al. (eds.) (2000), The Brokered World. Go-Betweens and Global Intelligence 1770–1820, Sagamore Beach

SCHARPF, FRITZ W. (1985), Die Politikverflechtungs-Falle: Europäische Integration und deutscher Föderalismus im Vergleich, in: Politische Vierteljahreszeitschrift (PVS) 26, 323–356

Schaumann, Johann C. G. (1792), Wissenschaftliches Naturrecht, Halle

Schelsky, Helmut (1957), Ist die Dauerreflektion institutionalisierbar? Zum Thema einer modernen Religionssoziologie, in: Zeitschrift für evangelische Ethik 1, 153–174, https://doi.org/10.14315/zee-1957-0126

Schimmelpfennig, Frank (2012), A Comparison of the Rule of Law Policies of Major Western Powers, in: Zürn et al. (eds.), 111–132

Schlieben-Lange, Brigitte (1996), Idéologie, révolution et uniformité de la langue, Liège

Schluchter, Wolfgang (1979), Die Entwicklung des modernen Rationalismus, Tübingen

Schluchter, Wolfgang (1985), Aspekte bürokratischer Herrschaft. Studien zur Interpretation der fortschreitenden Industriegesellschaft, Frankfurt am Main

Schmidt-Assmann, Eberhard, Marion Schöndorf-Haubold (eds.) (2005), Der Europäische Verwaltungsverbund, Tübingen

Schmitt, Carl (1943), Das Reich und Europa, Leipzig

Schmitt, Carl (1993), Über die drei Arten des rechtswissenschaftlichen Denkens, 2nd ed., Berlin (1st ed. 1934), https://doi.org/10.3790/978-3-428-07733-5

Schmitt, Carl (1996), Der Hüter der Verfassung, 4th ed., Berlin

Schmitt, Carl (2004), On the Three Types of Juristic Thought, translated by Joseph W. Bendersky, Contributions in Political Science No. 397, Westport

Schmitt, Carl (2006), The Nomos of the Earth in the International Law of the Jus Publicum Europaeum, Candor, NY

Schmitt, Carl (2008), Römischer Katholizismus und politische Form, 5th ed., Stuttgart (1st ed. 1923)

Schmitt, Carl (2009), Politische Theologie. Vier Kapitel zur Lehre von der Souveränität, 9th ed., Berlin

Schnabel, Franz (1949), Deutsche Geschichte im neunzehnten Jahrhundert, vol. II, 2nd ed., Freiburg

Schuppert, Fabian (2012), Reconsidering Resource Rights: The Case for a Basic Right to the Benefits of Life-Sustaining Eco-Systems Services, in: Journal of Global Ethics 8, 1–11

Schuppert, Fabian (2014), Beyond the National Resource Privilege: towards an International Court of Environment, in: International Theory 6, 68–97

Schuppert, Fabian (2015a), Being Equals. Analyzing the Nature of Social Egalitarian Relationships, in: Fourie, Carina et al. (eds.), Social Equality. On What it Means to be Equals, Oxford, 107–128

Schuppert, Fabian (2015b), Non-domination, Non-alienation and Social Equality: towards a Republican Understanding of Equality, in: Critical Review of International Social and Political Philosophy 18, 440–455

Schuppert, Gunnar Folke (1973), Die verfassungsgerichtliche Kontrolle der Auswärtigen Gewalt, Baden-Baden

Schuppert, Gunnar Folke (1980), Die öffentliche Aufgabe als Schlüsselbegriff der Verwaltungswissenschaft, in: Verwaltungsarchiv 71, 309–344

SCHUPPERT, GUNNAR FOLKE (1984), The Constituent Power, in: STARCK, CHRISTIAN (ed.), Main Principles of the German Basic Law, Baden-Baden, 37–64

SCHUPPERT, GUNNAR FOLKE (1992), Treuhandanstalt – Zum Leben einer Organisation im Überschneidungsbereich zweier Rechtskreise, in: Staatswissenschaften und Staatspraxis, 3. Jg., Heftnr. 2, 186–210

SCHUPPERT, GUNNAR FOLKE (1993), Verwaltungsrechtswissenschaft als Steuerungswissenschaft. Zur Steuerung des Verwaltungshandelns durch Verwaltungsrecht, in: HOFFMANN-RIEM, WOLFGANG et al. (eds.), Reform des Allgemeinen Verwaltungsrechts. Grundfragen, Baden-Baden, 65–114

SCHUPPERT, GUNNAR FOLKE (1995a), Rigidität und Flexibilität von Verfassungsrecht. Überlegungen zur Steuerungsfunktion von Verfassungsrecht in normalen wie in "schwierigen Zeiten", in: Archiv des öffentlichen Rechts (AöR) 120, 32–99

SCHUPPERT, GUNNAR FOLKE (1995b), Rückzug des Staates? Zur Rolle des Staates zwischen Legitimationskrise und politischer Neubestimmung, in: Die öffentliche Verwaltung (DöV) 48, 761–770

SCHUPPERT, GUNNAR FOLKE (1995c), Zur Anatomie und Analyse des Dritten Sektors, in: Die Verwaltung 28, 137–200

SCHUPPERT, GUNNAR FOLKE (1996), Grundrechte und Bekämpfung der Organisierten Kriminalität, in: BARFUSS, WALTER (ed.), Sicherheitsverwaltung. Drei-Länder-Tagung 1994 der Gesellschaft für Verwaltungswissenschaften Deutschlands, Vienna, 31–57

SCHUPPERT, GUNNAR FOLKE (1999), Schlüsselbegriffe der Perspektivenverklammerung von Verwaltungsrecht und Verwaltungswissenschaft, in: Die Verwaltung, Beiheft 2, 103–125

SCHUPPERT, GUNNAR FOLKE (2000), Verwaltungswissenschaft. Verwaltung, Verwaltungsrecht, Verwaltungslehre, Baden-Baden

SCHUPPERT, GUNNAR FOLKE (2001), Das Konzept der regulierten Selbstregulierung als Bestandteil einer als Regelungswissenschaft verstandenen Rechtswissenschaft, in: Die Verwaltung, Beiheft 4, 201–252

SCHUPPERT, GUNNAR FOLKE (2003), Staatswissenschaft, Baden-Baden

SCHUPPERT, GUNNAR FOLKE (2006), Bürokratisches Regieren – eine governancetheoretische Perspektive, in: VOSSKUHLE, ANDREAS (ed.), Entbürokratisierung und Regulierung, Baden-Baden, 6–40

SCHUPPERT, GUNNAR FOLKE (2007a), Governance as Communication. Das Beispiel von European Governance, in: JARREN, OTFRIED et al. (eds.), Entgrenzte Demokratie? Herausforderungen für die politische Interessenvermittlung, Baden-Baden, 287–308, https://doi.org/10.5771/9783845203119-287

SCHUPPERT, GUNNAR FOLKE (2007b), Souveränität – überholter Begriff, wandlungsfähiges Konzept oder 'born 1576, but still going strong', in: STEIN et al. (eds.), 251–269

SCHUPPERT, GUNNAR FOLKE (2007c), Was ist und wozu Governance?, in: Die Verwaltung 40, 463–512

SCHUPPERT, GUNNAR FOLKE (2007d), Governanceinfrastruktur durch Rechtsstaatlichkeit, in: BEISHEIM, MARIANNE, GUNNAR FOLKE SCHUPPERT (eds.), Staatszerfall und Governance, Baden-Baden, 194–222, https://doi.org/10.5771/978384520 1009-194

Schuppert, Gunnar Folke (2008a), Die bundesstaatliche Finanzverfassung zwischen Pfadabhängigkeit und Wandel, in: Hufen, Friedhelm et al. (eds.), Verfassungen – Zwischen Recht und Politik. Festschrift zum 70. Geburtstag für Hans-Peter Schneider, Baden-Baden, 285–301, https://doi.org/10.5771/9783845206462-285

Schuppert, Gunnar Folke (2008b), Politische Kultur, Baden-Baden, https://doi.org/10.5771/9783845209296

Schuppert, Gunnar Folke (2008c), Was ist und wie misst man Wandel von Staatlichkeit?, in: Der Staat 47, 325–358, https://doi.org/10.3790/staa.47.3.325

Schuppert, Gunnar Folke (2009), Zum Umgang mit unterschiedlichen Konzeptualisierungen der Rule of Law als Anwendungsfall normativer Pluralität, in: Kötter, Matthias, Gunnar Folke Schuppert (eds.), Normative Pluralität ordnen, Baden-Baden, 209–231, https://doi.org/10.5771/9783845219653-209

Schuppert, Gunnar Folke (2010), Staat als Prozess. Eine staatstheoretische Skizze in sieben Aufzügen, Frankfurt am Main

Schuppert, Gunnar Folke (2011a), Alles Governance oder was?, Baden-Baden, https://doi.org/10.5771/9783845230498

Schuppert, Gunnar Folke (2011b), Partnerships, in: Bevir, Mark (ed.), The SAGE Handbook of Governance, London, 286–299

Schuppert, Gunnar Folke (2012a), Can the Rule of Law Travel? Überlegungen zur Reisefähigkeit des Rechtsstaatsprinzips, unpublished manuscript, Erfurt

Schuppert, Gunnar Folke (2012b), Verwaltungsorganisation und Verwaltungsorganisationsrecht als Steuerungsfaktoren, in: Hoffmann-Riem, Wolfgang et al. (eds.), Grundlagen des Verwaltungsrechts, vol. I, 2nd ed., Munich, 995–1081

Schuppert, Gunnar Folke (2012c), When Governance meets Religion. Governancestrukturen und Governanceakteure im Bereich des Religiösen, Baden-Baden

Schuppert, Gunnar Folke (2013a), Einige Bemerkungen zur Allgemeinen Staatsverwirrung – ist er gegangen, kommt er zurück oder wird er nur neu gesehen?, in: Bach, Maurizio (ed.), Der entmachtete Leviathan. Löst sich der souveräne Staat auf?, Zeitschrift für Politik, Sonderband 5, Baden-Baden, 29–49

Schuppert, Gunnar Folke (2013b), Europäische Verwaltungsnetzwerke im Lichte der Grundsätze guter Verwaltung, in: Huber, Peter M. (ed.), Der Vertrag von Lissabon und das nationale Verfassungsrecht. Europäische Verwaltungsnetzwerke, Stuttgart, 133–164

Schuppert, Gunnar Folke (2014), Verflochtene Staatlichkeit. Globalisierung als Governance-Geschichte, Frankfurt am Main

Schuppert, Gunnar Folke (2015), Wege in die moderne Welt. Globalisierung von Staatlichkeit als Kommunikationsgeschichte, Frankfurt am Main

Schuppert, Gunnar Folke (2016a), Ordnung durch Bewegung – Recht als dynamisches System, in: Rechtswissenschaft 7, 177–210, https://doi.org/10.5771/1868-8098-2016-2-177

Schuppert, Gunnar Folke (2016b), The World of Rules. Eine etwas andere Vermessung der Welt, in: Max Planck Institute for European Legal History Research

Paper Series No. 2016–01 [English translation: The World of Rules. A Somewhat Different Measurement of the World, Global Perspectives on Legal History 10, Frankfurt am Main 2016]

Schuppert, Gunnar Folke (2017a), Buon Governo e Giustizia. Gerechtigkeit – ein Qualitätsmerkmal des Regierens? WZB Discussion Paper of the Research Unit Democracy and Democratization, Berlin

Schuppert, Gunnar Folke (2017b), Governance of Diversity. Zum Umgang mit kultureller und religiöser Pluralität in säkularen Gesellschaften, Frankfurt am Main

Schuppert, Gunnar Folke (2017c), Notwendiges Umdenken im Hause des Rechts: Schauplätze und Akteure, in: Ruppert, Stefan, Thomas Duve (eds.), Rechtswissenschaft in der Berliner Republik, Berlin, 182–211

Schuppert, Gunnar Folke (2018a), Staatswissenschaft(en), in: Voigt, Rüdiger (ed.), Handbuch Staat, Wiesbaden, 135–152, https://doi.org/10.1007/978-3-658-20744-1_13

Schuppert, Gunnar Folke (2018b), Umdenken im Hause des Rechts – das Beispiel des öffentlichen Rechts in der Berliner Republik, in: Duve, Thomas, Stefan Ruppert (eds.), Rechtwissenschaft in der Berliner Republik, 182–211

Schuppert, Gunnar Folke (2019), Rechtswissenschaft als Regelungswissenschaft, in: Möslein, Florian (ed.), Regelsetzung im Privatrecht, Tübingen, 31–58

Schuppert, Gunnar Folke (forthcoming), Gerechtigkeitsdiskurse als Gesellschaftskritik, in: Kneip, Sascha et al. (eds.), Festschrift für Wolfgang Merkel

Schuppert, Gunnar Folke (ed.) (1998), Das Gesetz als zentrales Steuerungsinstrument des Rechtstaates, Baden-Baden

Schuppert, Gunnar Folke (ed.) (2005), Governance-Forschung. Vergewisserung über Stand und Entwicklungslinien, Baden-Baden

Schuppert, Gunnar Folke, Christian Bumke (2000), Die Konstitutionalisierung der Rechtsordnung. Überlegungen zum Verhältnis von verfassungsrechtlicher Ausstrahlungswirkung und Eigenständigkeit des “einfachen” Rechts, Baden-Baden

Schüttpelz, Erhard (2007), Ein absoluter Begriff. Zur Genealogie und Karriere des Netzwerkbegriffs, in: Kaufmann, Stefan (ed.), Vernetzte Steuerung. Soziale Prozesse im Zeitalter technischer Netzwerke, Zurich, 25–46

Schwöbel, Christine E. J. (2011), The Appeal of the Project of Global Constitutionalism to Public International Lawyers, in: German Law Journal 13, 1–22, https://doi.org/10.1017/S2071832200020320

Secord, James A. (2004), Knowledge in Transit, in: Isis 95, 654–672, https://doi.org/10.1086/430657

Seel, Martin (2013), Narrative und (De-)Legitimation: Der zweite Irak-Krieg im Kino, in: Fahrmeir (ed.), 45–58

Seelmann, Kurt (2010), Rechtsphilosophie, 5th ed., Munich

Seibel, Wolfgang (2016), Verwaltung verstehen. Eine theoriegeschichtliche Einführung, Berlin

SEINECKE, RALF (2015), Das Recht des Rechtspluralismus, Grundlagen der Rechtswissenschaft 29, Tübingen

SELLERT, WOLFGANG (1997), Gewohnheit, Formalismus und Rechtsritual im Verhältnis zur Steuerung sozialen Verhaltens durch gesetztes Recht, in: MELVILLE, GERT, DURCHHARDT, HEINZ (eds.), Im Spannungsfeld von Recht und Ritual. Soziale Kommunikation im Mittelalter und Früher Neuzeit, Cologne, 23–47

SHETTY, SALIL (2017), Nicht nur Autokraten grenzen aus (Summary Amnesty Report 2016/2017), in: Amnesty Journal 04/05, 38–41

SIEGRIST, HANNES, DAVID SUGARMAN (ed.) (1999), Eigentum im internationalen Vergleich (18.–20. Jahrhundert), Göttingen, https://doi.org/10.13109/9783666357930

SKALLWEIT, STEPHAN (1957), Das Herrscherbild des 17. Jahrhunderts, in: Historische Zeitschrift (HZ) 184, 68–80, https://doi.org/10.1524/hzhz.1957.184.jg.65

SKINNER, QUENTIN (1978), The Foundations of Modern Political Thought, 2 vols., Cambridge, https://doi.org/10.1017/CBO9780511817878

SKINNER, QUENTIN (1988), Meaning and understanding in the history of ideas, in: TULLY, JAMES (ed.), Meaning and Context. Quentin Skinner and his Critics, Oxford, 29–67

SKINNER, QUENTIN (2002), Visions of Politics I., Cambridge, https://doi.org/10.1017/CBO9780511613784

SLAUGHTER, JOSEPH R. (2006), Enabling Fictions and Novel Subjects. The *Bildungsroman* and International Human Rights Law, in: Publications of the Modern Language Association of America 121, 1405–1423

SLAUGHTER, JOSEPH R. (2007), Narration and International Human Rights Law, in: Comparative Literature and Culture 9/1 (online only), http://docs.lib.purdue.edu/cgi/viewcontent.cgi?article=1031&context=clcweb&sei-redir=1#search=%22clc+web+jospeh+slaughter+narration%22

SMEND, RUDOLF (1994), Staatsrechtliche Abhandlungen, 3rd ed., Berlin, https://doi.org/10.3790/978-3-428-08080-9

SMITH, PAMELA H. (2009), Science on the Move: Recent Trends in the History of Early Modern Science, in: Renaissance Quarterly 62, 345–372, https://doi.org/10.1086/599864

SMITH, VANESSA (2013), Joseph Bank's Intermediaries. Rethinking Global Cultural Exchange, in: MOYN, SAMUEL, ANDREW SARTORI (eds.), Global Intellectual History, New York, 81–109

SPINDLER, MANUELA, SIEGFRIED SCHIEDER (2006), Theorien der Internationalen Beziehungen, 2nd ed., Opladen

STEGBAUER, CHRISTIAN (2002), Reziprozität, Wiesbaden, https://doi.org/10.1007/978-3-322-97106-7

STEIN, PETER (1999), Roman Law in European History, Cambridge, https://doi.org/10.1017/CBO9780511814723

STEIN, TINE et al. (eds.) (2007), Souveränität, Recht, Moral. Die Grundlagen politischer Gemeinschaft, Frankfurt am Main

STEINHAUSEN, GEORG (1968), Geschichte des deutschen Briefes. Zur Kulturgeschichte des Deutschen Volkes, 2nd ed., Zurich (1st ed. 1889)

Stichweh, Rudolf (1991), Der frühmoderne Staat und die europäische Universität. Zur Interaktion von Politik und Erziehungssystem im Prozess der Ausdifferenzierung (16.–18. Jahrhundert), Frankfurt am Main

Stollberg-Rilinger, Barbara (2016), Die Aufklärung. Europa im 18. Jahrhundert, 2nd ed., Stuttgart

Stollberg-Rilinger, Barbara (ed.) (2001), Vormoderne politische Verfahren, Berlin

Stolleis, Michael (1987), Gemeinwohl, in: Herzog, Roman et al. (eds.), Evangelisches Staatslexikon, 3rd ed., vol. 1, Stuttgart, col. 1061–1064

Stolleis, Michael (1988), Geschichte des öffentlichen Rechts in Deutschland. Vol 1: Reichspublizistik und Policeywissenschaft 1600–1800, Munich

Stolleis, Michael (1989), Die Entstehung des Interventionsstaates und das öffentliche Recht, in: Zeitschrift für neuere Rechtsgeschichte 11, 129–147

Stolleis, Michael (1990), Staat und Staatsräson in der frühen Neuzeit. Studien zur Geschichte des öffentlichen Rechts, Frankfurt am Main

Stolleis, Michael (1996), Die Idee des souveränen Staates, in: Mussgnug, Reinhard (ed.), Entstehen und Wandel verfassungsrechtlichen Denkens, Berlin, 63–85 (Der Staat, Beiheft 11)

Stolleis, Michael (2012), Rechtsstaat und Unrechtsstaat im 20. Jahrhundert, in: Starck, Christian (ed.), Recht und Willkür, Tübingen, 47–62

Stolleis, Michael (2014), Naturgesetz und Naturrecht – zwei Abkömmlinge der wissenschaftlichen Revolution des 17. und 18. Jahrhunderts, in: Armgardt, Matthias, Tilmann Repgen (eds.), Naturrecht in Antike und früher Neuzeit, Tübingen, 137–149

Strayer, Josef R. (1975), Die mittelalterlichen Grundlagen des modernen Staates, Cologne, https://doi.org/10.7788/boehlau.9783412306236

Stromseth, Jane et al. (2006), Can Might Make Rights? Building the Rule of Law after Military Intervention, Cambridge, https://doi.org/10.1017/CBO9780511803086

Stroumsa, Guy G. (2011), Das Ende des Opferkults. Die religiösen Mutationen der Spätantike, Berlin

Suchman, M. C. (1995), Managing Legitimacy: Strategic and Institutional Approaches, in: Academy of Management Review 20, 571–610, https://doi.org/10.5465/amr.1995.9508080331

Süsterhenn, Adolf (1947), Das Naturrecht, in: Die Kirche in der Welt 1, 55–62

Sylvest, Casper (2008), "Our Passion for Legality": International Law and Imperialism in Late Nineteenth-Century Britain, in: Review of International Studies 34, 403–423

Tamanaha, Brian (2007), A Concise Guide to the Rule of Law, St. John's University School of Law, Legal Studies Research Papers No. 07–0028

Thier, Andreas (2011), Hierarchie und Autonomie. Regelungstraditionen der Bischofsbestellung in der Geschichte des kirchlichen Wahlrechts bis 1140, Frankfurt am Main

Thurnwald, Richard (1934), Die menschliche Gesellschaft, vol. V, Berlin

TRUTE, HANS-HEINRICH et al. (2008), Der Governance-Ansatz als verwaltungsrechtswissenschaftliches Analysekonzept, in: SCHUPPERT, GUNNAR FOLKE, MICHAEL ZÜRN (eds.), Governance in einer sich wandelnden Welt, PVS-Sonderheft 41, Wiesbaden, 173–189

TYLOR, EDWARD B. (1871), Die Anfänge der Cultur: Untersuchungen über die Entwicklung der Mythologie, Philosophie, Religion, Kunst und Sitte, Leipzig

UTZ, ARTHUR FRIEDHELM (1951), Naturrecht im Widerstreit zum positiven Gesetz, in: Die Neue Ordnung in Kirche, Staat, Gesellschaft, Kultur 5, 313–329

VAN ITTERSEN, MARTINA (2006), Profit and Principle. Hugo Grotius, Natural Rights Theories and the Rise of Dutch Power in the East Indies (1595–1615), Leiden, https://doi.org/10.1163/9789047408949

VAN REYBROUCK, DAVID (2012), Kongo – eine Geschichte, Frankfurt am Main

VAN STADEN ALFRED, HANS VOLLAARD (2002), The Erosion of State Sovereignty: Towards a Post-territorial World?, in: KREIJEN, GERARD (ed.), State, Sovereignty, and International Governance, Oxford, 165–184

VESTING, THOMAS (2011a), Die Medien des Rechts: Schrift, Weilerswist

VESTING, THOMAS (2011b), Die Medien des Rechts: Sprache, Weilerswist

VESTING, THOMAS (2013), Die Medien des Rechts: Buchdruck, Weilerswist

VESTING, THOMAS (2015), Die Medien des Rechts: Computernetzwerke, Weilerswist, https://doi.org/10.5771/9783845277417

VESTING, THOMAS et al. (eds.) (2014), Grundrechte als Phänomene kollektiver Ordnung. Zur Wiedergewinnung des Gesellschaftlichen in der Grundrechtstheorie und der Grundrechtsdogmatik, Tübingen

VOIGT, STEFAN (2002), Institutionenökonomik, Munich

VORLÄNDER, HANS (1999), Verfassung und politische Kultur. Anmerkungen aus aktuellem Anlaß, in: GEBHARDT, JÜRGEN (ed.), Verfassung und politische Kultur, Baden-Baden, 75–84

VOSSKUHLE, ANDREAS (2001a), Der Dienstleistungsstaat. Über Nutzen und Gefahren von Staatsbildern, in: Der Staat 40, 495–523

VOSSKUHLE, ANDREAS (2001b), Regulierte Selbstregulierung – Zur Karriere eines Schlüsselbegriffs, in: Die Verwaltung, Beiheft 4, 197–201

VOSSKUHLE, ANDREAS et al. (eds.) (2013), Verabschiedung und Wiederentdeckung des Staates im Spannungsfeld der Disziplinen, Berlin (Der Staat, Beiheft 21), https://doi.org/10.3790/978-3-428-53944-4

VRIES, PETER (2009), Zur politischen Ökonomie des Tees. Was uns Tee über die englische und chinesische Wirtschaft der Frühen Neuzeit sagen kann, Vienna

WAHL, RAINER (1985), Rechtsschutz gegen den Staat, in: GRIMM, DIETER (ed.), Einführung in das öffentliche Recht, Heidelberg, 222–223

WAHL, RAINER (2001), Elemente der Verfassungsstaatlichkeit, in: Juristische Schulung (JuS) 11, 1041–1048

WALDHOFF, CHRISTIAN (2011), Die Gründungserzählung der Verfassung als Idee des Staates, in: DEPENHEUER (ed.), 61–79, https://doi.org/10.1007/978-3-531-92794-7_3

WALLERATH, MAXIMILIAN (2000), Die Änderung der Verwaltungskultur als Reformziel, in: Die Verwaltung 33, 351–413

Weinacht, Paul-Ludwig (1975), Fünf Thesen zum Begriff der Staatsräson. Die Entdeckung der Staatsräson für die deutsche politische Theorie (1604), in: Schnur, Roman (ed.), Staatsräson. Studien zur Geschichte eines politischen Begriffs, Berlin, 65–97

Weinkauff, Hermann (1951/52), Das Naturrecht in evangelischer Sicht, Zeitwende 23, 95–102

Wesel, Uwe (1985), Frühformen des Rechts in verstaatlichten Gesellschaften, Frankfurt am Main

Wesel, Uwe (1997), Geschichte des Rechts. Von den Frühformen bis zum Vertrag von Maastricht, Munich

Wetzstein, Thomas (2008), Wie die urba zum orbi wurde. Der Beitrag des Papsttums zur Entstehung neuer Kommunikationsräume im europäischen Hochmittelalter, in: Johrendt, Jochen, Harald Müller (eds.), Römisches Zentrum und kirchliche Peripherie. Das universale Papsttum als Bezugspunkt der Kirchen von den Reformpäpsten bis zu Innozenz III, Berlin, 47–75

Wieacker, Franz (1935), Wandlungen der Eigentumsverfassung, Hamburg

Wieacker, Franz (1953), Das Sozialmodell der klassischen Privatrechtsgesetzbücher und die Entwicklung der modernen Gesellschaft, Schriftenreihe der Juristischen Studiengesellschaft Karlsruhe, Heft 3, Karlsruhe

Wieacker, Franz (1960), Das Bürgerliche Recht im Wandel der Gesellschaftsordnungen, in: von Caemmerer, Ernst et al. (eds.), Hundert Jahre Deutsches Rechtsleben. Festschrift zum hundertjährigen Bestehen des Deutschen Juristentages, vol. II, Karlsruhe, 1–18

Wieacker, Franz (1967), Privatrechtsgeschichte der Neuzeit unter besonderer Berücksichtigung der deutschen Entwicklung, Göttingen

Wieacker, Franz (1996), A History of Private Law in Europe: With Particular Reference to Germany, Oxford

Wielsch, Dan (2001), Freiheit und Funktion. Zur Struktur- und Theoriegeschichte des Rechts der Wirtschaftsgesellschaft, Baden-Baden

Wielsch, Dan (2013), Grundrechte als Rechtfertigungsgebote im Privatrecht, in: Archiv für civilistische Praxis (AcP) 213, 718–759, https://doi.org/10.1628/000389914X13920224936212

Wiemer, Hans-Ulrich (ed.) (2006), Staatlichkeit und politisches Handeln in der römischen Kaiserzeit, Berlin, https://doi.org/10.1515/9783110926590

Willems, Ulrich (2012a), Normative Pluralität und Kontingenz als Herausforderungen politischer Theorie. Prolegomena zur Theorie eines Politischen Pluralismus, in: Toens, Katrin, Ulrich Willems (eds.), Politik und Kontingenz, Wiesbaden, 225–301, https://doi.org/10.1007/978-3-531-94245-2_14

Willems, Ulrich (2012b), Religionsfreiheit und Religionspolitik im Zeitalter religiöser und kultureller Pluralität. Ein Plädoyer für einen neuen religionspolitischen modus vivendi und modus procedendi, in: Berger, Daniel, Marianne Heimbach-Steins (eds.), Freiheit – Gleichheit – Religion: Orientierungen moderner Religionspolitik, Würzburg, 131–152

WILSON, ERIC (2008), Savage Republic. De Indis of Hugo Grotius, Republicanism and Dutch Hegemony within the Early Modern World-System (ca. 1600–1619), Leiden, https://doi.org/10.1163/ej.9789004167889.i-534

WILSON, JAMES Q. (1993), The Moral Sense, New York, https://doi.org/10.2307/2938952

WIRTH, UWE (ed.) (2002), Performanz. Zwischen Sprachphilosophie und Kulturwissenschaften, Frankfurt am Main

WOLF, ERNST (1947/48), Naturrecht und Gerechtigkeit, in: Evangelische Theologie 7, 233–253, https://doi.org/10.14315/evth-1947-1-623

WYDUCKEL, DIETER (1979), Princeps Legibus Solutus. Eine Untersuchung zur frühmodernen Rechts- und Staatslehre, Berlin

ZAJAC-SANNERHOLM, RICHARD (2012), Rule of Law Promotion after Conflict: Experimenting in the Kosovo Laboratory, in: ZÜRN et al. (eds.), 252–277

ZEH, JULI (2006), Alles auf dem Rasen. Kein Roman, Frankfurt am Main

ZEH, JULI (2012), Die Diktatur der Demokratie. Warum ohne Recht kein Staat zu machen ist, Hamburg

ZÜRCHER, CHRISTOPH (2005), Gewollte Schwäche. Vom schwierigen analytischen Umgang mit prekärer Staatlichkeit, in: Internationale Politik 60, 13–22

ZÜRN, MICHAEL (2011a), Perspektiven des demokratischen Regierens und die Rolle der Politikwissenschaft im 21. Jahrhundert, in: Politische Vierteljahresschrift (PVS) 52, 603–635

ZÜRN, MICHAEL (2011b), Vier Modelle einer Globalen Ordnung in kosmopolitischer Absicht, in: Politische Vierteljahresschrift (PVS) 52, 78–118

ZÜRN, MICHAEL et al. (eds.) (2012), Rule of Law Dynamics. In an Era of International and Transnational Governance, Cambridge

Permissions

All chapters in this book were first published in AGHILL, by Max Planck Institute for Legal History and Legal Theory by Gunnar Folke Schuppert; hereby published with permission under the Creative Commons Attribution License or equivalent. Every chapter published in this book has been scrutinized by our experts. Their significance has been extensively debated. The topics covered herein carry significant information for a comprehensive understanding. They may even be implemented as practical applications or may be referred to as a beginning point for further studies.

We would like to thank the editorial team for lending their expertise to make the book truly unique. They have played a crucial role in the development of this book. Without their invaluable contributions this book wouldn't have been possible. They have made vital efforts to compile up to date information on the varied aspects of this subject to make this book a valuable addition to the collection of many professionals and students.

This book was conceptualized with the vision of imparting up-to-date and integrated information in this field. To ensure the same, a matchless editorial board was set up. Every individual on the board went through rigorous rounds of assessment to prove their worth. After which they invested a large part of their time researching and compiling the most relevant data for our readers.

The editorial board has been involved in producing this book since its inception. They have spent rigorous hours researching and exploring the diverse topics which have resulted in the successful publishing of this book. They have passed on their knowledge of decades through this book. To expedite this challenging task, the publisher supported the team at every step. A small team of assistant editors was also appointed to further simplify the editing procedure and attain best results for the readers.

Apart from the editorial board, the designing team has also invested a significant amount of their time in understanding the subject and creating the most relevant covers. They scrutinized every image to scout for the most suitable representation of the subject and create an appropriate cover for the book.

The publishing team has been an ardent support to the editorial, designing and production team. Their endless efforts to recruit the best for this project, has resulted in the accomplishment of this book. They are a veteran in the field of academics and their pool of knowledge is as vast as their experience in printing. Their expertise and guidance has proved useful at every step. Their uncompromising quality standards have made this book an exceptional effort. Their encouragement from time to time has been an inspiration for everyone.

The publisher and the editorial board hope that this book will prove to be a valuable piece of knowledge for students, practitioners and scholars across the globe.

Index

A

Administrative State, 15, 105-106, 108, 114, 176, 207, 227

Ancient Constitution, 5, 57

B

Body Politic, 128, 203, 211-212

Brokered World, 80-81

Bureaucratic Administration, 91, 124, 206-207, 220, 224

C

Civil Code, 12, 114

Civil Law, 12, 88-89, 114, 260

Civil Service, 126, 227

Civil Society, 115, 140, 234, 263, 270

Cognitive Challenge, 79, 124

Communication Code, 53-56

Communication Spaces, 53, 55, 66-67, 69

Constituent Power, 65-66, 252-255

Constitutional History, 17, 105, 249, 252, 255

Constitutional Jurisdiction, 116, 251, 268, 271

Constitutional Law, 15, 17-18, 28, 45, 47-48, 66, 87-88, 92, 111, 116, 177, 202, 205, 207-208, 221-222, 229, 247-248, 251, 254, 259, 267, 270

Constitutional Theory, 65, 208, 253

Constitutionalization, 114, 117, 142

Criminal Law, 56, 88, 142, 167, 267

D

Democratic State, 103, 224

E

Ecclesiastical Law, 11, 256

Enlightenment, 45, 47, 75, 78-80, 106, 121-127, 129-131, 133-134, 137, 141, 215

Entangled History, 41-43, 51, 69-70, 124

Entanglement Actors, 72, 74, 80

Entanglement Research, 70-73

Entanglement Structures, 71-74

F

Fields Of Knowledge, 53, 69

Form Of Authority, 223, 225

G

Global Constitutionalism, 5-6, 31, 266

Global Governance, 29, 40, 171-173

Global Intellectual Fields, 42, 53, 57

Global Intellectual History, 70, 82

Global Justice, 25-27, 31, 266

Governance Structure, 125, 127

H

Human Rights, 5, 17, 20-23, 30, 39, 42, 45, 71, 121, 136, 140, 142, 147, 155, 172, 174-184, 187-199, 213, 218, 221, 239, 263-264, 267-269

Human Rights Activist, 21, 191

I

Idealism, 45, 147, 188

Imperial Court, 35, 227

Imperial Rule, 48, 225-226

Institutional Justice, 27, 208-209, 269

Institutionalized Contact Zones, 49-50

Interim Appraisal, 16, 24, 179

J

Jurisprudence, 8, 15-16, 19, 29, 104, 106, 112-113, 115, 127, 170, 172, 179, 229-230, 235, 238, 258, 261

Jus Commune, 58-60, 88

Justice Discourses, 24, 31, 266

L

Language Of Justice, 24, 84

Language Of Law, 1, 3-11, 14-17, 19-21, 24, 27, 30-31, 36, 48, 61, 145, 164, 169, 172, 190, 194, 198, 200, 220-221, 223, 235, 240, 243, 252, 256, 266, 270-272

Language Of Politics, 4, 8-9, 16, 20, 24, 31, 36, 61, 84, 104, 121, 127-128, 130-131, 135-136, 140-141, 143, 165, 190, 192, 205, 218, 249, 252, 266, 272

Language Of Rights, 16, 19, 21, 24, 84, 186, 192

Law Of Nations, 47, 79, 143

Lead Discipline, 44, 46, 127

Legal Code, 85, 89-90

Legal Pluralism, 6, 117-118, 120

Legal Protection, 16, 212

Legitimation Formula, 240, 270

M

Medieval Order, 236, 239-240

Modern International Law, 26, 46, 142, 152

Modern Territorial State, 46, 50, 91, 129, 244

N

New Global Order, 27, 30, 84

Non-state Law, 142, 268

O

Organizational Law, 175, 204, 220

P

Paradigmatic Shift, 25-26

Performative Language, 8-10, 16

Policy Programmes, 15, 207

Political Authority, 4-7, 20, 31, 84, 133-134, 198, 220, 246, 263, 266-267, 270-272

Political Change, 7-9, 84, 104, 147, 174, 180, 192

Political Developments, 103, 137, 173

Political Discourse, 3, 24, 48, 57

Political History, 44, 61, 121, 143, 174, 187, 198-199, 205, 208, 220, 237, 243, 265, 269, 272

Political Philosophy, 25, 44, 62, 87, 148, 221-222, 263, 270-271

Political Unity Formula, 240, 270

Politicization Of Law, 244-245

R

Realism, 45, 147

Religious Peace, 99-100

S

Self-government, 6, 124, 247

Semantic Shifts, 24, 109, 112, 146

Separation Of Powers, 137, 178, 193, 205-206, 212, 220, 246, 255, 269

Social Philosophy, 179, 222, 263

Sovereign State, 125, 228, 236, 240-241, 267, 269

Sovereignty, 48, 55, 106, 120, 138, 151, 160-161, 167, 191, 194, 197, 201, 221, 224, 232-233, 235-244, 259, 265, 269-270, 272

Sphere Of Resonance, 102-104, 106, 118

State Authority, 18, 28, 103, 136, 139, 178, 199, 212, 221, 223, 228-230, 238, 241-242, 267

State Nomads, 80-81

State Power, 179, 194, 199, 206

Statization, 105, 267

Statutory Law, 15, 251, 262

T

Taxation, 17, 24, 91, 226

Transnational Law, 142, 268

Transnationalization, 199, 235

www.ingramcontent.com/pod-product-compliance
Lightning Source LLC
LaVergne TN
LVHW011516200926
848484LV00001B/52
* 9 7 8 1 6 4 7 2 6 6 2 4 0 *